Lonely Planet Publications
Melbourne | Oakland | London

Damian Harper

Beijing

The Top Five

1 Temple of Heaven Park
Access Imperial China's foremost temple complex (p68)

2 Beijing's hutong
Wander through the city's maze of alleyways (p82)

3 Forbidden City
Discover the splendour of China's largest imperial palace (p76)

4 Summer Palace
Explore the superb landscape of the huge palace grounds (p98)

5 The Great Wall
Size up China's most celebrated fortification outside town (p165)

Contents

Published by Lonely Planet Publications Pty Ltd
ABN 36 005 607 983

Australia Head Office, Locked Bag 1, Footscray,
Victoria 3011, ☎ 03 8379 8000, fax 03 8379 8111,
talk2us@lonelyplanet.com.au

USA 150 Linden St, Oakland, CA 94607,
☎ 510 893 8555, toll free 800 275 8555,
fax 510 893 8572, info@lonelyplanet.com

UK 72–82 Rosebery Ave, Clerkenwell, London,
EC1R 4RW, ☎ 020 7841 9000, fax 020 7841 9001,
go@lonelyplanet.co.uk

The Authors

DAMIAN HARPER

After a stop-start career in bookselling, Damian studied Modern and Classical Chinese at London's School of Oriental and African Studies, graduating in 1995. His degree course took him to Beijing, laying the foundations for a deep affection for the city. He has since lived (and worked) in Beijing with his Shāndōng-born wife Dai Min and has travelled extensively through China, co-authoring several travel guides for Lonely Planet.

CONTRIBUTORS

JULIE GRUNDVIG
Julie has been living and travelling in Northeast Asia for the past 13 years. She has worked as editor of the *BC Asian Review* and is currently associate editor of the international journal *Yishu: Journal of Contemporary Chinese Art*. Julie currently lives in Vancouver, BC, Canada. Julie wrote the Food & Drink chapter and co-wrote the Arts & Architecture chapter.

DR TRISH BATCHELOR
Dr Trish Batchelor is a general practitioner and travel medicine specialist who works at the Ciwec Clinic in Kathmandu, Nepal. She is also a medical advisor to the Travel Doctor New Zealand clinics. Trish teaches travel medicine through the University of Otago and is interested in underwater and high-altitude medicine. She has travelled extensively through Southeast and East Asia. Trish wrote the Health section in the Directory chapter.

PHOTOGRAPHER

PHIL WEYMOUTH
Standing in the Forbidden City, photographing ballroom dancers in the park, eating dumplings and exploring the *hútong* – Beijing was a great experience for Phil.

Phil studied photography in Melbourne, worked as a photographer in Bahrain and spent several years working for a rural Australian media company. He now runs a freelance photojournalism business based in Melbourne, Australia.

Introducing Beijing

Capital of the most populous nation on earth and first city in a land that has long dazzled observers, Beijing is the striking metropolitan core of a country with one of the world's oldest civilizations.

For decades at the fringes of world events, Beijing now finds itself positioned in the spotlight as the dynamic nucleus of a country generating staggering gross domestic product (GDP) figures. Pundits talk of the 21st century as belonging to China; and China itself, as everyone knows, belongs to Beijing.

The city may have left the moneymaking to Shanghai and Shenzhen and the music making to Hong Kong and Taiwan, but as the dynastic capital since the 13th century, Beijing has an indisputable pedigree. Seat of power to the Mongol, Ming and Qing emperors, the city is no stranger to prestige. Annihilated by Genghis Khan, esteemed by Marco Polo, reshaped by the Ming, courted by the West and plunged into chaos by Mao – Beijing has had a dramatic and turbulent past, but its authority has rarely been in question.

But exactly where this city is now heading, no one knows for sure. The forest of cranes, thump of jackhammers, crackle of welding torches and pendulous sweep of the wrecking ball suggests a vigorous, yet incomplete, revolution. What *is* certain is that Beijing, for centuries a vast and introspective walled bastion, has long been stirring and is now moving forward in gigantic leaps.

Few cities on earth have undergone such rapid transformation as today's Beijing, and the convulsions of change have old-timers scratching their heads. With the 2008 Olympics – the Holy Grail of Beijing city planners – in the bag, the transformation has received new vigour.

Beijing – fondly called Peking by ageing Western diplomats, *The Times* and historians – still stumps first-time visitors who arrive expecting a ragged tableau of communist China. New arrivals are struck by both the city's modernity and immensity. Located on a vast plain that reaches as far south as the Yellow River, the city's chessboard flatness reinforces a sense that it goes on forever. This flat topography, coupled with broad, sweeping avenues, huge open spaces and one-storey *hútong* (alleyway) architecture traditionally gave the city a stumpy skyline. Since the capital's architects embraced height to augment China's growing stature, the city's once flat perspective is now punctuated by towers of glass and steel.

And it's not all just buildings and flyovers. The social fabric of the city – once stitched from a grey communist piece of cloth – now comes in brighter colours. Students who used to recite slogans instead spend hours fussing over their hair or the latest fad or lounging around in Internet cafés. Snappily dressed businessmen seal multimillion *yuan* deals over steak dinners and fine wine. The city's growing contingent of bars services an urban workforce that works and plays hard,

Lowdown

- **Population** 13.8 million
- **Time zone** GMT + 8 hours
- **Coffee** Y20-30
- **Subway ticket** Y3
- **Three-star room** Y400-600
- **Number of cars** Two million
- **Number of taxis** 63,000
- **Number of high-rise buildings under construction** 2000+
- **Expat population** 50,000

while Beijing's eclectic restaurant scene is proof that the rest of the world has come to town, further evinced by the mushrooming international community.

Today's Beijing is going places, but development remains patchy and lopsided. Investment and opportunity may swill about, but with one foot lodged in the past and the other set squarely in the future, Beijing has become a curious hybrid. Glittering high-rises cap the city's central and business districts, yet you don't have to go far into the suburbs to see donkey-drawn carts. The energy of the young generation contrasts with the resignation of the elderly. Many victims – migrant workers, the unemployed or those without hope – are caught in the abyss between the free market and the state-controlled economy. The city furthermore has a long tradition of wrecking itself (of more than 2,500 temples that once existed in and around Beijing, only several dozen survive today), and the current felling of *hutong* is reckless.

But in this headlong rush into the future, history – an increasingly precious commodity – has not been totally condemned. Within Beijing's environs you will find some of China's most stunning sights: the Forbidden City, the Summer Palace, Temple of Heaven Park, the Lama Temple and the Great Wall, to name just a few. Beyond Beijing, excursions to the erstwhile imperial encampment at Chéngdé and the Great Wall's finale at the sea at Shānhaiguān add additional historical allure.

The city also has its own human story to tell. The false dawn of communism was dazzling in its day, but today's Beijingers are a pragmatic bunch who have – with regard to Mao Zedong and his revolutionary zeal – been there, done that, moved on. Unpretentious and forthright, what locals lack in charisma and panache, they make up for with candour, modesty and erudition. Overwhelmingly polite and uncomplicated, Beijingers are a friendly and welcoming people. Enjoy your visit.

DAMIAN'S TOP BEIJING DAY

A strong coffee for breakfast and then a few forms of taichi to limber up. Then I'll jump on my bike and head to Zhongshan Park to take a seat and read a book in the shade of some trees. After walking round part of the Forbidden City's palace moat, a morning shopping trip to Wangfujing Dajie is a must for daily purchases and a newspaper, followed by lunch in a nearby restaurant. Qianhai Lake is easily reached by bike, where I'll lounge about in a lakeside café. In the afternoon, a visit to one of Beijing's temples affords a needed contrast to the city's increasing modernity. If it's a clear day, I'll stroll around Tiananmen Square at dusk before catching a taxi to Sanlitun for both dinner and an evening beer.

City Life

City Life

BEIJING TODAY

New arrivals to Hong Kong or Shànghǎi come primed for cities pumped up by both cliché and high expectations, while many first timers to Beijing arrive with no more than a hazy picture of their destination.

Visitors are bowled over by a skyline bristling with cranes and shimmering with glittering high-rises, as well as the energetic modernity and the sheer vigour of a city rediscovering its youth and sense of direction. The collision between communism and capitalism traditionally generates either fire and smoke or a bitter chill, but Beijing's way seems to have produced a unique kind of vitality that makes perfect sense. Once a stagnant backwater of the world economy and practically a global irrelevance, Beijing has found a prosperity and purpose that has grabbed the world's attention. There has never been such an exciting time to visit Beijing.

The city may not be a torchbearer, but it is proud of its distinguished history and heritage and assured of both its importance and significance as the national capital. In its dramatic reinvention, the city has taken a leaf from Shanghai's book, and seemingly found opportunity everywhere. A buzz is in the air, inspiring architecture is going up (take a look at Oriental Plaza), the art scene is adding its own splash of colour, cafés are commonplace and a lively music scene (p133) is keeping the city awake at night. Money is being ploughed into transport infrastructure in a frantic bid to bring the city up to date for the 2008 Olympics, with US$22 billion earmarked for projects to prettify Beijing before the athletes arrive.

The city has learned how to work and play hard, and the swelling middle and white-collar class has totally redefined the socioeconomic make-up of town. Fashion – once a vice of the decadent West and a household taboo – is now an indispensable lifestyle fad among the young and aspiring generation. Car ownership – despite the outlandish costs of purchasing and owning a vehicle – is going through the roof with over two million cars on Beijing's streets. Prostitution and other old evils have resurfaced, while yawning inequalities between the haves and have-nots grow wider daily.

Despite its slick overlays, Beijing is a mishmash of both the old and new and the rich and poor; among all the signs of prosperity lurk the ragged reminders of poverty. The youth of Beijing may be on a roll, but some Beijingers over the age of 40 feel the sting of disillusionment, created by the huge sacrifices made by their generation.

Development also has its price and Beijing's energetic expansion is giving the city's heritage a thrashing. Roads may need to be widened to facilitate transport, but at what cost? Beijing has only recently woken up to the importance of heritage conservation; in the 1950s the city's huge walls (some of the world's most magnificent) were levelled, along with numerous *páilou* (decorative archways, see p71). Today the residents of many *hútong* (alleyways) are being moved on as property developers bulldoze their homes to make way for uniform high-rise housing blocks for the new moneyed class. These small single-storey dwellings sit on valuable land that is like gold dust in a rising real estate market, especially as the *hutong* criss-cross Beijing's central districts. More than 10,000 homes are vanishing every year and huge pockets of history are obliterated.

In recent years there has been an effort to reconstruct historical sites. The irony of reconstructing and repackaging the Ming

Hot Conversation Topics

- Money, money, money
- The newest, best restaurant to spend some of the above in
- The latest quality pirate DVD on sale on a Beijing flyover or underpass
- Beijing's pernicious traffic conditions
- Just why CCTV9 news is so execrably bad
- The latest mother of all spring sandstorms to billow through town

City Wall between the Southeast Corner Watchtower and Chongwenmen and Dongbianmen is, however, surely not lost on the old folk of Beijing. But scores of Buddhist temples are gone for good, their former sites now built over.

GDP figures make for a spectacular fanfare, but the age of the true free market – where the fittest survive and the failing and moribund fade away – has yet to arrive. The baubles of success may dazzle and it is easy to forget Beijing is the capital of a communist state. The city's economic machine glitters, but the cogs and wheels – the apparatus that channels its moneymaking energy – is still a 1950s socialist-capitalist hybrid. In its bid to survive, the government has made great concessions, but it knows that reform can only go so far before the seeds of its own extinction are sown. There are limits to reform.

The tremendous strides that Beijing has made since the early 1980s are awesome, but they conceal the limping progress of other development indicators such as democratic reform, effective anti-corruption measures, freedom of the press and freedom of speech.

A cyclist passes a cinema billboard

CITY CALENDAR

China follows both the Gregorian *(yánglì)* and the lunar calendar *(yīnlì)*. Traditional Chinese festivals and holidays (p201) are calculated according to the lunar calendar and fall on different days each year according to the Gregorian calendar.

JANUARY & FEBRUARY

SPRING FESTIVAL
Chūn Jié

Also known as Chinese New Year, this festival is the highpoint of the year, kicking off on the first day of the first lunar month. The festival usually falls sometime between late January and mid-February and ushers in a new year marked by one of the 12 animals of the Chinese zodiac. The weeks in the build-up to the festival are an explosion of colour, with *chūnlián* (spring couplets) pasted on door posts, door gods brightening up *hutong* and shops glistening with red and gold decorations. Colleagues at work and relatives present each other with red envelopes *(hóngbāo)* of money, the streets ring with cries of '*gōngxǐ fācái*' ('congratulations – make money') and Beijing residents don their fanciest attire. The White Cloud Temple (p89), the Lama Temple (p81) and other temples in Beijing stage entertaining temple fairs *(mi'àohu'ì)*. Celebrations are also held in parks such as Ditan Park (p75). Although officially lasting only three days, many people take a week or more off work. Although the city is vacated by legions of Chinese heading to the provinces to visit relatives and it can be bitterly cold, the Spring Festival can be a fascinating time to be in Beijing. Air and rail transport however can be booked solid, hotel accommodation is harder to come by and many businesses shut up shop for a week or so.

LANTERN FESTIVAL
Yuánxiāo Jié
23 Feb 2005; 12 Feb 2006

Celebrated two weeks after the first day of the Spring Festival, this festival (also known as Dēng Jié or Shàngyuán Jié) is not a public holiday, but can be a very colourful time to visit Beijing. The Chinese visit *dēnghuì* (lantern shows) in the evening and devour gorgeous *yuánxiāo* (glutinous rice dumplings with soft, sweet fillings).

MARCH & APRIL

GUANYIN'S BIRTHDAY
Guānshìyìn Shēngrì
28 Mar 2005; 18 Mar 2006
The birthday of Guanyin (Sanskrit Avalokitesh-vara), the Buddhist Goddess of Mercy (p185), is a fine time to visit Buddhist temples, many of which have halls dedicated to the divinity. Puning Temple (p183) is entirely dedicated to Guanyin and sees important celebrations on the occasion of her birthday, held on the 19th day of the second moon.

TOMB SWEEPING DAY
Qīng Míng Jié
5 Apr (4 Apr in leap years)
A day for worshipping ancestors, the festival falls near the date of Easter; people visit and clean the graves *(sǎomù)* of departed relatives.

The Chinese often place flowers on the tomb and burn ghost money for the departed. There may be increased vigilance in Tiananmen Square during the festival, as public displays of mourning for the dead of 4 June 1989 remain prohibited.

SEPTEMBER & OCTOBER

MID-AUTUMN FESTIVAL
Zhōngqiū Jié
18 Sep 2005; 6 Oct 2006
Also known as the Moon Festival, this festival is marked by eating tasty *yuèbǐng* (moon cakes), gazing at the full moon and gathering together with relatives for family reunions. It is also a traditional holiday for lovers and takes place on the 15th day of the eighth lunar month.

BIRTHDAY OF CONFUCIUS
Kǒngzi Shēngrì
The great sage has his birthday on the 27th day of the eighth month, an occasion marked by celebrations at Confucian temples.

CULTURE

CONNECTIONS

Within their daily life, Chinese people often have to compete for goods or services in short supply and many have been assigned jobs for which they have zero interest and often no training. Those who have *guānxì* (connections) usually get what they want because the connections network is, of course, reciprocal.

Obtaining goods or services through connections is informally referred to as 'going through the back door' *(zǒu hòu mén)*. Guanxi is lavishly cultivated by way of banquets and fuelled by *báijiǔ* (white spirit) and the best smokes on the market. As foreign investment in China has grown, gift giving for *guanxi* has become more and more wasteful. Cadres and officials are very well placed for this activity, but exploiting *guanxi* can easily lead to corruption.

IDENTITY

You may get the impression that Beijing is laid back and even indolent, but it has repeatedly been the source of tempestuous historical events, from the May 4 Movement to the Cultural Revolution and the student democracy movement of 1989. Beijing is – unlike buzzing Hong Kong or Shanghai – a city of slowly brewing *latent* energy that slowly accumulates before spilling over.

Beijingers know that they live in the cultural, political and psychological centre of China. They are not only *Zhōngguórén* (Chinese), they are *shǒudūrén* (citizens of the capital) and in the top spot. Throughout the land the Chinese chat in *Pǔtōnghuà* (based on the Beijing dialect), set their watch according to Beijing Time *(Běijīng Shíjiān)* and act on enigmatic directives from the capital.

Beijing people see themselves as more politically astute than the rest of China and chat more about politics than elsewhere. Confident of their pre-eminence, they feel superior *(gāorén yīděng)* to those unfortunate enough to live outside town. *Běijīnghuà* – the local dialect – they think is infinitely superior to *putonghua* and revel in the complexities of the Beijing dialect and how it instantly distinguishes outsiders. To be a Beijinger is to be the genuine article, while everyone else, Chinese included, is a *wàidìrén* (from outside town) or even worse, a *tǔbāozi* (country bumpkin).

Beijingers have a reputation among their fellow Chinese for being blunt and straightforward *(zhíjié liǎodàng)*, honest, well-read and cultivated, if just a bit conservative. Beijingers scorn the calculating *(suànji)* shrewdness of Hong Kong Chinese and the notorious stinginess of the Shanghainese. They take pride in being generous *(dàfang)* and amicable *(yǒushàn)*, and this is nowhere more evident than when dining out. Beijingers will fight to pay for the bill with loud choruses of '*wǒ lái, wǒ lái, wǒ fù qián*' ('I'll pay') and will never split the bill (as may happen in Shanghai). Beijingers are also prone to excess, cooking more than they need and binning the rest. It's all part of their big-hearted mindset. Ostentatious displays of wealth don't go down so well in Beijing as in Hong Kong, however. Like the city in which they live, Beijingers are unpretentious and modest. Beijing has left the construction of record-breaking high-rise towers to Taiwan, Hong Kong and Shanghai.

LIFESTYLE

Changes in the way of life of Beijing residents have matched the city's economic transformation over the past 20 years. Modern Beijing offers young people a new and exciting world of fashion, music, dance, sport, new slang, drugs and lifestyle experimentation. Many of those over the age of 40, however, often feel trapped between the familiar expectations of their genera-

Chinese Etiquette

The Chinese are very polite and will naturally appreciate it if you are polite in return. Reserved in their behaviour and expression, the Chinese eschew public displays of emotion and grand gestures. Face saving (avoidance of shame) is important to the Chinese psyche and forcing a Chinese person to back down prompts loss of face.

Meals are important occasions where friendships and business deals are often forged. The host – or the person sitting next to you – is likely to serve you food and ensure your glass is refilled. Relentless toasting is common, often performed standing up and accompanied by a chorus of '*gānbēi*', which is the signal for you to drain your glass. But if you can only handle half a glass, say '*gǎn bànbēi*' which literally means 'drink half a glass'. Don't forget to do a toast in return, a few minutes after you have been toasted. Even if you have been invited out make a gesture to pay the bill. It will be appreciated but refused. Don't, however, insist on paying the bill as your host will need to pay. For reasons of face, it is terribly important for Chinese to settle the bill as a sign of generosity and hospitality. Smoking at meal time is generally OK, as it can establish a rapport among smokers.

A landmine to be wary of is political discussion. The Chinese may secretly agree with you that the Communist Party is a band of good-for-nothings, but these are sentiments they probably won't want to voice. This works both ways, so say you don't want to talk politics (if you are being grilled on US foreign policy) unless there is quid pro quo. Even if you are not on business, name cards are very important, so make sure you have a stack printed up with Chinese on one side and English on the reverse. The Chinese present and receive business cards with the fingers of both hands.

tion and the widening horizons of the city's youth. The unpleasantness of the Cultural Revolution encourages parents in this age group to protect their children from strife and unexpected misfortune. The following domestic sketch may not be as common as it was 10 years ago, but this is still how many Beijing residents live.

Old Mr Zhao is in his late 60s, smokes 10 *Zhongnanhai* cigarettes a day and lives in a one-storey courtyard house east of Wangfujing Dajie. He lives off a pension of Y800 a month – 90% of his basic salary when he worked as a machinist. He shares a room with his wife, Liang Min, a retired nurse who also earns a pension of around Y800. Mr Zhao rises at 5.30am to practice some *taichi* in a nearby park, before returning to his courtyard to read the newspaper.

Mr Zhao and his wife live with their son, Zhao Yongqiang and his wife, Liu Yan. In his late 30s, Zhao Yongqiang is actually the owner of the house, which was allocated to him by his work unit *(dānwèi)*. Zhao's parents moved in when they got too old to live by themselves. Zhao Yongqiang earns Y2000 a month as a teacher at a local middle school and takes the bus or cycles to work every day. His 35-year old wife drops their 10-year old daughter off at school every day of the week and works part-time as a shop assistant in a pharmacy, earning Y1200 a month. In the hope that their daughter can get into university, they both put money aside for private English lessons, their greatest expense.

The entire family is careful with money and save as much as they can. You won't find a single credit card in the household and no one is in debt. With little spare money for entertainment, the Zhao family watch TV in the evenings or sit around in the courtyard chatting with neighbours. Watching TV is usually a tussle between Zhao Yongqiang, who wants to watch football, and his father, who prefers to tune into Beijing opera. To break the deadlock, they tune into an imported Korean soap opera or drama, which satisfies the women of the household.

The courtyard houses eight families in all, so there's always someone dropping by for a game of chess or cards or a few bottles of Beijing Beer. On Saturday morning, Zhao Yongqiang prepares lamb kebabs from locally bought meat in preparation for lunch attended by the entire courtyard (everyone chips in for the meat and beer).

Recent road widening topped and tailed the *hutong* in which Mr Zhao lives with his family, but the modest residence he calls home was spared. Many local friends and associates were moved into modern high-rise housing in the suburbs, but the Zhao family is happy to remain here, despite the small size of their dwelling. They love the sense of community and the undeniable charm of their Qing dynasty courtyard home. To top it all, the location slap bang in the centre of town is peerless!

FASHION

The fashion industry in Beijing has exploded over the past 10 years. Whereas in the early 1990s a fashion industry barely existed, the annual Beijing Fashion Week, featuring innovative and inspiring creations from Chinese designers, has become a fixture on the international fashion circuit.

Despite the turnaround, Beijing is inherently less international than either Shanghai or Hong Kong, so it is unlikely it will ever rank as a leading fashion city. But with over 20 schools and colleges with fashion departments, the city takes its clothing seriously.

On the streets the picture is less certain but no less interesting. Many Beijing youths cling to a home-grown rather than an international sense of style, with less reverence of designer labels and mass market fashion trends and more emphasis on a happy-go-lucky medley of styles and designs. Men over the age of 40 will still wear black, brown or grey jackets and trousers (all of the time), while the moneyed class shop for labels and young, hip Beijingers are individualistic in their tastes. The Beijing-dominant rock/punk music subculture has a strong influence on the young and the way they dress.

Traditional Chinese-style clothes are perennially popular, influencing legions of Beijing designers and filling shops with clothing inspired by classic garments such as the *cheongsam*. Other essential fashion items include skin whitening creams and parasols and, increasingly, cosmetic surgery.

Traditional Chinese-style clothing

ECONOMY & COSTS
'HE WHO IS NOT IN CHARGE OF IT DOES NOT INTERFERE IN ITS BUSINESS.'
Confucius

Beijing is the national capital of the world's fastest growing economy and the city chosen to host the 2008 Olympic Games. Glowing economic predictions portray China as the world's largest economy by 2020 if it maintains its current trajectory.

With the Olympics in the bag, the local government has seized the nettle to activate a vast investment blueprint that will shake up Beijing. The facts and figures alone are breathtaking: in the run-up to the Olympics, US$6.7 billion is to be spent on Beijing's public transport system and road construction, US$4.4 billion is earmarked for environmental protection, US$18.2 billion is planned for the expansion of manufacturing and high-tech industries, while the development of new urban areas is expected to cost an awesome US$96.8 billion.

Tourism is becoming an increasingly important source of revenue, with 110 million domestic visitors arriving in 2003, spending around US$90 billion. With China tipped to be the world's top tourist destination by 2020, the potential for growth is huge.

Facts and figures aside, Beijing remains China's political heart rather than its economic frontline and its pulse is more measured than, say, Shanghai's. Vigilant about its own affairs and scrupulous at reigning in more strident trends nationwide, the economic environment of Beijing is far from laissez-faire. Regularly published peons to China's robust economy may paint a different picture, but Beijing remains a staid, bureaucratic environment where much economic development is propelled by state investment and large scale public works programmes rather than by market forces. Many of the labour intensive and high investment programmes that will shape the Beijing Olympic Economy fall into this category.

A similar formula powers much of China's spectacular GDP growth. The conspicuous manifestations of such development – high-rise towers, chic designer clothing stores and Bentley showrooms – are eye catching, but much of the economy remains under the control of the socialist state and its army of bureaucrats.

Several major obstacles to growth exist, some of which represent local problems, while others are part of larger national dilemmas. All of them impinge on the city's economic performance, discourage investment and hamper Beijing's efforts to become a major international financial centre.

Beijing has a largely unfavourable geographical location – neither on the coast nor on a major waterway – and never developed a great trading economy like that of Shanghai or Hong Kong.

Water and land are two natural resources that are being rapidly depleted, restricting Beijing's development potential, while the ongoing problem of migrant labourers coming to Beijing in search of work and opportunity is swelling unemployment levels and straining resources. Local labour authorities were preparing for an influx of more than 200,000 migrant labourers in 2004.

Beijing is investing considerable sums in transport infrastructure, from laying new roads and widening existing roads to expanding the subway system. But economic development itself has revealed the limitations of Beijing's road and transport systems. The number of vehicles in Beijing topped two million in 2003 (a figure that is rapidly growing) and 16,789 traffic jams were officially recorded in 2002. Congestion charges – along the lines of London's successful model – are being considered in a bid to ease congestion. Cars are already prohibitively expensive and any further measures to control the number of cars on Beijing's roads will antagonise the automobile industry (a major contributor to national economic growth).

Corruption not only erodes GDP but is a major cause of public dissatisfaction

Beijing's Economic Stats

- Beijing's GDP US$43 billion (2003)
- 2003 total retail consumption exceeded US$22.9 billion
- Annual expenditure on housing US$6.1 billion

with the government. One of the principal complaints of the 1989 Tiananmen demonstrators, the problem of corruption, has not been solved despite some high-profile imprisonments and executions.

As a city hell-bent on modernising, Beijing can be shockingly expensive. You can pay criminal prices: up to Y45 (US$5.50) for a coffee or Y50 (US$6) for a bowl of noodles at Capital Airport; Y1.2 million (US$150,000) for a bottom-rung Porsche or US$8500 a month for a plush three-bedroom apartment.

Foreigners (and the Chinese nouveau riche) are targeted for their hard-earned cash, so don't just dish it out. Look around, learn to get savvy and get a feel for where locals shop, and quickly try to get a sense of proportion. Working with a new currency, take your time to accurately convert prices.

Hotels are going to be the biggest expense, but food and transport can add up quickly too. Excluding the cost of getting to Beijing, ascetics can survive on as little as US$15 per day – that means staying in dormitories, travelling by bus or bicycle rather than taxi, eating from street stalls or small restaurants and refraining from buying anything. At the time of writing, the cheapest dorm bed was Y15 and a basic meal in a run-of-the-mill streetside restaurant cost around Y20 to Y30.

At the opposite end of the spectrum, five-star hotel rooms can reach US$300 per day and upmarket restaurant meals around US$50. And there is an increasing number of expensive department stores. If you want to spend money you won't have a problem.

Beer at corner shops *(xiǎomàibù)* – often buried down *hutong* – should cost around Y1.5 for a bottle of Beijing or Yanjing Beer. Drinking at bars is much more expensive, where a small bottle of Beijing or Tsingtao will cost around Y15 to Y25. Unlike cigarettes in countries such as the UK, where prices for cigarettes are by and large the same, there is great variation in Chinese cigarette prices (Y3 to Y70).

Pirate DVDs usually retail for around Y8 but be warned that quality is often a problem.

GOVERNMENT & POLITICS

'A REVOLUTION IS NOT A DINNER PARTY, OR WRITING AN ESSAY, OR PAINTING A PICTURE, OR DOING EMBROIDERY; IT CANNOT BE SO REFINED, SO LEISURELY AND GENTLE, SO TEMPERATE, KIND, COURTEOUS, RESTRAINED AND MAGNANIMOUS. A REVOLUTION IS AN INSURRECTION, AN ACT OF VIOLENCE BY WHICH ONE CLASS OVERTHROWS ANOTHER.'

Mao Zedong

Beijing is the seat of political power in China and all the important decisions that affect the rest of the land are made here.

Precious little is known about the inner workings of the Chinese government, but what is known is that the entire monolithic structure, from grass roots work units to the upper echelons of political power, is controlled by the Chinese Communist Party (CCP) and its power base is Beijing.

The highest authority rests with the Standing Committee of the CCP Politburo. The Politburo comprises 25 members and below it is the 210-member Central Committee, made up of younger party members and provincial party leaders. At the grass roots level the party forms a parallel system to the administrations in the army, universities, government and industries. Real authority is exercised by the party representatives at each level in these organisations. They, in turn, are responsible to the party officials in the hierarchy above them, thus ensuring strict central control.

The day-to-day running of the country lies with the State Council, which is directly under the control of the CCP. The State Council is headed by the premier and beneath the premier are four vice-premiers, 10 state councillors, a secretary-general, 45 ministers and various other agencies. The State Council implements the decisions made by the Politburo.

Approving the decisions of the CCP leadership is the National People's Congress (NPC), the principal legislative body that convenes in the Great Hall of the People (p65). It comprises a 'democratic alliance' of both party members and non-party members including intellectuals, technicians and industrial managers. In theory they are empowered to amend the constitution and to choose the premier and members of the State Council. The catch is that all these office holders must first be recommended by the Central Committee, and thus the NPC is only an approving body.

The Chinese government is also equipped with a massive bureaucracy. The term 'cadre' is usually applied to bureaucrats, and their monopoly on power means that wide-ranging perks are a privilege of rank for all and sundry – from the lowliest clerks to the shadowy puppet masters of Zhongnanhai. China's bureaucratic tradition is a long one.

The wild card in the system is the army. Comprising land forces, the navy and the air force, it has a total of around 2.9 million members. China is divided into seven military regions, each with its own military leadership – in some cases with strong regional affiliations.

ENVIRONMENT

China's breakneck economic growth over the past few decades has both depleted resources and generated vast quantities of pollution. Long-distance train travellers through China will be familiar with a bleak landscape of fields and trees choked with shredded non-biodegradable plastic bags. Successful economic renewal provides the Communist Party with a tenuous mandate to rule, so green issues and sustainable development policies have long taken a back seat in short-term political planning. Rules and laws for protecting the environment exist, but are often not rigorously enforced.

Beijing is under tremendous pressure to clean itself up for the 2008 Olympics. Various measures have been introduced to clean the air, including encouraging the use of natural gas and electricity rather than the traditional circular coal briquettes (fēngwōméi) for winter heating, replacing diesel buses with environmentally friendly vehicles and closing heavily

Dune

You've heard of the Gobi and you may have heard of the Takla Makan, but did you know that Beijing may one day be another of China's deserts? The nearest patch of desert is only 18km from Beijing; winds are blowing the sands towards the capital at a rate of 2km a year, with dunes up to 30m high wriggling ever closer.

Anyone who has visited Beijing in spring will be familiar with the yellow clouds billowing down the streets. Even the sight of Beijing residents with plastic bags over their heads is commonplace. The storms can be fierce; sandstorm forecasts are now broadcast on TV to alert the public. In February 2001, sand particles from a sandstorm in north China reached Taiwan.

Experts blame overgrazing and deforestation; without grassland and tree cover, and with a dropping water table, the deserts are on a roll, overwhelming villages in north China. The Gobi Desert is expanding towards the south at a rate of 2.4% per year, extinguishing the grasslands. Every month, 200 sq km of arable land in China becomes desert.

According to the United Nation's Office to Combat Desertification and Drought (UNSO), one-third of China is subject to desertification – the process by which previously semi-arable or arable land gradually becomes depleted of plant and animal life.

The Chinese government has been jolted into pledging a massive US$6.8 billion to stop the spread of the sand. A green wall, which will eventually stretch 5700km – longer than the Great Wall – is being planted in northeastern China to keep back the sand, though some experts argue that it is not tree, but grass cover that best binds the soil.

polluting industries. Beijing's skies may be losing their customary pall, but certain measures (eg stricter exhaust emission controls) have to be weighed against the burgeoning volume of cars on Beijing's streets.

Compared to just five years ago, however, Beijing is a much more pleasant and greener city to live in. Grass has appeared in wisps and patches, splashing the city's usual greys and browns with lushly watered vivid green. Beijing aims to increase the amount of green space in the city by 50% come 2010. The prettification has extended to rebuilding a section of the Ming dynasty city wall (earlier felled by the communists) and the development of more parks.

Apart from the occasional summer rainstorm soaking, Beijing is dusty and dehydrated. In fact, it is so arid it's baffling how anything grows at all. Beijing and much of north China currently faces an acute water shortage, with dropping water tables and shrinking reservoirs. Increased water use in and around Beijing – and upstream along the Yellow River – has resulted in increased amounts of water being extracted from the ground. Experts warn that Beijing's water supply will be exhausted in another six years unless something is done. Posters around town exhort residents to save every drop of water and the local government has implemented water recycling measures, but with an estimated 30% to 40% of water lost through leaking underground pipes, it's an uphill struggle. The gargantuan south–north water transfer project will help supply Beijing with water directly pumped from the flood-prone Yangzi River in 2010, but sustainable water use is just as critical.

URBAN PLANNING

The demands of a rapidly increasing population and ballooning vehicle numbers have put Beijing's transport and housing infrastructure under duress. But netting the 2008 Olympics has given the city a chance to grab the bull by the horns. Millions of square feet of real estate space are currently under construction, with the total amount of office space expected to double by 2008. In the first nine months of 2003, real estate development in Beijing was chalked up at US$8.8 billion. The subway is undergoing extension and roads are being widened, with the Chinese character *chāi* (for demolition) daubed in white on condemned buildings city-wide.

But Beijing's metamorphosis is not all roses – huge building projects have relocated over 100,000, often elderly, urban residents. Some have moved willingly while others have tried to resist, but with the state owning all property in Beijing, protesters can do little in the face of the police (and widespread apathy). A third of Beijing's *hutong* within the Second Ring Rd have been demolished and, because the remainder sit on immensely valuable land, they continue to fall at a rate of 10,000 properties a year. One example is Chaoyangmen Nanxiaojie, once a narrow and bustling street lined with hole-in-the-wall restaurants, kebab outlets and *hutong* openings, and now a wide avenue overlooked by modern housing units.

Beijing planners say that it's easy for foreign observers to condemn the destruction, remarking that Beijing needs to modernise like any other city. Nonetheless, the identity of the city is undergoing an irreversible transformation. The nostalgic rebuilding of part of the Ming City Wall is a synthetic and limited undoing of the gargantuan demolition act that destroyed it. And with artificial *sihéyuàn* (courtyard house) restaurants materializing in the city's five-star hotels, perhaps the death knell for *hutong* is already on the Beijing breeze, among all the construction dust.

Arts & Architecture

Arts & Architecture

ARTS

Like other aspects of life in Beijing, the art scene has experienced a renaissance over the past 20 years. Alongside China's impressive social and economic developments, a yearning for innovation and creative expression has nurtured a transformation in cinema, theatre and music. If you want to fathom the artistic psyche of the Chinese people, Beijing provides an excellent opportunity. Nonetheless, restraint and compromise have inhibited the full growth of Beijing's cultural scene, a situation compounded by a traditionally cautious Chinese attitude to self-expression.

LITERATURE

Some of China's most important 20th-century writers have made their homes in Beijing, including Lao She, Lu Xun, Mao Dun and Guo Moruo. Beijing today remains an important centre of literary activity, despite the upheavals and turmoil artists and writers have faced over the past century. The city is home to an eclectic group of authors, many young and upcoming, who write with an outspokenness and creative energy that is helping to redefine Chinese literature in the 21st century.

After China came under the control of the communists, most writing in 20th-century China tended to echo the Communist Party line, with formulaic language and predictable plotlines. Writers were required to fill their work with stock phrases such as 'the great, glorious, correct Communist Party' and create characters that were models of political ideals. Writing was rigid and unimaginative, with little allowance for creative embellishment.

Things changed after Mao's death in 1976, when Chinese artists and writers were finally able to throw off political constraints and write more freely. Writers for the first time dared to explore the traumatic events of the Cultural Revolution, creating a movement called 'Scar Literature', a genre that would continue throughout the 1980s. Another literary movement also emerged called 'New Realism', which explored issues that were previously taboo, such as AIDS, party corruption and other contemporary social problems. One of the most controversial novels to appear in the 1980s was *Half of Man is Woman,* by Zhang Xianliang and translated into English by Martha Avery, a candid exploration of sexuality and marriage in contemporary China. Zhang has been called the Chinese Milan Kundera and his book became an international bestseller. Another of Zhang's works that has been translated into English is *Getting Used to Dying* (1989), about a writer's new found sexual freedom, also translated by Martha Avery.

One of China's most famous female authors, Zhang Jie, first drew the attention of literary critics in the late 1970s with the publication of her daring novella *Love Must Not be Forgotten* (1979). The book challenged the traditional structure of marriage with its intimate portrayal of a middle-aged woman and her love of a married man. Chinese authorities disparaged the book, calling it morally corrupt, but the book proved extremely popular with readers and went on to win a national book award. Zhang went on to write the novels *Heavy Wings* (1980) and *The Ark* (1981). *The Ark*, about three women separated from their husbands, has been compared to Doris Lessing's *The Golden Notebook*, and established Zhang as China's 'first feminist author'.

During the 1980s writers not only felt the freedom to explore off-limits topics in their work but also to experiment with language and symbolism for the first time. A group of poets, including Bei Dao, Gu Cheng, Yang Lian and Shu Ting, became identified as the 'Misty Poets' and used deliberately elusive images and logic in their writing. Bei Dao (Zhao Zhenkai), one of the most famous of the Misty Poets, was born in Beijing and served as a Red Guard during the Cultural Revolution. In the early 1970s he began to write poems, using several different pseudonyms, criticising the official literature of his time. Bei Dao

Beijing Book Reviews

- **Diary of a Madman and Other Stories**, Lu Xun, translated by William Lyell (1990) Lu Xun is considered the father of modern Chinese literature and this classic was the first of its kind to be written in a first-person narrative. The story is a criticism of Confucian repression in pre-revolutionary China.
- **Camel Xiangzi**, Lao She, translated by Shi Xiaoqing (1981) A masterpiece by one of China's most beloved authors about a rickshaw puller living in early 20th-century China.
- **Blades of Grass: The Stories of Lao She**, translated by William Lyell (2000) This collection contains 14 stories by Lao She, poignant descriptions of people living through times of political upheaval and uncertainty.
- **Black Snow**, Liu Heng, translated by Howard Goldblatt (1993) Liu Heng, author of the story that formed the basis for the film, *Ju Dou*, wrote this compelling novel about workers in contemporary Beijing. A superbly written book and a fine translation.
- **Empress Orchid**, Anchee Min (2004) Historical novel about Empress Tzu Hsi and her rise to Empress of China during the last days of the Qing dynasty. Good historical background of Beijing and entertaining to read.
- **Old Madam Yin: A Memoir of Peking Life 1926–1938**, Ida Pruitt (1979) The story of the friendship between an American hospital worker and a Chinese woman from an upper-class family in pre-revolutionary Beijing. The writing is a bit stilted but overall a fairly good read.
- **Jade and Fire**, Raymond James Burnett (1987) A historical mystery in 1948 Beijing about a police inspector investigating the murder of a Daoist priest. Interesting because of its incorporation of political events and persons into the narrative.
- **Third Messiah**, Christopher West (2000) Set in Beijing, this fast-paced crime novel about a police detective searching for his missing sister-in-law provides an insightful look into contemporary Chinese society.
- **Flower Net**, Lisa See (1998) This is a unique contemporary thriller about a Chinese woman detective investigating the death of the American ambassador's son in Beijing. It's a light read and certainly not great literature but it's good to kill time.
- **Summer of Betrayal**, Hong Ying, translated by Martha Avery (1999) This novel is about a young woman's involvement in the events of Tiananmen Square and the summer following the incident. The book has received mixed reviews from readers who found the writing a bit sentimental.
- **Peking Story: The Last Days of Old China**, David Kidd (2003) This is a true story of a young man who marries the daughter of an aristocratic Chinese family in Beijing two years before the 1948 Communist Revolution. The writing is simple, yet immersive.
- **Around the Bloc, My Life in Moscow, Beijing, and Havana**, Stephanie Elizondo Griest (2004) Light-hearted account of a young journalist and her escapades through the communist bloc.

became involved with the Democracy Movement and his poetry of the time expresses a desire for freedom and the disillusionment of his generation. The poet rose to international acclaim in the late 1970s when his poetry began to be published in international poetry journals. Despite being a primary target of China's 'Anti-Spiritual Campaign' in 1983, Bei Dao continued to publish and travelled throughout Europe and the United States giving readings and lectures. Several of his books were received enthusiastically in the international community but were banned in China for their pessimistic take on China's political climate. During the 1989 student uprising in Tiananmen Square, democracy advocates circulated his poetry and he was accused of helping to incite the events that followed. Soon after, the poet decided to live in exile in the United States where he still lives today. Much of Bei Dao's work has been translated into English, including *The August Sleepwalker* (1986) and *Old Snow* (1991), both translated by Bonnie S McDougall.

After the tragic events of 1989 the desire for a more 'realist' type of literature grew in China, paving the way for a new group of writers, such as the now internationally recognised 'hooligan author' Wang Shuo, sailor turned fiction writer, who has become known for his satirical stories about China's underworld and political corruption. Wang's stories, which are dark, gritty and take jabs at just about every aspect of contemporary Chinese society, have made him none too popular among Chinese authorities, who believe him to be a 'spiritual pollutant' and a bad influence on his readers. One of Wang's most controversial novels, *Please Don't Call Me Human*, first published in 1989, was written after the events of Tiananmen Square and provides a mocking look at the failures of China's state security system. Wang's works appeal to a broad spectrum of Chinese society, despite being banned. He has written over 20 books as well as screenplays for television and film. Books available in English include *Playing for Thrills* (2000) and *Please Don't Call Me Human* (1998), both translated by Howard Goldblatt.

China's economic progress and the excessive materialism of the 1990s has spawned a new generation of authors in Beijing, many of whom remember little about the Cultural Revolution and instead are most affected by the day-to-day realities of growing up in the city. Growing up without war or poverty, young writers are instead writing about the loneliness and decadence of urban life. Novels such as *Beijing Doll* (2002), by Chun Shu, depict disaffected youth in contemporary Beijing. The provocative novel is about an 18-year-old who lives a life of sex, drugs and alcohol, rejecting the traditional Chinese values she was versed in. Called a 'punk memoir', the book is currently banned in China for its disturbing accounts of teenagers caught up in Beijing's dark underbelly.

'Cyber literature' is another form of writing that has taken hold of China's new generation of authors. Increasing numbers of writers are putting their work online, because of the difficulties of finding a publisher. While some writers consider net publication a lesser form of art, some net authors have found themselves discovered in Web magazines and have moved on to have their works published. Writer Ning Ken's story *The Veiled City* was posted online and landed him the Lao She Literary Award, one of the most prestigious awards in China.

VISUAL ARTS

Beijing has a flourishing art scene, with privately run galleries competing with government-run museums and exhibition halls. Beijing artists are increasingly catching the attention of the international art world and joint exhibitions with European or American artists are now common. The Beijing Biennale, held in the autumn of 2003, was the first international exhibit of its kind to showcase artworks from over 40 countries and serve as a representative platform for some of China's top artists. While traditional Chinese art is still practised in the capital, Beijing is also home to a large community of artists practising a diverse mix of art forms including performance art, installation, video art and film.

Similar to what was happening in the Chinese literary scene, artists in China experienced a creative renaissance after the death of Mao in 1976. Some painters began using the realist techniques they learned in China's art academies to portray the harsh realities of Chinese peasant life in modern day China. Others broke away from the confines of 'socialist realism' and moved into broader territory, experimenting with a variety of contemporary forms. Many turned to the West for inspiration and tried to incorporate Western ideas into their works.

One such group, the Stars, found inspiration in Picasso and German Expressionism. The short-lived group was very important for the development of Chinese art in the 1980s and 1990s, leading the way for the New Wave movement that appeared in 1985. New Wave art-

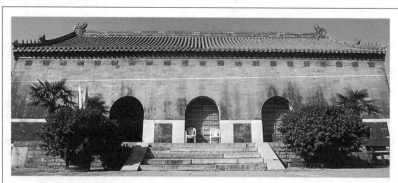

Wan Fung Art Gallery (p65)

ists were greatly influenced by Western art, especially Marcel Duchamp, and through their work challenged traditional Chinese aesthetics. One New Wave artist, Huang Yongping, became known for destroying his works at exhibitions, in an effort to escape from the notion of 'art'. Some New Wave artists transformed Chinese characters into abstract symbols while others used graphic images in their work to shock viewers. Performance art also became popular, with many artists wrapping themselves in plastic or tape to symbolise the repressive realities of modern day China.

The pivotal turning point for contemporary Chinese art came in 1989. In February of that year, Beijing's China Art Gallery (p74) sponsored an exhibit devoted exclusively to Chinese avant-garde art for the first time, inviting all of the important artists of the past decade to exhibit. On the opening day of the exhibition, artists Tang Song and Xiao Lu fired pistol shots at their own installations and the exhibition closed. Both artists were arrested but released several days later.

The upsetting events that followed in June 1989 caused many artists to become disillusioned with the current political situation in China and idealism soon soured into cynicism. This attitude is reflected through the 1990s and art works are permeated with feelings of loss, loneliness and social isolation. Two of the most important Beijing artists to characterise this period of 'Cynical Realism' are Fang Lijun and Yue Minjun. Both created grotesque portraits of themselves and friends that convey a sense of boredom and mock joviality.

Top Ten Beijing Art Galleries

- **Courtyard Gallery** – This contemporary Chinese art gallery is across from the East Gate of the Forbidden City.
- **Red Gate Gallery** (p67) – Founded by an Australian, this gallery has a focus on contemporary Chinese art.
- **25000 Cultural Transmission Center** – Also known as 'The Long March Space,' the 25000 Cultural Transmission Center promotes artistic works often excluded from Beijing's mainstream art scene.
- **Beijing Art Museum** (p95) – Located within Wanshou Temple, this museum carries exhibits aimed at promoting Chinese cultural heritage.
- **Wan Fung Art Gallery** (p65) – Gallery representing contemporary artists working in traditional painting, oil painting, watercolour painting, sculpture and mixed media.
- **China National Museum of Fine Arts** – Built in 1962, this recently renovated museum carries works by modern and contemporary Chinese artists as well as Chinese masters.
- **Creation Gallery** – Innovative art space showcasing Chinese contemporary artists.
- **798 Art Space** – German Bauhaus warehouse with over 1200 sq metres of art space exhibiting works of Chinese contemporary artists.
- **China Art Archives and Warehouse** – Exhibition space devoted to experimental art in China.
- **Beijing Tokyo Art Projects** – Branch of the Tokyo Gallery that originally opened in Ginza, Tokyo in 1950 by curator Takashi Yamamoto.

Experiments with American-style pop art were another reaction to the events of 1989. Inspired by Warhol, some artists took symbols of socialist realism and transformed them into kitschy visual commentary. Images of Mao appeared against floral backgrounds and paintings of rosy-cheeked peasants and soldiers were interspersed with ads for Canon cameras and Coca Cola. Artists were not only responding to the tragedies of the Tiananmen massacre but also to the rampant consumerism that was sweeping the country.

Reaction to the rapid modernisation that is affecting Beijing as well as other Chinese cities has been a current theme of much of the art from the 1990s to the present day. Urban development and accompanying feelings of isolation and dislocation are themes of Beijing video artist Zhu Jia. In his video titled 'Double Landscape,' a man is being served coffee by a mannequin dressed as a woman. The banality of the video and its lack of drama or narrative are meant to be representative of the meaninglessness of urban existence.

Yin Xiuzhen is one of the most influential female artists based in Beijing. She began showing her work in the late 1980s and has exhibited in a large number of art spaces around China. Yin's work is also a reaction to the dramatic changes taking place in Beijing and elsewhere. Often her pieces are a response to the destruction of Beijing's traditional architecture as well as environmental issues. One of her works, a commentary on urban waste, was to collect old clothing from Beijing residents, wash the clothing and then hang the clothes from an old pagoda to dry, letting the drips of water fall onto a mound of plaster

Traditional Chinese Painting

The origins of Chinese painting lie in the Bronze Age, beginning with representational figures of humans, animals and demons inscribed on bronze vessels. The emphasis on brushwork and line in these works was and remains the defining element of traditional Chinese painting. In fact, the character *hua*, 'to paint', represents a brush tracing the boundaries of a field. While Western painting values colour, composition and texture, the quality of a Chinese painting has shown from early on the great importance placed on brush technique.

Painting flourished during the Tang dynasty (AD 618–907). The most painted subjects were scenes of court life, as well as animals. The Tang also saw a rise in the popularity of landscape painting. The idyllic natural worlds depicted in Tang landscapes are beautifully detailed in brilliant washes of blues and greens.

During the Northern (AD 960–1127) and Southern Sung (1127–1279) dynasties landscape painting rose to new heights of excellence. Sung painters preferred moody, romantic landscapes with swirling mist-covered mountains and imaginary locales.

With the invasion of the Mongols in the 13th century, Yuan dynasty (1279–1368) painting took on a much different tone to that of the Sung dynasty. Yuan paintings have large empty spaces and are quite austere compared to those of the Tang and Sung.

The Ming (1368–1644) and Qing dynasties (1644–1911) saw a return to earlier styles of painting. Conventional subject matter was conveyed in startling new ways, with more emphasis on patterns and bright colours.

---

of Paris placed below. As the water came into contact with the plaster of Paris, it hardened, becoming a hill of cement. Another of her works was to gather old furniture and household items from destroyed houses in Beijing and create a mock 'city of debris', one that has been abandoned and near forgotten.

In the early 1990s many Beijing artists found escape from political scrutiny on the grounds of the Old Summer Palace, where they could rent cheap houses and work freely. Because of increasing recognition of some of the artists who lived there, police raids became more common and the artistic community was broken up. Forced to move out of their haunts, many found less bureaucratic control in the suburbs.

Dashanzi, a factory zone on the north-eastern edge of Beijing, in the Chaoyang district, became the favourite spot of many. Over the past several years, this quiet enclave has transformed into a thriving neighbourhood of lofts, galleries, bookshops, design studios, cafés and bars, all tucked into a small section of Dashanzi called 798 – named after Factory 798, a disused electronics factory complex built in the 1950s by East German architects. Here, Mao's ideals are reinterpreted through the artistic works of China's new visionaries, resulting in a lively, enigmatic and sometimes controversial community that is increasingly catching the attention of the international art world. Unfortunately, the Dashanzi art community is currently facing an uncertain future. Despite its growing reputation as China's 'new Soho', the entire area is scheduled for demolition in 2005 to make way for more of the luxury high-rise apartment buildings that dot the Beijing landscape.

MUSIC

In 1986 during a 'World Peace' music concert held in Beijing, a young trumpet player named Cui Jian walked on stage, strapped on a guitar and played a song that would forever change the sound and look of Chinese popular music. With its distinctly abrasive vocal style and lyrics describing feelings of loneliness and alienation, *Nothing To My Name (Yi Wo Suo You)* was unlike any song ever performed by a mainland Chinese musician.

For other early Chinese rock bands like Tang Dynasty and Black Panther, the pounding riffs and power chords of heavy metal from the 1970s and '80s (i.e. Led Zeppelin and Rush) provided the inspiration to pick up guitars, grow long hair and start a band. This 'First Generation' of Chinese rock bands not only took inspiration from classic rock and heavy metal, but also from punk's aggression and abrasiveness.

Since those early days Chinese rock has continued to flourish and Beijing has gained the reputation as China's rock-music mecca. Acts like ambient break-beaters Supermarket, post punk outfit SUBS, metal groups Spring and Autumn (Chunqiu), Suffocation (Zhixi) and Ritual Day (Shijiao Ri), and the Nirvana- and Doors-influenced Cold Blooded Animals, share the stage at Beijing's numerous live-music venues (see p133) with rockers Tongue (Shetou), Sand (Shazi), Handsome Black, the highly popular Second Hand Roses (Ershou Meigui) and more established acts. Look out also for hip-hop acts Dragon Tongue, CMBC and Kung Fu.

DJ culture has also come to China with Beijing's new wave of clubs. Club-goers can now get their grooves on to the booming sounds of hip-hop, house, drum-and-bass, techno and trance in addition to the popular sounds of home-grown Chinese house music.

This infusion of new styles and sounds has left an indelible impression on Chinese society, especially its youth culture. Today the sight of a long-haired Beijing homeboy with a guitar strapped to his back is about as common as that of a cigarette vendor or taxi driver. Television music programmes and radio shows play songs by rock acts almost as frequently as they do pop crooners and divas, while even hotel bars feature rock bands on a regular basis. Indeed, with such an infusion of new sounds and styles it appears that Chinese rock is here to stay.

Traditional Chinese zither

Traditional Chinese Music

The Chinese believed that the chimes of the large sets of bells (seen in Confucian temples and at the Great Bell Temple in Beijing) corresponded with the *dào* (way). A concordant pitch would signify all was well between heaven and earth. Similarly, the Chinese believe that all music influences the equilibrium of the *dào*.

Historically, music served a ceremonial or religious function, rather than as entertainment. Confucian students studied music not to rouse the emotions, but to seek inner quietude and balance. *The Book of Song (Shijing)* and the *Book of Rites (Lǐjì)*, two books of the Confucian canon, dwell on song, the rhythms of life and the function of music. It fell to folk song traditions to reflect the musical enjoyment of the common people and China's rich ethnic mix.

Traditional Chinese musical instruments include the two-stringed fiddle (*èrhú*) – famed for its desolate wail – the two-stringed viola (*húqín*), the vertical flute (*dòngxiāo*), the horizontal flute (*dízi*), the four-stringed lute (*pípa*) and the Chinese zither (*zhēng*).

To appreciate traditional music in Beijing, catch performances at the **Lao She Teahouse** (p132) or the **Sanwei Bookstore** (p132).

Festivals worth looking out for include the MIDI Music Festival at the Beijing MIDI School of Music (☎ 6259 0101, 6259 0007) – held during the first three days of May every year since 2000 (apart from 2004, when it was cancelled), when a vast array of bands perform live.

For classical music and opera lovers, the Beijing Music Festival (www.bmf.org.cn) is held for around 30 days during the months of October and November. For live music venues, see p134.

CINEMA & TV

The cinematic output of Fifth Generation directors, whose works were received with standing ovations worldwide in the 1980s and 1990s, was a high-water mark for Chinese film. *Farewell My Concubine* (1993), directed by Chen Kaige, and *Raise the Red Lantern* (1991), directed by Zhang Yimou, were garlanded with praise and reaped several major film awards. The lavish tragedies, starring icons such as Gong Li, radiated a beauty that entranced Western audiences and made their directors the darlings of Cannes.

Sixth Generation film directors shunned the exquisite beauty and lush palette of the Fifth Generation and rendered instead the angst and grimness of modern urban Chinese life. Their independent, low-budget works put an entirely different spin on mainland Chinese film-making, but their dour subject matter and harsh film style (frequently in black and white) left many Western viewers cold. To cap it all, many Sixth Generation films went unseen inside China.

Beijing Bastards (1993), directed by Zhang Yuan, focussed on the preoccupations and drug-taking lifestyle of Beijing's youth while *Frozen* (1995), directed by Wang Xiaoshuai, dwelled on suicide. *Beijing Bicycle* (2001), also directed by Wang Xiaoshuai and inspired by De Sica's *Bicycle Thieves*, is a tale of a Beijing youth seeking to recover his stolen bike.

Both Fifth- and Sixth-Generation directors constantly ran into problems with the authorities and the most controversial were clipped by the censors or banned outright. Other retaliatory measures included revoking their passports so they could not attend foreign film festivals.

By the late 1990s Hong Kong (the films of Wong Kar-wai and Stanley Kwan) and Taiwan cinema (the works of Edward Yang, Hou Hsiao-hsien, Tsai Ming-liang and Ang Lee) had continued to surge ahead. *Crouching Tiger, Hidden Dragon* (2000) shrewdly fielded to Western audiences by Ang Lee, was one of the Taiwan director's masterstrokes (as was the 1995 movie *Sense and Sensibility*). But it seemed that mainland Chinese cinema had come up against the buffers.

Today's Chinese film-makers are seeking the assistance and financing of international film companies, aiming to tap the vast local demand for thrillers, action films, dramas and comedies, rather than winning international acclaim or producing arthouse cinema. Eschewing politically risqué material or ambiguous subject matter, the new wave of films will try not to rile the Chinese censor.

Set in Beijing, Feng Xiaogang's works – *Big Shot's Funeral* (2001, starring Donald Sutherland) and *Be There or Be Square* (1998) – are typical of the new drift. But making money

Top Five Films

- *Beijing Bicycle* (2001) – Eschewing the lavish colour of Fifth-Generation directors and observing Beijing through a realist lens, Wang Xiaoshuai's film follows young and hapless courier Guo on the trail of his stolen mountain bike.
- *The Last Emperor* (1987) – Bernardo Bertolucci's celebrated (seven Oscars including best director, best costume design and best cinematography) and extravagant epic charts the life of Henry Puyi during his accession and the ensuing disintegration of dynastic China.
- *Beijing Bastards* (1993) – Starring rocker Cui Jian, Yuan Zhang's documentary-style cinematography tags along with a rock band in Beijing, grittily capturing the energy of Beijing's alienated and discontented youth.
- *The Gate of Heavenly Peace* (1995) – Using original footage from the six weeks preceding the Tiananmen massacre, Richard Gordon and Carma Hinton's moving three-hour tribute to the spirit of the student movement and its annihilation is a must-see.
- *Farewell My Concubine* (1993) – Charting a dramatic course through 20th-century Chinese history from the 1920s to the Cultural Revolution, Chen Kaige's film is a sumptuous and stunning narrative of two friends from the Beijing opera school whose lives are framed against social and political turmoil.

in China's film market is a tall order, considering the rampant piracy. Beijing street vendors hawk pirate DVDs of films on virtually the same day as their cinema premiers (it's not just Hollywood films that suffer). With such a lawless economy eating into revenue, the future of film-making for the China market alone is uncertain.

On television, most Chinese prefer to watch contemporary sitcoms and soaps imported from South Korea or Japan (collectively called *rìhánjù*, literally 'series from Japan and South Korea') or films made in Hong Kong and Taiwan (collectively called *Gǎngtáipiān*), rather than those produced locally. Chinese productions portraying contemporary life fail to depict the world realistically, but Chinese viewers lap up the ubiquitous Chinese historical costume dramas.

PERFORMING ARTS

Theatre

As spoken drama is a recent introduction to China (see p134) and opera traditionally took the place of storytelling, theatre remains an emergent art. An increasing number of theatrical companies are coming to Beijing from abroad, however, and local theatre companies are staging more and more productions, many of which are influenced by Western technique and content. For stage events in Beijing, consult the stage listings of *That's Beijing* (www.thatsmagazines.com).

Opera

Beijing opera is still regarded as the *crème de la crème* of all the opera styles prevalent in China and has traditionally been the opera of the masses. Intrigues, disasters or rebellions usually inspire themes, and many have their source in the fairy tales and stock characters and legends of classical literature.

The music, singing and costumes are products of the opera's origins. Formerly, opera was performed mostly on open air stages in markets, streets, teahouses or temple courtyards. The orchestra had to play loudly and the performers had to develop a piercing style of singing, which could be heard over the throng. The costumes are a garish collection of sharply contrasting colours because the stages were originally lit by oil lamps.

The movements and techniques of the dance styles of the Tang dynasty are similar to those of today's opera. Provincial opera companies were characterised by their dialect and style of singing, but when these companies converged on Beijing they started a style of musical drama called *kunqu*. This developed during the Ming dynasty, along with a more popular variety of play-acting pieces based on legends, historical events and popular novels. These styles gradually merged by the late 18th and early 19th centuries into the opera we see today.

The musicians usually sit on the stage in plain clothes and play without written scores. The *èrhú*, a two-stringed fiddle that is tuned to a low register and has a soft tone, generally supports

The Who's Who of Beijing Opera

There are four types of actors' role: the *shēng, dàn, jìng* and *chǒu*. The *shēng* are the leading male actors and they play scholars, officials, warriors and the like. They are divided into the *laoshēng*, who wear beards and represent old men, and the *xiǎoshēng*, who represent young men. The *wénshēng* are the scholars and the civil servants. The *wushēng* play soldiers and other fighters, and because of this are specially trained in acrobatics.

The *dàn* are the female roles. The *lǎodàn* are the elderly, dignified ladies such as mothers, aunts and widows. The *qīngyī* are aristocratic ladies in elegant costumes. The *huādàn* are the ladies' maids, usually in brightly coloured costumes. The *dǎomǎdàn* are the warrior women. The *cǎidàn* are the female comedians. Traditionally, female roles were played by male actors, but now they are almost always played by females.

The *jìng* are the painted-face roles and they represent warriors, heroes, statesmen, adventurers and demons. Their counterparts are the *fújìng*, ridiculous figures who are anything but heroic.

The *chou* is basically the clown. The *cǎidàn* is sometimes the female counterpart of this male role.

the *húqin*, a two-stringed viola tuned to a high register. The *yùeqín*, a sort of moon-shaped four-stringed guitar, has a soft tone and is used to support the *èrhú*. Other instruments are the *shēng* (a reed flute) and the *pípa* (lute), as well as drums, bells and cymbals. Last but not least is the *ban*, a time-clapper that virtually directs the band, beats time for the actors and gives them their cues.

Apart from the singing and the music, the opera also incorporates acrobatics and mime. Few props are used, so each move, gesture or facial expression is symbolic. A whip with silk tassels indicates an actor riding a horse. Lifting a foot means going through a doorway. Language is often archaic Chinese, music is ear splitting (bring some cotton wool), but the costumes and make-up are magnificent. Look out for a swift battle sequence – the female warriors involved are trained acrobats who leap, twirl, twist and somersault into attack.

There are numerous other forms of opera. The Cantonese variety is more 'music hall', often with a 'boy meets girl' theme. Gaojia opera is one of the five local operatic forms from the Fújiàn province and is also popular in Taiwan, with songs in the Fújiàn dialect but influenced by the Beijing opera style.

If you get bored after the first hour or so, check out the audience antics – spitting, eating apples, plugging into a transistor radio (important sports match perhaps?) or loudly slurping tea. It's lively audience entertainment fit for an emperor. For recommended theatres that stage performances of Beijing opera see p131.

ARCHITECTURE

Traditional architecture in Beijing is a legacy of the Ming and Qing dynasties (1368-1911), as seen in the magnificent Forbidden City, Summer Palace and the remaining *hútong*, small alleys and courtyard style homes, in the centre of the city. The government's eagerness to modernise has meant that many traditional buildings have been razed to make way for imposing steel and glass skyscrapers and upmarket shopping centres.

The building frenzy in Beijing began in the early 1980s but didn't really accelerate until the 1990s, with a housing renovation policy that resulted in thousands of old-style homes and Stalinist concrete structures from the 1950s being torn down and replaced by modern apartment buildings. During the 1990s Beijing destroyed so much of its architectural heritage it was denied a World Heritage listing in 2000 and 2001. This prompted the government to establish 40 protection zones throughout the older parts of the city to protect the remaining heritage buildings. Regulations were also created to control the appearance and height of buildings around the central part of the city.

Few buildings now stand in Beijing that predate the Ming dynasty. Because early buildings were constructed with wood and paper, most were not meant to last very long. The longest standing structure in Beijing is the Great Wall, built in 3 BC. One of the best places to see the ancient architecture of China is at the **Beijing Ancient Architecture Museum** (Map pp239-41; 21 Dongjing Lu; Y15; ☯ 9am-4pm; bus 15 to Nanweilu stop), which has exhibits of architecture ranging from early mud huts to examples of Ming and Qing palaces.

Roof detail, Forbidden City (p76)

Basic principles of Chinese architecture were formed as early as the Neolithic period. Roofs were commonly supported with brackets set on columns, which were lavishly decorated with carvings. The roof with the upturned 'swallowtail eaves' that most Westerners identify as being Chinese, appeared during the Han dynasty (206 BC–AD 220).

Chinese architecture normally falls into four categories: residential, imperial palaces, temples and recreational. Residences in Beijing were once *siheyuan*, houses situated on four sides of a courtyard. The houses were aligned exactly – the northern house was found directly opposite the southern, the eastern directly across from the western. *Siheyuan* can still be found in a few remaining pockets in central Beijing, though most have disappeared.

Traditionally the Chinese followed a basic ground plan when they built their homes. In upper class homes as well as in palaces and temples, buildings were surrounded by an exterior wall and designed on a north–south axis, with an entrance gate and a gate built for spirits that might try to enter the building. Behind the entry gates in palaces and residential buildings was a public hall and behind this were private living quarters built around a central court with a garden. The garden area of upper-class gentry and imperial families spawned an entire subgenre of 'recreational architecture', which included gardens, pavilions, pagodas, ponds and bridges. The Forbidden City (p76) and Summer Palace (p98) remain the finest examples of imperial architecture remaining in Beijing. In fact, the Forbidden City is the largest architectural complex in China, covering over 72 hectares. The best example of temple architecture is at the Beihai Park (p73).

Hidden under dust and scaffolding, today's Beijing is a schizophrenic hodgepodge of old and new. With ultramodern skyscrapers dominating the skyline and grandiose plans in the works to prepare for the 2008 Olympics, it's possible that in a few years the entire city will resemble the set of a futuristic sci-fi movie. Authorities are putting into play an entire makeover of the city with the addition of a new light rail and subway system, a Fifth and Sixth Ring Rd, a new expressway and the expansion of streets in the downtown urban core. Some of these

Beijing's Top Ten Most Notable Buildings

- **Forbidden City** (p76) To many, this elegant Ming dynasty palace is the symbol of Beijing. Its grand scale and traditional architecture provide a marvellous glimpse into China's imperial history.
- **Summer Palace** (p98) With its majestic halls, gardens and galleries painted with scenes from Chinese mythology, this is one of the loveliest spots in the city to see traditional Chinese architecture.
- **Peking University** Designed in 1919 by an American architect, the university follows traditional Chinese design, combined with Western features such as a pitched roof and large windows.
- **Peace Hotel** Built in 1953, this hotel is regarded as the first modern building in Beijing. It launched an era of Soviet-influenced architecture that lasted through the 1950s.
- **Great Hall of the People** (p65) One of many buildings erected during Mao's Great Leap Forward. Its massive size is symbolises the power and strength of the Chinese people.
- **National Swimming Centre** Some call it the 'water cube', others a 'box of bubbles'. This facility, estimated to be finished in 2006, will be the largest venue ever created for the Olympics, with five swimming pools and seating for up to 17,000 people.
- **National Stadium** Locals dislike this building, not just for its US$500 million price tag, but for its curved, intermeshed steel walls and 'bird's-nest' appearance that many say does not fit in with the local landscape.
- **CCTV Building** A one-of-a-kind in China, this futuristic building is shaped like a gigantic 'Z' and has generated an unprecedented amount of controversy that it is just not Chinese enough.
- **National Theatre** The designers of this theatre want the building to represent a 'new China' – modern and progressive without straying from traditional ideals. The circular roof, meant to symbolise 'earth', contrasts with the square lake it sits upon, symbolising balance and harmony.
- **Bank of China Headquarters** The son of notable architect I.M. Pei has designed this striking building with an airy atrium and innovative indoor garden.

construction plans have lain dormant for years but with the Olympics on the horizon, there's a strong urge to show Beijing off to the rest of the world as a city of the future.

Critics of all this new development make the claim that while Beijing should move forward, it should also try to retain its unique cultural heritage. Chang'an Ave has already been dubbed by some as an 'architectural hall of shame' because of its flashy steel and chrome buildings that, to many, contain little style and don't capture the essence of the city. Regardless of the criticism, plans are going ahead to recreate the city landscape. Contracts have been signed with a number of foreign architectural firms who are designing some of the most innovative, yet controversial buildings in China.

Some of the projects planned for the 2008 Olympics are truly fantastic in nature. The Olympic Stadium, dubbed a 'bird's nest' by locals, was designed by the Swiss architectural firm Herzog & De Meuron. Bowl shaped and covered with a transparent membrane, it will hold up to 100,000 spectators. Another building causing a stir is the National Swimming Centre, built as a shimmering 'cube' of water and designed by the Australian firm PTW. One of the most controversial buildings is the new National Theatre, designed by French architect Paul Andreu, which is being built on the west side of Tiananmen Square. The $US300 million dollar dome-shaped building, called 'the egg', is considered an eye-

Modern architecture, Dongcheng

sore by many, who see it as not fitting in with the traditional architecture of the Forbidden City nearby and looking too out of place next to the Great Hall of the People.

Beijing's desire to hire foreign architects to design these new buildings rather than hire local firms has much to do with its desire to modernise rapidly and prove to the rest of the world that it is on par with other great international cities. It may also be due to that fact that architecture is a fairly new field of study in China and many people feel that China's own architects are too young or inexperienced to pull off the type of striking structures required to catch the attention of the world.

With all of these construction projects currently under way, it's uncertain what the face of Beijing will look like in the not so distant future. Questions remain unanswered about how long the furious pace of construction will last and whether or not the city will be able to hold onto its distinctive cultural heritage while moving into the 21st century. Without a doubt, the city is in the process of transforming itself and for the next few years, at least until the Olympics, will continue to be an experimental playground for international architects.

Food & Drink

Food & Drink

Long gone are the days of drab communal dining halls and tasteless food dished up for the masses. Beijing today offers a dazzling array of local and global cuisines served with a flavour and fervour on par with most international cities. The capital offers something for everybody – from inexpensive food stalls to five-star gourmet restaurants.

Beijing cuisine combines the best of cuisines from around China, with a preference for warm, filling dishes, due to its northerly location. Many dishes reflect the influence of the Mongols, with an emphasis on mutton and flat breads. Wheat-based noodles, buns and dumplings are preferred over rice and, of course, Beijing's most famous dish is Peking duck (see p116), a must-try for anyone visiting the capital.

Eating well in Beijing doesn't have to cost a king's ransom. Budget eats can be found in the night markets and down small side streets where a bowl of noodles or dumplings will cost very little. A formal restaurant, with tablecloths and waiting staff, will be more expensive but provide more choices and have air conditioning.

Steamed buns are readily available

Restaurants featuring international cuisines will be the priciest. Regardless of the establishment, always verify prices before ordering. Prices for certain items like seafood can vary from place to place and you don't want a shock when you see the bill.

Most top-end restaurants in Beijing have some kind of English menu, although translations from Chinese are often literal and rather amusing (anyone for 'fried pig stomach on cabbage'?). Smaller restaurants will provide a menu in Chinese or have placards posted on the wall featuring daily specials. For help with Chinese menus check out the menu decoder (p38) or go with Chinese friends and let them order. In general, it is always better to eat Chinese food in a group as you'll be served a wider variety of dishes.

CULTURE

ETIQUETTE

Traditionally, the Chinese had a number of taboos regarding table etiquette. Nowadays these rules are much more relaxed and foreigners are given special allowances for social gaffes. However, there are some basic rules to follow when eating with Beijing friends or colleagues that will make things at the table go more smoothly.

Everyone receives an individual bowl and a small plate and teacup. It's quite acceptable to hold the bowl close to your lips and shovel the contents into your mouth with chopsticks. If the food contains bones or seeds, just put them out on the tablecloth or in a dish reserved for this purpose. Restaurants are prepared for the mess and staff change the tablecloth after each customer leaves.

Chopstick skills are a necessary means of survival when eating out in Beijing. If you haven't mastered the tricky art of eating with two sticks you could find yourself on a crash diet without even trying! Don't despair if at first much of the food lands on the table or in your lap and not in your bowl. Eating this way takes practice and most Chinese are understanding when it comes to foreigners and chopstick problems. They certainly have their own problems when it comes to steak knives and forks. When eating from communal dishes, don't use your chopsticks to root around in a dish for a piece of food. Find a piece by sight and go directly for it without touching anything else. And remember that while dropping food is OK, never drop your chopsticks as this is considered bad luck.

Most Chinese think little of sticking their own chopsticks into a communal dish, though this attitude is changing because of SARS. Many restaurants in Beijing now provide separate serving spoons or chopsticks to be used with communal dishes. If these are provided, be sure to use them. Never use a personal spoon to serve from a communal plate or bowl.

Eating Dos & Don'ts

- Don't wave your chopsticks around or point them at people. This is considered rude.
- Don't drum your chopsticks on the side of your bowl – only beggars do this.
- Never commit the terrible faux pas of sticking your chopsticks into your rice. Two chopsticks stuck vertically into a rice bowl resemble incense sticks in a bowl of ashes and is considered an omen of death.
- Do wait to be seated when entering a restaurant.
- Don't discuss business or unpleasant topics at dinner.
- Do try and sample all dishes, if possible.
- Don't let the spout of a teapot face towards anyone. Make sure it is directed outward from the table or to where nobody is sitting.
- Never flip a fish over to get to the flesh underneath. If you do so, the next boat you pass will capsize.

Don't be surprised if your Chinese host uses their chopsticks to place food in your bowl or plate. This is a sign of friendship and the polite thing to do is to smile and eat whatever has been given you. If for some reason you can't eat it, leave it in your bowl or hide it with rice.

Remember to fill your neighbours' teacups when they are empty, as yours will be filled by them. You can thank the pourer by tapping two fingers on the table gently. On no account serve yourself tea without serving others first. When your teapot needs a refill, signal this to the waiter by taking its lid off.

Probably the most important piece of etiquette comes with the bill: the person who extended the dinner invitation is presumed to pay, though everyone at the table will put up a fight. Don't argue with your host too hard; it's expected that at a certain point in the future the meal will be reciprocated.

Banquets

The banquet is the apex of the Chinese dining experience. Virtually all significant business deals in China are clinched at the banquet table.

Dishes are served in sequence, beginning with cold appetisers and continuing through 10 or more courses. Soup, usually a thin broth to aid digestion, is generally served after the main course.

The idea is to serve or order far more than everyone can eat. Empty bowls imply a stingy host. Rice is considered a cheap filler and rarely appears at a banquet – don't ask for it, as this would imply that the snacks and main courses are insufficient, causing embarrassment to the host.

It's best to wait for some signal from the host before digging in. You will most likely be invited to take the first taste. Often your host will serve it to you, placing a piece of meat, chicken or fish in your bowl. If a whole fish is served, you might be offered the head, the cheeks of which are considered to be the tastiest part. Try and at least take a taste of what was given to you.

Never drink alone. Imbibing is conducted via toasts, which will usually commence with a general toast by the host, followed by the main guest reply toast, and then settle down to frequent toasts to individuals. A toast is conducted by raising your glass in both hands in the direction of the toastee and crying out *gānbēi*, literally 'dry the glass'. Chinese do not clink glasses. Drain your glass in one hit. It is not unusual for everyone to end up very drunk, though at formal banquets this is frowned upon. Raising your tea or water glass in a toast is not very respectful so, unless you have deep-rooted convictions against alcohol, it's best to drink at least a mouthful.

Don't be late for a formal banquet; it's considered extremely rude. The banquet ends when the food and toasts end – the Chinese don't linger after the meal. You may find yourself being applauded when you enter a large banquet. It is polite to applaud back.

HOW BEIJING PEOPLE EAT

To the Chinese, eating is a way to socialise and friendships are made at the dinner table. Restaurants are noisy, crowded places where people get together with family and friends to unwind and enjoy themselves. Eating is a time of relaxation, away from the pressures of work and school. It is a social lubricant, an opportunity for the nouveaux riches to flaunt their wealth and the nouveau chic to prove their cool. While friends in the West go out for a beer, the Chinese will opt for a 'hot and noisy' meal punctuated with increasingly vociferous shots of rice wine.

Typically, the Chinese sit at a round table and order dishes from which everyone partakes; ordering a dish just for yourself would be unthinkable. It's not unusual for one person at the table to order on everyone's behalf. Usually among friends only several dishes will be ordered, but if guests are present the host will order at least one dish per person, possibly more. At formal dinners, be prepared for a staggering amount of food, far more than anyone could eat.

Epicureans will tell you that the key to ordering is to ask for a variety and balance of textures, tastes, smells, colours and even temperatures. Most Chinese meals start with some snacks, perhaps some peanuts or pickles. Following the little titbits are the main courses, usually some meat and vegetable dishes. Soup is often served at the end of the meal as well as noodles or rice.

Most Chinese eat early, often as early as 11am for lunch and 5pm for dinner, but lots of trendy late-night Beijing eateries buzz for 24 hours. Breakfast is the one meal that many foreigners have problems with. Chinese breakfasts generally include dumplings, *yóutiáo* (fried breadsticks), *congee*, pickles, peanuts and soya bean milk. Bear this in mind before you get too excited about your two-star hotel buffet breakfast. If you can't face this there are cafés where you can get Western breakfasts. Every mid-range or top-end hotel offers a breakfast buffet.

Although Chinese restaurants have a reputation in the West for being noisy, tasteless and basic (Formica tables, tacky calendars and plastic chopsticks), this only shows that Westerners don't appreciate the same things when going out to eat. While most Westerners need to feel they've got value for money by the quality of the ambience and service, for most Chinese the quality of the food is paramount. Good restaurants gain a reputation solely for the quality of their food, no matter what the décor or location.

STAPLES

NOODLES

Noodles are a staple in Beijing and eaten more than rice, which is more commonly eaten in southern China. Noodles can be made by hand or by machine but many people agree that hand-pulled noodles (*la mian*) are the tastiest. Watching the noodles being made is almost as much a treat as eating them. First the cook stretches the dough in his hands, shakes it gently up and down and swings it so the dough twists around itself many times until it becomes firm. The dough is pulled and stretched until it becomes very fine.

Noodles are thought to have originated in northern China during the Han dynasty (206 BC–AD 220), when the Chinese developed techniques for large-scale flour grinding. Not only were noodles nutritious, cheap and versatile, they were portable and could be stored for long periods. Legend credits Marco Polo with having introduced noodles to Italy in 1295.

The Chinese like to eat noodles on birthdays and during the New Year because their long thin shape symbolises longevity. That's why it's bad luck to break noodles before cooking them.

RICE

There's a saying in Chinese that 'precious things are not pearls or jade but the five grains'. An old legend about the origin of rice claims that rice is actually a gift from the animals. The story goes that centuries ago, China was overwhelmed by floods that destroyed all the crops and caused massive starvation. One day some villagers saw a dog running towards them and on the dog's tail were bunches of long yellow seeds. When the villagers planted the seeds the rice grew and hunger disappeared.

The Chinese revere rice not only as their staff of life but also for its aesthetic value. Its mellow aroma is not unlike bread. Its texture when properly done – soft yet offering some resistance, the grains detached – sets off the textures of the foods that surround it. Flavours are brought into better focus by its simplicity. Rice is the unifier of the table, bringing all the dishes into harmony.

Rice comes in many different preparations – as a porridge *(congee)* served with savouries at breakfast, fried with tiny shrimps, pork or vegetables and eaten at lunch or as a snack. But plain steamed white rice – fragrant yet neutral – is what you should order at dinner.

REGIONAL CUISINES

All of China's cuisines are available in Beijing. Some of those most commonly represented are Sichuan, Shanghai and Cantonese cuisines. Muslim foods are also easily found, particularly foods of the Uyghurs, who come from China's northwestern Xinjiang province.

BEIJING

Beijing cuisine is classified as a 'northern cuisine' and typical dishes are made with wheat or millet, whose common incarnations are as steamed dumplings *(jiǎozi)* or noodles, while arguably the most famous Chinese dish of all is Peking duck. Vegetables are limited, so there

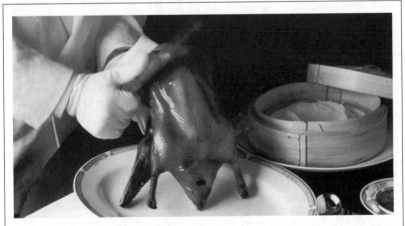

Beijing's most famous dish, Peking duck (p116)

is a heavy reliance on freshwater fish and chicken; cabbage and turnips are some of the most ubiquitous vegetables found on menus as well as yams and potatoes.

Not surprisingly, the influence of the Mongols is felt most strongly in Beijing and two of the region's most famous culinary exports – Mongolian barbecue and Mongolian hotpot – are adaptations from Mongol field kitchens. Animals that were hunted on horseback could be dismembered and cooked with wild vegetables and onions using soldiers' iron shields on top of hot coals as primitive barbecues. Alternatively, each soldier could use his helmet as a pot, filling it with water, meat, condiments and vegetables to taste. Mutton is now the main ingredient in Mongolian hotpot.

Roasting was once considered rather barbaric in other parts of China and is still more common in the northern areas. The main methods of cooking in the northern style, though, are steaming, baking and 'explode-frying'. The last of these is the most common, historically because of the scarcity of fuel and, more recently, due to the introduction of the peanut, which thrives in the north and produces an abundance of oil. Although northern-style food has a reputation for being unsophisticated and bland, it has the benefit of being filling and therefore well-suited to the cold climate.

SICHUANESE

Sichuan food is known as the hottest of all China's cuisines, so take care when ordering. Lethal red chillies (introduced by Spanish traders in the early Ch'ing dynasty), aniseed, peppercorns and pungent 'flower pepper' (huājiāo) are used; and dishes are simmered to give the chilli peppers time to work into the food. Meats are often marinated, pickled or otherwise processed before cooking, which is generally by stir- or explode-frying.

Famous dishes include camphor-smoked duck (zhāngchá yāzi), Granny Ma's tofu (mápó dòufu) and spiced chicken with peanuts (gōngbào jīdīng). Sichuan is a long distance from the coast, so pork, poultry, legumes and soybeans are commonly used, and supplemented by a variety of wild condiments and mountain products, such as mushrooms and other fungi, as well as bamboo shoots. Seasonings are heavy: the red chilli is often used in conjunction with Sichuan peppercorns, garlic, ginger and onions.

CANTONESE

This is what non-Chinese consider 'Chinese' food, largely because most émigré restaurateurs originate from Guangdong (Canton) or Hong Kong. Cantonese flavours are generally more subtle than other Chinese styles – almost sweet – and there are very few spicy dishes. Sweet-and-sour and oyster sauces are common. The Cantonese are almost religious about the importance of fresh ingredients, which is why so many restaurants are lined with tanks full of finned and shelled creatures. Stir-frying is by far the most favoured method of cooking, closely followed by steaming. Dim sum, now a worldwide Sunday institution, originated in this region; to go yám cha (Cantonese for 'drink tea') still provides most overseas Chinese communities with the opportunity to get together at the weekend. Dim sum can be found in restaurants around Beijing.

Fresh noodles being made at one of Beijing's many street stalls (p113)

Expensive dishes – some that are truly tasty, others that appeal more for their 'face' value – include abalone, shark's fin and bird's nest. Pigeon is a Cantonese specialty served in various ways but most commonly roasted.

UYGHUR

The Uyghur style of cooking reflects the influences of Xinjiang's chequered past. Yet, despite centuries of sporadic Chinese and Mongol rule, the strongest influence on ingredients and methods is still Turkic or Middle Eastern, which is evident in the reliance on mutton for protein and wheat for the staple grain. When rice is eaten, it is often in the Central Asian version of pilau (*plov*). Nevertheless, the influence of Chinese culinary styles and ingredients makes it probably the most enjoyable region of Central Asia in which to eat.

Uyghur bread resembles Arabic *khoubz* (Indian naan) and is baked in ovens based on the *tanour* (Indian tandoor) model. It is often eaten straight from the oven and

Kebabs for sale on Wangfujing Snack Street (p118)

sprinkled with poppy seeds, sesame seeds or fennel. Uyghur bakers also make excellent bagels (*girde nan*). Wheat is also used for a variety of noodles. *Laghman* are the most common: noodles cooked *al dente*, thick and topped with a combination of spicy mutton, peppers, tomatoes, eggplant, green beans and garlic. *Suoman* are noodle squares fried with tomatoes, peppers, garlic and meat, sometimes quite spicy. *Suoman goshsiz* is the vegetarian variety.

Kebabs are common, as they are throughout the Middle East and Central Asia, both shashlik- and tandoori-style. Samsas or samsis are the Uyghur version of samosas: baked envelopes of meat. Meat often makes an appearance inside dumplings (*chuchura*), which can be steamed or fried.

VEGETARIAN

China has a long history of Daoist and Buddhist philosophers who abstained from eating animals, and vegetarianism can be traced back over 1000 years. The Tang dynasty physician Sun Simiao extolled the virtues of vegetarianism in his 60-volume classic, 'Prescriptions Worth More Than Gold'. Legend has it that Sun lived to the ripe old age of 101. However, try telling this to your waiter who brings out a supposedly pristine veggie or tofu dish decorated with strips of pork or chicken. The majority of Chinese have little understanding of vegetarianism and many consider it a strange Western concept.

Because of China's history of poverty and famine, eating meat is a status symbol, and symbolic of health and wealth. Many Chinese remember all too well the famines of the 1950s and 1960s when having anything to eat was a luxury. Eating meat (as well as milk and eggs) is a sign of progress and material abundance. Even vegetables are often fried in animal-based oils and soups are most commonly made with chicken or beef stock. Saying you don't eat meat confuses many Chinese who may interpret this to mean seafood is OK, or even chicken or pork. Trying to explain the reasons behind why you don't eat meat brings even more confusion. Men especially are looked down upon because not eating meat is thought to decrease sexual virility.

However, in larger cities such as Beijing, Shanghai or Guangzhou, vegetarianism is slowly catching on and there are new chic vegetarian eateries appearing in fashionable restaurant districts. These are often expensive establishments and you pay for ambience as well as the food. In Beijing the oldest vegetarian restaurant is the Gongdelin Vegetarian Restaurant (p116), which serves excellent food and has a lengthy menu.

Chinese vegetarian food often consists of 'mock meat' dishes made from tofu, wheat gluten and vegetables. Some of the dishes are quite fantastic to look at, with vegetarian ingredients sculpted to look like spare ribs or fried chicken. Sometimes the chefs go to great lengths to create 'bones' from carrots and lotus roots. Some of the more famous vegetarian dishes include vegetarian 'ham', braised vegetarian 'shrimp' and sweet and sour 'fish'.

SNACKS

Snacking in Beijing is great fun and a good way to explore the local cuisine. Some popular snacks often eaten with beer or wine are fried tripe *(bào dù)*, filled sausages *(guàn cháng)* and fried liver *(chǎo gān)*. A tasty Muslim treat are lamb kebabs *(kǎo yángròu chuàn)*, often sold in night markets or outdoor restaurants.

Beijing has plenty of tasty breads, such as bread stuffed with leeks and eggs *(jiǔ cài bǐng)*, thin and crunchy pancakes *(jiān bǐng)* and bread filled with diced pork *(ròu bǐng)*. If some of these sound a little too carnivorous, there's also plenty of sweets such as 'rolling donkey' *(lú dá gǔn)*, a type of cake made with sticky rice dipped in soybean flour. It's supposed to resemble a donkey rolling in the dust. During winter it's common to see people eating sugar-coated crab apples on a stick and roasted sweet potatoes *(hóngshǔ)*, which are sold by the roadside.

DESSERTS & SWEETS

The Chinese do not generally eat dessert, but fruit is considered to be an appropriate end to a good meal. Western influence has added ice cream to the menu in some upmarket establishments, but in general sweet stuff is consumed as snacks and is seldom available in restaurants.

One exception to the rule is caramelised fruits, including apples *(bāsī pínggǔo)* and bananas *(bāsī xiāngjiāo)*, which you can find in a few restaurants. Other sweeties include shaved ice and syrup *(bīngshā)*; a sweet, sticky rice pudding known as Eight Treasure Rice *(bābaófàn)*; and various types of steamed bun filled with sweet bean paste.

DRINKS

NONALCOHOLIC DRINKS

Tea is a fundamental part of Chinese life. In fact, an old Chinese saying identifies tea as one of the seven basic necessities of life, along with fuel, oil, rice, salt, soy sauce and vinegar. The Chinese were the first to cultivate tea, and the art of brewing and drinking tea has been popular since the Tang dynasty (AD 618–907).

Most cheaper restaurants serve on-the-house pots of weak jasmine or green tea. Higher quality brands of tea are available in teashops or in supermarkets. China has three main types of tea: green *(lǜ chá)* or unfermented; black tea *(hóng chá)*, which is fermented; and wulong *(wūlóng)*, or semifermented. In addition, there are other variations, including jasmine *(cháshuǐ)* and chrysanthemum *(júhuā chá)*. Traditionally,

Tea displays at Ten Fu's Tea Shop (p146)

Chinese would never put milk or sugar in their tea but things are changing. Now 'milk tea' *(nǎi chá)* is available everywhere in Beijing, often served cold with a whopping amount of sugar.

Coffeehouse chic has hit the city in a big way and Western-style coffee houses have sprouted up all over the city. The coffee chain Starbucks has become fashionable for trendy urban youth. A cup of semidecent coffee should set you back around Y20, depending upon the establishment.

Soft drinks, such as Sprite, Coca-Cola and local fizzy drinks like Jianlibao, a honey sweetened drink, are easily found along with ice teas and fruit drinks. Bottled water is on sale all over the place but check the cap to see if it's sealed before buying.

Milk is available fresh or powdered from supermarkets and convenience stores. Popular are sweet yoghurt drinks in bottles sold in stores or fresh yoghurt sold at some street stalls.

ALCOHOLIC DRINKS

If tea is the most popular drink in the PRC then beer must be number two. By any standards the top brands are good. The best known is Tsingtao, made with a mineral water that gives it a sparkling quality. It's essentially a German beer since the town of Qingdao (formerly spelled 'Tsingtao'), where it's made, was once a German concession and the Chinese inherited the brewery. Experts claim that draught Tsingtao tastes much better than the bottled stuff. Locally brewed beer in Beijing includes the brands Yanjing Beer, Beijing Beer and Wuxing beer. A bottle will normally cost Y1.5 to Y2 in street shops, around Y15 to Y20 in a bar.

China has cultivated vines and produced wine for an estimated 4000 years. Chinese wine-producing techniques differ from those of the West. Quality-conscious wine producers in Western countries work on the idea that the lower the yield the higher the quality of the wine produced. But Chinese farmers cultivate every possible square centimetre of earth; they encourage their vines to yield heavily and also plant peanuts between the rows as a cover crop for half the year. The peanuts sap much of the nutrient from the soil and in cooler years the large grape crop fails to ripen sufficiently to produce good wine.

Western producers try to prevent oxidation in their wines, but oxidation produces a flavour that Chinese tipplers find desirable and go to great lengths to achieve. Chinese diners are also keen on wines with different herbs and other materials soaked in them, which they drink for their health and for restorative or aphrodisiac qualities.

The word 'wine' gets rather loosely translated – many Chinese 'wines' are in fact spirits. Rice wine is intended mainly for cooking rather than drinking.

Drinking in the City

Beer *(píjiǔ)* is Beijing's favourite tipple (see p38), but besides imported brands, you'll have to settle for the Chinese beers, of which Yanjing Beer, Beijing Beer and Tsingtao are the best-selling labels. Canned and bottled in brown and green bottles, Yanjing Beer is both watery and unremarkable, but it is extraordinarily cheap.

China's drinkers are slowly developing a taste for wine *(pútaojiǔ)*, but good labels are still in short supply or outrageously expensive. Several of Beijing's top-notch restaurants also have fine wine lists. China furthermore ferments its own wine, with Dynasty and Great Wall the best known. Many Chinese brands, however, are too sweet and cling to the teeth.

To aid digestion and get rapidly sozzled, Chinese men often drink *báijiǔ* with lunch and dinner. Despite being loosely translated as wine, the potent potion is in fact a clear spirit fermented from sorghum (a type of millet). *Báijiǔ* is used for toasts at banquets; if you are invited to *gānbēi*, you will be expected to drain your glass. The drink is a searing, eye-wateringly strong tipple that will quickly have you sliding off your seat and taking the tablecloth with you, so go easy on it.

Rice wine *(mǐjiǔ)* is intended more for cooking than drinking. Other wines contain pickled lizards, bees or snakes, all of which are noted for their tonic effects.

Imported alcohol (such as Johnny Walker Black Label or fine wines) is highly prized by the Chinese for its prestige value; such bottles make a perfect gift. Steep import taxes, however, translate into ludicrous prices, so take advantage of your duty-free allowance on arrival.

Avoid rowdy displays of public drunkenness. The loud, drunken lager lout at large wins no brownie points and could lead to a run-in with the police. Chinese hard-core drinkers sociably congregate in packs and are the last to be bundled out of restaurants as the shutters crash down. Chinese finger-guessing games require little intelligence and become the last resort of the seriously drunk in eateries the land over.

Chinese Beer

Despite the ample girth of its beer market, inhabitants of the Middle Kingdom can only claim to be newborns at beer (*píjiǔ*) drinking. Beer is not indigenous to China, so the hops, yeast and tinkering at the German Qingdao (Tsingtao) brewery would have set many a curtain twitching when it opened in 1903.

Even by the 1970s the liquid was still derided as *mǎniào* (horse piss) and shelved in favour of the local rocket fuel (*báijiǔ*). But beer gradually dislodged the competition and today is pretty much the drink of choice for a Chinese get-together, outselling *báijiǔ* for the first time in 1998. Even by 1993 China was the world's second largest consumer of beer after the United States.

Lured by such huge market potential, foreign breweries raced to cash in during the euphoria of the 1990s. 'International brewers had arrived in China like stampeding wildebeest,' notes Joe Studwell in his *The China Dream: The Elusive Quest for the Greatest Untapped Market on Earth* (Profile Books Ltd; 2003). Most incurred huge losses, however, as beer drinkers in China stuck to the almost unfeasibly cheap local brews and shunned the foreign beers.

Flavourwise, Chinese beer may be drab, but it can be lauded as a remarkable feat of socialist standardisation, for it tastes the same pretty much wherever you go in China. The nation's most famous beer is the Shandong-brewed Tsingtao (Qingdao), esteemed by all other Chinese breweries. You can buy it in draught (*zhāpí*) pint glasses from bars around town, or in cans and bottles. There are also a few brands of Chinese dark beer, brewed in the northeast.

Depending on where you shop, you can pick up a bottle of Yanjing Beer for Y1.5, with a deposit of five *máo* on the bottle. Cheap restaurants usually charge around Y3 for a bottle; but they hang on to the deposit. A small bottle of Beijing Beer or Tsingtao will cost you around Y15 to Y25 in a Sanlitun bar.

Despite their small market share, widely available foreign brands include Beck's, Carlsberg, Heineken, Corona, San Miguel and Budweiser. A growing selection of rarer foreign beers can be sunk at bars around town – see p126 for a rundown on bars in Beijing. Supermarkets also generally stock a range of foreign beers and more famous brands of beer from around China.

If you want a cold beer, ask for '*liáng píjiǔ*', and if you want it really arctic, '*bīngzhèn píjiǔ*'. At a watery 3.4% proof, Chinese beer isn't strong and experienced beer drinkers will drink bath loads of the stuff. You may still, however, get the occasional dodgy bottle that seems to bring on a hangover all by itself – and watch out for explosive bottles during the heat of summer.

Hejie Jiu (lizard wine) is produced in the southern province of Guangxi; each bottle contains one dead lizard suspended perpendicularly in the clear liquid.

Wine with dead bees or pickled snakes is also desirable for its alleged tonic properties – in general, the more poisonous the creature, the more potent the tonic effects. Maotai, a favourite of Chinese drinkers, is a spirit made from sorghum (a type of millet) and used for toasts at banquets.

MENU DECODER
USEFUL WORDS & PHRASES

I don't want MSG.	*wó bú yào wèijīng*	我不要味精
I'm vegetarian.	*wǒ chī sù*	我吃素
not too spicy	*bù yào tài là*	不要太辣
menu	*càidān*	菜单
bill (cheque)	*mǎidān/jiézhàng*	买单/结帐
set meal (no menu)	*tàocān*	套餐
let's eat	*chī fàn*	吃饭
cheers!	*gānbēi*	干杯
chopsticks	*kuàizi*	筷子
knife	*dàozi*	刀子
fork	*chāzi*	叉子
spoon	*tiáogēng/tāngchí*	调羹/汤匙
hot	*rède*	热的
ice cold	*bīngde*	冰的

STAPLES
Rice Dishes

jīdàn chǎofàn	鸡蛋炒饭	fried rice with egg
jīchǎofàn	鸡炒饭	fried rice with chicken
jīdàn mǐfàn	米饭	steamed white rice
shūcài chǎofàn	蔬菜炒饭	fried rice with vegetables
xīfàn zhōu	稀饭/粥	watery rice porridge (congee)

Noodle Dishes

hún tún miàn	馄饨面	wontons and noodles
jīsī chǎomiàn	鸡丝炒面	fried noodles with chicken
jīsī tāngmiàn	鸡丝汤面	soupy noodles with chicken
májiàng miàn	麻酱面	sesame paste noodles
niúròu chǎomiàn	牛肉炒面	fried noodles with beef
niúròu miàn	牛肉汤面	soupy beef noodles
ròusī chǎomiàn	肉丝炒面	fried noodles with pork
shūcài chǎomiàn	蔬菜炒面	fried noodles with vegetables
tāngmiàn	汤面	noodles in soup
xiārén chǎomiàn	虾仁炒面	fried noodles with shrimp
zhájiàng miàn	炸酱面	bean and meat noodles

Bread, Buns & Dumplings

cōngyóu bǐng	葱油饼	spring onion pancakes
guōtiē	锅贴	pot stickers/pan-grilled dumplings
mántóu	馒头	steamed buns
ròu bāozǐ	肉包子	steamed meat buns
shāobǐng	烧饼	clay oven rolls
shuǐjiān bāo	水煎包	pan grilled buns
shuǐjiǎo	水餃	boiled dumplings
sùcài bāozǐ	素菜包子	steamed vegetable buns

Soup

húntún tāng	馄饨汤	wonton soup
sān xiān tāng	三鲜汤	three kinds of seafood soup
suānlà tāng	酸辣汤	hot and sour soup

CUISINES
Beijing & Other Northern-style Dishes

peking kǎoyā	北京烤鸭	Peking duck
jiāo zhá yángròu	焦炸羊肉	deep-fried mutton
jiǔ zhuǎn dàcháng	九转大肠	spicy braised pig's intestine
qīng xiāng shāo jī	清香沙烧鸡	chicken wrapped in lotus leaf
sān měi dòufu	三美豆腐	sliced beancurd with Chinese cabbage
shuàn yángròu	涮羊肉	lamb hotpot
sì xǐ wánzi	四喜丸子	steamed and fried pork, shrimp and bamboo shoot balls
yuán bào lǐ jí	芫爆里脊	stir-fried pork tenderloin with coriander
zào liū sān bái	糟溜三白	stir-fried chicken, fish and bamboo shoots

Top Ten Restaurants

- **Xiao Wang's Home Restaurant** (pp117-8) Award-winning Beijing and eclectic Chinese cuisine, great atmosphere and an individual style. Two locations.
- **Courtyard** (p119) Boasting a top-notch wine list and delectable fusion dishes, this stylish restaurant has a spectacular location just east of the Forbidden City, a downstairs art gallery and an upstairs cigar divan.
- **Huang Ting** (p120) Its simulated *hútòng* setting may be a sham, but the ambience is nonetheless elegant and the food excellent.
- **Baguo Buyi** (p119) The searing flavours of Sichuan delivered in an original and entertaining setting.
- **Quanjude Roast Duck Restaurant** (p120) Not the huge touristy outlet on Qianmen Dajie, but this more personable branch on Shuaifuyuan Hutong serves some excellent Peking duck.
- **Tiandi Yijia** (p117) Imperial location and superb styling, this exclusive eatery has a diverse Chinese menu and an old Peking ambience.
- **Liqun Roast Duck Restaurant** (p116) Petite Peking duck restaurant offering fine fowl and an individual character.
- **Lao Hanzi** (p123) Popular Hakka restaurant in the Sanlitun area.
- **Gongdelin Vegetarian Restaurant** (p116) Buddhist vegetarian cuisine at particularly palatable prices.
- **Beijing's back alleys** Not a restaurant! Wander at will down Beijing's *hutong* and hunt down spicy lamb kebabs, meat buns, noodles, baked sweet potatoes and more.

Shanghai Dishes

jiāng cōng chǎo xiè	姜葱炒蟹	stir-fried crab with ginger and scallions
mìzhī xūnyú	蜜汁熏鱼	honey-smoked carp
níng shì shànyú	宁式鳝鱼	stir-fried eel with onion
qiézhī yúkuài	茄汁鱼块	fish fillet in tomato sauce
qīng zhēng guìyú	清蒸鳜鱼	steamed Mandarin fish
sōngzǐ guìyú	松子鳜鱼	Mandarin fish with pine nuts
suānlà yóuyú	酸辣鱿鱼	hot and sour squid
yóubào xiārén	油爆虾仁	fried shrimp
zhá hēi lǐyú	炸黑鲤鱼	fried black carp
zhá yúwán	炸鱼丸	fish balls

Cantonese Dishes

bái zhuó xiā	白灼虾	blanched prawns with shredded scallions
dōngjiāng yánjú jī	东江盐焗鸡	salt-baked chicken
gālí jī	咖喱鸡	curried chicken
háoyóu niúròu	蚝油牛肉	beef with oyster sauce
kǎo rǔzhū	烤乳猪	crispy suckling pig
mì zhī chāshāo	密汁叉烧	roast pork with honey
shé ròu	蛇肉	snake
tángcù lǐjī/gǔlǎo ròu	糖醋里脊/咕老肉	sweet and sour pork fillets
tángcù páigǔ	糖醋排骨	sweet and sour spare ribs

Sichuanese Dishes

bàngbàng jī	棒棒鸡	shredded chicken in a hot pepper and sesame sauce
dàsuàn shàn duàn	大蒜鳝段	stewed eel with garlic
gānshāo yán lǐ	干烧岩鲤	stewed carp with ham and hot and sweet sauce
gōngbào jīdīng	宫爆鸡丁	spicy chicken with peanuts
huíguō ròu	回锅肉	boiled and stir-fried pork with salty and hot sauce
málà dòufu	麻辣豆腐	spicy tofu

shuǐ zhǔ niúròu	水煮牛肉	fried and boiled beef, garlic sprouts and celery
yúxiāng ròusī	鱼香肉丝	'fish-resembling' meat
zhàcài ròu sī	榨菜肉丝	stir-fried pork or beef tenderloin with tuber mustard
zhāngchá yā	樟茶鸭	camphor tea duck

Beef Dishes

háoyóu niúròu	蚝油牛肉	beef with oyster sauce
hóngshāo niúròu	红烧牛肉	beef braised in soy sauce
niúròu fàn	牛肉饭	beef with rice
tiébǎn niúròu	铁板牛肉	beef steak platter
gānbiàn niúròu sī	干煸牛肉丝	stir-fried beef and chilli
tiébǎn niúròu	铁板牛肉	sizzling beef platter

Chicken & Duck Dishes

háoyóu jīkuài	蚝油鸡块	diced chicken in oyster sauce
hóngshāo jīkuài	红烧鸡块	chicken braised in soy sauce
jītuǐ fàn	鸡腿饭	chicken leg with rice
níngméng jī	柠檬鸡	lemon chicken
tángcù jīdīng	糖醋鸡丁	sweet and sour chicken
yāròu fàn	鸭肉饭	duck with rice
yāoguǒ jīdīng	腰果鸡丁	chicken and cashews

Pork Dishes

biǎndòu ròusī	扁豆肉丝	shredded pork and green beans
guōbā ròupiàn	锅巴肉片	pork and sizzling rice crust
gūlǔ ròu	咕噜肉	sweet and sour pork
háoyóu ròusī	耗油肉丝	pork with oyster sauce
jiàngbào ròudīng	酱爆肉丁	diced pork with soy sauce
jīngjiāng ròusī	京酱肉丝	pork cooked with soy sauce
mùěr ròu	木耳肉	wood-ear mushrooms and pork
páigǔ fàn	排骨饭	pork chop with rice
qīngjiāo ròu piàn	青椒肉片	pork and green peppers
yángcōng chǎo ròupiàn	洋葱炒肉片	pork and fried onions

Seafood Dishes

gélì	蛤蜊	clams
gōngbào xiārén	宫爆虾仁	diced shrimp with peanuts
háo	蚝	oysters
hóngshāo yú	红烧鱼	fish braised in soy sauce
lóngxiā	龙虾	lobster
pángxiè	螃蟹	crab
yóuyú	鱿鱼	squid
zhāngyú	章鱼	octopus

Vegetable & Bean Curd Dishes

báicài xiān shuānggū	白菜鲜双菇	bok choy and mushrooms
cuìpí dòufu	脆皮豆腐	crispy skin bean curd
hēimùěr mèn dòufu	黑木耳焖豆腐	bean curd with wood-ear mushrooms
jiāngzhī qīngdòu	姜汁青豆	string beans with ginger
lúshuǐ dòufu	卤水豆腐	smoked bean curd
shāguō dòufu	砂锅豆腐	clay pot bean curd

tángcù ǒubǐng	糖醋藕饼	sweet and sour lotus root cakes
hóngshāo qiézi	红烧茄子	red cooked aubergine
sùchǎo biǎndòu	素炒扁豆	garlic beans
sùchǎo sùcài	素炒素菜	fried vegetables
yúxiāng qiézi	鱼香茄子	'fish-resembling' aubergine
jiācháng dòufu	家常豆腐	'home style' tofu

DRINKS

píjiǔ	啤酒	beer
báijiǔ	白酒	Chinese spirits
kěkǒu kělè	可口可乐	Coca-Cola
yézi zhī	椰子汁	coconut juice
nǎijīng	奶精	coffee creamer
kāfēi	咖啡	coffee
niúnǎi	牛奶	milk
kuàngquán shuǐ	矿泉水	mineral water
hóng pútáo jiǔ	红葡萄酒	red wine
mǐjiǔ	米酒	rice wine
qìshuǐ	汽水	soft drink (soda)
dòujiāng	豆浆	soya bean milk
chá	茶	tea
kāi shuǐ	开水	water (boiled)
bái pútáo jiǔ	白葡萄酒	white wine
suānnǎi	酸奶	yoghurt

History

History

FROM THE BEGINNING

Positioned outside the central heartland of Chinese civilisation, Beijing only emerged as a cultural and political force that would shape the destiny of China with the 13th century Mongol occupation of China. Prior to Genghis Khan's destruction and restoration of Beijing, the Chinese and the tribes that invaded from the north largely chose to establish dynastic capitals elsewhere in China: in Luòyáng, Xī'ān, Nánjīng, Dàtóng, Kāifēng and, during the dynasty of the Southern Sung (AD 1127–1279), in Hángzhōu.

Settlements in the Beijing area, however, long predate the Yuan (Mongol) dynasty. Although the area southwest of Beijing was inhabited by early humans some 500,000 years ago, the earliest recorded settlements in Chinese historical sources date from 1045 BC. Ancient Chinese chronicles refer to a state called Yōuzhō u ('secluded state') during the reign of the mythical Yellow Emperor, one of nine states that existed at the time.

The capital of the state of Yān, one of the warring states of the Eastern Zhou period, was also nearby and was known as Yānjīng ('Capital of Yan'). The name Yan is still associated with northern Héběi province and Beijing itself, as is the name Yanjing (the name of one of Beijing's most popular beers). The capital of the state of Yan was also known as Jì or Jìchéng ('the city of Jì'), a name that referred to the marshy features of the surrounding area at the time.

When China's first emperor, Qinshi Huangdi, united China for the first time in the 3rd century BC, he divided the country into 36 prefectures and Jicheng became the seat of local government of Guǎngyáng prefecture. The city gradually rose in importance during the Han (206 BC–AD 220), Wei (AD 220–265) and Jin dynasties (265–420) and by the time of the Sui dynasty (581–618), Jìchéng emerged as the seat of government of the Zhuō prefecture. During the prosperous Tang period (618–907) the city was again known as Youzho u.

LIAO & JIN DYNASTY BEIJING

The city's strategic location on the edge of the North China Plain did not escape the attention of the war-faring northern tribes, and Beijing was successively occupied by foreign forces, promoting its development as a major political centre. In 938 the non-Chinese Khitan Mongol Liao dynasty (907–1125) established Beijing as an auxiliary capital, when it was known both as Nanjing (Southern Capital) and Yanjing. In 1153 the Manchurian Jurchen Jin dynasty (1115–1234) moved their capital here, calling it Zhōngdū (Middle Capital).

It was during the Liao and the Jin dynasties that Beijing underwent significant transformation into a key political and military city. This was due in part to the rapid decline of Chang'an (present day Xi'an) as the political centre of China and the growing strategic significance of this part of north China. The Liao developed Beijing – then called Nanjing – as a fortified stronghold against the Northern Sung (960–1127) and as a base for launching attacks across the Central Plains.

The city was enclosed within fortified walls for the first time, accessed by eight gates. In their confrontation with the Southern Sung who ruled from Hangzhou, the Jin further developed Beijing and expanded the city walls so they encompassed an urban area around twice the size of the earlier Liao city. The Jin City Wall only partially followed the outline of the earlier wall, incorporating its northerly boundary, but expanding to the south, east

44

and west. Its complement of gates – connected to each other by roads that threaded across the city (rather like present day Kāifēng or Xi'an) – expanded to 12.

Within the Imperial City was the palace, accessed via four gates and containing ceremonial and administrative halls, drum and bell towers, gardens, temples and pagodas. Wanning Gong (Palace of Eternal Peace) was the name of the auxiliary imperial palace, built outside the main palace grounds, on the site of today's Beihai Park and Zhonghai (now part of Zhongnanhai, see p88). Beyond the city walls lay four altars at the four cardinal points, dedicated to the worship of the sun, moon, heaven and earth.

MONGOL BEIJING

In 1215 the great Mongol warrior Genghis Khan and his formidable army descended on Zhōngdū, razing the city and the Imperial City with all its palaces and halls to the ground. Despite the destruction, the event marked Beijing's first transformation into a powerful capital of the entire country, a status it would enjoy to the present day, bar 21 years of Nationalist rule in the 20th century.

The first emperor of the Yuan dynasty, Kublai Khan (1215–1294), came to Zhongdu in 1260, residing in a hall on Qionghua Island in present day Beihai Park (p73). Out of the ruins of Zhongdu, he decided to transform the city into the magnificent capital of the Yuan dynasty, shifting it slightly to the northeast. Designed by Liu Bingzhong, the city came to be called Dàdū (Great Capital), also assuming the Mongol name Khanbalik (the Khan's town). By 1279 Kublai Khan had made himself ruler of the largest empire the world has ever known, with Dadu its capital. Surrounded by a vast rectangular wall punctured by three gates on either side, the city was centred on the drum and bell towers (near to their surviving Ming dynasty counterparts), its regular layout a paragon of urban design and a form that survives in today's Beijing.

Although nothing remains of the Mongol era Imperial City, historical records have preserved a picture of its layout and appearance. Featuring both Mongol and Han Chinese design elements, the Mongol Imperial City was positioned on either side of the lakes of Beihai and Zhonghai, then called Tàiyè Chí. In terms of location and plan, the palace halls to the east of the lakes – called the Danei ('Great Inner') – were used by the emperor and were the forebears of the Ming and Qing dynasty Forbidden City. The main palace gate was called Chongtian Men, in front of which stood three bejewelled bridges and three pathways, the middle one carved with a coiling dragon. The most magnificent hall in the palace was the Daming Dian, 200 *chi* wide (one *chi* equals a third of a metre), 120 *chi* deep and 90 *chi* high. East of the lakes was the Fulong Gong (Fulong Palace) and Xinglong Gong (Xinglong Palace), residence of the empress and imperial concubines. Surrounding the Imperial City grounds ran a long wall called a *xiaoqiang* – the precursor of the Ming and Qing dynasty Imperial City Wall. The eastern wall of the Imperial City ran along the western flank of modern Beijing's Nanheyan and Beiheyan Dajie (Map pp232-3). Beyond it rose the mighty city wall.

The marvellous palace of Dadu no longer survives, but the Italian traveller Marco Polo claims to have seen it, describing what he saw to an amazed Europe: 'The building is altogether so vast, so rich, and so beautiful, that no man on earth could design anything superior to it. The outside of the roof also is all coloured with vermilion and yellow and green and blue and other hues, which are fixed with a varnish so fine and exquisite that they shine like crystal, and lend a resplendent lustre to the Palace as seen for a great way round'.

Polo was equally dazzled by the innovations of gunpowder and paper money. History's first case of paper currency inflation occurred when the last Mongol emperor flooded the country with worthless bills. This, coupled with a large number of natural disasters, provoked an uprising led by the mercenary Zhu Yuanzhang who took Beijing in 1368 to found the Ming dynasty.

AD 938	1153	1215	1260
Beijing established as auxiliary capital of the Liao dynasty; city walls first built	Beijing becomes Jin dynasty capital; city walls expanded	The Mongols, under Genghis Khan, sack Beijing	The first Yuan emperor, Kublai Khan, transforms the city and names it Dàdū

MING DYNASTY BEIJING

After seizing Beijing, the first Ming emperor Hongwu (r 1368–1398; the reigning title of Zhu Yuanzhang) renamed the city Běipíng (Northern Peace) and established his capital in Nanjing in present-day Jiāngsū province to the south. It wasn't until the reign of the Yongle emperor (r 1403–25) that the court moved back to Beijing. Seeking to rid the city of all traces of 'Yuan Qi' (literally 'breath of the Yuan dynasty'), the Ming levelled the fabulous palaces of the Mongols along with the Imperial City, while preserving much of the regular plan of the Mongol capital. Millions of taels of silver was spent in the city's reconstruction. The city was expanded southwards, its northern extents shrunk and it was renamed Beijing (Northern Capital), but was also known as Shùntiān. The Ming was the only pure Chinese dynasty to rule from Beijing, as the Liao, Jin, Yuan and later Qing dynasties were all periods of foreign rule.

Yongle is credited with being the true architect of the modern city, and much of Beijing's hallmark architecture, such as the Forbidden City and the Temple of Heaven, were first built in his reign. The Temple of Heaven (p68) is just one of five altars in Beijing, each positioned according to a cardinal point, that date from the Ming dynasty. The countenance of Ming dynasty Beijing was flat and low-lying – a feature that would remain till the 20th century – as law forbade the construction of any building higher than the Forbidden City's Hall of Supreme Harmony (p76).

The Ming Imperial City and its walls were largely constructed on the same site as its Mongol precursor. Nonetheless, adjustments were made to the Imperial City and its expansion north and south (to the gate of Chengtian Men – renamed the Gate of Heavenly Peace in the Qing dynasty; see p61) expanded the city in size. Furthermore, the Supreme Temple (p72) and the Altar to the God of the Land and the God of Grain (p72) were moved to new positions either side of the Gate of Heavenly Peace. Several waterways now flowed into the imperial grounds that were previously outside the Imperial City and the lakes were renamed.

The Imperial City was rectangular in shape, save for a lopped-off southwestern corner occupied by a massive Buddhist temple called the Ci'en Temple (Ci'en Si) that dated from the Yuan era. Pierced by four gates – Chengtian Men, Bei'an Men, Dongan Men and Xi'an Men – the Imperial City Wall now extended for around 9km. South of Chengtian Men – the main gate leading to the Forbidden City – a tract of the palace wall in the shape of a 'T' extended into the space today occupied by Tiananmen Square (p70), accessed at its southernmost tip via the huge gate of Daming Men. The marble bridges, lions and marble columns (huábiǎo) in front of the Gate of Heavenly Peace all date from the Ming dynasty.

During this time, the basic grid of present-day Beijing was laid and the city adopted a guise that would survive until the communist era.

At the start of the Ming dynasty, China was outward looking and explorative. The reign of Yongle saw the dispatch of seven maritime expeditions abroad, led by the Mus-

1368	1368–1644	1403–25	1644
Mercenary Zhu Yuanzhang takes Beijing and founds the Ming dynasty	City wall reshaped and the Great Wall rebuilt and extended under Ming rule; basic layout of contemporary Beijing established	Reign of Ming emperor Yongle sees first construction of the Forbidden City and Temple of Heaven	Founding of the Qing dynasty

lim general Zheng He (1371–1433). Reaching as far as Aden, the expeditions were later curtailed when Yongle died and Ming China began to look inward. Fearful of attack from northern tribes, money and manpower was poured into rebuilding and extending the Great Wall (the distinctive brick-clad wall that can be visited outside Beijing dates from Ming times), which was lengthened by 600 miles in the second half of the 15th century.

Enfeebled by corruption and a court paralysed under the sway of powerful eunuchs, China was further weakened and destabilised by a succession of natural disasters in the early 17th century that sparked peasant uprisings. United and consolidated into an efficient fighting force by Nurhachi (1559–1626), the Manchus to the northeast had voraciously eyed China's growing vulnerability. With disorder mounting in China, the Manchus seized the initiative and penetrated the Great Wall's defences at Shānhǎiguān (p177). Beijing fell in 1644 to the peasant rebel Li Zicheng, as the last Ming emperor hanged himself on Jingshan Hill north of the Forbidden City.

QING DYNASTY BEIJING

ANY ONE PASSING WITHOUT PROPER AUTHORIZATION THROUGH ANY OF THE GATES OF THE FORBIDDEN CITY INCURS A HUNDRED BLOWS OF THE BAMBOO. THE LAW IS INVARIABLY ENFORCED…DEATH BY STRANGULATION IS THE PUNISHMENT DUE TO ANY STRANGER FOUND IN ANY OF THE EMPEROR'S APARTMENTS.

Society in China, R K Douglas (1901)

Unlike their Mongol and Ming forebears, the non-Chinese Manchu left the halls, palaces and walls of Beijing largely untouched and preserved the earlier layout of the city. The inner city wall enclosed the Manchu sector of Beijing and became known as the Tartar City Wall, while the outer city wall to the south was also called the Chinese City Wall, surrounding as it did the Chinese (non-Manchu) quarter of town. The walls of the Imperial City maintained their Ming dynasty extents, enclosing the Forbidden City, the lakes of Beihai and Zhonghai, Jingshan Hill, and bordered to the east along today's Imperial Wall Foundation Ruins Park (along Beiheyan Dajie and Nanheyan Dajie, p76), to the west along Xihuangchenggen Beijie and Xihuangchenggen Nanjie, to the north along today's Di'anmen Dajie and to the south along Chang'an Jie. It was during the Qing dynasty that the Summer Palace (p98) was conceived.

In the last 120 years of Manchu rule, Beijing and much of China were subject to invasion and rebellion: the Anglo-French troops who destroyed the Old Summer Palace (p97) during the Second Opium War (1856–60); the Taiping Rebellion (1850–68), which killed an estimated 20 million people and brought the Qing dynasty to the brink of collapse; and the disastrous Boxer Rebellion that was finally quashed in 1900. A xenophobic group culled from the secret societies (many of which had originally been established to oppose the Manchu Qing) and violently opposed to foreigners and missionaries in China, the Boxers were finally championed by the corrupt court of the Empress Dowager Cixi (1835–1908). The Boxers entered Beijing in June 1900 and the famous siege of the Foreign Legation Quarter was only successfully lifted by a multinational army in August. Beijing suffered and much of the Foreign Legation Quarter (p63) was left devastated. In a failed attempt to smoke out the besieged foreigners, Chinese Hui (Muslim) soldiers torched China's greatest library, the Hanlin Library.

1850–68	1860	1900	1908
Taiping Rebellion	Anglo-French troops destroy the Old Summer Palace during the Second Opium War	Boxer Rebellion and siege of the Foreign Legation Quarter	Empress Dowager Cixi bequeaths power to two-year-old Puyi, the last Chinese emperor

DAWN OF THE MODERN ERA

When Cixi died she bequeathed power to two-year-old Puyi (Aisin Gioro Puyi), who was to be China's last emperor. The brutal and corrupt Qing dynasty quickly collapsed, assailed by the revolution of 1911 that ostensibly brought the Kuomintang (Nationalist Party) to power and the Republic of China (ROC) was declared with Sun Yat-sen as president. Real power, however, remained in the hands of warlords who carved China up into their own fiefdoms.

One of these warlords was General Yuan Shikai, who attempted to declare himself emperor in Beijing in 1915, after performing the imperial rites at the Temple of Heaven (p68):

UNFORTUNATELY, THE CEREMONY WAS SHORN OF MUCH OF ITS TRADITIONAL BEAUTY AND STATELINESS BY THE FACT THAT YUAN THOUGHT IT NECESSARY TO ENSURE HIS OWN SAFETY BY PROCEEDING FROM THE PALACE TO THE ALTAR OF HEAVEN IN AN ARMOURED CAR.

Twilight in the Forbidden City, Reginald F Johnston (1934)

Yuan's designs ended abruptly on his death in 1916, but other warlords continued to control most of northern China and the Kuomintang held power in the south.

China's continuing poverty and control by warlords and foreigners, coupled with its reluctance to adapt, was a recipe for revolt. Beijing University became a hotbed of intellectual dissent, attracting scholars from all over China. Karl Marx's *The Communist Manifesto*, translated into Chinese, became the basis for countless discussion groups. One of those attending was a library assistant named Mao Zedong (1893–1976).

The communists, including Mao, later established a power base in Shànghǎi and entered into an uneasy alliance with the Kuomintang to reunify China.

In 1926 the Kuomintang embarked on the Northern Expedition to wrest power from the remaining warlords. Chiang Kai-shek (1886–1975) was appointed commander-in-chief by the Kuomintang and the communists. The following year, Chiang turned on his communist allies and slaughtered them en masse in Shanghai; the survivors carried on a civil war from the countryside. By the middle of 1928 the Northern Expedition had reached Beijing, where a national government was established with Chiang holding both military and political leadership. Chiang changed the name Beijing back to Beiping to distinguish the city from the nationalist capital of Nanjing.

During 1937 the Japanese invaded the city (again renaming it Beijing and staying there until 1945, doing little damage to the city's buildings and temples) and by 1939 had overrun eastern China. The Kuomintang retreated west to the city of Chóngqìng, which became China's temporary capital during WWII. After Japan's defeat in 1945

Soldier in front of the Gate of Heavenly Peace (p64)

1911	1911	1926	1937
Collapse of the Qing dynasty	Sun Yat-sen declared president of the Republic of China	The Kuomintang embark on the Northern Expedition to unify China	Japanese occupation of Beijing

the Kuomintang returned (renaming the city Beiping), but their days were numbered: by this time the Chinese Civil War was in full swing. The communists, now under the leadership of Mao Zedong, achieved victory in 1949, and as the People's Liberation Army (PLA) marched into Beijing, the Kuomintang leaders fled to Taiwan. On 21 September 1949 Beiping was once more renamed Beijing and on 1 October, Mao Zedong proclaimed the People's Republic of China (PRC) to an audience of 500,000 in Tiananmen Square. Beijing was once again capital.

AFTER THE REVOLUTION

After 1949 came a period of catastrophic historical destruction in Beijing. The huge city walls were pulled down and the commemorative arches followed. Hundreds of temples and monuments were destroyed. Blocks of buildings were reduced to rubble to widen the boulevards and Tiananmen Square. Soviet technicians poured in and left their mark in the form of Stalinesque architecture.

The carte blanche to devastate traditional Chinese culture was extended in 1966 when Mao launched the Cultural Revolution. China was to remain in the grip of chaos for the next decade. It wasn't until around 1979 that Deng Xiaoping – a former protégé of Mao who had emerged as a pragmatic leader – launched a 'modernisation' drive. The country opened up and Westerners were finally given a chance to see what the communists had been up to for the past 30 years.

Temples, monuments and libraries in Beijing that had suffered perennial neglect or had been wrecked during the Cultural Revolution were restored in the 1980s and 1990s. Much had gone for good, but what was left was dusted down, painted and touched up for tourist consumption and to restore national pride. The city also embarked on a massive construction boom that saw glittering towers and high-rises erupt across the city. China's

The Four Gates of the Imperial City

The now largely vanished Imperial City Wall originally had four gates, with the **Gate of Heavenly Peace** (Tiānānmén; p64) the sole survivor and the principle gate lying to the south. Lying on the same meridian line, **Dian Men** was the northern gate located at the junction of today's namesake Dianmen Dajie (Dian Gate St) and Dianmennei Dajie (Inside Dian Gate St). During the Ming dynasty the gate was known as Beian Men (Gate of Northern Peace) and was a broad single-eaved and yellow glazed gateway. It was pulled down in 1955.

Dongan Men (Gate of Eastern Peace) was the eastern gate situated at the intersection of the Imperial Wall Foundation Ruins Park and Donganmen Dajie. Nothing remains of the gate (p76), save for a few miserable bricks. Dongan Men and Xian Men were both built in the same style as Dian Men. The bodies of Qing dynasty emperors would be conveyed through Dongan Men and on to the Eastern Qing Tombs, if they were to be buried there. The gate tower of Dongan Men was burnt down during a mutiny orchestrated by Yuan Shikai (the first president of the Republic of China) in February 1912. After its torching it was never repaired and was later pulled down.

Providing access on the eastern Imperial City wall was **Xian Men**, which stood on at the intersection of today's Xianmen Dajie and Xihuangcheng Beijie. Unlike Dongan Men, which lay on the same east–west line as Donghua Men (the still extant eastern gate of the Forbidden City), Xian Men was north of Xihua Men because the lake of Zhōnghǎi blocked a direct line of exit from the palace gate. As a result, Xian Men and Dongan Men were not symmetrically balanced and lay on separate latitudes. Chinese accounts record that the north side of the portal accidentally burnt down in 1950, the fault of a careless stallholder working in the nearby market. The entire gate was razed shortly afterwards. Subsidiary gates of the Imperial City included **Changan Zuo Men**, **Changan You Men** and **Daming Men** (p70), which all lay to the south and were pulled down after 1949.

1949	1950s	1966	1976
Communist victory over the Kuomintang; founding of the People's Republic of China	Most of Beijing's city walls and gates are levelled to make way for roads	The Cultural Revolution is launched	Death of Mao; death of Premier Zhou Enlai sparks spontaneous protests

spectacular reform drive is possibly, however, the final straw for legions of Beijing's historic *hútong* (alleyways). With the explosion in car ownership and the need to modernise the city's transport infrastructure to meet the demands of an increasingly mobile population, road-widening schemes are set to again redraw the map of Beijing.

The mood in today's Beijing seems very different from the Tiananmen Square spring student demonstrations of 1989, when Beijing was the focal point of international condemnation as images of army troops in full battle gear and tanks rolling into the Square were beamed around the world.

In the fallout of the 1989 student uprising, political reshuffling saw former engineer and Soviet-educated Jiang Zemin move through Communist Party ranks towards ultimate leadership of the country. Jiang took power upon Deng's death in 1997 and privatisation of some of China's many industries began.

While economic responses have proceeded full tilt, the government has managed to keep a tight reign on the policy. There's a conspicuous absence of protest in today's Beijing and you won't see subversive graffiti or wall posters. The imprisonment of followers of the banned quasi-Buddhist Falun Gong in recent years proves political dissent exists, but unrelenting government coercion has consigned it to some deeply subterranean level where it has become practically unconscious.

But some of Beijing's largest problems could, however, be environmental rather than political. The Gobi desert is coming to town (see boxed text p15) and Beijing is also one of the world's most polluted cities. The need for speedy economic expansions, magnified by preparations for the 2008 Olympics, is putting extra pressure on an already degraded environment. A staggering US$181.4 billion has been earmarked for Olympic-related development of the public transport system, roads, manufacturing and high-tech industries and urban areas, as well as environmental protection. But it is clear there will be continuing environmental impacts of the push to beautify the city for the Olympics. For example, attempts to 'green' the city are already placing pressure on Beijing's dwindling water supply. Only time will tell just how the Olympics will shape the next phase of Beijing's history.

1979	1980s	1989	2001
Deng Xiaoping's reformist agenda commences	Temples and monuments restored to encourage tourism; construction boom begins	Tiananmen Square Massacre	Beijing chosen to host the 2008 Olympic Games

1 *Exploring the Forbidden City (p76)* **2** *Man in traditional costume at Prince Gong's Residence (p94)* **3** *Phoning home, Dongcheng (p72)* **4** *Cycling Beijing's hutong (p82)*

1 *Red Gate Gallery, Southeast Corner Watchtower (p67)*
2 *Fortress walls, Southeast Corner Watchtower (p67)* 3 *Weathered doors, Imperial Archives (p65)*
4 *Water calligraphy, Jingshan Park (p81)*

1 *Sculptured column, Gate of Heavenly Peace (p64)* **2** *Soldier on guard, Tiananmen Square (p70)* **3** *Pedestrians passing portraits of former political leaders* **4** *School children in front of the Monument to the People's Heroes (p66)*

1 Food stall, Donghuamen Night Market (p21) 2 Pickles on display at Liubiju (p145) 3 Street stall spruikers (p113) 4 Diners on Wangfujing Snack Street (p118)

1 Walking through the Forbidden City (p76) *2* Artistic detail, Summer Palace (p98) *3* Ornate roofs, Forbidden City (p76) *4* Marco Polo Bridge (p175)

1 Sunrise over the Great Wall, Badaling (p167) 2 Security guard, Forbidden City (p76) 3 Stone bridge near the Gate of Heavenly Peace (p64) 4 Temples near the Imperial Summer Villa, Chengde (p181)

1 Shrine clouded in incense smoke, White Cloud Temple (p89) *2* Beijing opera performance (p25) *3* Worshipper at Dongcheng's Lama Temple (p81) *4* Traditional lanterns, Prince Gong's Residence (p94)

1 *Temple of Heaven Park (p68)*
2 *Early morning dancing, Beihai Park (p73)* 3 *Beijing Botanical Gardens (p95)* 4 *Paddle boats on Beihai Lake (p73)*

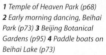

Neighbourhoods

Neighbourhoods

The neighbourhoods of Beijing, a flat city of largely uniform character uninterrupted by major waterways or hilly terrain, are not clearly delineated by distinct boundaries or physical features, yet the city is divided into numerous historical districts (*qu*).

The Forbidden City acts as the cartographic and physical focus of Beijing, the bull's-eye around which the city's notable historic sights cluster and the city's five ring roads radiate concentrically. Beijing's most historic quarters surround the Forbidden City and Tiananmen Square, within the looping boundary of the Second Ring Rd and the Circle Line of the subway.

Xicheng (West City) is the district to the west of the Forbidden City and the Drum Tower. Dongcheng (East City) is conversely the neighbourhood to the east of the Forbidden City and Drum Tower. Both Xicheng and Dongcheng are the city's central districts, which contain Beijing's most ancient monuments, famous lakes and *hútong* (alleyways) and enclose the former territory of the Imperial City.

For all practical purposes, north and south Beijing are divided by Chang'an Jie (becoming Jianguomennei Dajie and Jianguomenwai Dajie in the east and Fuxingmennei Dajie and Fuxingmenwai Dajie in the west), along which runs the East-West

Traditional architecture inside the Forbidden City (p76)

Line of the subway. The district of Chongwen, containing the Temple of Heaven, lies south of Dongcheng, and Chaoyang is a huge neighbourhood to the north, east and southeast of both Dongcheng and Chongwen.

South of Xicheng and Dongcheng is the district of Xuanwu, largely enclosed within the Second Ring Rd, and the huge district of Fengtai which covers a huge swathe of southwest Beijing. The colossal district of Haidian, sprawling west and north of Xicheng, contains some of Beijing's premier sights, including the Summer Palace, the Old Summer Palace and Fragrant Hills Park.

ITINERARIES

One Day

Beijing's top sight is undeniably the **Forbidden City** (p76), and you will need (at least) the entire morning to cover the palace and the nearby sights of **Tiananmen Square** (p70). Then take the subway from Tiananmen Xi to **Wangfujing Dajie** and lunch at **Quanjude Roast Duck Restaurant** (p120) or **Wangfujing Snack St** (p118). Walk off your meal browsing shops along Wangfujing Dajie before taking a taxi to the **Temple of Heaven Park** (p68) for a few hours. Try to squeeze in a performance of Chinese acrobatics at the **Universal Theatre** (p136) before rounding off the evening by wining and dining in **Sanlitun** (p122).

Three Days

Spend your morning exploring the **Forbidden City** (p76) and the monuments of **Tiananmen Square** (p70), before lunching at one of the roast duck restaurants in the vicinity of Qian Men. In the afternoon, take your time on a walking tour around the **Foreign Legation Quarter** (p63) and **Wangfujing Dajie** on our walks (p103). In the evening, head west back towards the Forbidden City and dine perched next to the east gate of the Forbidden City at the **Courtyard** (p119) or pick up some snacks at **Donghuamen Night Market** (p121). To round off the day, take a taxi to **Sanlitun** (p129) and find a bar.

On day two take a day trip to the **Great Wall** (p165) and the **Ming Tombs** (p171) outside town. Back in Beijing, spend the evening enjoying **Beijing opera** (p131) at one of the city's numerous theatres and dine at **Xiao Wang's Home Restaurant** (p117).

On day three make an early morning visit to the **Temple of Heaven Park** (p68) before browsing the stalls and bric-a-brac shops of **Liulichang** (p149). In the afternoon, pay a visit to the **Summer Palace** (p98); alternatively, walk along the restored **Ming City Wall** (p65) from Chongwenmen to the **Southeast Corner Watchtower** (p66) and then, if you have the time or the energy, visit the **Lama Temple** (p81) or wander at will around Beijing's **hutong**. Cap the day with a meal at the traditionally designed **Huang Ting** (p119) just off Wangfujing Dajie.

CHONGWEN & SOUTH CHAOYANG

Eating p115; Shopping p143; Sleeping p154

This part of Beijing covers the historic swathe south and southeast of the Forbidden City, largely within the loop of the Huchenghe (City Moat) and the route of the now vanished Chinese City Wall. It also incorporates parts of Dongcheng (East City), Xicheng (West City) and Xuanwu districts.

The area north of Qianmen Xidajie and Qianmen Dongdajie and within the loop of the Second Ring Rd (following the former Tartar City Wall, now marked by the subway stations of the Circle Line) was the historic Manchu sector of Beijing. It is within the southern extents of the old Tartar City that you can find the Gate of Heavenly Peace and Imperial City artefacts, including the Supreme Temple and the Imperial Archives.

Not surprisingly, this core district also contains the city's brashest Communist Party symbols, including the imposing portrait of Mao Zedong, his turgid mausoleum building, the Great Hall of the People and Tiananmen Square itself. It is also where the foreign powers chose to establish their legation quarters in the 19th century, and edifices of the era can be seen east of Tiananmen Square. Some of Beijing's finest hotels can be found along Chang'an Jie, also east of Tiananmen Square.

The area south of Qianmen Xidajie and Qianmen Dongdajie is a coarser region than the districts embraced by the Second Ring Rd. It belongs to the old Chinese quarter, south of the Qing dynasty Tartar City Wall and well beyond the imperial zone, which was bounded by the Imperial City Wall. Historically a district of the common people, it remains a more down-at-heel and shabby area, threaded by small *hutong* and home to the shops and bazaars of Dashilar. Yet this district also belongs in the south, an aspect facing the sun and indicative of *yáng* (the male and positive principle). The direction is symbolised in the official name of Front Gate (Qian Men, also called Zhengyang Men – or Sun-facing Gate). Blessed with such positive attributes, it is not surprising that Beijing's principle imperial shrine, the Temple of Heaven, is also located here.

A salient feature of this area are the names associated with the old Tartar City Wall and its few surviving remnants. The subway stations of Qianmen, Chongwenmen and Jianguomen recall several of the city wall's vast and imposing gates, of which only Qianmen survives, along with Dongbianmen (Southeast Corner Watchtower) to the southeast. The length of city wall between Chongwenmen and the Dongbianmen watchtower has been restored and can be visited. The road looping south from Jianguomen, following the line of the city moat marks the outline of the levelled Chinese city wall, whose gates are recalled in such street names as Guangqumen Nanbinhe Lu, Zuo'anmen Xibinehe Lu and Yondingmen Dongbinhe Lu.

ANCIENT OBSERVATORY

Map pp239–41

Gǔ Guānxiàngtái

☎ 6524 2202; adult Y15; ⏰ 9.30-11.30am & 1-4.30pm Wed-Sun; subway Jianguomen

Mounted on the battlements of a watchtower, Beijing's Ancient Observatory forlornly overlooks the traffic-clogged Second Ring Rd near Jianguomennei Dajie, hemmed in by gargantuan building projects and stranded by traffic loops and shuddering flyovers.

The observatory dates back to Kublai Khan's days when it lay north of the present site. Khan – like later Ming and Qing emperors – relied heavily on astrologers to plan his military moves. The present observatory was built between 1437 and 1446 to facilitate both astrological predictions and seafaring navigation.

Navigational equipment used by Chinese ships is displayed downstairs, and on the roof is an array of Jesuit-designed astronomical instruments. The Jesuits, scholars as well as

Temple of Heaven (p68)

Top Five Chongwen & South Chaoyang

- Taking an early morning or twilight stroll around immense **Tiananmen Square** (p70).
- Spend the morning sizing up the imposing grandeur and cosmic overtones of the **Temple of Heaven Park** (p68).
- Sample the European flavours of the **Foreign Legation Quarter** (p63).
- Tour the restored Ming dynasty city wall from Chongwenmen to the stalwart bastion of Dongbianmen (Southeast Corner Watchtower) at the **Ming City Wall Ruins Park** (p66).
- Peruse the exhibition commemorating the Imperial City at the **Imperial City Museum** (p65), before taking a peek at the nearby **Imperial Archives** (p65) and the artistic offerings of its Wan Fung Art Gallery.

---

proselytisers, came to town in 1601 when Matteo Ricci and his associates were permitted to work with Chinese scientists. Outdoing the resident calendar-setters, they were given control of the observatory and became the Chinese court's official advisers.

The instruments on display date from 1669 to 1673, and are embellished with sculptured bronze dragons and other Chinese handiwork – a unique mix of East and West. Of the eight on view (including an equatorial armillary sphere, celestial globe and altazimuth), six were designed and constructed under the supervision of the Belgian priest Ferdinand Verbiest, who came to China in 1659 as a special employee of the Qing court.

The azimuth theodolite was supervised by Kilian Stumpf, also a missionary. The eighth instrument, the new armillary sphere, was completed in 1744 by Ignaz Kögler. It's not clear which instruments on display are the originals.

During the Boxer Rebellion, the instruments disappeared into the hands of the French and Germans. Some were returned in 1902, and others were returned after WWI, under the provisions of the Treaty of Versailles (1919).

BEIJING UNDERGROUND CITY

Map pp239–41

Běijīng Dìxiàchéng

between 64 & 62 Xidamo Changjie; adult Y20; ⏰ 8am-5.30pm; subway Chongwenmen

By 1969, as the USA landed men on the moon, Mao had decided the future for the Beijing people lay underground. Alarmist predictions of nuclear war with Russia dispatched an army of Chinese beneath the streets of Beijing to burrow a huge warren of bombproof tunnels. The task was completed Cultural Revolution-style – by hand – and was finished in 1979, just as Russia decided to bog down in Afghanistan instead.

A section of the tunnels can now be visited. The entry point, in an unremarkable building along an alley east of Qianmen Dajie and south of Taijichang Dajie, is hard to spot, so look out for its English sign.

The complex is a tremendous achievement, and even though many tunnels are blocked off, you get a distinct idea of the scale of the endeavour.

There's not much to see, but if you speak Chinese the guide will take you for a 20-minute circuit. You'll pass chambers labelled with their original function (cinema, hospital, arsenal etc), although it's difficult to discern much. You'll also make out signposts to major landmarks reached by the tunnels (Tiananmen Square, the Forbidden City), but these routes are inaccessible. Also punctuating the route are the occasional flood-proof gates. The tunnels are also aerated with 2,300 ventilation shafts, many of which poke up into neighbouring shops and eateries from which you can hear snatches of conversation.

CHAIRMAN MAO MAUSOLEUM

Map pp239–41
Máo Zhǔxí Jìniàntáng
☎ 6513 2277; southern side of Tiananmen Square; admission free; ☸ 8.30-11.30am Mon-Sat, 2-4pm Mon, Wed & Fri; subway Tiananmen Xi, Tiananmen Dong or Qianmen

Chairman Mao died in September 1976, and his mausoleum was constructed shortly thereafter on the site of the Daming Gate (see Tiananmen Square, p70).

However history judges Mao, his influence was enormous. Easy as it now is to vilify his deeds and excesses, many Chinese show deep respect when confronted with the physical presence of the man. China International Travel Service (CITS; Zhōngguó Guójì Lǚxíngshè) guides freely quote the old 7:3 ratio on Mao that first surfaced in 1976: Mao was 70% right and 30% wrong (what, one wonders, are the figures for CITS itself?), and this is now the official Party line.

Although admission is free, you have to pay Y10 to check your bags and camera across

the way. Join the enormous queue of Chinese sightseers, but don't expect more than a quick glimpse of the body as you file past the sarcophagus. At certain times of the year the body requires maintenance and is not on view.

EXPLORASCIENCE Map pp239–41
Suǒní Tànmèng
☎ 8518 2255; 1st fl, Oriental Plaza, Wangfujing Dajie; adult/child Y30/20; ☸ 9.30am-5.30pm Mon-Fri, 10am-7pm Sat & Sun, closed 2nd Mon & Tue every month; subway Wangfujing

This Sony-sponsored interactive hands-on science exhibition is in the fun Oriental Plaza shopping mall. ExploraScience is full of gadgets and is perfect for inquisitive children and little Einsteins.

FOREIGN LEGATION QUARTER
Map pp239–41
subway Chongwenmen, Qianmen or Wangfujing

As James Ricalton noted in the Foreign Legation district soon after the Boxer Rebellion:

> Here the fire was as hot as anywhere. A cannon ball came through the wall of this legation and carried off the head of Mr Wagener, a gentleman in the customs service. I was told by good authorities that this burned district, destroyed ruthlessly and uselessly, represented, at a low estimate, five million dollars' worth of property.

The former Foreign Legation Quarter, where the foreign powers of the 19th century had their embassies, schools, post offices and banks, lay to the east of Tiananmen Square. The entire district became a war zone during the Boxer Rebellion. A stroll in the area around Taijichang Dajie and Zhengyi Lu will reveal some of its European flavour (see the Foreign Legation Quarter Walk p102).

Probably the greatest cultural loss during the Boxer Rebellion was the destruction by fire of the Hanlin Academy, the centre of Chinese learning and literature. Ricalton stated: 'The Classics of Confucius inscribed on tablets of marble were treasured there; these are gone; the 20,000 volumes of precious literature are gone; and this venerable institution, founded a thousand years before the Christian era…is a heap of ruins. The loss of thousands of volumes of ancient records recalls the destruction of the Alexandrian Library as an irreparable loss; not so many precious books, perhaps, yet the Hanlin College antedated the Alexandrian Library by nearly seven hundred years'.' The library was torched by Muslim Huí troops who were trying to flush out the besieged Western inhabitants of the legations.

On the northern corner of Taijichang Toutiao's intersection with Taijichang Dajie there is a brick in the wall engraved with the road's former foreign name: **Rue Hart**. This modest street sign somehow evaded both the 1949 Liberation and the Cultural Revolution.

At the junction of Taijichang Dajie and Dongjiaomin Xiang stands the twin-spired grey **St Michael's Church** (🕐 after 6pm) also called Dongjiaomin Catholic Church. Opposite are the many buildings of the former Belgian Embassy. Along the western reaches of Dongjiaomin Xiang you'll pass the former French Legation (behind bright red doors), and further along on the right is the former **French Post Office** (now the Jingyuan Restaurant) – a building crying out to be converted into a pub.

FRONT GATE Map pp239–41
Qián Mén

☎ 6525 3176; adult Y10; 🕐 8.30am-4pm;
subway Qianmen

Front Gate actually consists of two gates. The northernmost of the two gates, 40m-high **Zhengyang Men** (Sun-facing Gate) dates from the Ming dynasty and was the largest of the nine gates of the inner city wall separating the inner, or Tartar (Manchu), City from the outer, or Chinese, City. Partially destroyed during the Boxer Rebellion of 1900, the gate was once flanked by two temples that have since vanished. With the disappearance of the city walls, the gate sits out of context, but you can climb it for views over the square, and the interior houses mod-

els and photos of old Beijing. Similarly torched during the Boxer Rebellion, the **Arrow Tower** (Jiàn Lóu) to the south also dates from the Ming and was originally connected to Zhengyang Men by a semicircular enceinte, which was demolished in the 20th century. To the east is the former British-built Qian Men Railway Station (Lǎo Chēzhàn), now housing shops, an Internet café and the **Old Station Theater** (p131), where you can watch performances of Beijing Opera.

GATE OF HEAVENLY PEACE Map pp239–41
Tiānānmén

☎ 6309 9386; adult Y15; 🕐 8.30am-4.30pm;
subway Tiananmen Xi or Tiananmen Dong

Hung with a vast likeness of Mao, the double-eaved Gate of Heavenly Peace is a potent national symbol. Built in the 15th century and restored in the 17th century, the gate was formerly the largest of the four gates of the Imperial City Wall (Huáng Chéng). Called Chengtian Men during the Ming dynasty, it was renamed Tiananmen during the reign of emperor Shunzhi at the dawn of the Qing dynasty. Of the two **stone lions** that guard the gate, legend records that the westerly stone creature blocked the path of Li Chuangwang when he invaded Beijing at the end of the Ming dynasty. Li fended the lion off by stabbing its belly with his spear while on horseback, leaving a mark that can still be seen. Some locals dispute this story, arguing that it is a bullet hole – the work of allied force guns after troops entered Beijing to quell the Boxer Rebellion in 1900.

There are five doors to the gate, fronted by seven bridges spanning a stream. Each of these bridges was restricted in its use, and only the emperor could use the central door and bridge.

Transport

Subway East-West Line: Tiananmen Xi and Tiananmen Dong subway stops serve Tiananmen Square, the Forbidden City, the Imperial Wall Museum and the Imperial Archives; Wangfujing subway stop serves Wangfujing Dajie, and you can backtrack into the Foreign Legation Quarter from here; get off at the Jianguomen stop (both East-West and Circle Lines) for the Ancient Observatory, Southeast Corner Watchtower and the restored Ming City Wall Ruins Park. Circle Line: The Qianmen stop takes you to the Front Gate; Chongwenmen puts you at the commencement of the Ming City Wall Ruins Park that leads to the Southeast Corner Watchtower; alight at the Beijingzhan stop for the Henderson Center and Beijing Train Station. The Circle Line intersects with the East-West Line at Jianguomen.

Bus Services along Chang'an Jie include buses 1 and 4, travelling from Sihuizhan along Jianguomenwai Dajie, Jianguomennei Dajie and Chang'an Jie; bus 20 travels from Tianqiao via Qianmen to Wangfujing, Dongdan and Beijing Train Station; bus 54 goes from Beijing Train Station past Dongbianmen (Southeast Corner Watchtower) to Chongwenmen, Zhengyi Lu, Qianmen, Dashilar and the Temple of Heaven Park.

Today's political coterie review mass troop parades from here, and it was from this gate that Mao proclaimed the People's Republic on 1 October 1949. The dominating feature is the gigantic portrait of the ex-chairman, to the left of which run the poetic slogans 'Long Live the People's Republic of China' and to the right 'Long Live the Unity of the Peoples of the World'. The portrait was famously pelted with paint-filled eggs during the 1989 demonstrations in the square; the iconoclasts were workers from Mao's home province of Húnán. A number of spares of the portrait exist, and a fresh one was speedily requisitioned after the 1989 incident.

You pass through Tiananmen on your way to the Forbidden City (assuming you enter from the southern side). Climb up to excellent views of Tiananmen Square, and peek inside at the impressive beams and overdone paintwork. Other diversions include video presentations and paintings of the Tiananmen Square flag-raising ceremony, featuring jubilant representatives of China's ethnic minorities.

There is no fee for walking through the gate, but if you climb Tiananmen you will have to buy an admission ticket and pay (Y2) to store your bag at the kiosk inconveniently located about 30m away from the ticket office. Security is intense with metal detectors and frisking awaiting visitors. A list of prohibited items includes Xerox documents (to prevent seditious fliers drifting down onto the square below, perhaps?).

GREAT HALL OF THE PEOPLE

Map pp239–41
Rénmín Dàhuìtáng
☎ 6309 6668; western side of Tiananmen Square; adult Y20; ☺ times vary, usually 9am-3pm; subway Tiananmen Xi

On a site previously occupied by Taichang Temple, the Jinyiwei (Ming dynasty secret service) and the Ministry of Justice, the Great Hall of the People is the venue of the legislature, the National People's Congress. The 1959 architecture is monolithic and intimidating, and the tour parades visitors past a choice of 29 of its lifeless rooms named after the provinces that make up the Chinese universe. Also on the billing is the 5000-seat banquet room where US President Richard Nixon dined in 1972, and the 10,000-seat auditorium with the familiar red star embedded in a galaxy of lights in the ceiling. The Great Hall of the

People is closed to the public when the People's Congress is in session.

IMPERIAL ARCHIVES Map pp239–41

Huángshǐ Chéng
136 Nanchizi Dajie; admission free; ☺ 9am-7pm; subway Tiananmen Dong

Tucked away on the right-hand side of the first road to the east of the Forbidden City is the old Imperial Archives. This is the former repository for the imperial records, decrees, the 'Jade Book' (the imperial genealogical record) and huge encyclopaedic works, including the *Yongle Dadian* and the *Daqing Huidian*. You can peer through the closed door and make out the chests in which the archives were stored. With strong echoes of the splendid imperial palace, the courtyard contains well-preserved halls and the **Wan Fung Art Gallery** (www.wanfung.com.cn; ☺ 12-6pm Mon & 10am-6pm Tue-Sun).

IMPERIAL CITY MUSEUM Map pp239–41

Huáng Chéng Yìshùguǎn
☎ 8511 5104/5114; 9 Changpu Heyan; adult/student Y20/10, audio tour Y50; ☺ 9am-4.30pm; subway Tiananmen Dong

This important museum is devoted to the Imperial City (Huáng Chéng), which – apart from a few brief stretches – no longer exists. The recently opened museum is the centrepiece of a surviving section of the Imperial City Wall that has been dolled up and converted into a park. It might be contrived and *faux* old Peking, but **Changpu River Park** (Chāngpú Hé Gōngyuán) is a long and pleasant strip running along Dongchang'an Jie. The park is decorated with a graceful marble bridge, rock features, paths, a stream, willows, magnolias, scholar trees and walnut trees. Apart from a visit to the museum, a stroll in the park makes for a relaxing sojourn before or after a visit to the Forbidden City.

The museum functions as a memorial to the demolished wall, gates and buildings of the Imperial City (see the boxed text p49). A **diorama** in the museum reveals the full extent of the yellow-tiled Imperial City Wall, which encompassed a vast chunk of Beijing nearly seven times the size of the Forbidden City. Within its walls were lakes (Nánhǎi, Zhōnghǎi and Běihǎi), rivers (Jīnshuǐ Hé and Yù Hé), the Imperial Archives (p65), the Supreme Temple (Tài Miào; see the Workers Cultural Palace, p72), the Altar to the God of the Land and God of Grain (see Zhongshan Park, p72), Jingshan

It's Free Top Five

Badly off or broke in Beijing? Try the following for free thrills:

- File past the embalmed body of Chairman Mao in the **Chairman Mao Mausoleum** (p63) and then do a circuit of **Tiananmen Square** (p70).
- Pay a visit to the grand **Imperial Archives** (p65) and the art exhibition at the on-site Wan Fung Art Gallery.
- You don't *have* to buy anything wandering along **Wangfujing Dajie** (p143), and **St Joseph's Church** (p85) is still on the house.
- Explore the **Foreign Legation Quarter** (p63) at your leisure or take our Legation Quarter Walk (p102).
- Stretch a leg without at the **Ming City Wall Ruins Park** (p65).

Park (p81), official residences and a vast array of now vanished temples. In its heyday, 28 large temples could be found in the Imperial City alone, along with many smaller shrines. Many of these can be observed on the diorama, including a large temple in the northwest of the Imperial City with a double-eaved hall similar to the Hall of Prayer for Good Harvests at the Temple of Heaven Park (p68).

Also of note are the **illustrations** outlining the Liao, Jin and Yuan dynasty city walls. Period photos of the old gates of Beijing (including Daqing Men, Zuo Changan Men, You Changan Men and Dongan Men) and images of the halls and pavilions in Zhongnanhai (p90) are hung on the walls. Also worth exploring are two Ming and Qing dynasty maps of Beijing charting no longer extant temples. Note the huge Shanchuan Tan altar complex (also known as the Xian Nong Tan or Temple of Agriculture) to the west of the Temple of Heaven, which was pulled down in the 1950s. Conspicuously absent from the museum are images of the destruction of the Imperial City Wall, the inner or Tartar City Wall, the outer or Chinese City Wall and all the now-vanished temples and buildings that were levelled; had they been preserved, there would be no need for such an exhibition.

Further galleries have exhibits of imperial ornaments such as *ruyi* (sceptres), porcelain and enamelware, and the weapons and armour of the imperial guards. There are also small exhibitions on Beijing's *hutong* and Beijing's pigeons (their rearing is a traditional local pastime) and displays exhibiting sandal-wood and mahogany Ming and Qing furniture. There's also a bookshop and an elevator for disabled access.

MING CITY WALL RUINS PARK

Map pp239–41
Míng Chéngqiáng Yízhǐ Gōngyuán
Chongwenmen Dongdajie; ☼ 24 hr;
subway Chongwenmen

Running the entire length of the northern flank of Chongwenmen Dongdajie is this slender new park containing a long section of the Ming inner city wall (originally 40km in length), which was restored in 2002. At the time of writing, the wall was still being rebuilt and finishing touches made. The irony of its reconstruction will hardly be lost on Beijing's senior citizens. Levelled in the 1950s to facilitate transport and eliminate the legacy of earlier dynasties, this section of the wall has been rebuilt to restore grandeur to Beijing and attract the tourist dollar.

South of Beijing Train Station, the park runs all the way from the former site of **Chongwen Men** (Chongwen Gate; one of the nine gates of the inner city wall) to the **Southeast Corner Watchtower** (p67). You can walk the park's length, taking in its higgledy-piggledy contours and examining the interior layers of stone in parts of the wall that have collapsed. The restored sections run for around 2km, rising up to a height of around 15m and interrupted every 80m with buttresses *(dun tai)*, which extend to a maximum depth of 39m. The most interesting sections of wall are those closer to their original and more dilapidated state; restored parts of the wall are too uniform and well finished. You can hunt down a further section of original, collapsing wall if you follow Jianguomen Nandajie north of the Southeast Corner Watchtower. The dishevelled wall runs to your left as you walk north up Jianguomen Nandajie. Take a left onto Beijingzhan Dongjie where you can see the wall come to a halt as it meets the pavement through a gap in the modern perimeter wall.

MONUMENT TO THE PEOPLE'S HEROES Map pp239–41

Rénmín Yīngxióng Jìniànbēi
Tiananmen Square; subway Tiananmen Xi, Tiananmen Dong or Qianmen

North of Mao's mausoleum, the Monument to the People's Heroes was completed in 1958. The 37.9m-high obelisk, made of Qīngdǎo

granite, bears bas-relief carvings of key pa-
triotic and revolutionary events (such as Lin
Zexu destroying opium at Hǔmén in the 19th
century and Taiping rebels), as well as appropriate calligraphy from communist bigwigs
Mao Zedong and Zhou Enlai. Mao's eight-
character flourish proclaims 'Eternal Glory to
the People's Heroes'. The monument is illuminated at night.

MUSEUM OF CHINESE HISTORY & MUSEUM OF THE CHINESE REVOLUTION Map pp239–41

Zhōngguó Lìshǐ Bówùguǎn; Zhōngguó Gémìng Lìshǐ
Bówùguǎn

☎ 6512 8986; eastern side of Tiananmen Square;
admission Y30 each; ☷ 8.30am-4.30pm Tue-Sat;
subway Tiananmen Dong

The propagandist Museum of Chinese History
and the Museum of the Chinese Revolution
are clumped together in a sombre building,
served by individual ticket offices. From 1966
to 1978 the museums were closed so that history could be revised in the light of recent
events, and the tradition continues with frequent closures. Several halls of the Museum
of Chinese History stage temporary art and
culture exhibitions.

NATURAL HISTORY MUSEUM

Map pp239–41

Zìrán Bówùguǎn

☎ 6702 4431; 126 Tianqiao Nandajie; adult Y15;
☷ 8.30am-5pm, last entry 4pm;
subway Qianmen

The main entrance hall to the overblown,
creeper-laden 1950s Natural History Museum
is hung with portraits of great natural historians, including Darwin and Linnaeus (here spelt
Linnacus). Outside, a grove of fossilised trees
has been erected.

Some of the exhibits, such as the spliced
human cadavers and genitalia, are best seen
on an empty stomach, or not at all (depending
on the strength of your stomach). Otherwise
check out the dinosaurs that used to roam
China before party officials replaced them.
There's the possibly beer-drinking *Tsingtao-
saurus* (*Qingdaolong*) named after the beach
resort and its cousin the *Shantongosaurus*, also
from Shāndōng. The dinosaur exhibits are on
the ground floor and downstairs.

Other exhibition halls offer a ghastly men-
agerie of creatures suspended in formalde-
hyde. The pickled fish are no different from the

many you see floating belly up in restaurant
aquariums throughout China.

Coming at you in the human evolution
chamber upstairs is a posse of apemen in Socialist Realist pose. There are limited English
captions.

SOUTHEAST CORNER WATCHTOWER

Map pp239–41

Dōngnán Jiǎolóu

☎ 8512 1554; Dongbianmen; adult Y10; ☷ 9am-5pm;
subway Jianguomen or Chongwenmen

This splendid fortification, with a green-tiled,
twin-eaved roof rising up imperiously south
of the Ancient Observatory as Jianguomen
Nandajie loses itself in a knot of junctions,
dates back to the Ming dynasty. Clamber up
the steps for views alongside camera-wielding
Chinese train spotters eagerly awaiting rolling
stock grinding in and out of Beijing Train Station. Mounting the battlements, two forlorn
stumps of flag abutments and a cannon or
two can be seen, but really worth hunting out
are the **signatures** etched in the walls by allied forces during the Boxer Rebellion. Look
for the brass plaque in Chinese and a sheet
of Perspex nailed to the wall near the top of
the steps. You can make out the name of a
certain P Foot; 'USA' is also scrawled on the
brickwork. The international composition of
the eight-nation force that relieved Beijing
in 1900 is noted in names such as 'André',
'Stickel' and what appears to be a name in
Cyrillic. One brick records the date 'Dec 16
1900'. Allied forces overwhelmed the redoubt
after a lengthy engagement. Note the drain-
age channels poking out of the wall along
its length. You can reach the watchtower
from the west through the **Railway Arch**, which
was built for the first railway that encircled
Beijing.

The watchtower is punctured with 144
archers' windows, and attached to it is a
100m section of the original inner city wall,
beyond which stretches the restored **Ming City
Wall** extending all the way to Chongwenmen.
Inside the highly impressive interior is some
staggering carpentry: huge red pillars surge
upwards, topped with solid beams. The 1st
floor is the site of the **Red Gate Gallery** (☎ 6525
1005; www.redgategallery.com; admission
free; ☷ 10am-5pm); the 2nd floor gallery is
devoted to a small Chinese language exhibition on the watchtower and the Chongwen
District, while the 3rd floor gallery contains
additional paintings.

TEMPLE OF HEAVEN PARK Map pp239–41

Tiāntán Gōngyuán

☎ 6702 8866; Tiantan Donglu; low season Y10-30, high season Y15-35; ☺ park 6am-9pm, sights 8am-6pm; subway Chongwenmen or Qianmen

The most perfect example of Ming architecture, Tiāntán – literally 'Altar of Heaven' but commonly called Temple of Heaven – has come to symbolise Beijing. Its outline has decorated countless pieces of tourist literature, and its name serves as a brand name for a wide range of products ranging from balm to plumbing fixtures. It originally functioned as a vast stage for the solemn rites performed by the Son of Heaven, who came here to pray for good harvests, seek divine clearance and atone for the sins of the people. In the 1970s the complex was given a face-lift and was freshly painted. It is set in a 267-hectare park, with a gate at each

point of the compass, and bounded by walls to the north and east.

The Temple of Heaven's unique architectural features will delight numerologists, necromancers and the superstitious – not to mention acoustic engineers and carpenters. Shape, colour and sound combine to take on symbolic significance. Seen from above the temples are round and the bases square, a pattern deriving from the ancient Chinese belief that heaven is round and earth is square. Thus the northern end of the park is semicircular and the southern end is square. The **Temple of Earth**, also called Ditan (see Ditan Park p75), is on the northern compass point, and the **Temple of Heaven** is on the southern.

The Temple of Heaven was considered sacred ground and it was here that the emperor performed the major ceremonial rites.

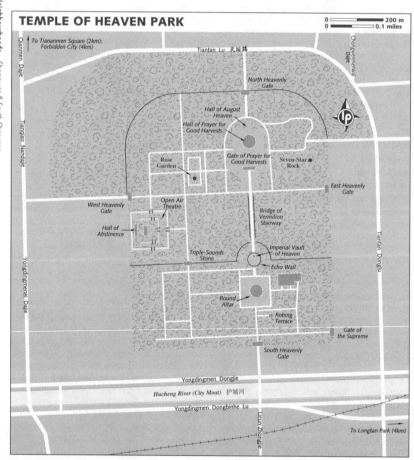

TEMPLE OF HEAVEN PARK

The most important ceremony of the year was performed just before the winter solstice when the emperor and his enormous entourage passed down Qianmen Dajie to the **Imperial Vault of Heaven** in total silence. Commoners were not permitted to view the ceremony and remained cloistered indoors. The procession included elephant and horse chariots and long lines of lancers, nobles, officials and musicians dressed in their finest, with flags fluttering. The next day the emperor waited in a yellow silk tent at the southern gate while officials moved the sacred tablets to the **Round Altar**, where the prayers and sacrificial rituals took place. It was thought that this ritual decided the nation's future; hence a hitch in any part of the proceedings was regarded as a bad omen.

The Temple of Heaven is still an important meeting place. Get here at 6.30am (before the ticket booth opens) to see *tàijíquán* (also known as *taichi*), dancing to Western music and various other games being played. This is how Beijing awakens; by 9am it becomes just another Chinese park.

Round Altar

The 5m-high Round Altar (Yuán Qiū) was constructed in 1530 and rebuilt in 1740. It is composed of white marble arrayed in three tiers, and its geometry revolves around the imperial number nine. Odd numbers were considered heavenly, and nine is the largest single-digit odd number. The top tier, thought to symbolise heaven, has nine rings of stones. Each ring is composed of multiples of nine stones, so that the ninth ring has 81 stones. The middle tier – earth – has the 10th to 18th rings. The bottom tier – humanity – has the 19th to 27th rings, ending with a total of 243 stones in the largest ring. The number of stairs and balustrades are also multiples of nine. If you stand in the centre of the upper terrace and say something, the sound waves bounce off the marble balustrades, making your voice appear louder (by nine times?).

Echo Wall

Just north of the altar, surrounding the Imperial Vault of Heaven, is the Echo Wall (Huíyīn Bì), 65m in diameter. Its form enables a whisper to travel clearly from one end to the other – that is, if there's not a tour group in the middle. In the courtyard are the **Triple-Sounds Stones** (Sānyīn Shí). It is said that if you clap or shout standing on the stones, the sound is echoed once from the first stone, twice from the second stone

and thrice from the third stone. Queues can get long at this one.

Imperial Vault of Heaven

The octagonal Imperial Vault of Heaven (Huáng Qióng Yǔ) was built at the same time as the Round Altar, and is structured along the same lines as the older Hall of Prayer for Good Harvests. It used to contain spirits used in the winter solstice ceremony.

Proceeding up from the Imperial Vault is a walkway: to the left is a molehill composed of excess dirt dumped from digging air-raid shelters, and to the right is a rash of souvenir shops.

Hall of Prayer for Good Harvests

The crown of the whole complex is the Hall of Prayer for Good Harvests (Qínián Diàn), a magnificent piece mounted on a three-tiered marble terrace. Built in 1420, it was burnt to cinders in 1889 and heads rolled in apportioning blame. The cause seems to have been lightning. A faithful reproduction based on Ming architectural methods was erected the following year, the builders choosing Oregon fir for the support pillars, as explained by Lucian S. Kirtland in *Finding the Worthwhile in the Orient* (1926):

> When it was desired to rebuild the temple, and the Manchus were determined to copy in detail the building which had been destroyed, it was found that China's forests were bereft of timbers which could uphold the heavy tiled roof. After much argument with themselves, the necromancers of the court finally decided that pine logs from the forests of Oregon would constitute proper *feng-shui*. This decision very happily corresponded with the best engineering advice, and the New World furnished the pillars which you now see.

The four central pillars symbolise the seasons, the 12 in the next ring denote the months of the year, and the 12 outer ones represent the day, broken into 12 'watches'. Embedded in the ceiling is a carved dragon, a symbol of royalty. The patterning, carving and gilt decoration of this ceiling and its swirl of colour is a dizzying sight.

All this is made more amazing by the fact that the wooden pillars ingeniously support the ceiling without nails or cement – quite an accomplishment for a building 38m high and 30m in diameter.

TIANANMEN SQUARE Map pp239–41
Tiānānmén Guǎngchǎng
subway Tiananmen Xi, Tiananmen Dong or Qianmen
Tiananmen Square 1989, as captured in excerpts from Thirty-Eighth Group Army *Accomplish the Mission, Conscientiously Complete the Martial Law Task* report to the Central Military Commission, 8 June 1989 (*Tiananmen Papers*, edited by Andrew J. Nathan and Perry Link):

> Before they cleared the Square, the various movements of the group army's 10,800 officers and soldiers and forty-five armoured vehicles crushed the blazing arrogance of the riot elements, smashed their lines of defense on the west, and struck fear into the hearts of the diehards who were entrenched in the Square.

The world's largest public square, Tiananmen Square is a vast desert of paving stones at the heart of Beijing and a poignant epitaph to China's hapless democracy movement. It may be a grandiose Maoist tourist trap, but there's more than enough space to stretch a leg. And the view can be breathtaking, especially on a clear day and at nightfall when the square is illuminated. Kites flit through the sky, children stamp around on the paving slabs and Chinese out-of-towners huddle together for the obligatory photo opportunity with the great helmsman's portrait.

The square is laid out on a north–south axis. Threading through the **Front Gate** (Qián Mén) to the south, the square's meridian line is straddled by the **Chairman Mao Mausoleum** (p63), cuts through the **Gate of Heavenly Peace** (Tiānānmén; p64) to the north and cleaves through the Forbidden City spread out behind.

In the square, one stands in the symbolic centre of the Chinese universe. The rectangular arrangement, flanked by halls to both east and west, echoes the layout of the Forbidden City. As such, the square employs a conventional plan that pays obeisance to traditional Chinese culture, but its ornaments and buildings are largely Soviet-inspired.

Tiananmen Square as we see it today is a modern creation. During Ming and Qing times part of the Imperial City Wall (Huáng Chéng) called the Thousand Foot Corridor (Qiānbù Láng) poked deep into the space today occupied by the square, enclosing a section of the imperial domain. The wall took the shape of a 'T', emerging from the two huge, and now absent, gates that rose up south of the Gate of Heavenly Peace – Chang'an Zuo Men and Chang'an You Men – before running south to the vanished

Gate of Heavenly Peace (p64)

Beijing's Decorative Archways

Many of Beijing's streets, alleys and place names are named after temples, city gates, markets and bridges, some of which have survived to the present, but many have not. Chaoyangmen Nandajie and Chaoyangmen Beidajie in Chaoyang district mean, respectively, 'the street south of Chaoyang Gate' and 'the street north of Chaoyang Gate'. Nothing is actually left of Chaoyang Gate since it was pulled down in the 1950s, and it survives in road names alone. Baiyun Lu is named after its namesake Taoist temple, the White Clouds Temple (Baiyun Guan; p89), which survives to this day. Tianqiao, Hufangqiao, Ganshiqiao and Dazhiqiao are place names that derive from now-vanished bridges (qiáo).

The etymology of such street names may be easy to trace, but not many Beijing youngsters know how Xisi, Dongsi, Xidan and Dongdan came to be named. In fact, these place names recall the now-levelled *pailou*, or decorative arches, that used to stand there.

Pailou, still visible along the street that runs just south of the Confucius Temple (p75) on Guozijian Jie, were erected at entrances to numerous streets and alleys of note in Beijing. Also known as *páifāng*, *pailou* served no practical purpose and were purely decorative objects adorned with a horizontal inscription board. Few survive today, but at one time Beijing had more *pailou* than any other city in China.

Dongdan and Xidan, which respectively mean 'East Single' and 'West Single' recall the individual *pailou* that stood at each location. Dongsi and Xisi, which mean 'East Four' and 'West Four', refer to the four *pailou* that were erected at the crossroads at each spot. At both the Dongsi and Xisi crossroads, four wooden *pailou* were constructed, facing the four points of the compass. The *pailou* survived until the 1950s, when they came down to make way for road widening. The single *pailou* that existed at Dongdan and Xidan – each three bays wide and supported by four huge pillars – dated to the reign of Ming emperor Yongle. They were similarly levelled for road widening.

The Arrow Tower and Zhengyang Gate at today's Qianmen can still be seen, but a huge *pailou* also formerly stood there. Some older Beijing residents still refer to Qianmen as Wupailou (five *pailou*), referring to the now-vanished five-bay Ming dynasty archway that rose up south of Zhengyang Gate. The *pailou* was torched when Qianmen was set on fire as foreign troops entered Beijing in 1900 to quell the Boxer uprising. The archway was reconstructed when Cixi returned to Beijing in 1901, but came down for good in the 1950s when Qianmen Dajie was widened. Other *pailou* that have disappeared include the three archways that stood outside the Dagaoxuan Temple at the western end of Jingshan Qianjie.

Apart from those on Guozijian Jie and a marvellous glazed archway in the Imperial College (p75) itself, several other *pailou* survive in today's Beijing. The archway in Zhongshan Park (p72) is a three-bay, four-pillar *pailou*, with triple eaves and tiled in blue. It used to stand at the western entrance to Xizongbu Hutong in Dongdan, before being moved to the park in 1919. Three *pailou* stand in front of the Lama Temple (p81), a vast *pailou* can be seen in front of the White Clouds Temple (p89) and across from the entrance to Dongyue Temple (p86), on the other side of Chaoyangmenwai Dajie.

Daming Men (Daming Gate). Called Daqing Men during the Qing dynasty and Zhonghua Men during the Republic, the Daming Gate had three watchtowers and upturned eaves and was guarded by a pair of stone lions. It was pulled down after 1949, a fate similarly reserved for Chang'an Zuo Men and Chang'an You Men. East and west of the Thousand Foot Corridor stood official departments and temples, including the Ministry of Rites, the Ministry of Revenue, Honglu Temple and Taichang Temple.

Mao conceived the square to project the enormity of the Communist Party, so it's all a bit Kim Il-Sungish. During the Cultural Revolution, the chairman, wearing a Red Guard armband, reviewed parades of up to a million people here. In 1976 another million people jammed the square to pay their last respects to Mao. In 1989 army tanks and soldiers forced pro-democracy demonstrators out of the square. Although it seems likely that no one was actually killed *within* the square itself, possibly thousands were slaughtered *outside* the square. In more recent years members of the banned quasi-Buddhist Falun Gong brought their protests here, only to be hauled off to prison. Despite being a public place, the square remains more in the hands of the government than the people; it is monitored by closed circuit TV cameras, and plainclothes police are primed to paralyse the first twitch of dissent.

West of the **Great Hall of the People** (p65), the **future Beijing Opera House** is nearing completion, set to compete with Shànghǎi's fine example.

If you get up early you can watch the **flag-raising ceremony** at sunrise, performed by a troop of People's Liberation Army (PLA) soldiers drilled to march at precisely 108 paces per minute, 75cm per pace. The same ceremony in reverse is performed at sunset, but you can hardly see the soldiers for the throngs gathered to watch.

Unless you want a map you will have to sidestep determined map-sellers and their confederates – the incessant learners of English – and just say no to the 'poor' art students press-ganging tourists to view their exhibitions.

Bicycles cannot be ridden across Tiananmen Square (apparently tanks are OK), but you can walk your bike. Traffic is one way for north–south avenues on either side of the square.

WORKERS CULTURAL PALACE
Map pp239–41
Láodòng Rénmín Wénhuà Gōng
☎ 6525 2189; northeast of Tiānānmén; adult Y2;
🕑 6.30am-7.30pm; subway Tiananmen Dong

On the Forbidden City's south-eastern flank opposite Zhongshan Park and away from the hubbub is the Workers Cultural Palace. Despite the uninviting name, this was the site of the emperor's premier place of worship, the **Supreme Temple** (Tài Miào). The huge halls of the temple remain, their roofs enveloped in imperial yellow tiles. Rising up to the splendid **Front Hall**, the scene of imperial ceremonies of ancestor worship, are three flights of steps. Only gods could traverse the central plinth; the emperor was consigned to the left-hand flight. The plaque above the Front Hall is inscribed in both Chinese and Manchu. Sadly this hall, as well as the **Middle Hall** and **Rear Hall** behind, is inaccessible. As with Zhongshan Park, the northern perimeter of the park abuts the palace moat (tōngzi hé), where you can find a bench and park yourself in front of a fine view. Take the northwest exit from the park and find yourself just by the Forbidden City's Meridian Gate (p77) and point of entry to the palace.

ZHONGSHAN PARK Map pp239–41
Zhōngshān Gōngyuán
☎ 6605 4594; west of Tiānānmén; adult Y3;
🕑 6am-9pm; subway Tiananmen Xi

This lovely little park sits to the west of the Gate of Heavenly Peace, with a section hedging up against the Forbidden City moat. Clean, tranquil and tidy, it's a refreshing prologue or conclusion to the magnificence of the adjacent imperial residence. The park was formerly the sacred Ming-style Altar to the God of the Land and the God of Grain (Shèjìtán), where the emperor offered sacrifices. The square altar (wǔsè tǔ) remains, bordered on all sides by walls tiled in various colours. Near the park entrance stands a towering dark blue tiled **páilou** (decorative archway) with triple eaves that originally commemorated the German foreign minister Baron von Ketteler, killed by xenophobic Boxers in 1900. The pailou (see boxed text p71), now rededicated and called the Peace-Defending Archway, is inscribed with the four characters 'Defend Peace', penned by writer Guo Moruo. A nearby brass plaque inconspicuously reminds visitors of the memorial's original dedication to von Ketteler, misspelling his name as Kolind. In the eastern section of the park is the **Forbidden City Concert Hall** (p134). Take the north-eastern exit from the park and find yourself by the Forbidden City's **Meridian Gate**; from here you can reach the **Workers Cultural Palace** and the **Supreme Temple**.

DONGCHENG

Eating p119; Shopping p146; Sleeping p156

Bounded to the north and east by the Second Ring Rd and by Chang'an Jie to the south, Dongcheng (East City) is one of Beijing's most historic districts. Formerly marking the centre of Yuan dynasty Beijing, a city whose east-west axis later shifted south, the Drum and Bell Towers rise up from an area riddled with charming hútòng (alleyways) and lanes. In fact, hutong crisscross the entire district, and wandering in the resulting maze is one of the best ways to appreciate the city (our bike ride on p107 will take you through much of Dongcheng). Several of the district's old museums and temples lie buried down hutong, and digging them out is part of the fun.

The centrepiece of this district, however, is the Forbidden City, which forms a massive and imperious chunk of the southwest. At the heart of the former Imperial City (a large part of which belongs to Dongcheng), the rectangular outline of the imperial palace and its moat imprints itself on the rest of Dongcheng. Progressively larger squares and parallelograms of streets radiate out from the Forbidden City, culminating in the boxlike boundary of the Second Ring Rd.

The top right corner of the old Imperial City, the eastern boundary of which ran along Donghuangchenggen Nandajie and Donghuangchenggen Beidajie and then west along Dianmen Dongdajie and Dianmen Xidajie, is in Dongcheng. None of the four gates of the Imperial City wall survive, but a few fragments of Dongan Men (p76) can be seen near the Forbidden City's west gate (Donghua Men). Also part of the erstwhile Imperial City, Jingshan Park and Beihai Park have strong imperial connections. Qianhai Lake, across the road north from Beihai Park, lay just outside the Imperial City. The area around the lake, which is also called Shichahai (Sea of the Ten Buddhist Temples, presumably denoting the shrines that once stood here), has developed a prosperous bar and café industry thriving on its picturesque and historic ambience.

The district is rich in temple architecture, although in earlier ages there were considerably more temples than today. Beijing's finest temple, the Lama Temple, lies just within the Second Ring Rd to the northeast, and a short walk south is Beijing's Confucius Temple.

Dongcheng also hosts Beijing's premier shopping street: Wangfujing Dajie (also known as Jin Jie – Gold St), with its host of top-name shops and department stores. To the east runs Dongdan Dajie (also called Yin Jie – Silver St). Road widening schemes are altering the face of Dongcheng, with *hutong* being topped and tailed in the process, but the Beijing Cultural Relics Protection Association protects *hutong* with particularly historic *sìhéyuàn* (courtyard houses).

BEIHAI PARK Map pp232–3
Běihǎi Gōngyuán

☎ 6407 1415; northwest of the Forbidden City; adult Y5, Jade Islet Y10; ☼ 6.30am-8pm, buildings to 4pm; subway Tiananmen Xi, then bus 5

Beihai Park is a relaxing place to stroll around, grab a snack, sip a beer, rent a rowing boat, or watch calligraphers practising characters on the paving slabs and couples cuddling on a bench in the evening. It's crowded at weekends, and in winter there's ice skating.

Approached via four gates, Beihai Park is largely lake, or more specifically the lake of Beihai (which literally means "North Sea"). The associated South and Middle Seas to the south together lend their name to the nerve centre of the Communist Party west of the Forbidden City, Zhongnanhai.

The park, covering an area of 68 hectares, was the former playground of the emperors. **Jade Islet** in the lower middle is composed of the heaped earth excavated to create the lake – some attribute this to Kublai Khan.

The site is associated with the Great Khan's palace, the navel of Beijing before the creation of the Forbidden City. All that remains of the Khan's court is a large jar made of green jade in the **Round City** near the park's southern entrance.

Dominating Jade Islet on the lake, the 36m-high **White Dagoba** was originally built in 1651 for a visit by the Dalai Lama, and was rebuilt in 1741. You can reach the dagoba through the **Yongan Temple** (included in Beihai Park ad-

mission). Enter the temple through the Hall of the Heavenly Kings, past the Drum and Bell Towers to the Hall of the Wheel of the Law, with its central effigy of Sakyamuni and flanked by bodhisattvas and 18 luohan (p90). At the rear is a bamboo grove and a steep

Pedestrian tunnel, Beihai Park (left)

BEIHAI PARK

0 — 200 m
0 — 0.1 miles

Londou Huyie

Qianhai Lake

Dianmen Xidajie

North Gate 北门
Can Altar 蚕坛

Rowboat Dock 游船码头
Painted Boat Studio 画肪斋
Five Dragon Pavilion 五龙亭
Boat House 船坞
Beihai Lake
Rowboat Dock 游船码头

Jade Islet
East Gate 东门
Jingshan Park

Round City

West Gate 西门
Wenjin Jie
South Gate 南门

Zhonghai Lake

Forbidden City

flight of steps up through a decorative archway, emblazoned with the characters 'Long Guang' on one side. Head up the steps to the Zhengjue Hall, which contains a statue of Milefo and Weituo (p90). Puan Hall, the next hall, houses a statue of Tsong Khapa, founder of the Yellow Hat sect of Tibetan Buddhism, flanked by statues of the fifth Dalai Lama and the Panchen Lama. Eight golden effigies on either flank include some Tantric statues and the goddess Heinumu, with her necklace of skulls. The final flight of steep steps leads to the dagoba.

On the northeastern shore of the islet is the handsome, double-tiered **Painted Gallery** (Huàláng). Near the boat dock is the **Fangshan**

Restaurant (p119), a restaurant that dishes up imperial recipes favoured by Empress Cixi. She liked 120-course dinners with about 30 kinds of desserts.

Xitian Fànjing, on the lake's northern shore, is one of the city's most captivating temples (admission is included in your park ticket). Taichi (tàijíquán) practitioners can frequently be seen practising outside the main entrance. The first hall, the Hall of the Heavenly Kings, takes you past Milefo, Weituo and the four Heavenly Kings. The **Dacizhenru Hall** dates to the Ming dynasty and contains three huge statues of Sakyamuni, the Amithaba Buddha and Yaoshi Fo (Medicine Buddha). The golden statue of Guanyin at the rear is sadly unapproachable. The hall is supported by huge wooden pillars (nánmù), and you can make out where the original stone pillars existed. At the very rear of the temple is a glazed pavilion and a huge hall that are both unfortunately out of bounds.

The nearby **Nine Dragon Screen** (Jiǔlóng Bì), a 5m-high and 27m-long spirit wall, is a glimmering stretch of coloured glazed tiles.

BELL TOWER Map pp232–3
Zhōnglóu
☎ 6401 2674; north end Dianmenwai Dajie; adult Y15; 9am-4.30pm; bus 5, 58 or 107

Fronted by a Qing dynasty stele, the Bell Tower sits just behind the Drum Tower (down an alley directly north). It was originally built at the same time as the Drum Tower but later burnt down. The present structure dates to the 18th century. Legend has it that the bell maker's daughter plunged into the molten iron before the 42-ton bell was cast. Her father managed to grab her shoe as she slid into the furnace; since then it is said that the Ming dynasty bell's soft chime miraculously resembles that of the Chinese word for 'shoe' (xié). Note that most Buddhist temples in China have their own drum and bell towers, as do a number of other cities (such as Xi'an).

CHINA ART GALLERY Map pp232–3
Zhōngguó Měishùguǎn
☎ 6401 7076/2252; 1 Wusi Dajie; adult Y4; 9am-5pm Tue-Sun, last entry 4pm; bus 103, 104, 106 or 108 to Meishu Guan stop

Back in the old days, one of the safest hobbies for an artist was to retouch classical landscapes with red flags, belching factory chimneys or bright red tractors. But the China Art Gallery has a more progressive range of paintings and occasional photographic exhibitions. The museum – housed in a largely traditional style building with upturned eaves – underwent a revamp in 2003, a high priority as the setting was regularly outclassed by the frequently colourful and vivid works on view. The absence of a permanent collection means that all exhibits are temporary. Foreign pieces may seem somewhat naive, but the Chinese works can be fresh and invigorating. There are no English captions, but it's still a first-rate place to see modern Chinese art and, maybe just as importantly, to watch the Chinese looking at art.

CONFUCIUS TEMPLE & IMPERIAL COLLEGE Map pp232–3

Kǒng Miào; Guózǐjiàn

☎ 8401 1977; 13 Guozijian Jie; adult Y10; 🕙 8.30am-5pm; subway Yonghegong

Stroll down the *hutong* opposite the gates of the Lama Temple to the former Confucius Temple. The temple, forlorn and untended, is a quiet sanctuary from Beijing's congested, smoggy streets and snarling traffic. The temple might not be worth a trip in itself, but its proximity to the Lama Temple makes it a haven from the bustling crowds at the latter. It's also the second largest Confucian temple in China after the venerable example at Qūfù in Shāndōng province. The paintwork and general upkeep of the temple is pitiful. Where on earth does the revenue from tickets sales go?

The grounds are home to cypresses and hundreds of stelae that record the names of successful candidates of the highest level of the official Confucian examination system. It was the ambition of every scholar to see his name engraved here, but it wasn't easy. Each candidate was locked in one of about 8000 cubicles, measuring roughly 1.5 sq metres, for a period of three days. Many died or went insane during their incarceration. Many of the stele pavilions are bricked up alongside gnarled cypresses that claw at the sky.

Inside the main hall, called the **Hall of Great Achievement** (Dacheng Dian), sits a statue of Kongzi (Confucius). When last visited, a worshipper had made the unlikely offering of two bottles of Erguotou (the strongest Beijing spirit money can buy) on the small red offering table in front of the sage (not known for his benders). A small museum of musical instruments can be also visited in a side hall, and at the rear is a forest of 190 stelae recording the 13 Confucian classics consisting of 630,000 Chinese characters. Emperor Qianlong commissioned the stone tablets, and it took the scholar who made them 12 years to complete.

Some of Beijing's last remaining *pailou* (p71), or ornamental arches, bravely survive in the *hutong* outside (Guozijian Jie), braced for a possible denouement with future roadwidening schemes.

West of the Confucius Temple is the **Imperial College** (Guózǐjiàn), where the emperor expounded the Confucian classics to an audience of thousands of kneeling students, professors and court officials – an annual rite. Built by the grandson of Kublai Khan in 1306, the former college was the supreme academy during the Yuan, Ming and Qing dynasties and was the only institution of its kind in China. On the site is a marvellous glazed, three-gate, single-eaved decorative archway called a *liúli páifāng* (glazed archway). The **Biyong Hall** beyond is a twin-roofed structure with yellow tiles surrounded by a moat and topped with a gold knob. Pop inside and take in the huge and impressive ceiling.

In the vicinity of the Lama Temple and Guozijian Jie are numerous religious artefact and souvenir shops where you can pick up effigies of Buddhist deities and bodhisattvas along with Buddhist keepsakes and talismans (hùshēnfú).

DITAN PARK Map pp232–3

Dìtán Gōngyuán

☎ 6421 4657; east of Andingmenwai Dajie; park Y1, altar Y5; 🕙 9am-9pm; subway Yonghegong

Cosmologically juxtaposed with the Temple of Heaven (Tiāntán), the Altar of the Moon (Yuètán), the Altar of the Sun (Rìtán) and the

Transport

Subway Circle Line: The Yonghegong stop takes you right to the Lama Temple and the Confucius Temple to the south, and it's not too far to walk north to Ditan Park.

Bus The double-decker bus 2 (shangxing) runs along Dongdan Beidajie and Dongsi Nandajie; Dongsi Beidajie to the Confucius Temple and the Lama Temple; bus 5 travels from Deshengmen to the Bell Tower, down to Dianmen Xidajie and Jingshan Houjie (for Jingshan Park), on to Beihai Park and Xihua Men (west gate of the Forbidden City), before heading further south to Zhongshan Park and Qianmen; bus 13 can take you from the Lama Temple along Dianmen Xidajie to Beihai Park; bus 103 can take you from Sundongan Plaza on Wangfujing Dajie to Dengshikou, on to the China Art Gallery, the Forbidden City, Jingshan Park and then Beihai Park; bus 107 runs from Beihai Park to the Drum Tower and then along to Jiaodaokou Dongdajie to Dongzhimen subway station.

Altar of the Country (Shèjìtán), Ditan is the Temple of the Earth. The park, site of imperial sacrifices to the Earth God, lacks the splendour of the Temple of Heaven Park but is worth a stroll if you've just been to nearby Lama Temple. During Chinese New Year, a temple fair is held here, and in winter, a sparkling ice festival is staged. The park's large **altar** (fāngzé tán) is square in shape, symbolising the earth.

DONGAN MEN REMAINS Map pp232–3
Míng Huáng Chéng Dōngān Mén Yízhǐ
Imperial Wall Foundation Ruins Park, intersection of Donghuamen Dajie and Beiheyan Dajie; 🕐 24 hr; subway Tiananmen Dong

In an excavated pit just northeast of the Cui Ming Zhuang Hotel (p157) sits a pitiful stump, all that remains of the magnificent Dongan Men, the east gate of the Imperial City. Before being razed, the gate was a single-eaved, seven-bay wide building with a hip and gable roof capped with yellow tiles. The on-site English caption dodges the gate's fate, saying it 'was lost later', giving the impression it just fell down when in fact it was damaged by fire (see the boxed text, p49). The remains of the gate – just two layers of 18 bricks – make for dull viewing but serve as a headstone to the recklessness of the era that swept it – and most of Beijing's other gates – away. Of more interest in the pit are the bricks of the exca-

vated **Ming dynasty road** that used to run near to Dongan Men. The road is around 2m lower than the current road level, and the expertly made bricks are typical of precisely engineered Ming dynasty brickwork. Also preserved here are some remains of the **Huangen Bridge** that crossed the Jade River (Yù Hé) just west of Dongan Men and a marble map of the old Imperial City wall. The remains are located in the Imperial Wall Foundation Ruins Park, a thin strip of park that follows a large part of the course of the east wall of the Imperial City Wall from Datianshuijing *Hutong* all the way north to Dianmen Dongdajie.

DRUM TOWER Map pp232–3
Gǔlóu
☎ 6401 2674; Gulou Dongdajie; adult Y20; 🕐 9am-4.30pm; bus 5, 58 or 107

The Drum Tower was originally built in 1273 and marked the centre of the old Mongol capital Dàdū. Since being rebuilt in 1420, the tower has been repeatedly destroyed and restored. Stagger up the incredibly steep steps for long views over Beijing's rooftops. The drums of this later Ming dynasty version were beaten to mark the hours of the day – in effect the Big Ben of Beijing. Time was kept with a water clock and an idiosyncratic system of time divisions. On view is a large array of drums, including the large and dilapidated **Night Watchman's Drum** (gēnggǔ; gēng being one of the five two-hour divisions of the night) and a big array of reproduction drums. Originally there were 25 watch drums here and damage to the drums is blamed on allied forces that engaged the Boxers in battle back in 1900. There is also an analysis of the ancient Chinese seasonal divisions and an exhibition relating to old Beijing. When ascending or descending the Drum Tower, watch out for slippery steps.

FORBIDDEN CITY Map pp232–3
Zǐjìn Chéng
☎ 6513 2255; adult from Y40; 🕐 8.30am-4pm May-Sep, 8.30am-3.30pm Oct-Apr; subway Tiananmen Xi or Tiananmen Dong

The spectacular Forbidden City, so called because it was off limits to commoners for 500 years, occupies a primary position in the Chinese psyche. To the Han Chinese, the Forbidden City is a contradictory symbol. It's a politically incorrect yarn from a pre-revolutionary dark age, but it's also one spun from the very pinnacle of Chinese civilisation. It's not therefore surprising that more violent forces during the Cultural Revolution wanted to trash the place. Perhaps hearing the distant tinkle of the tourist dollar, Premier Zhou Enlai did the right thing by stepping in to keep the Red Guards at bay.

This gargantuan palace complex – the largest and best preserved cluster of ancient buildings in China – was home to two dynasties of emperors, the Ming and the Qing, who didn't stray from their pleasure dome unless they absolutely had to. A bell jar dropped over the whole spectacle maintained a highly rarefied atmosphere that nourished its elitist community. A stultifying code of rules, protocol and superstition deepened its otherworldliness, perhaps typified by its twittering band of eunuchs. The rest of China was governed from within these walls until the 1911 revolution gatecrashed the party, bringing with it the last orders for the Qing dynasty.

Its mystique diffused (the Beijing authorities insist on prosaically calling the complex the Palace Museum), entry to the palace is no longer prohibited. In former ages the price for uninvited admission would have been instant death; these days Y40 will do.

Watch out for unscrupulous characters who will do their best to convince you that you must have an official guide to see the palace; it isn't true. You can get a personal introduction from Roger Moore (ex-007) instead. For Y40, rent a cassette tape narrated by Her Majesty's spy for a self-guided tour. For the tape to make sense you must enter the Forbidden City from the south gate and exit from the north.

Don't confuse the Gate of Heavenly Peace (p64) with the Forbidden City entrance. Some visitors purchase a Gate of Heavenly Peace admission ticket by mistake, not realising that this admits you only to the upstairs portion of the gate. To find the Forbidden City ticket booths, walk north until you can't walk any further without paying. Toilets can be found within the Forbidden City. Exterior photography is no problem, but photographing the interior of halls is often disallowed.

History

Constructed on the site of a palace dating to Kublai Khan and the Mongol Yuan dynasty, the Ming emperor Yongle established the basic layout of the Forbidden City between 1406 and 1420. The grandiose emperor employed battalions of labourers and crafts workers – by some estimates there may have been up to a million of them – to build it. The palace lay at the heart of the Imperial City, a much larger,

walled enclosure reserved for the use of the emperor and his personnel (see the History chapter). From here the emperors governed China, often erratically and haphazardly, as authority drifted into the hands of court officials, eunuchs and anyone else skulking in these corridors of power.

Most of the buildings you see now are post-18th century, like many of Beijing's restored or rebuilt structures. The largely wooden palace was a tinderbox and was constantly going up in flames – a lantern festival combined with a sudden gust of Gobi wind would easily do the trick, as would a fireworks display. Fires were also deliberately lit by court eunuchs and officials who could get rich off the repair bills.

It was not just the buildings that went up in smoke but also rare books, paintings and calligraphy. Libraries and other palace halls and buildings housing combustible contents were tiled in black; the colour represents water in the five-element (wǔxíng) theory, and its symbolic presence is thought to prevent conflagrations. In the 20th century there were two major lootings of the palace by Japanese forces and the Kuomintang. Thousands of crates of relics were removed and carted off to Taiwan, where they remain on display in Taipei's National Palace Museum (worth seeing). Perhaps this was just as well, since the Cultural Revolution turned much of China's precious artwork into confetti.

Layout

The palace is so large (720,000 sq metres, 800 buildings, 9000 rooms) that a permanent restoration squad moves around repainting and repairing it. It's estimated to take about 10 years to do a full renovation, by which time they have to start repairs again. It is possible to explore the Forbidden City in a few hours, but it's so big that a full day will keep you occupied and the enthusiast will make several trips. Whatever you do, try not to miss the delightful courtyards, pavilions and mini-museums within them on each side of the main complex.

The palace's ceremonial buildings lie on the north–south axis of the Forbidden City, from the **Gate of Heavenly Peace** in the south to **Divine Military Genius Gate** (Shénwǔmén) to the north.

Restored in the 17th century, **Meridian Gate** (Wǔ Mén) is a massive portal that in former times was reserved for the use of the emperor. Gongs and bells would sound imperial comings and goings, while lesser mortals used lesser gates: the military used the west gate, civilians the east gate. The emperor also reviewed his

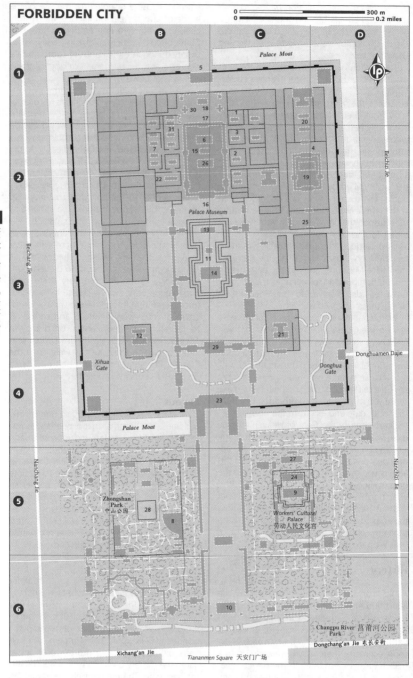

FORBIDDEN CITY

0   300 m
0   0.2 miles

Palace Moat

Béchízí Jie

Béichang Jie

Palace Museum

Donghuamen Dajie

Xihua Gate

Donghua Gate

Palace Moat

Nanchang Jie

Nanchízi Jie

Zhongshan Park 中山公园

Workers' Cultural Palace 劳动人民文化宫

Changpu River 菖蒲河公园 Park

Xichang'an Jie

Tiananmen Square 天安门广场

Dongchang'an Jie 东长安街

armies from here, passed judgment on prisoners, announced the new year's calendar and oversaw the flogging of troublesome ministers.

Across the Golden Stream, which is shaped to resemble a Tartar bow and is spanned by five marble bridges, is **Supreme Harmony Gate** (Tàihé Mén). It overlooks a massive courtyard that could hold an imperial audience of up to 100,000 people.

Raised on a marble terrace with balustrades are the **Three Great Hall**s (Sān Dàdiàn), the heart of the Forbidden City. The **Hall of Supreme Harmony** (Tàihé Diàn) is the most important and the largest structure in the Forbidden City. Built in the 15th century and restored in the 17th century, it was used for ceremonial occasions, such as the emperor's birthday, the nomination of military leaders and coronations. Flanking the entrance to the hall are bronze incense burners. The large bronze turtle in the front is a symbol of longevity and stability. It has a removable lid, and on special occasions incense was lit inside it so that smoke billowed from its mouth.

To the west of the terrace is a small pavilion with a bronze grain measure and to the east is a sundial; both are symbolic of imperial justice. On the corners of the hall's roof, as with other buildings in the city, you'll see a mounted figure with his retreat cut off by mythical and actual animals, a story that relates to a cruel tyrant hanged from one such eave.

Inside the Hall of Supreme Harmony is a richly decorated **Dragon Throne** (Lóngyǐ) from which the emperor would preside (decisions final, no correspondence entered into) over trembling officials. The entire court had to touch the floor nine times with their foreheads (this was the custom known as kowtowing) in the emperor's presence. At the back of the throne is a carved Xumishan, the Buddhist paradise, signifying the throne's supremacy.

Behind the Hall of Supreme Harmony is the smaller **Hall of Middle Harmony** (Zhōnghé Diàn), which was used as a transit lounge for the emperor. Here he would make last-minute preparations, rehearse speeches and receive close ministers. On display are two Qing dynasty sedan chairs, the emperors' mode of transport around the Forbidden City. The last of the Qing emperors, Puyi, used a bicycle and altered a few features of the palace grounds to make it easier to get around.

The third hall is the **Hall of Preserving Harmony** (Bǎohé Diàn), used for banquets and later for imperial examinations. It now houses archaeological finds. The Hall of Preserving Harmony has no support pillars, and to the rear is a 250-tonne marble imperial carriageway carved with dragons and clouds, which was moved into Beijing on an ice path. The emperor was conveyed over the carriageway in his sedan chair as he ascended or descended the terrace. The outer housing surrounding the Three Great Halls was used for storing gold, silver, silks, carpets and other treasures.

The basic configuration of the Three Great Halls is echoed by the next group of buildings. Smaller in scale, these buildings were more important in terms of real power, which in China traditionally lies at the back door or, in this case, the back gate.

The first structure is the **Palace of Heavenly Purity** (Qiánqīng Gōng), a residence of Ming and early Qing emperors, and later an audience hall for receiving foreign envoys and high officials.

Immediately behind it is the **Hall of Union** (Jiāotài Diàn), which contains a clepsydra – a water clock made in 1745 with five bronze vessels and a calibrated scale. There's also a mechanical clock built in 1797 and a collection of imperial jade seals on display.

At the northern end of the Forbidden City is the **Imperial Garden** (Yùhuā Yuán), a classical Chinese garden with 7000 sq metres of fine landscaping, including rockeries, walkways and pavilions. This is a good place to take a breather as it has a café, toilets and souvenir shops. Two more gates lead out to the large Divine Military Genius Gate.

The western and eastern sides of the Forbidden City are the palatial former living quarters, once containing libraries, temples, theatres, gardens and even the tennis court of the last emperor. These buildings now function as museums requiring extra admission fees (around Y10). The clock exhibition hall (Zhōngbiǎo Guǎn) contains a fascinating collection of elaborate timepieces, many of which were presents to the Qing emperors from overseas. Opening hours are irregular, and no photos are allowed without prior permission. Special exhibits sometimes appear in other palace museum halls, so check the expat mags (p204) for details.

Behind the Wall

If ceremonial and administrative duties occupied most of the emperor's working hours, it was the pursuit of pleasure behind the high walls of the Forbidden City that occupied much of his attention during the evenings. With so many wives and consorts to choose from, a system was needed to help the emperor choose his bed-time companion. One method was to keep the names of royal wives, consorts and favourites on jade tablets near the emperor's chambers. By turning the tablet over the emperor made his request for the evening, and the eunuch on duty would rush off to find the lucky lady. Stripped naked and therefore weaponless, the little foot-bound creature was giftwrapped in a yellow cloth, piggybacked over to the royal boudoir and dumped at the feet of the emperor; the eunuch recording the date and time to verify the legitimacy of a possible child.

Aside from the emperor having fun, all this activity had a more serious purpose: prolonging the life of the emperor. An ancient Chinese belief that frequent sex with young girls could sustain one's youth even motivated Mao Zedong to follow the same procedure.

Financing the affairs of state probably cost less than financing the affairs of the emperor, and keeping the pleasure dome functioning drew heavily on the resources of the empire. During the Ming dynasty an estimated 9000 maids of honour and 70,000 eunuchs were serving the court.

Apart from the servants and the prize concubines, there were also the royal elephants to maintain. Pocketing the cash was illegal, but selling elephant dung for use as shampoo was not – it was believed to give hair that

extra sheen. Back in the harem the cosmetic bills piled up to 400,000 liang of silver. Then, of course, the concubines who had grown old and were no longer in active service were still supposed to be cared for. Rather than cut back on expenditure, the emperor sent out eunuchs to collect emergency taxes whenever money ran short.

As for the palace eunuchs, the royal chop was administered at the Eunuch Clinic near the Forbidden City, using a swift knife and a special chair with a hole in the seat. The candidates sought to better their lives in the service of the court, but half of them died after the operation. Mutilation of any kind was considered grounds for exclusion from the next life, so many eunuchs carried around their appendages in pouches, believing that at the time of death the spirits might be deceived into thinking them whole.

FORMER HOME OF LAO SHE

Map pp232–3
Lǎo Shě Jìniànguǎn
19 Fengfu Hutong, off Dengshikou Xijie; adult Y5;
🕑 9am-4pm Tue-Sun

An interesting diversion for those doing Wangfujing Dajie is this little courtyard museum dedicated to one of Beijing's most famous 20th-century writers. Author of *Rickshaw Boy* and *Tea House*, and former teacher at London's School of Oriental and African Studies, Lao She (1899–1966) tragically committed suicide by throwing himself into a Beijing lake during the Cultural Revolution (some say he was murdered). One troubling photo reveals Lao She's humiliation at the hands of Red Guards on 23 August 1966 (the eve of his death). Along with some other artists, he was dressed in Beijing opera dress and forced to kneel in front of a fire at the Confucius Temple before being beaten (a scene reproduced in Chen Kaige's film *Farewell My Concubine*). Sadly for English speakers, the museum's captions are in Chinese, but there are a large number of first editions on view, along with photos and personal effects.

GUO MORUO FORMER RESIDENCE

Map pp232–3
Guō Mòruò Gùjū
☎ 6666 4681, 6618 2523; 18 Qianhai Xiyan; adult Y6;
🕑 9am-4pm Tue-Sun, closed winter; subway Gulou

Born Guo Kaizhen, Guo Moruo (1892–1978) was one of communist China's most politically correct writers. From a wealthy landlord family, he received an elite education in Japan, but in spite of his ruling-class roots he founded the Marxist-inspired Creation Society in 1921. In the same year, a collection of Guo Moruo's poetry, *The Goddesses* (Nůshén), was partially translated into English. When the communists came to power in 1949, Guo was made director of the Chinese Academy of Sciences. In 1951 he was awarded the Stalin Peace Prize (an oxymoron if ever there was one). He was given several other high-level posts during his twilight years. Unlike many other writers, he survived the Cultural Revolution with barely a scratch.

Guo lived in a garden-like compound in Beijing. His house has been preserved along with many of his books and manuscripts.

JINGSHAN PARK Map pp232–3
Jǐngshān Gōngyuán

☎ 6403 3225; Jingshan Qianjie; adult Y2;
🕙 6am-9.30pm; subway Tiananmen Xi, then bus 5

Jingshan Park, with its priceless views, was shaped from the earth excavated to create the palace moat. During legation days, the mound was called Coal Hill and was Beijing's highest point during the Ming dynasty. Clamber to the top of this regal pleasure garden for a magnificent panorama of the capital and an unparalleled overview of the russet roofing of the Forbidden City. In the early morning at weekends, groups of elderly Chinese flock here to sing.

On the eastern side of the park a locust tree stands in the place where the last of the Ming emperors, Chongzhen, hung himself as rebels swarmed at the city walls. The hill supposedly protects the palace from the evil spirits – or dust storms – from the north (the billowing dust clouds in the spring have to be seen to be believed).

LAMA TEMPLE Map pp232–3
Yōnghé Gōng

☎ 6404 4499, ext 252; 28 Yonghegong Dajie; adult Y25, audio guide Y20; 🕙 9am-4pm; subway Yonghegong

The Lama Temple is Beijing's largest and most spectacular temple. Ornamented with intriguing statuary, stunning frescoes, tapestries, incredible carpentry and a great pair of Chinese lions, it was once the official residence of Count Yin Zhen. In 1723 the count became emperor and moved to the Forbidden City. His name was changed to Yongzheng, and his former residence became Yonghe Palace. In 1744 it was converted into a lamasery and

became home to legions of monks from Mongolia and Tibet.

In 1792 the Emperor Qianlong, having quelled an uprising in Tibet, instituted a new administrative system involving two golden vases. One was kept at the renowned Jokhang Temple in Lhasa, to be employed for determining the reincarnation of the Dalai Lama, and the other was kept at the Lama Temple for the lottery used for choosing the next the Panchen Lama. The Lama Temple thus assumed a new importance in ethnic minority control.

The lamasery has three richly worked archways and five main halls, each taller than the preceding one. Styles are mixed – Mongolian, Tibetan and Han – with courtyard enclosures and galleries.

Journeying China at the time of the Boxer Rebellion, photographer James Ricalton noted with distaste: 'My own opinion is that it is one of the most dirty, dingy, smoky, ramshackle establishments in the whole world and filled with one thousand five hundred Mongolian and Tibetan ignorant fanatics, called priests.' This is certainly not the mood in the temple today.

The first hall, **Lokapala**, houses a statue of the future Buddha, Maitreya, flanked by celestial guardians. The statue facing the back door is Weituo, the guardian of Buddhism, carved from white sandalwood. In the courtyard beyond is a pond with a bronze mandala depicting Xumishan, the Buddhist paradise.

The second hall, **Yonghe Hall** (Yōnghé Diàn), is overseen by three figures of Buddha – past, present and future.

The third hall, **Yongyou Hall** (Yǒngyòu Diàn), has statues of the Buddha of Longevity and the Buddha of Medicine (to the left). The courtyard beyond features galleries with some *nandikesvaras*, or joyful Buddhas, tangled up in multi-armed close encounters. These are coyly draped lest you be corrupted by the sight, and can be found in other discreet locations.

The **Hall of the Wheel of the Law** (Fǎlún Diàn) further north contains a large bronze statue of Tsong Khapa (1357–1419), founder of the Gelukpa or Yellow Hat sect, and frescoes depicting his life. This Tibetan-style building is used for study and prayer. (Note that the Chinese name of the hall is echoed in the name of Falun Gong, pointing to the organisation's Buddhist roots).

(Continued on page 85)

Beijing's Hutong

If you want to plumb Beijing's homely interior and move beyond the must-see sights and shopping mall glitz of town, voyage into the land of the city's *hútòng* (alleyways). Many of these charming alleyways remain, crisscrossing east-west across the city and linking to create a huge, enchanting warren of one-storey ramshackle dwellings and historic courtyard homes.

Hutong may still be the stamping ground of a quarter of Beijing's residents, but many are sadly being swept aside in Beijing's race to manufacture a modern city of white tile high-rises. Marked with white plaques, some historic *hutong* and *sìhéyuàn* (courtyard homes) are protected by the Beijing Cultural Relics Protection Association, but for many others, a way of life is being ruthlessly bulldozed, at a rate of more than 10,000 dwellings a year.

History

These humble passageways first covered Beijing in the Yuan dynasty, after Genghis Khan's army reduced the city then known as Zhōngdū to rubble. The city was redesigned, with alleys or *hutong* running east–west. By the Qing dynasty, there were more than 2000 such passageways riddling the city, leaping to around 6000 by the 1950s; now the figure has dwindled again to around 2000.

The story of Beijing's *hutong* is almost as fascinating as a visit to the lanes themselves. The original meaning of the word '*hutong*' is uncertain. It is based on the Mongolian, and derives from the time when the Khan's horsemen camped in the new capital of the Yuan dynasty. It might have referred to a passageway between gers (or 'yurts', the Russian term). Or it might come from *hottog*, meaning a well – wherever there was water in the dry plain around Beijing, there were inhabitants.

The more historic *hutong* have the oldest *siheyuan*, but the more recent post-1949 courtyards are more functionally designed and have little or no ornamentation. *Hutong* land is now a hodgepodge of the old and the new, with Qing dynasty courtyards riddled with modern brick outhouses and socialist-era conversions, cruelly overlooked by grim apartment blocks. Most *hutong* lie within the loop of the Second Ring Rd, which largely follows the outline of the flattened Tartar City Wall.

Siheyuan

Old walled courtyards, or *siheyuan*, are the building blocks of this delightful world. A number of old courtyards have been preserved as museums, but many are still lived in and hum with activity. From spring to autumn, men collect outside their gates, drinking beer, playing chess, smoking and chewing the fat. Inside, trees soar aloft, providing shade and a nesting ground for birds.

Most of the old courtyards date from the Qing dynasty, although a few have struggled through from the Ming. Particularly historic and noteworthy *siheyuan* boast a white marble plaque near the gates identifying them as being protected.

Particularly notable courtyards are entered by a number of gates, but the majority have just a single door. More venerable courtyards are fronted by large, thick, red doors, outside of which perch either a pair of Chinese lions or drum stones (*bǎogǔshí*; two circular stones resembling drums, each on a small plinth and occasionally topped by a miniature lion or a small dragon head). Many of these courtyards were the residences of officials, wealthy families and even princes; the residence of Prince Gong is one of the more celebrated examples.

Beijing's more historic courtyard gates are accessed by a set of steps and topped with and flanked by ornate brick carvings. The generosity of detail indicates the social clout of the courtyard's original inhabitants.

Courtyards used to house just one family of the noblesse, but today many belong to the 'work unit' (*dānwèi*), which apportions living quarters to its workforce. Others belong to private owners, but the state still ultimately owns all property in China, explaining why *hutong* are knocked down with such ease.

Foreigners (*lǎowài*) have cottoned on to the charm of courtyards and have breached this very conservative bastion (see Hutong Life p156). But many have been repelled by poor heating, no hot water, no cable TV, dodgy sanitation and no place to park the four-wheel drive. Many *hutong* homes still lack toilets, and this explains the multitude of malodorous public loos strung out along the alleyways. Other homes have been thoroughly modernised and sport varnished wood floors, fully fitted kitchens, a Jacuzzi and air-con. Those seeking to live in a courtyard dwelling can consult the classified pages of the expat magazines where real estate agents advertise (two bedroom lodgings start at around US$1000 per month, but remember that expats are charged much more than Chinese occupants).

Many old courtyard houses have been divided into smaller units, but many of their historical features remain, especially their roofs. Courtyard communities are served by small shops (*xiǎomàibù*) and restaurants strung out along *hutong*, while the children gather at local kindergartens and schools.

Wind-water Lanes

Hutong nearly all run east–west to ensure that the main gate faces south, satisfying *fēng shuǐ* requirements. This south-facing aspect guarantees a lot of sunshine and protection from more negative forces from the north. This positioning also mirrors the layout of all Chinese temples, nourishing the *yáng* (the male and light aspect) while checking the *yīn* (the female and dark aspect).

Little connecting alleyways that run north–south link the main alleys. The rectangular waffle-grid pattern that results stamps the points of the compass on the Beijing psyche. You may hear a local saying, '*wǒ gāoxìng de wǒ bù zhī běi le*', meaning 'I was so happy, I didn't know which way was north' (an extremely disorientating state of joy).

Many courtyards used to be further protected by rectangular stones bearing the Chinese characters for Tài Shān (Mount Tai) to vanquish bad omens. Some courtyards still preserve their screen walls – feng shui devices erected in front of the main gate to deflect roaming spirits.

Trees provide much-needed shade in summer and *qì* (energy), and most old courtyards have a locust tree at the front, which would have been planted when the *siheyuan* was constructed.

Names

Hutong names spring from many roots. Some are christened after families, such as Zhaotangzi *Hutong* (Alley of the Zhao Family). Others simply took their name from historical figures or local features, while others have more mysterious associations, such as Dragon Whiskers Ditch Alley. Others reflect the merchandise plied at local markets, such as Ganmian Hutong (Dry Flour Alley) or Chrysanthemum Lane.

Around the Forbidden City there were some rather unusual industries. Wet Nurse Lane was full of young mothers who breast-fed the imperial offspring. These young mothers were selected from around China on scouting trips four times a year. Clothes Washing Lane was where the women who did the imperial laundry lived. The maids, having grown old in the service of the court, were packed off to faraway places until their intimate knowledge of royal undergarments was out of date.

Hutong Dimensions

Despite an attempt at standardisation, Beijing's alleys have their own personalities and proportions. The longest alley extends for 3km (Dongjiaomin Xiang in Dongcheng; see the Tiananmen Square and Foreign Legation Quarter walk p102), while the shortest – unsurprisingly called Yichi Dajie (One Foot St) – is a very brief 25m. Some people contest that Guantong Xiang (Guantong Alley), near Yangmeizhu Xijie in Xuanwu district (east of Liulichang Dongjie), is even shorter at 20m.

Some *hutong* are wide and leafy boulevards, whereas others are narrow, claustrophobic corridors. Beijing's broadest alley is Lingjing Hutong (Fairyland Alley), with a width of 32m, but the aptly named Xiaolaba Hutong (Little Trumpet Alley) is a squeeze at 50cm. And chubby wayfarers could well get wedged in Qianshi Hutong not far from Qiánmén – it's narrowest reach is a mere 40cm. The alley with the most twists and turns is Jiuwan Hutong (Nine Bend Alley), while Beijing's oldest *hutong* is Zhuanta Hutong (Brick Pagoda Alley). Dating from Mongol times, it can be found west off Xisi Nandajie.

Hutong Tour

A perusal of Beijing's *hutong* is an unmissable experience. The best way is just to wander around the centre of Beijing as the alleyways riddle the town within the Second Ring Rd. Otherwise limit yourself to historic areas, such as around the Drum Tower (p76), the area around the Lusongyuan Hotel (p159) or the roads branching east and west off Chaoyangmen Nanxiaojie, east of Wangfujing Dajie.

Alternatively, hire a bike and delve into this historic world on your own set of wheels (p107). Or do the pedicab tourist trip with the **Beijing Hutong Tour Co Ltd** (☎ 6615 9097, 6400 2787; ✆ day tours 8.50am & 1.50pm, evening tours 6.50pm May-Oct), whose acolytes depart from a point 200m to the west of the north entrance of Beihai Park (p73). Day tours usually take two to three hours, and the evening tour takes 1½ hours. Any number of other pedicab touts infest the roads around the Shichahai Lakes – they will circle you like hyenas, baying, '*Hutong, hutong*'. Tours typically cost Y180 and will also take in the Drum Tower (p76) and Prince Gong's Residence (p94). You can also ask about tours at your hotel.

For many *hutong*, Beijing's successful 2008 Olympic bid was the kiss of death. Those who want to get a taste of courtyard life while staying in Beijing can check into one of the hotels that occupy *siheyuan* – check out the Sleeping chapter for details – such as the **Lusongyuan Hotel** (p159) or the **Haoyuan Guesthouse** (p157).

The Hutong of the Imperial City

Although the Imperial City failed to survive the convulsions of the 20th century, the *hutong* that threaded through the imperial enclave survive, many of their names denoting their former function. Zhonggu Hutong (Bell and Drum Alley) was responsible for the provision of bells and drums to the imperial household. Jinmaoju Hutong (Cloth and Cap Department Alley) handled the caps and boots used by the court while Zhiranju Hutong (Weaving and Dying Department Alley) supplied its satins and silks. Jiucuju Hutong (Wine and Vinegar Department Alley) managed the stock of spirits, vinegar, sugar, flour and other culinary articles.

Also scattered within the Imperial City were numerous storehouses, surviving in name only in such alleys as Lianziku Hutong (Curtain Storehouse Alley), Denglongku Hutong (Lantern Storehouse Alley) and Duanku Hutong (Satin Storehouse Alley). Candles were vital items during Ming and Qing times, their supply handled by the Laku (Candle Storehouse), which operated from Laku Hutong. The Cui Ming Zhuang Hotel (p157) sits on the former site of the Ciqiku (Porcelain Storehouse), which kept the Forbidden City stocked with porcelain bowls, plates, wine cups and other utensils.

To the west of Beihai Park (p73), the large road of Xishiku Dajie, upon which sits the dignified North Cathedral (p93), gets its name (which literally means West Ten Storehouse St) from the assortment of storehouses that were scattered along its length during Ming times. Among items supplied to the Imperial City from warehouses here were paper, lacquer, oil, copper, leather and weapons, including bows, arrows and swords.

There are also the *hutong* named after the craft workers who supplied the Forbidden City with its raw materials, such as Dashizuo Hutong (Big Stonemason's Alley). The stonemasons here fashioned the stone lions, terraces, imperial carriageways and bridges of the Imperial City.

Now-vanished temples are also recalled in *hutong* names, such as the Guangming Hutong south of Xi'anmen Dajie, named after the huge Guangming Dian (Guangming Temple) that is no more.

Cycling through Beijing's hutong

(Continued from page 81)

The last hall, **Wanfu Pavilion** (Wànfú Gé) has a stupendous 18m-high statue of the Maitreya Buddha in his Tibetan form, clothed in yellow satin and reputedly sculpted from a single block of sandalwood. You may find yourself transported to Tibet, where the wood for this statue originated, thanks to the smoke curling up from yak butter lamps.

At the rear of the temple there is a display of Tibetan artefacts, statues and other Buddhist accoutrements. A typically demure multi-armed statue of Guanyin can be seen, along with more exotic Tantric offerings. Also revealed is a rundown on the gold lots used for choosing the next Lama, whose genealogical tree can be traced along the wall (spot the photo of the 11th Panchen Lama shaking hands with Li Peng).

Photography is not permitted inside the temple buildings, but the postcard industry thrives. English-speaking guides can be found in the office to the left of the entrance gate or loitering near the temple entrance.

MAO DUN FORMER RESIDENCE

Map pp232–3
Máo Dùn Gùjū
☎ 6404 0520/4089; Jiaodaokou Nandajie, 13 Houyuan Ensi Hutong; adult Y5; ⏰ 9am-4pm Tue, Thu & Sat; subway Andingmen

Deep in the heart of a historic *hutong* quadrant southeast of the Drum and Bell Towers is this small and unassuming museum. Mao Dun, a homophone for the Chinese word 'contradiction', was the pen name of Shen Yanbing (1896–1981), who was born into an elite family in Zhèjiāng province but educated in Beijing. In 1920 he helped found the Literary Study Society (the earliest literary society of the New Literature Movement), an association promoting literary realism. Mao Dun joined the League of Left Wing Writers in 1930, becoming solidly entrenched in the bureaucracy after the communists came to power. He lay low during the Cultural Revolution, but briefly returned to writing in the 1970s. The museum is typically parsimonious and low-key.

ST JOSEPH'S CHURCH Map pp232–3

Dōng Táng
74 Wangfujing Dajie; ⏰ 6.30-7am Mon-Sat, 6.30-8am Sun; subway Wangfujing

One of the four principal churches in Beijing, St Joseph's Church is also called the East Cathedral. Originally built during the reign of Shunzhi in 1655, it was damaged by an earthquake in 1720 and rebuilt. The luckless church also caught fire in 1807, was destroyed again in 1900 during the Boxer Rebellion, and restored in 1904, only to be shut in 1966. The church has been fully repaired and is now a more sublime feature of Wangfujing Dajie's commercial facelift. A large square in front swarms with children playing and Chinese models in bridal outfits posing for magazine covers. You can take in the church through the steam of a cappuccino or latte at the Starbucks opposite.

WEN TIANXIANG TEMPLE Map pp232–3

Wén Tiānxiáng Cí
☎ 6401 4968; 63 Fuxue Hutong; adult Y5; ⏰ 9am-5pm Tue-Sun; subway Andingmen

Tucked away in a *hutong* not far to the east of Mao Dun's former home is this serene family shrine. Dedicated to Southern Song poet and patriot Wen Tianxiang (1236–83), who was captured by the Mongols and incarcerated in Beijing, the shrine is a quiet preserve of courtyards, halls and steles. In the temple grounds stands an ancient jujube tree (much favoured by *hutong* dwellers) supposedly cultivated by Wen Tianxiang himself. The area around the temple is worth exploring for its rich *hutong* textures and sense of history.

CHAOYANG

Eating p122; Shopping p147; Sleeping p159
This district covers a vast swathe of Beijing east and northeast of the Second Ring Rd. As Chaoyang lay outside the old city walls, it is not a historic district and contains only a few sights of note. But the Sanlitun bar streets can be found here as well as the top-end hotels around the embassy area. The southern part of Chaoyang, containing the Jianguomen Embassy Area and its associated restaurants and hotels, is incorporated on the Chongwen and South Chaoyang map (pp234-5).

Neighbourhoods – Chaoyang

Top Five Chaoyang

- Step into another world at Beijing's most distinctive Taoist temple, **Dongyue Temple** (below).
- Peruse the sacred beauty of the bodhisattva effigies at the **Poly Art Museum** (right) and admire its fine collection of ancient bronzes.
- Wander in low gear around **Ritan Park** (opposite).
- Lunch or dine scrumptiously at **Xiao Wang's Home Restaurant** (p123).
- Spend an evening wining and dining around **Sanlitun** (p122).

BLUE ZOO BEIJING Map pp234–5
Fùguó Hǎidǐ Shìjiè

☎ 6591 3397; Workers Stadium south gate; adult/child Y75/50; ☼ 8am-10pm

Aquatic Blue Zoo is a good alternative for the little ones when they are beginning to tire of the restaurant aquarium. The live **shark feeding** (10am and 2.30pm) is a drawcard, and the marine tunnel is quite an eye-opener. Diving lessons are also available for adults (Y380), but instruction is in Chinese only.

DONGYUE TEMPLE Map pp234–5
Dōngyuè Miào

☎ 6553 2184; 141 Chaoyangmenwai Dajie; adult Y10; ☼ 9am-4.30pm Tue-Sun; subway Chaoyangmen

The morbid Taoist shrine of Dongyue Temple is an unsettling albeit fascinating experience. With its roots somewhere in the Yuan dynasty, what's above ground level has been recently revived with care, attention and a huge amount of cash. The temple is an active place of worship where Taoist monks attend to a world entirely at odds with the surrounding glass and steel high rises. Note the temple's huge *páifāng* (memorial archway) lying to the south, divorced from its shrine by the intervention of Chaoyangmenwai Dajie.

Stepping through the entrance pops you into a Taoist Hades, alongside tormented spirits reflecting on their wrong-doing and atonement beyond reach. Take your pick: you can muse on life's finalities in the **Life and Death Department** or the **Final Indictment Department**. Otherwise get spooked at the **Department for Wandering Ghosts** or the **Department for Implementing 15 Kinds of Violent Death**. Alternatively get roasted for bad grammar at the **Department of the Hell**.

It's not all doom and gloom: the luckless can check in at the **Department for Increasing Good Fortune and Longevity**. Ornithologists will be birds of a feather with the **Flying Birds Department**, while the infirm can seek a cure at the **Deep-Rooted Disease Department**. The **Animal Department** has a colourful and lively band of fauna.

Other halls are no less fascinating. The **Hall of Taishan Fujun** is dedicated to a Taoist god in charge of the souls of the departed who flee to the holy mountain of Tài Shān. **Divinity Mao Hall** is where a likeness of Mao Ying, founding master of the mysterious Maoshan Taoist School, resides.

Don't forget to stride over the **Copper Beam Stone** (Xiǎo Jīn Dòuzi); patrons of the temple insist that it brings good luck. English explanations detail each department's function.

A good time to visit the temple is during festival time, especially during the Chinese New Year and the Mid-Autumn Festival.

POLY ART MUSEUM Map pp234–5
Bǎolì Yìshù Bówùguǎn

☎ 6500 8117; www.polymuseum.com; Poly Plaza; 14 Dongzhimen Nandajie; Y15; ☼ 9am-4.30pm; subway Dongsishitiao

Up the escalator on the 2nd floor of the Poly Plaza is this excellent new-generation museum. It might be small, but it ranks as one of

Decorated face inside Dongyue Temple (left)

Beijing for Children

Many children will dig their heels in when confronted with the measureless museum-style torpor of the Forbidden City and the Ming Tombs. Thanks to China's one-child policy, however, Beijing's poor sibling-less tykes are spoiled rotten by their parents, and the city is bursting with activities to keep all those demanding little egos occupied. **Beijing Aquarium** (p92) and **Blue Zoo Beijing** (p86) are aquatic options for a rainy day. **ExploraScience** (p63) in Oriental Plaza is a hands-on foray into the world of science. Alternatively put your children on ice for a while at **Le Cool Ice Rink** (p138). If your kids think the Great Wall is a colossal bore, you can always plonk them on the 3km downhill toboggan ride at the Simatai section (see Excursions p169). The dinosaurs at the **Natural History Museum** (p67) should go down well, but steer the little ones away from the more grisly displays. In the evenings, the **China Puppet Theatre** (p135) regularly casts a spell over its audience of little (and not-so-little) ones. If your children are fed up with window-shopping, take them along to the **New China Children's Toy World** (p146), a huge and extravagant emporium of toys on Wangfujing Dajie. For further toys, try **Kids World** (6th fl, Lufthansa Center Youyi Shopping City) and the stalls on the 4th floor of the Sanlitun Yashou Clothing Market (p148). Current and forthcoming events and attractions – from plays to arts and crafts events and seasonal parties – for children in Beijing are listed in the monthly English-language culture magazine **That's Beijing** (www.thatsmagazines.com). Note also that many museums and attractions have a cheaper rate for children, usually applying to children shorter than 1.3m, so ask.

China's best collections. The well-lit displays consist of **bronzes** and carved stone **Buddhist effigies** sculpted between the Northern Wei and Tang dynasties, although at the time of writing the latter were on tour in the USA. The bronzes, dating from the Shang dynasty (1700 to 1100 BC) and passing through the Zhou period, include an impressive range of patina-coloured vessels, including *ding*, *jue*, *gui*, *xu* and other containers and bells (*zhong*). Several pieces are decorated with the elaborate, animistic patterns called *taotie*, creating a swirl of animal motifs. The 'Square *ding* with animal faces' and the '*zun* with bovine motifs' are both magnificent pieces. Also on view are early bells with animal faces, a rare, small *zun* vessel in the shape of a rabbit and a marvellous gilt dragon head ornament from a canopy frame. A couple of bodhisattva effigies can be viewed in the foyer downstairs, and if the rest of the stone effigies are back from abroad, you will be able to view what appears from the catalogue to be a beautiful collection of contemplative bodhisattvas, seated and standing Buddha statues.

RITAN PARK Map pp234–5
Rìtán Gōngyuán

☎ 8563 5038; Ritan Lu; adult Y1; ⏰ 6am-9pm; subway Chaoyangmen

This park is one of Beijing's oldest and was built in 1530 as an altar for ritual sacrifice to the sun. The **altar**, typically surrounded by kite flyers and children playing, is ringed by a circular wall while the rest of the park is given over to pines and quietude.

ZHIHUA TEMPLE Map pp234–5
Zhìhuà Sì

☎ 6513 5207; 5 Lumicang Hutong; adult Y5; ⏰ 8.30am-4.30pm Tue-Sun; bus 24 to Lumicang stop

Buried deep down a *hutong*, Zhihua Temple is a quiet 15th-century Ming dynasty temple noted for its deep-blue roof tiling. The coffered ceiling of the third hall of the Growth of Intellect Temple is not there – it's in the USA. Inside the **Ten Thousand Buddha Hall** is a constellation of Buddhas surrounding a large copper effigy of the Maitreya Buddha. The temple is in the Yabao Lu area, east of Chaoyangmen Nanxiaojie; take bus No 24 to the Lumicang bus stop.

Transport

Subway Circle Line: The Poly Art Museum is just north of the Dongsishitiao stop, and Dongyue Temple is a 10-minute walk east of the Chaoyangmen stop; Dongsishitiao is the closest subway stop to the bars and restaurants of Sanlitun. To save walking take a cab or bus 115.

Bus Double-decker bus 3 takes you from the Jingguang New World Hotel, past Tuanjiehu Park and the Agricultural Exhibition Center to the Lufthansa Center; bus 110 runs from Chaoyangmen subway station along Chaoyangmen Dajie, past the Dongyue Temple and then north along Gongrentiyuchang Donglu via the Workers Stadium and up Xin Donglu; bus 115 runs east along Gongrentiyuchang Beilu from the Dongsishitiao subway stop to Sanlitun.

FENGTAI & XUANWU

Eating p124; Shopping p149; Sleeping p161

Fengtai and Xuanwu occupy the southeast of Beijing, an area that might not see Beijing at its prettiest or most historic. But travellers will enjoy rummaging for curios in the stalls and shops of Liulichang (p149) and experiencing the ancient Taoist mysteries of the White Cloud Temple (opposite). The district around the Niujie Mosque (opposite) is distinctive for its Huí (Chinese Muslim) character. The quarter focuses on the street of Niu Jie (Cow St), which is named after the local predilection for beef (and avoidance of pork).

Neighbourhoods – Fengtai & Xuanwu

FAYUAN TEMPLE

Map pp236–8

Făyuán Sì

☎ 6353 3966/4171; 7 Fayuansi Qianjie; adult Y5; ☼ 8.30-11.30am & 1.30-3.30pm Thu-Tue; bus 6 to Niu Jie or bus 10 to Libaisi stop

In a lane east of Niujie Mosque is this bustling temple originally constructed in the 7th century and still a hive of activity. It's now the **China Buddhism College**, but the temple was originally built to honour Tang soldiers who had fallen during combat against the northern tribes. A visit here is like going to a college campus – students playing Ping-Pong during breaks, hanging out and chatting – except that the students are monks dressed in Buddhist yellow robes. Don't miss the hall at the very back of the temple, which houses an unusual **copper-cast Buddha** seated on a thousand-petal lotus flower. From the entrance of Niujie Mosque, walk left 100m then turn left into the first *hutong*. Follow the *hutong* for about 10 minutes, and you'll arrive at Fayuan Temple.

GRAND VIEW GARDEN

Map pp236–8

Dàguānyuán Gōngyuán

☎ 6354 3168, 6355 5874; 12 Nancaiyuan Jie; adult Y10; ☼ 8.30am-4.30pm; bus 59

Unlike most of Beijing's parks, which date back to imperial days, the Grand View Garden dates back only to the 1980s. The park was built as a replica of the family gardens described in the classic Chinese novel *Dream of the Red Mansions* (also known as *The Story of the Stone*), written by Cao Xueqin in the late 18th century. Although the park is not steeped in history, it could be of interest if you've read the novel. Otherwise, just relax and enjoy the birds, trees and colourful pavilions. The Grand View Garden is in the southwest corner of town just inside the Second Ring Rd.

MILITARY MUSEUM

Map pp236–8

Jūnshì Bówùguǎn

☎ 6851 4441; 9 Fuxing Lu; adult Y5; ☼ 8.30am-5pm, last entry 4pm; subway Junshibowuguan

Wandering into the Military Museum you are greeted by a statue of Mao and his car, plus huge portraits of fellow travellers Lenin, Marx and Stalin. Beyond are Cold War-era F-5 fighters (as featured in parks all over China), the much larger F-7 and F-8s, tanks and, near the stairs, two large surface-to-air HQ-2 (Red Flag-2) missiles. Upstairs bristles with further weaponry and a heavy-going gallery of statues of military and political top brass. Two large halls tackle historic wars, including the war against US involvement in Korea, while the top floor has the most arresting exhibition on recent conflicts, including the Opium War, the Taiping and the Boxer Rebellion. There are limited English captions only in the upper gallery.

Cynics would no doubt like to know that the museum is not far from Muxidi, the site of the greatest civilian bloodletting by the military during the 1989 Tiananmen demonstrations.

Top Five Fengtai & Xuanwu

- Make a foray into the huge **White Cloud Temple** (opposite) and enter a world of Taoist myth, faith and superstition.
- Visit **Niujie Mosque** (opposite) – Beijing's premier mosque and place of veneration for the city's sizeable Huí population.
- Rummage through the stalls, shops and bazaars of **Liulichang** (p149).
- Join the audience at the noble **Zhengyici Theatre** (p132) for a night of Beijing opera.
- Admire the impressive spectacle of the **South Cathedral** (p89).

NIUJIE MOSQUE Map pp236–8

Niújiē Lǐbài Sì

☎ 6353 2564; 88 Niu Jie; adult Y10, free for Muslims;
⏲ 8am-sunset; bus 6 to Niu Jie or bus 10 to Libaisi stop

This engaging mosque was designed with a Chinese temple style guide in hand. With a history dating back to the 10th century, the mosque is the largest in town, and is also the burial site for a number of Islamic clerics. The mosque is given over to a profusion of greenery, as well as flourishes of Arabic. There is a main prayer hall (which you can enter only if you are Muslim), women's quarters and the Building for Observing the Moon (Wàngyuèlóu), from where the lunar calendar was calculated. There is estimated to be around 180,000 ethnic Chinese Muslims (a minority called the 'Huí') in Beijing, and there are 40 mosques in town. The Huí differ from the Muslim Uyghurs from Xīnjiāng, who are ethnically Turkic in origin. Dress appropriately (no shorts or short skirts) and be particularly respectful on Fridays, or save your visit for another day of the week.

SOUTH CATHEDRAL Map pp236–8

Nántáng

141 Qianmen Xidajie; ⏲ mass in Latin 6am Sun-Fri,
English 10am Sun; subway Xuanwumen

Beijing's South Cathedral was built on the site of the house of Matteo Ricci, the Jesuit missionary who introduced Christianity to China. Since being completed in 1703, the church has been destroyed three times, including being burnt down in 1775 and enduring a trashing by anti-Christian forces during the Boxer Rebellion in 1900. Enter the grounds near a statue of Virgin Mary. The stone in front of her is etched in Chinese with the words '10,000 blessings'. Nearby are the Chinese words 'alailuya' (Halleluja). The church itself is now decorated with modern stained glass, fake marbling, portraits of the Stations of the Cross and cream-coloured confessionals. Note the Buddhist influence in the patterns on the stained glass down the west side of the church. Opposite the Catholic Arts Center (shut at the time of research) you can buy religious artefacts near the gate at the **Holy Things Handicraft Department** (shèngwù gōngyìpǐn bù); inside you can pick up effigies of Jesus and the Virgin Mary and other Catholic accoutrements. At the time of writing, the entire block north of the church to the Marco Polo Hotel had been demolished, leaving a vast wasteland. Don't enter by the very front door but by the traditional-looking door to the left.

Transport

Subway Circle Line: You can reach the South Cathedral at the Xuanwumen stop.

East-West Line: Get off at the Junshibowuguan stop for the Military Museum.

Bus Double-decker bus 1 runs from Beijing West Train Station, past the Military Museum, east past Xidan and onto Tiananmen and beyond along Chang'an Jie; bus 10 connects Niu Jie with Wangfujing Dajie, running through Tiananmen, Xidan and Changchun Jie.

WHITE CLOUD TEMPLE Map pp236–8

Báiyún Guàn

☎ 6346 3531; Baiyun Lu; adult Y10; ⏲ 8.30am-4.30pm May-Sep, 8.30am-4pm Oct-Apr

White Cloud Temple, once the Taoist centre of northern China, was founded in AD 739. It's a lively, huge and fascinating temple complex of numerous shrines and courtyards, tended by distinctive Taoist monks with their hair twisted into topknots. As with many of China's temples, the White Cloud Temple has repeatedly been destroyed. Today's temple halls date principally from the Ming and Qing dynasties.

The halls at the temple, centre of operations for the Taoist Quanzhen School and abode of the China Taoist Association, are dedicated to a host of Taoist officials and marshals. The **Hall of the Jade Emperor** celebrates this most famous of Taoist deities, while Taoist housewives cluster earnestly at the **Hall to the God of Wealth** to divine their financial future. Depictions of the Taoist Hell festoon the walls of the **Shrine Hall for the Saviour Worthy**, so comparisons with Hieronymus Bosch can be made.

Drop by White Cloud Temple during the Spring Festival (p9) and be rewarded with the spectacle of a magnificent temple fair (miàohuì). Worshippers funnel into the streets around the temple in their thousands, lured by artisans, street performers, wǔshù (martial arts) acts, craft workers, traders and a swarm of snack merchants. Near the temple entrance, a vast, patient queue of people (a rare occurrence in China) snakes slowly through the gate for a chance to rub a polished stone carving for good fortune. Beyond, throngs of worshippers further fortify their luck by tossing metal discs at bell-adorned oversize coins (Y10 for 50) suspended from a bridge (you can imagine the ruckus this makes during the Spring Festival).

To find the temple, walk south on Baiyun Lu and across the moat. Continue along Baiyun

Lu and turn into a curving street on the left; follow it for 250m to the temple entrance.

ZHONGNANHAI

Map pp236–8

Zhōngnánhǎi; subway Tiananmen Xi

Just west of the Forbidden City is China's new forbidden city, Zhongnanhai. The interior is off limits to tourists, but you can gawk at the entrance. The name means the 'Central and South Seas', after the two large lakes in the compound. The southern entrance is via **Gate of New China** (Xinhuamen) on Xichang'an Jie,

guarded by two PLA soldiers and fronted by a flagpole. The gate was built in 1758 and was then known as the Tower of the Treasured Moon.

Since the founding of the People's Republic in 1949, Zhongnanhai has been the site of the residence and offices of the highest ranking members of the Communist Party. The unexpected gathering of thousands of Falun Gong followers in spring 1999 outside Zhongnanhai led to the movement's christening as a 'cult' and its subsequent humiliation at the hands of the authorities.

Sacred Beijing – the Spiritual Heart of the City

In the tumult of transition, it's easy to get swept away by the cyclone of change sweeping Beijing's streets. Wherever one looks, the city's ancient patina is being feverishly scrubbed away by a municipal government hell-bent on repackaging Beijing. As the 2008 Olympics glitters on the horizon, the vision of a modern metropolis is taking shape, delivered by massive injections of cash. But if you truly want to get off the merry-go-round and skirt the flood of construction and consumerism, it's time to foray into Beijing's sacred realm, where islets of tradition temptingly survive.

It's in Beijing's temples that you can discern the millennia-old face of the city lying beneath recent cosmetic overlays. It's a profound, mystical and magical world – a colourful sphere designed by the laws of *fēng shuǐ*, guarded by menacing door gods, instilled with a devotion wreathed in plumes of incense, and peopled by legions of praying monks.

Temple Layout

The place of prayer for Buddhist, Taoist or Confucian worshippers, Chinese temples tend to follow a strict, schematic pattern. Most importantly, all Buddhist, Taoist and Confucian temples are laid out on a north–south axis in a series of halls, with the main door of each hall facing south. Beijing's *hútong* (alleyway) courtyards were traditionally also constructed along the same axis.

One striking difference between Chinese temples and Christian churches is their open plan, consisting of numerous buildings interspersed with breezy open-air courtyards. This allows the climate (rain, sunshine, fog, dew, frost, snow, sleet etc) to permeate and conduct the overall mood. Seasons therefore play an essential role in defining the disposition of a temple; this is also true of Beijing's palaces, such as the Summer Palace and the Forbidden City. The open-air layout furthermore allows the *qì* (energy) to circulate, dispersing stale air and allowing incense to be liberally burned.

Buddhist Temples

Most temples in Beijing are Buddhist. Buddhist temples such as the Lama Temple typically (but not exclusively) introduce themselves at the entrance by way of the chubby Milefo, popularly known as the Laughing Buddha. He sits in the first hall at the entrance to the temple, flanked by the ferocious and intimidating Four Heavenly Kings. The first hall then yields to the first courtyard, where the drum and bell towers stand and one or two braziers (*lúzi*) for the burning of incense are positioned. The largest hall in a Buddhist temple is often called the Great Treasure Hall (Dàxióngbǎo Diàn). This hall shelters a trinity of golden Buddhist statues, the central effigy being Sakyamuni, the Historical Buddha. The eighteen *luohan* (arhats) are often found here, and in other temples they appear in a multitude of 500, housed in a separate hall.

In the rear of the same hall, a statue of Guanyin (Goddess of Mercy) often faces north, standing on a fish's head or a rocky outcrop. Guanyin is often celebrated in her own hall behind. The goddess is most impressively commemorated by her colossal statue in the Mahayana Hall in Puning Temple in Chéngdé (p181).

Pagodas

Originally built to house the remains of Buddha and later other Buddhist relics, pagodas (*tǎ*) were also used for storing sutras, religious artefacts and documents. They are common features of Buddhist temples, and generally rise at the rear of the compound. Numerous pagodas stand alone throughout China, their adjacent temples destroyed, such as the Yongyousi Pagoda in Chéngdé (p181). Dagobas (stupas) served a similar function and can be found in a few temples like the Miaoying Temple White Dagoba (p93), and Beijing's most famous example, the Yongan Temple in Beihai Park (p73).

If you want to immerse yourself in Buddhist temple architecture, a two-day visit to Chéngdé (p181) should be on your itinerary, especially if you want to see more of the Tibetan influence that characterises the Lama Temple. If you don't have the time, the Summer Palace (p98) is a more manageable alternative, and the Lama Temple (p81) is certainly worth a visit.

Buddhas & Bodhisattvas

- **Sakyamuni** The Historical Buddha is usually the central statue in the main hall (*dàxióngbǎo diàn*) of Buddhist temples. The effigy represents Gautama Siddhartha, who became Buddha. He is sometimes represented reclining and about to enter Nirvana, as in the recumbent figure at Sleeping Buddha Temple in the Beijing Botanical Gardens (p95).
- **Milefo** The Future or Laughing Buddha, the amiable and chubby Milefo, is the rotund, often golden figure at the entrance to Buddhist temples. Milefo's jovial mission is often proclaimed by twin vertical sets of Chinese characters on either side of his corpulent frame. Milefo is a bodhisattva whose time is yet to come.
- **Weituo** The defender of Buddhism, Weituo stands back-to-back with Milefo, holding a staff or a sword.
- **Guanyin** Known as Avalokiteshvara in Sanskrit, Guanyin (Goddess of Mercy, p185) lives on earth in the Dalai Lama and calls the Potala Palace in Tibet her home. In China, she is associated with the Buddhist island of Pǔtuó Shān. In temples, she often faces north at the rear of the main hall, or has her own shrine. She dispenses mercy to worldly mortals, her Chinese name meaning 'Listening to the Cries'. Guanyin is generally depicted as being female, although early carvings portray her as male.
- **Wenshu** Ruling bodhisattva of the sacred Buddhist mountain of Wǔtái Shān, Wenshu (Manjushri) often sits to the left of Sakyamuni in the trinity of Buddhist statues in the main hall of Buddhist temples. He represents wisdom and is often depicted carrying a sword and riding a lion.
- **Luohan** Usually seen in two rows of nine on either side of the trinity of Buddhist statues in the main hall of Buddhist temples, the *luohan* (*arhat*) have been freed from the cycle of rebirth and await the coming of the future Buddha. Luohan are also seen in constellations of 500.
- **Four Heavenly Kings** These ferocious, colourful temple guardians stand in pairs on either side of Milefo. Gargantuan in size, they wield weapons or pluck musical instruments.

Taoist Temples

Taoism predates Buddhism, and much of its religious culture connects with a distant animism and shamanism, despite the purity of its philosophical school. The religion's primordial origins survive in its many cosmic myths and legends and its huge number of deities, many of which are worshipped in temples. Some of China's sacred Buddhist mountains (eg, Éméi Shān) were originally peopled by Taoist hermits who gradually surrendered their mountainous retreats to Buddhists. One old legend says that Laotzu journeyed west on an ox to India to become Buddha.

Although their layout echoes that of their Buddhist siblings, Taoist temples are governed by a separate pantheon of gods and are equipped with a distinct set of motifs, such as circular *bāguà* (eight trigrams) formations, reflected in eight-sided pavilions and halls. The *yīn/yáng* diagram can often be seen, along with statues of Laotzu and the Jade Emperor, like at the White Cloud Temple (p89). Other characters popularly associated with Taoist myth are the Eight Immortals and the God of Wealth.

Taoist temple entrances are often guarded by Taoist door gods, similar to Buddhist temples, and the main hall is usually called the Hall of the Three Clear Ones or Three Pure Ones and is devoted to a triumvirate of Taoist gods.

Beijing's two main Taoist temples, the Dongyue Temple (p860) and White Cloud Temple (p89), are more netherworldly than most Buddhist temples, and there is more of an atmosphere of superstition and magic. Dongyue Temple in particular is an outlandish and unsettling domain.

It's also worth noting that the ancient Chinese martial arts of *tàijíquán (taichi)* and *bāguà zhǎng* are Taoist in inspiration, unlike many other arts that draw on Buddhism. If you are interested in learning *tàijíquán*, it could be worth inquiring at Taoist temples for instruction.

Taoist monks are easily distinguished from their shaven-headed Buddhist confreres by their long hair, sometimes tied into a topknot, straight trousers and squarish jackets.

Taoist Gods & Goddesses

- **Laotzu** The founding father of philosophical Taoism, Laotzu is always depicted in Taoist temples. He is often seen riding on the back of an ox on his famous journey to the west.
- **Jade Emperor** Typically depicted in the main hall of Taoist temples, the effigy of the Jade Emperor, the paramount Taoist deity, is usually found alongside statues of Laotzu and the Yellow Emperor. Together the triumvirate is known as the Three Pure Ones.
- **Eight Immortals** This legendary group of immortals is often celebrated in Taoist temples, portrayed crossing the sea.
- **Queen of Heaven** Tianhou is a Taoist goddess associated with sailors and the sea. She is celebrated chiefly in the seaboard provinces of southern China.

Confucian Temples

Confucian temples are not as active or as colourful as their Taoist or Buddhist cousins, and often seem rather musty and neglected. Perhaps this is because the authorities still ambiguously see Confucius as a critic of absolute state power while he also serves as a model for virtuous citizens. Neither purged nor feted in contemporary China, Confucius finds himself rather sidelined.

Confucian temples bristle with stelae celebrating local scholars, some supported on the backs of *bìxì* (mythical tortoise-looking dragons). A statue of Kongzi (Confucius) usually resides in the main hall, overseeing rows of musical instruments and flanked by disciples. Cypresses are commonly planted in the grounds of Confucian temples, and a mythical animal, the *qílín* (a statue exists at the Summer Palace), is commonly seen. The *qílín* was a hybrid animal that appeared on earth only in times of harmony.

Other Faiths

Christianity made a series of tentative toeholds in China, but it was not until the 17th century that the Jesuits arrived in Beijing. Church architecture followed, and many of Beijing's churches utilised the European styles of baroque and Gothic, while others tried to blend a Western structure with traditional Chinese decorative styles.

There are a few historic mosques in Beijing, designed largely in the Chinese style, the Niujie Mosque (p89) being the most famous. These mosques act as the focal point of worship for the Huí minority, Chinese descendents of Muslims travelling the silk routes.

HAIDIAN & XICHENG

Eating p124; Sleeping p162

Xicheng occupies the western flank of Beijing's central district, including part of the Imperial City and sites around the Qianhai and Houhai lake area. Haidian district occupies the northwest of Beijing, an area noted for the famous Beijing and Qinghua Universities, and incorporating the Zhongguancun high-tech district.

BEIJING ZOO & BEIJING AQUARIUM

Map pp230–1

Běijīng Dòngwùyuán

☎ 6831 4411; 137 Xizhimenwai Dajie; adult Y10, pandas Y5 extra; 7.30am-5.30pm; subway Xizhimen

All zoos are animal prisons, but Beijing Zoo seems like death row. Most of the design features date from the 1950s – concrete and glass cells – but the pandas have plusher living quarters for good behaviour.

The polar bears pin their hopes on graduating from their concrete hell to the marvellous **Beijing Aquarium** (☎ 6833 8742; adult/child Y100/50; low season 9am-5.30pm, high season 9am-6pm), a first-class addition in the northeastern corner of the zoo – it's the largest inland aquarium in the world. On view is an imaginative Amazon rainforest (complete with piranha), coral reefs, a shark aquarium (where you can dive with the flesh eaters), and a marine mammal pavilion. The latter hosts lively aquatic animal displays. If you have kiddies in tow and they reckon the Temple of Heaven is a colossal bore, bring them here – they'll love it.

East of the zoo is the distinctive **Beijing Exhibition Hall** (Běijīng Zhǎnlǎn Guǎn), designed in the days when Chinese architects were party ideologues. Enthusiasts of Soviet-era monuments will admire its guileless overture.

GUANGJI TEMPLE Map pp230–1
Guǎngjì Sì
☎ 6616 0907; cnr Xisi Beidajie & Fuchengmennei Dajie; admission free; ⏰ 8.30am-4.30pm; subway Fuchengmen

Guangji Temple has been the headquarters of the Chinese Buddhist Association since 1953. With a history of more than 800 years, this simple temple has an assortment of stelae in its tree-shaded courtyard and Buddhist gifts from numerous nations.

LU XUN MUSEUM Map pp230–1
Lǔ Xùn Bówùguǎn
☎ 6616 4168; 19 Gongmenkou Ertiao; adult Y5; ⏰ 9am-4pm Tue-Sun; subway Fuchengmen

Not far from Miaoying Temple White Dagoba is this museum dedicated to the iconoclastic writer Lu Xun, the 'No 1 Thinking Person's Revolutionary'. Lu Xun (1881–1936), born in Shàoxìng in Zhèjiāng province, is often regarded as the father of modern Chinese literature. Before his literary innovations, first used to great dramatic effect in the chilling *Diary of a Madman*, literati had composed in stultifyingly complex classical Chinese. As a writer, Lu Xun, who first trained in medicine, articulated a deep yearning for reform by mercilessly exposing the foibles of the Chinese people's character. He aligned himself with the communist cause, and is chiefly remembered for his most famous work, *The True Story of Ah Q*.

Top Five Haidian & Xicheng

- Make an early morning visit to the graceful **Prince Gong's Residence** (p94) and embark on our Lakeside Walk (p106).
- Pay your respects at the **North Cathedral** (right), one of Beijing's most important Christian monuments.
- Appreciate the fine Buddhist statues and effigies at the **Wanshou Temple and Beijing Art Museum** (p95).
- Take the kids along to the **Beijing Aquarium** (opposite) for a fun day out.
- Admire the collection of Tibetan Buddhist Statuary at the **Miaoying Temple** (right).

Transport

Subway Circle Line: offers access to the Xu Beihong Museum, the Lu Xun Museum and the Miaoying Temple White Dagoba.

Bus Double-decker bus 4 runs from Beijing Zoo past the Exhibition Center and then south along the Second Ring Rd to Qianmen (for Tiananmen Square); several westbound buses from Xizhimen can get you to the zoo, including buses 105 and 111.

Hampered by a shortage of English captions, the museum's collection of photos and manuscripts remains largely impenetrable to all but the most erudite.

MEI LANFANG FORMER RESIDENCE
Map pp230–1
Méi Lánfāng Jìniàn Guǎn
☎ 6618 0351; 9 Huguosi Lu; adult Y2; ⏰ 9-11.30am & 1-4pm Tue-Sun Apr-Nov; subway Jishuitan

Place of pilgrimage for Beijing opera aficionados, this former *sìhéyuàn* (courtyard house) of actor Mei Lanfang is tucked away in a *hutong* named after the nearby remains of Huguo Temple. Beijing opera (p131) was popularised in the West by Mei Lanfang (1894–1961), who played *dàn* or female roles, and is said to have influenced Charlie Chaplin. His former residence has been preserved as a museum, replete with costumes, furniture and old opera programmes.

MIAOYING TEMPLE WHITE DAGOBA
Map pp230–1
Miàoyìng Sì Báitǎ
☎ 6616 0211; 171 Fuchengmennei Dajie; adult Y10; ⏰ 9am-4pm; subway Fuchengmen, bus 13, 101, 102 or 103 to Baita Si

The Yuan dynasty white dagoba of the Miaoying Temple is similar to that in Beihai Park (p73). The highpoint of a visit here, however, is its riveting collection of thousands of **Tibetan Buddhist statues**. A population of bronze luohan figures also inhabits the temple. There is liberal use of English captions.

NORTH CATHEDRAL Map pp230–1
Běitáng
Xishiku Dajie; subway Fuchengmen, bus 14 or 55 to Xianmen stop

Also called the Cathedral of Our Saviour, this august cathedral was built in 1887 but was badly damaged during the Cultural Revolution before being converted into a factory warehouse. Despite being covered in gaudy grey, flaking paint, the cathedral is well worth a look-see. One of Beijing's four main churches, the North Cathedral was the only one located within the grounds of the Imperial City. You can walk all the way around to the rear at the left, where there appears to be a small nunnery. Some stained glass survives, and the cathedral is open to the faithful. There are services in Latin and Chinese early in the morning. The metal gate leading to the cathedral might appear locked, but give it a shove and it should open.

PRINCE GONG'S RESIDENCE
Map pp230–1
Gōngwáng Fǔ
☎ 6616 8149, 6601 6132; 14 Liuyin Jie; adult Y20; tour Y60; ☷ 8.30am-4.30pm; subway Gulou, then bus 60
Reputed to be the model for the mansion in Cao Xueqin's 18th-century classic, *Dream of the Red Mansions*, the residence is one of Beijing's largest private residential compounds. Despite skulking ice cream sellers and pantomime costume hire, it can be a quiet and introspective place, especially if you visit in the morning and avoid the tour groups. This remains one of Beijing's more attractive retreats, being decorated with rockeries, plants, pools, pavilions, corridors and elaborately carved gateways. Guided tours include tea tasting and a sample of Beijing opera. Full performances of Beijing opera are held regularly in the Qing dynasty

Actors in costume at Prince Gong's Residence (left)

Grand Opera House (☎ 6618 6628; adults Y80-120; ☷ 7-30pm, Mar-Oct) in the east of the grounds. Roughly 500m to the east of the residence is the quaint **Silver Ingot Bridge** (Yínding Qiáo) that bisects willow-lined Qiánhǎi and Hòuhǎi Lakes. There are numerous cafés and restaurants in the vicinity worth hunting down for a bite to eat or a drink.

Gong, But Not Forgotten

Prince Gong is known for being the last emperor's father, but he also earned an unflattering footnote in history as a failed negotiator with the British. The issue was who might live in Beijing's splendid *sihéyuàn* (courtyard houses).

With the forced signing of the infamous Tianjin Treaty (1858), China was expected to permit foreign ambassadors to reside in the capital. Most clauses of the treaty – tolerance of Christian missionaries, more 'open' trade and the continued sale of opium (illegal in China) – could be conceded. But although the British were no longer to be referred to as *yí* (barbarians), allowing them to live in the Son of Heaven's city was too much.

Unimpressed, British troops pushed the issue by force, attacking seaside forts east of Beijing. When this didn't work, the British sent negotiators to the capital, some of whom were promptly arrested and executed. By now the situation was critical; the emperor (who had fled to Manchuria) sent his brother Prince Gong to negotiate, but the Prince's efforts were doomed. The leader of the British delegation was the son of the same Lord Elgin who had removed the Parthenon's famous statuary (the Elgin Marbles) to England 'for safekeeping'. After allowing British and French troops to pillage what they could, the younger Elgin ordered the burning of the Summer Palace.

This act was distressing enough to the Qing, but it might have been worse. The Forbidden City was spared only because its destruction would have brought down the entire dynasty, and the British considered this would have been bad for business. Prince Gong immediately agreed to all the Tianjin Treaty's terms, and further pledged a large payment of silver plus part of Kowloon to British Hong Kong. In exchange, the British agreed to protect their new gains by supporting the Qing against the dangerous Taiping Rebellion.

Russ Kerr

SONG QINGLING FORMER RESIDENCE Map pp230–1

Sòng Qìnglíng Gùjū

☎ 6403 5858; 46 Beiheyan Lu; adult Y8; ⓧ 9am-4pm Tue-Sun; subway Gulou or Jishuitan

Madam Song is lovingly venerated by the Chinese as the wife of Sun Yat-sen, founder of the Republic of China. Her house is rather dormant and moth-eaten; on display are personal items, pictures, clothing and books. You can find the museum on the northern side of Houhai lake and within reach of the Xu Beihong Museum (p95), Prince Gong's Residence and a bunch of bars set up near the lakes.

WANSHOU TEMPLE & BEIJING ART MUSEUM Map pp230–1

Wànshòu Sì & Běijīng Yìshù Bówùguǎn

☎ 6841 3380/3379; Suzhou Jie; adult Y10; ⓧ 9am-4.30pm Tue-Sun

Ringed by a red wall on the southeastern corner of Suzhou Jie (off the Third Ring Rd), the Ming dynasty Wanshou Temple was originally consecrated for the storage of Buddhist texts. Recently restored, the temple's name echoes the Summer Palace's Longevity Hill; in fact, from Qing times the imperial entourage would put their feet up here and quaff tea en route to the palace.

The highlight of a visit here, however, is its prized collection of bronze **Buddhist statuary** in halls that offer a tour through the Buddhist pantheon. On show are some quite splendid effigies of Buddhist deities and Bodhisattvas, including Guanyin (in bronze and *déhuà*, or blanc-de-Chine), Wenshu, Sakyamuni and some exotic Tantric pieces. Worth noting is the decidedly masculine-looking Guanyin at the rear of the **Mahavira Hall** (she is usually, but not exclusively, female). The octagonal pavilion at the rear once housed a 5m-high gold-lacquered brass statue now long gone; in its place is a miniature pagoda alloyed from gold, silver, zinc and lead. Some of China's holy mountains (including Pǔtuó Shān and Éméi Shān) in the form of small rockeries can also be found.

WUTA TEMPLE Map pp230–1

Wǔtǎ Sì

☎ 6217 2894/3543; 24 Wutasi Cun; adult Y10; ⓧ 9am-4.30pm; subway Xizhimen

The Indian-style Wuta Temple, dating from 1473, sits in a small park and is decorated with a fine collection of stone stelae and *bìxì*, mythical tortoise-like reptiles often seen in Confucian temples. The temple, also known as the Carved Stone Museum (Shíkē Bówùguǎn), can be easily reached by crossing the canal bridge directly opposite the rear exit of Beijing Zoo (p92).

XU BEIHONG MUSEUM Map pp230–1

Xú Bēihóng Jìniàn Guǎn

☎ 6225 2187/2042; 53 Xinjiekou Beidajie; adult Y5; ⓧ 9am-noon & 1-5pm Tue-Sun; subway Jishuitan

The Chinese artist Xu Beihong (1895–1953), best remembered for his galloping horses that injected dynamism into previously static forms of Chinese brushwork, is commemorated in this intriguing museum. Exposed to foreign (principally European) painting styles, Xu possessed one of 20th-century China's more fertile imaginations. The communists feted Xu, which partly explains the success and longevity of his name. His success is celebrated here in seven halls and remembered in a collection of oils, gouache, pen and ink sketches, and portraits.

AROUND BEIJING

BEIJING BOTANICAL GARDENS

Map pp228–9

Xiāng Shān Zhíwùyuán

☎ 6259 1283; 2km east of Fragrant Hills Park; adult Y5; ⓧ 6am-8pm; subway Pingguoyuan then bus 318, bus 333 from the Summer Palace or bus 360 from Beijing Zoo

The well-tended and clean botanical gardens, set against the backdrop of the Western Hills, make for a pleasant outing among bamboo fronds, pines and lilacs. The **Beijing Botanical Gardens Conservatory** (Y50; ⓧ 8.30am-4pm) built in 1999, contains 3000 different types of plants and a rainforest house.

Top Five Around Beijing

- Spend a day sizing up the colossal elegance of the **Summer Palace** (p98).
- Wander by the lakes and pick your way through the desolate ruins of the **Old Summer Palace** (p97).
- Hike around **Fragrant Hills Park** (p96) and visit the impressive temple architecture of the Azure Clouds Temple.
- Stoll at leisure through the **Beijing Botanical Gardens** (above) and make your way to its centrepiece Sleeping Buddha Temple.
- Take a trip to the mother of all Chinese bells at the **Great Bell Temple** (p96).

Within the grounds and about a 15-minute walk from the front gate (follow the signs) is **Sleeping Buddha Temple** (Wòfó Sì; ☎ 6259 1561; adult Y5; ⏰ 8am-5pm daily). The temple, first built during the Tang dynasty, has a huge reclining effigy of Sakyamuni weighing 54 tonne as a centrepiece. It is said to have 'enslaved 7000 people' in its casting.

On each side of Buddha are arrayed some sets of gargantuan shoes, gifts to Sakyamuni from various emperors in case he went for a stroll. Above him are the apt characters 'Zizai Dàdé', meaning 'great accomplishment comes from being at ease'. Other halls include effigies of Milefo and Weituo, the Four Heavenly Kings, some Golden Buddhas and Guanyin. The temple is near the Magnolia Garden, which flowers profusely in spring.

On the eastern side of the gardens is the **Cao Xueqin Memorial** (Cáo Xuěqín Jìniànguǎn; ☎ 6259 1561, ext 2083; 39 Zhengbaiqi; admission free; ⏰ 8am-5pm) where Cao Xueqin lived in his latter years. Cao (1715–63) is credited with penning the classic *Dream of the Red Mansions*, a vast and prolix family saga set in the Qing period.

FRAGRANT HILLS PARK Map pp228–9
Xiāng Shān Gōngyuán
☎ 6259 1283; adult Y5; ⏰ 7am-6pm;
subway Pingguoyuan then bus 318, bus 333 from the Summer Palace or bus 360 from Beijing Zoo

Easily within striking distance of the Summer Palace are the **Xī Shān** (Western Hills), another former villa-resort of the emperors. The part of Xi Shan closest to Beijing is known as **Fragrant Hills** (Xiāng Shān). This is the last stop for the city buses – if you want to get further into the mountains, you'll have to walk, cycle or take a taxi. You can either scramble up the slopes to the top of **Incense-Burner Peak** (Xiānglú Fēng) or take the **chairlift** (one way/return Y30/50; ⏰ 8.30am-5pm). From the peak you get an all-embracing view of the countryside, and you can leave the crowds behind by hiking further into the Western Hills. Beijingers love to flock here in autumn when the maple leaves saturate the hillsides in great splashes of red.

Near the north gate of Fragrant Hills Park is the excellent **Azure Clouds Temple** (Bìyún Sì; ☎ 6259 1155, ext 470; adult Y10; ⏰ 8am-5pm), which dates back to the Yuan dynasty. It took a hammering during the Cultural Revolution and reopened in 1979. The **Mountain Gate Hall** contains two vast protective deities: Heng

and Ha. Beyond is a small courtyard containing the drum and bell towers, leading to a hall with a wonderful statue of Milefo: it's bronze, but coal black with age. Only his big toe shines from numerous inquisitive fingers.

The next hall contains statues of Sakyamuni and Bodhisattvas Manjushri, Samantabhadra and Guanyin (Avalokiteshvara), plus 18 luohan; a marvellous golden carved dragon soars above Sakyamuni. A statue of Guanyin stands at the rear, atop a fish.

The **Hall of Bodhisattvas** contains Wenshu, Guanyin, Dashizhi, Puxian and Dizang, plus other immortals. The Sun **Yat-sen Memorial Hall** contains a statue and a glass coffin donated by the USSR on the death of Mr Sun.

At the very back is the marble **Vajra Throne Pagoda**, where Sun Yat-sen was interred after he died and before his body was moved to its final resting place in Nánjīng. The **Hall of Arhats** is well worth visiting, as its contains 500 luohan statues, each crafted with an individual personality.

Southwest of the Azure Clouds Temple is the Tibetan-styled **Temple of Brilliance** (Zhào Miào), and not too far away is a glazed tile pagoda. Both survived visits by foreign troops intent on sacking the area in 1860 and 1900. Less historic features of the park include an artificial ski slope.

If the climb took the stuffing out of you, it's possible to stay overnight at the park at the **Fragrant Hills Hotel** (Xiāngshān Fàndiàn; ☎ 6259 1166) near the main gate. The hotel was designed by the architect IM Pei, who also designed the definitive Bank of China Tower in Hong Kong (and its less well-known sibling in Xīdān).

GREAT BELL TEMPLE Map pp228–9
Dàzhōng Sì
☎ 6255 0819/0843; 31a Beisanhuan Xilu; adult Y10; ⏰ 8.30am-4.30pm Tue-Sun; bus 300, 302 or 367

This temple houses the biggest bell in China, 6.75m tall and weighing a hefty 46.5 tonnes. The bell is inscribed with Buddhist sutras, comprising more than 227,000 Chinese characters, and decorated with Sanskrit incantations. Clamber up to the **circular hall** (Y2), where there's a small exhibition on bell casting (with some English captions), and chuck a coin through the opening in the top of the bell for luck.

The bell was cast during the reign of Ming Emperor Yongle in 1406, and the tower was built in 1733. Getting the bell from the foundry to the temple proved difficult. A shallow canal was built, and when it froze over in winter, the bell was moved across the ice by sled.

Also on view in other halls are collections of bells from all over China, including bells belonging to the Marquis Zeng of Yi, similar to those at the Hubei Provincial Museum in Wǔhàn.

OLD SUMMER PALACE Map pp228–9
Yuánmíng Yuán
☎ 6262 8501; Qinghua Xilu; adult Y10, palace ruins Y15; ☼ 7am-7pm; subway Xizhimen then bus 375, minibus from Summer Palace

Located northwest of the city centre, the original Summer Palace was laid out in the 12th century. Resourceful Jesuits were later employed by Emperor Qianlong to fashion European-style palaces for the gardens, incorporating elaborate fountains and baroque statuary. During the Second Opium War, British and French troops destroyed the palace and sent the booty abroad. Today pieces still occasionally surface at auction houses. Much of the palace went up in flames, but a melancholic array of broken columns and marble chunks remain.

Trot through the southern gate and past the stretch of hawkers and arcade games to the more subdued ruins of the European

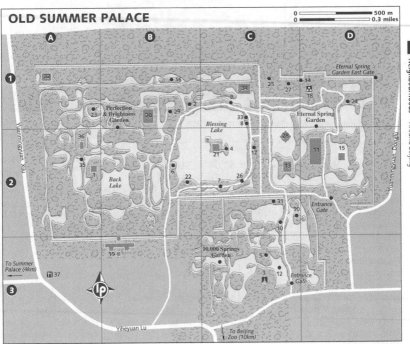

OLD SUMMER PALACE

Inside the grounds of the Old Summer Palace (p97)

Palace in the **Eternal Spring Garden** (Chángchūn Yuán) to the northeast. Alternatively enter by the east gate, which leads to the palace vestiges. The mournful composition of tumbledown palace remains lies strewn in a long strip; alongside are black-and-white photos displaying before and after images of the residence. It's here that you can find the **Great Fountain Ruins**, considered the best-preserved relic in the palace.

West of the ruins you can lose your way in an artful reproduction of a former labyrinth called the **Garden of Yellow Flowers**.

The palace gardens cover a huge area – 2.5km from east to west – so be prepared for some walking. Besides the ruins, there's the western section, the **Perfection and Brightness Garden** (Yuánmíng Yuán) and in the southern compound, the **10,000 Spring Garden** (Wànchūn Yuán).

You can take some pleasant trips in the area by public transport. Take bus No 332 from the zoo to both the old and new Summer Palaces; change to bus No 333 for Fragrant Hills Park; from Fragrant Hills Park change to bus No 360 to go directly back to Beijing Zoo.

Another route is to take the subway to Pingguoyuan (the last stop in the west), and from there take bus No 318 to Fragrant Hills Park; change to No 333 for the Summer Palace, and then to bus No 332 for the zoo.

SUMMER PALACE Map pp228–9
Yíhé Yuán

☎ 6288 1144; 19 Xinjian Gongmen, Haidian; admission Y40-Y50, audio guides Y30; 🕑 8.30am-5pm; subway Xizhimen, then bus 375, or direct on buses 303, 330, 332, 333, 346, 362, 801, 808 and 817

One of Beijing's most visited sights, the immense park of the Summer Palace deserves at least a day of your time.

Nowadays teeming with tour groups from all over China and beyond, this domain of palace temples, gardens, pavilions, lakes and corridors was once a playground for the imperial court. Royalty came here to evade the insufferable summer heat that roasted the Forbidden City. The site had long been a royal garden and was considerably enlarged and embellished by Emperor Qianlong in the 18th century. He deepened and expanded **Kunming Lake** (Kūnmíng Hú) with the help of 100,000 labourers, and reputedly surveyed imperial navy drills from a hilltop perch.

Anglo-French troops badly damaged the buildings during the Second Opium War in 1860. Empress Dowager Cixi began a refit in 1888 with money earmarked for a modern navy, but the extravagant marble boat at the edge of the lake was her only nautical concession.

Foreign troops, incensed by the Boxer Rebellion, had another go at roasting the Summer

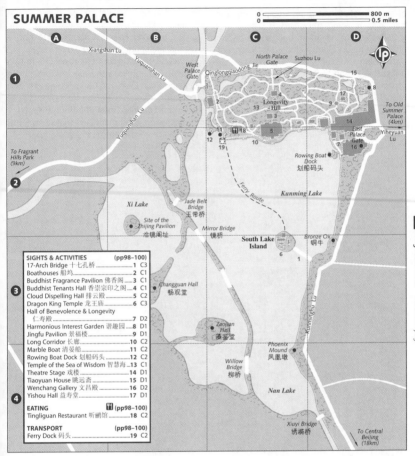

SUMMER PALACE

0 _____ 800 m
0 _____ 0.5 miles

Xiangshan Lu

Yuquanshan Lu

West Palace Gate

Qinglongqiaodong Jie

North Palace Gate

Suzhou Lu

Longevity Hill

To Old Summer Palace (4km)

East Palace Gate

Yiheyuan Lu

To Fragrant Hills Park (9km)

Yuquanshan Lu

Rowing Boat Dock
划船码头

Kunming Lake

Ferry Route

Xi Lake

Jade Belt Bridge
玉带桥

Site of the Zhijing Pavilion
冶镜阁址

Mirror Bridge
镜桥

South Lake Island

Bronze Ox
铜牛

Kunminghu Lu

SIGHTS & ACTIVITIES   (pp98–100)

17-Arch Bridge 十七孔桥 1	C3
Boathouses 船坞 2	C1
Buddhist Fragrance Pavilion 佛香阁 3	C1
Buddhist Tenants Hall 香崇宗印之阁 4	C1
Cloud Dispelling Hall 排云殿 5	C2
Dragon King Temple 龙王庙 6	C3
Hall of Benevolence & Longevity	
仁寿殿 7	D2
Harmonious Interest Garden 谐趣园 8	D1
Jingfu Pavilion 景福楼 9	D1
Long Corridor 长廊 10	C2
Marble Boat 清晏舫 11	C2
Rowing Boat Dock 划船码头 12	C2
Temple of the Sea of Wisdom 智慧海 .13	C1
Theatre Stage 戏楼 14	D1
Tiaoyuan House 眺远斋 15	D1
Wenchang Gallery 文昌殿 16	D2
Yishou Hall 益寿堂 17	D1

EATING   🍴 (pp98–100)
Tingliguan Restaurant 听鹂馆 18 C2

TRANSPORT   (pp98–100)
Ferry Dock 码头 19 C2

Changguan Hall
畅观堂

Zaojian Hall
藻鉴堂

Phoenix Mound
凤凰墩

Willow Bridge
柳桥

Nan Lake

Xiuyi Bridge
绣漪桥

To Central Beijing (18km)

Palace in 1900, prompting more restoration work. In 1949 there was a major overhaul, by which time the palace had once more fallen into disrepair.

Three-quarters of the park is occupied by Kunming Lake and the most notable structures reside near the east gates. The main building is the **Hall of Benevolence and Longevity** (Rénshòu Diàn) by the east gate, which houses a hardwood throne and is fronted by a courtyard decorated with bronze animals, including the mythical *qílín* (a hybrid animal that appeared on earth only at times of harmony). The hall, sadly, is barricaded off so you can only peer in.

Along the lake's northern shore, the **Long Corridor** (Cháng Láng) is trimmed with a plethora of paintings, while the slopes and crest of **Longevity Hill** (Wànshòu Shān) behind are

decorated with several temples. Slung out uphill on a north–south axis are **Buddhist Fragrance Pavilion** (Fóxiāng Gé) and **Cloud Dispelling Hall** (Páiyún Diàn), which are connected by corridors. At the crest sits the **Buddhist Temple of the Sea of Wisdom** (Zhì Huìhǎi) with glazed tiles depicting Buddha. Many, sadly, have had their heads obliterated.

The graceful **17-arch bridge** spans 150m to **South Lake Island** (Nánhú Dǎo) from the eastern shore of the lake. Cixi visited the island's **Dragon King Temple** (Lóngwáng Miào) to beseech the temple's statue for rain in times of drought. You can traverse Kunming Lake by boat from the island to the northern shore where you can see Cixi's **marble boat**, north of which survive some fine Qing boathouses.

The **Wenchang Gallery** (☎ 6288 1144, ext 224; adult Y20; ⏱ 8.30am-4.30pm) to the south

99

of the entrance is a quiet escape from the hordes rampaging through the palace. The galleries, set in a clean and engaging pocket of reproduction Qing architecture, comprise a porcelain exhibition, a jade gallery and an unusual selection of Qing artefacts (including some of Cixi's calligraphy), plus some decent bronzes. Some of the artefacts were looted during the Opium War and were returned from private collections abroad only recently. Towards the North Palace Gate (Sūzhōu Jiē) is

a fun diversion of riverside walkways, shops and eateries.

The Summer Palace is about 12km northwest of the centre of Beijing. You can get here by bicycle from the centre of town (1½ to two hours). Cycling along the road following the Beijing-Miyun Diversion Canal is pleasant, and in summer there's the option of taking a boat from the **Exhibition Center** (☎ 6823 2179, 6821 3366; one way/return Y45/75, including Summer Palace admission) near the zoo.

Walking & Cycling Tours

Walking & Cycling Tours

Beijing might be flat as a chessboard, but walking around town can be a hard slog, especially in the heat and traffic fumes of summer. The following walks are short and easy to manage, and take in some of Beijing's most characteristic and charming areas.

TIANANMEN SQUARE & FOREIGN LEGATION QUARTER WALK

Start from the **Gate of Heavenly Peace 1** (p64) and take the underground tunnel beneath Dongchang'an Jie to Tiananmen Square. To your west rises the monolithic mass of the **Great Hall of the People 2** (p65), its columned pomposity mirrored to your east by the **Museum of Chinese History and the Museum of the Chinese Revolution 3** (p67). Ahead of you stands the **Monument to the People's Heroes 4** (p66), last

Walk Facts

Start Gate of Heavenly Peace
End Beijing Hotel; Wangfujing Dajie
Distance 2.5km
Time Two hours

stand of the 1989 student demonstrators before they were driven from the square. Further south is the squat **Chairman Mao Mausoleum 5** (p63) and beyond it Zhengyang Men and the Arrow Tower, together known as **Front Gate 6** (p64). Walk to the east side to the square and, if you wish, fortify yourself with a meal of Peking duck at the branch of **Quanjude Roast Duck Restaurant 7** (p117) just south of the entrance to Dongjiaomin Xiang (Dongjiaomin Alley). Enter Dongjiaomin Xiang (formerly known as Legation St). Ahead on your right-hand side at No 40 is a green-roofed, orange brick building that was the site of the **former Dutch Legation 8**. Further along on your left hand side is the **Supreme Court 9** (Zuìgāo Rénmín Fǎyuàn), and on the other side of the road stands a building with huge pillars, the former address of the First National City Bank of New York (Huāqí Yínháng), now serving as the **Beijing Police Museum 10** (☎ 8522 2223; 36 Dongjiaomin Xiang; ☯9am-4pm Tue-Sun). About 20m up the road at No 34 (on your right) is an imposing, red brick building with pillars, the former address of the **Banque de L'Indo-Chine 11** (Dōngfāng Huìlǐ Yínháng). Look very carefully under the window

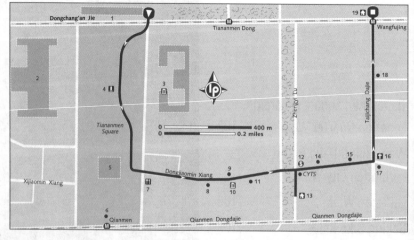

on the right, and you will be able to make out ghostly, faded Chinese characters that say 'Long live the mighty leader Chairman Mao'. Under the window on the left are the discernible characters 'Love live the mighty Chinese Communist Party'. Keep walking east to the domed **Minsheng Bank 12** at 4a Zhengyi Lu, on the corner of Zhengyi Lu and Dongjiaomin Xiang, which was the Yokahama Specie Bank during legation days. Pop in and take a look at the period features adorning the interior, especially the ceiling. North up Zhengyi Lu on the right-hand side of the road was the former Japanese Legation, opposite the British Legation to the west, now occupied by the Ministry of State Security and the Ministry of Public Security. South down Zhengyi Lu and beyond the branch of CYTS is the **Huafeng Hotel 13** (p155), on the site of the former Grand Hotel des Wagon-Lits (Liùguó Fàndiàn). Backtrack and continue along Dongjiaomin Xiang. The low, grey building at No 19 is the former **French post office 14**, now serving as the Jingyuan Sichuan Restaurant. Further ahead behind the grey wall is the **former French Legation 15**. The main gate stands at No 15, a big red entrance guarded by a pair of stone lions and impassive security guards. The Capital Hotel on the other side of the road sits on the grounds of the former German Legation. Ahead of you at No 11 rise up the twin spires of the Gothic **St Michael's Church 16** (Dongjiaomin Catholic Church). The green roofs and ornate red brickwork of the buildings in the compound opposite are the structures of the **former Belgian Legation 17** (until recently, one of these buildings functioned as the Ruijin Guesthouse, but it no longer takes foreigners). Walk north along Taijichang Dajie (formerly Rue Marco Polo) and look out for the brick street sign embedded in the northern wall of Taijichang Toutiao, carved with the old name of the road, **Rue Hart 18**. Located along the north side of Rue Hart was the Austro-Hungarian Legation, south of which was the site of the Peking Club, entered through a gate on Taijichang Dajie. At the north end of Taijichang Dajie and across Dongchang'an Jie is the **Beijing Hotel 19** (p154), parts of which date back to 1900.

WANGFUJING DAJIE TO THE FORBIDDEN CITY WALK

This walk guides you along Beijing's most famous shopping street before leading you to the Forbidden City via historic backstreets and sights. You continue from the conclusion of the Tiananmen Square and Foreign Legation Quarter Walk, or simply take the subway to Wangfujing station where this expedition commences.

Facing north up Wangfujing Dajie, on your left is the Beijing Hotel, while to your east is **Oriental Plaza 1** (p145), a gargantuan shopping mall that extends the entire block to Dongdan Beidajie. This was formerly the site of the world's largest McDonald's, but it and other businesses were forced out to accommodate this colossal construction project. Follow the throng of shoppers if you wish and spend an hour or so exploring Asia's largest shopping mall. The mall is crowned with the elegant and sophisticated Grand Hyatt Hotel (p154) and fountain displays attract crowds on the pavements along Dongchang'an Jie during the summer months.

Just north of Oriental Plaza is the **Wangfujing Bookstore 2**, one of Beijing's largest bookstores and a great place to pick up maps. Just beyond the large McDonald's (where the pedestrianised part of Wangfujing Dajie begins) is the **Beijing Arts and Crafts Central Store 3** (p144), containing several floors of arts and crafts. On the corner here is a branch of **Donglaishun 4**, a well-known Muslim restaurant specialising in hotpot. Next along the same side of the road is **Chenggu Zhai 5**, a jade and jadeite outlet over two floors, opposite the huge **Haoyou Emporium 6** (Hǎoyǒu Shìjiè Shāngchǎng). South of the Haoyou Emporium, a **páilóu 7** (decorative archway) leads to **Wangfujing Snack St 8** (p118), a bustling open-air corner of food stalls and take-away restaurants. Further into Wangfujing Snack St, alleyways are given over to the Haoyuan Market (p144) where you can trawl for souvenirs, collectibles and odds and ends. Also here is the **Jingdezhen**

Walk Facts

Start Oriental Plaza
End Forbidden City
Distance 2.8km
Time Two to three hours

Ceramic City 9 (p145), a store covering several floors selling brightly lit ceramics and porcelain pieces (some are gaudy, others are of interest).

If you need calories, buried down Shuaifuyuan Hutong (Shuaifuyuan Alley) just beyond the Zhongguo Zhaoxiang photographic shop on the right-hand side of Wangfujing Dajie is a branch of **Quanjude Roast Duck Restaurant 10** (p117) and **Goubuli 11** (p119), restaurant chains with nationwide reputations. Continue along Shuaifuyuan Hutong and you will see the Chinese-style Beijing Union Hospital. Back on Wangfujing Dajie is a branch of **Ten Fu's Tea 12** (p146), a Chinese tea store where you can pop in and taste their brews before purchasing. A bit further along on the same side of the street, you will find the **New China Children's Toy World 13** (p146), a frantic sprawl of children's games and gadgets on the other side of the road.

Ahead on the other side of the road is the **Beijing Department Store 14** (Běijīng Bǎihuò Dàlóu), in ages past Beijing's largest department store. A further branch of Goubuli (p119), where you can snack on Tianjin's renowned *baozi* (filled buns), sits on Dayuanfu Hutong just to the south. On the east side of Wangfujing Dajie stretches the long mass of the **Dong An Plaza 15** and the **Sundongan Plaza 16**, all the way to Jinyu Hutong. Head to the top floor of Sundongan Plaza for its large food court, or enjoy a film at Sundongan Cinema City (p136) on the 5th floor.

Keep strolling north along Wangfujing Dajie to the dignified presence of **St Joseph's Church 17** (p85), also known as the East Cathedral. Until just a few years ago, the church was derelict and buried away, but the place of worship has been spruced up and restored, adding inestimable character and history to Wangfujing Dajie.

Backtrack south and head along Donganmen Dajie to the congregation of vocal stallholders at the **Donghuamen Night Market 18** (p121) plying their snacks and culinary exotica from the four corners of China on the right-hand side of the road. At the junction of Donganmen Dajie and Donghuangchenggen Nanjie is the thin strip of the **Imperial Wall Foundation Ruins Park 19** (Huáng Chéng Gēn Yízhǐ Gōngyuán), which traces the foundations of the Imperial City Wall all the way north to Diananmen Dongdajie. Cross the road over the hollow at the foot of the park as it divides to allow traffic to pass from Donghuamen Dajie to Dongan-

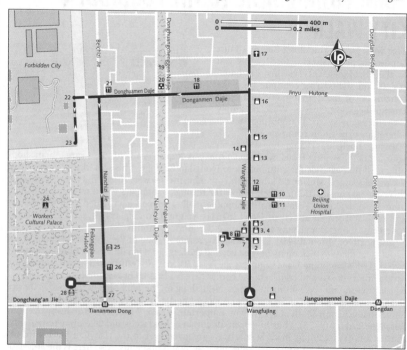

Walking across the cobblestones, Forbidden City (p76)

men Dajie, descend the stairs and examine the pitiful remains of **Dongan Men 20** (p76) – the razed east gate of the Imperial City.

Traverse the road, pass the Cui Ming Zhuang Hotel (p157) and continue west along Donghuamen Dajie to the **Courtyard Restaurant 21** (p119), hidden behind a frond of bamboo. From here you can peruse the contemporary and minimalist art gallery in the basement or appreciate the view over the lake of the Forbidden City from one of the leather sofas in the cigar room upstairs. Just west over the bridge that straddles the Forbidden City moat is the twin-eaved **Donghua Men 22**, the east gate of the Forbidden City. Moat-side stone seats are located here, so you can take the weight off your feet and enjoy the vista.

From here, you can (if you wish) follow the wall of the Forbidden City (the last intact city wall of Ming and Qing dynasty Beijing) all the way south to the Meridian Gate (p77); on the way you will pass one of the intricate **decorative corner towers 23** of the Forbidden City wall. Alternatively, head south down Nanchizi Dajie. With its attractive historic rooftops and brickwork, regularly spaced trees and narrow *hutong* openings, the street is thick with the flavours of traditional Beijing, and the foliage affords comfortable shade in summer. Walk past its numerous restaurants, tobacconists, barbers and teashops, and if you want, hang a right into the **Supreme Temple 24** (p72) in the Workers' Cultural Palace through the park's east gate.

On the other side of the road are the **Imperial Archives 25** (Huángshǐ Chéng; p65) and the Wan Fung Art Gallery, both well worth a visit. The small *hútong* (alleyway) just opposite the south gate of the Imperial Archives has the splendid name of Feilongqiao Hutong (Flying Dragon Bridge Alley). Just south on the corner of the Imperial Archives is the lavish **Tiandi Yijia restaurant 26** (p117), housed in elegant, restored architecture. Running to the east and west along Dongchang'an Jie is **Changpuhe Park 27** (Chāngpú Hé Gōngyuán). If you turn west, you can visit the **Imperial City Museum 28** (p65) and then continue along to the **Gate of Heavenly Peace** (p64), **Tiananmen Square** (p70) and the **Forbidden City** (p76).

LAKESIDE WALK

Begin your walk at the **Prince Gong's Residence 1** (p94) on the east side of Liuyin Jie, a broad and dignified willow-lined alley with many *sìhéyuàn* (courtyard houses) to the west of Qianhai Lake (also called Shichahai or the Ten Buddhist Temple Sea). Three of the People's Liberation Army 'Ten Great Marshals' used to live on this alley, which today resembles a parking lot for tour buses.

Walk Facts

Start Prince Gong's Residence
End Beihai Park
Distance 3km
Time Two to three hours

Walking south away from Prince Gong's Residence, the road becomes Qianhai Xijie, a thoroughfare that was formerly known as Yùhé Gùdào (Old Course of the Jade River). Rounding the corner, heading north away from you is **Tanzi Hutong 2** (Carpet Alley) named after the erstwhile local produce. This *hútòng* (alleyway) leads north to Dongmeichang Hutong (East Coal Factory Alley), and north of that lies the more poetically named Daxiangfeng Hutong (Large Circling Phoenix Alley).

Further on, Qianhai Xijie takes an abrupt turn south past the **Guo Moruo Former Residence 3** (p80). Relentless pedicab *hutong* operators might swarm around you at this stage; just fend them off unless you need a tour. Keep walking east along the alley now called Qianhai Beiyan, and you'll see a bike rental outlet on your left, opposite the bulky Shuaifu Restaurant. Just beyond the restaurant is the north entrance to **Lotus Lane 4** (p119), a restored lakeside stretch of cafés, including Kosmo (p120), and shops looping south to Dianmen Xidajie; it's worthy of a diversion for coffee or some lunch.

Continue along Qianhai Beiyan and you will shortly arrive at Qianhai Lake, with shops and the occasional café on your left. From here whenever inviting *hutong* openings appear, you can dive in and explore whenever you feel like it. Small, carved stone seats have been positioned facing the lake for you to admire the view.

Follow the waterline and then round the corner and amble along Houhai Nanyan, which runs along the south side of Houhai Lake. The lakeside perch is now littered with cafés, bars and crafts shops virtually along its entire length, so take your pick from the selection. There's the Hutong Bar, Jack's Bar, the Wave Café, the Houhai Café & Bar (p128) and others. A smaller and more limited operation is taking off on the opposite bank.

Head back towards Qianhai Lake to cross **Silver Ingot Bridge 5**, and then hang a right onto Yandai Xijie (Chinese Pipe Cross-St) with its shops, bars and cafés, which are quickly dislodging the dilapidated businesses that once operated here. The ancient and diminutive **Guangfuguan Taoist Temple 6** has now been converted into a café called the Guangfuguan Greenhouse (p128), run by an artist; it's on your left as you walk down Yandai Xijie – look out for the rounded archway. The road is an amazing confluence of old and new Beijing with Tibetan and ethnic jewellery shops and cafés cheek by jowl with bicycle repair workshops and dazed-looking locals.

Exiting onto bustling Dianmenwai Dajie, you will see the **Drum Tower 7** rising massively to the north, obscuring the **Bell Tower 8** behind; both are worth a visit. Dianmenwai Dajie is named after Dian Men, the north gate of the Imperial City. The meridian line that once bisected old Beijing ran through the Front Gate, the Gate of Heavenly Peace, the main halls of the Forbidden City, Dian Men and the Drum and Bell Towers, so they all lie on the same north–south axis.

Traditional lanterns, Prince Gong's Residence (p94)

Head back to Silver Ingot Bridge and walk south along the east bank of Qianhai Lake, past the famous Muslim restaurant **Kaorouji 9** (p120) and the Mongol dynasty **Wanning Bridge 10** to your left, with its original stonework dating from 1285. The weather-beaten stone beasts that lie prone on either side of the bank appear to be water dragons. Further on you will encounter another bike rental outfit and then, exiting onto Dianmen Xidajie, you can cross the road and make your way into **Beihai Park 11** (p73), with its host of attractions.

BEIJING BIKE RIDE

Beijing's sprawling distances and scattered sights can make for blistering sightseeing on foot, but voyaging the city's streets and alleyways by bike allows you to take it all in at just the right speed. Hop on a pair of wheels, get that bell jangling and tour past some of the city's finest monuments and through rarely visited reaches off the beaten track.

Bike Ride Facts

Start Donghua Men
End Arrow Tower
Distance 12km
Time Three hours

Start at **Donghua Men 1**, the east gate of the Forbidden City, and cycle south between the moat and the red walls of the palace, observing in particular the **southeast corner tower 2** of the wall of the Forbidden City. The walls around the palace, 10m high and containing 12 million bricks, are adorned at each corner with one such tower (*jiǎolóu*). Each tower is of highly elaborate construction with exceptional roof arrangements, supporting three eaves.

The trip around the moat is a spectacular route with unique views of historic Beijing. When you reach the large gate of **Quezuo Men 3** you might have to dismount, but you can push your bike through and past the face of the **Meridian Gate 4** (Wǔmén; p73), the entrance to the Forbidden City. Tour guides and hawkers might pounce, so push on through unless you want to park your wheels and tour the palace. Traversing the courtyard, take your bike through the gate of **Queyou Men 5** to continue your jaunt along the moat. At the junction with Xinhuamen Dajie is the **Purple Vine Teahouse 6** (p120), promising restorative cups of *chá*. Straight ahead to the west are the eastern gates to **Zhongnanhai 7** (p90), the strictly out-of-bounds

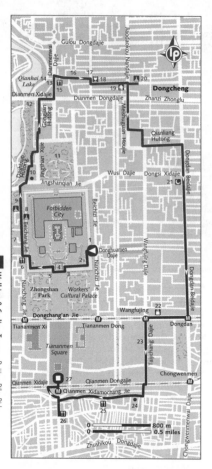

(without official invitation) nerve centre of political power in Beijing.

Head north onto Beichang Jie, west of the Forbidden City, and spot the bright red doors and brass knockers of several *sìhéyuàn* (courtyard homes) strung out along the road. You'll pass **Fuyuo Temple 8** (Fúyòu Sì) to your right – sadly locked away behind closed gates and the palace wall; but you can catch a glimpse of its roofs. Built at the start of the Qing dynasty, the temple was once a study for the Kangxi emperor and later served as a Lama temple. It was also known as the Rain God Temple (Yǔshén Miào).

On your left at No 39 are the now crumbling remains of the **Wanshouxinglong Temple 9** (Wànshòuxīnglóng Sì) – its band of monks long gone and now stripped of its holiness and occupied by Beijing residents. Dating from the reign of the Kangxi emperor, the temple was built on the site of a Ming dynasty arsenal and after 1949 served as the residence for surviving imperial eunuchs. Look for its white-painted archway, graced with full-form Chinese characters on the plaque above. Other temples of the Imperial City could also be found on this road; at 81 Beichang Jie was the Ming dynasty **Jingmo Temple**, which has disappeared.

When you reach the T-junction with Jingshanqian Jie and Wenjin Jie, bear right onto Jingshan Qianjie. The huge Taoist Dagaoxuan Temple once occupied this portion of Jingshan Qianjie, its eastern wall hedging up against Jingshan Xijie and its western wall enclosed by Dashizuo Hutong. Bounded to the north by Zhishanmen Jie (on a level with the east gate of Beihai Park), it was a huge rectangular complex occupying 1500 sq m. Fronted by a huge *páifāng* (memorial archway), the temple was badly damaged by foreign soldiers during the Boxer Rebellion (according to Chinese sources) and was eventually pulled down in 1956 when Jingshan Qianjie was widened.

Continuing along Jingshan Qianjie, take the first small *hutong* on the left just to the east of a restaurant and the orange shells of some public phones); the alley bends to the right, then left. This small *hutong*, called **Dashizuo Hutong 10** (Big Stonemason's Alley), where the stone for the Forbidden City was carved, is like many in Beijing – a mix of tumbledown dwellings and charmless modern blocks. Follow the *hutong* to the end, and exit opposite the west gate of **Jingshan Park 11** (p81); park your bike if you want and clamber up the hill for unparalleled views over the Forbidden City.

Cycle north along Jingshan Xijie and at the northern tip of the street head up Gongjian Hutong; its entrance is virtually straight ahead of you. You will exit the alley on Dianmen Xidajie. Turn left if you want to visit **Beihai Park 12** (p73). Push your bike along the southern side of Dianmen Xidajie, and you'll soon arrive at the northern gate of the park, from where you can easily reach the Buddhist Xītiān Fànjìng (p74), a temple well worth a perusal.

Continuing north, you can push your bike over the zebra crossing, then cycle along Qianhai Nanyan running along the east shore of Qianhai and take your bike through the district covered on the Lakeside Walk (p106). Or you can cycle east and then head up Dianmenwai Dajie (look out for the Drum Tower straight ahead with the Bell Tower behind it). You will soon cross the ancient **Wanning Bridge 13** (Wànníng Qiáo) straddling a small strip of water bled from the lake. Look over the sides of the bridge and note the worn statues of water dragons on either bank. This historic bridge dates from the Yuan dynasty, when it was originally made of wood. Note that part of the bridge has been restored with new marble, although much of the original Mongol era stonework survives. Also look directly to the west where you will see the small, restored white marble **Jinding Bridge 14** (Gold Ingot Bridge).

Just north of Wanning bridge on the eastern side of the road is a branch of the restaurant chain **Tianwaitian Roast Duck Restaurant 15** (p121), where you can restore some calories with a good-value plate of roast duck. Take the first right after the restaurant onto **Mao'er Hutong 16**. Despite being quite modern in its earlier section, it gradually emerges into something more traditional. Ahead, you'll pass a wall-mounted brass plaque that gives you a rundown on the history of Mao'er Hutong. Note the impressive brick carvings on the door of No 3; No 5 is a Qing dynasty courtyard house with a very well-preserved spirit wall (*yǐngbì*). One of Beijing's few famous historic gardens, Keyuan, lies along the alley at Nos 9 to 11; sadly, it is not open to the public. No 13 was the former address of Feng Guozhang, a famous northern warlord, while No 45 was the former Qing military commander's government office.

At the first main junction along Mao'er Hutong, the alley changes its name to Beibing Masi Hutong (famous for being the location of three of Beijing's theatres). The two alleys are divided by the north–south-running **Nanluogu Xiang 17**, one of Beijing's most famous alleyways. Cycle down Nanluogu Xiang and, if you want to rest your feet, take in a coffee in relaxed, snug courtyard surrounds by popping into the **Passby Bar 18** (p128). The café-bar, delightfully installed in an old courtyard home, sits on the corner of the second *hutong* turning on your left as you cycle south. Also look out for hole-in-the-wall kebab sellers that cook sizzling lamb kebab skewers along the alley; these shouldn't cost you more than Y0.50 each and are an economical and tasty way to stave off hunger.

Take the second turn on your left just beyond the Passby Bar at the street sign that says 'Police Station'. You are now cycling along Banchang Hutong, a charming stretch of old *sìhéyuàn*, a number of which are adorned with plaques attesting to their historic significance. You'll pass the old **Lusongyuan Hotel 19** (p159) at No 22, an old courtyard house now serving as a hotel.

Cycling through Beijing's busy streets

As Banchang Hutong meets Jiaodaokou Nandajie, it's worth taking a small detour north and into the first *hutong* entrance on your right – Fuxue Hutong. A very short way along the alley on the left-hand side is the **Wen Tianxiang Temple 20** (p85). The temple is fronted by a huge, recently restored *páilou* (decorated archway) emblazoned with the characters 'Lingxing Men'.

Head south along Jiaodaokou Nandajie, cross the junction with Dianmen Dongdajie and continue south down Meishuguan Houjie. Take the fourth street on your left and follow the promisingly named Dafosi Dongjie (Big Buddha Temple East St). Enter the alley and follow it around as it turns south. Sadly, there's not a lot to see along this stretch, but as you head south take the second left into the courtyard-studded alley of Qianliang Hutong. Exiting Qianliang Hutong, hang a right onto Dongsi Beidajie, a lively stretch of shops and restaurants. As you head south, cross the intersection with Dongsi Xidajie and continue along Dongsi Nandajie, past the **Dongsi Mosque 21** on your right (the mosque guardians might be fickle about admitting non-Muslims).

Continuing down Dongsi Nandajie, the road becomes known as Dongdan Beidajie. Busy with shops and shoppers, it meets Dongchang'an Jie at the eastern end of **Oriental Plaza 22** (p145). Turn right onto Dongchang'an Jie. At the western extent of Oriental Plaza, and the start of Wangfujing Dajie, turn left and instead cycle down Taijichang Dajie into the former **Foreign Legation Quarter 23** (p63). See the Tiananmen Square and Foreign Legation Quarter Walk (p102) for a rundown of sights in this district.

At the end of Taijichang Dajie, cross Qianmen Dongdajie and keep heading south down Ximi Hutong (Little Rice Alley). Turn right into Xidamochang Jie and head west. After around 250m, you'll see the entrance for **Beijing Underground City 24** (p62) on your left, between 64 and 62 Xidamochang Jie. This vast subterranean labyrinth, which dates back to the 1960s, is worth a visit, and tours are available.

Continue west along Xidamochang Jie to its conclusion, which ends in a babble of vocal restaurant owners urging you in for a bite to eat. You could also seek out **Liqun Roast Duck Restaurant 25** (p116) on Beixiangfeng Hutong, or alternatively Beijing's most famous roast duck restaurant – **Qianmen Quanjude Roast Duck Restaurant 26** (p117) – is just round the corner on Qianmen Dajie.

Your bike ride ends at the busy and frantic swell of Qianmen Dajie, overlooked by the enormous and brooding **Arrow Tower** of **Front Gate 27** (Qian Men; p64). Hope you enjoyed the trip!

Eating

Eating

TWO POINTED STICKS OF IVORY OR EBONY, DO THE OFFICE OF KNIFE AND FORK; THEIR MEATS ARE CUT INTO SMALL SQUARE PIECES, AND SERVED UP IN BOWLS; THEIR SOUPS ARE EXCELLENT, BUT THEY USE NO SPOONS; SO THAT AFTER SIPPING THE THIN, THE GROSSER PARTS OF IT ARE DIRECTED TO MOUTH BY THEIR CHOPSTICKS.

An Historical Account of the Embassy to the Emperor of China, Sir George Staunton (1797).

The Chinese can seem prudish and straight-laced (read Confucian), but if there's one big steamy love affair in their lives, it's got to be food. Dining is a kind of social lubricant where the Chinese are most relaxed. It's the meeting ground for romance, the context in which business deals are cemented, old friendships revived and new acquaintances forged. As a commodity, food in China has periodically been in very short supply and there's a collective memory of shortages and famine. Food is life and as such life is food.

If you want to catch the Chinese in their element, take in a Chinese restaurant in full swing. Mealtimes buzz with energy, for dining is a social event that sees the Chinese at their most gregarious and appealing. There's no shortage of theatre: from the demure bow of the *xiǎojie* (waitress), clad from ankle to nape in a ruby red, figure-hugging *cheongsam*, to the energetic ritual of toasts, fuelling laughter and applause, and the selfless histrionics that welcome the tab. Dinners are warm, relaxed and communal occasions where dishes are shared, cigarettes liberally handed round, glasses punctiliously refilled by the host and there's never any squabbling over the bill.

Beijing cuisine (*jīngcài*) is one of the four major Chinese styles of cooking (p33) so home town specialities should be obligatory engagements for all visitors. Ballooning incomes and the droves of foreigners coming to town have, however, provoked a Cultural Revolution of sorts in Beijing's restaurant scene. Even the most insistent diners will meet their match in Beijing's doggedly inventive restaurants. There was a time when Beijing's humdrum restaurant selection was enough to make you throw in the tea towel. Times have changed and once you've sampled the institutional delicacy of Peking duck you can indulge in whatever takes your fancy.

The kitchen gloves have truly come off; with more money sloshing around town, chefs from afar have congregated in Beijing to feed the latest fad. If it's Chinese you want, you

Dining on Wangfujing Snack Street, Dongcheng (p118)

Street Food Beijing Style

Off the main roads and in Beijing's alleys is a world teeming with steaming food stalls and eateries buzzing with activity. Be adventurous and eat this way, and you will be dining as most Beijingers do.

Breakfast can be easily catered for with a *yóutiáo* (deep-fried dough stick), a sip of *dòuzhī* (bean curd drink) or a bowl of *zhōu* (rice porridge). Other snacks include the crunchy, pancake-like and filling *jiānbing*; *jiānbing* vendors are easily spotted as they cook from tricycle-mounted white painted wooden stalls where pancakes are fried on a large circular griddle. The heavy meat-filled *ròubǐng* (cooked bread filled with finely chopped pork) are lifesavers and very cheap. A handy vegetarian option is *jiǔcài bǐng* (bread stuffed with cabbage, chives, leek or fennel and egg). *Dàbǐng* (a chunk of round, unleavened bread sprinkled with sesame seeds) can be found everywhere and of course there's *mántou* (steamed bread). *Málà tàng* is a spicy noodle soup (very warming in winter) with chunks of *dòufu* (tofu), cabbage and other veggies; choose your own ingredients from the trays. Also look out for *ròu jiamò*, a scrumptious open-your-mouth-wide bun filled with diced lamb, chilli and garlic shoots. Another must are *kǎo yángròu chuàn* (lamb kebabs), which make for a scrumptious and cheap snack or meal. You can find kebab chefs all over town; you can try the more expensive **Donghuamen Night Market** (p121), **Wangfujing Snack Street** (p118) or cheaper options that are hidden away down Beijing's alleyways (look for the billowing plumes of smoke), where you can pick up a skewer for around Y0.50. If you want your kebabs spicy ask for *là*; if you don't, ask for *búlà*. Vendors usually belong to either the Muslim Huí or Uyghur minority.

Hóngshǔ (baked sweet potatoes) are cheap, filling snacks (Y2) sold at street stalls throughout the city during winter. Vendors attach oil drums to their bikes which have been converted into mobile ovens. Choose a nice soft sweet potato and the vendor will weigh it and tell you how much it costs.

can't choose a better place to start, for chefs from all over the land are in town. And don't fret if you crave more variety, China's open door policy kicked open the kitchen hatch to world food long ago. Just about any fickle fancy meets its match, so plunge in and start twiddling those chopsticks – some of your best Beijing memories could well be tabletop ones.

Opening Hours

Beijing restaurants are generally open from around 10am to 10pm or 11pm, but it is quite common for establishments to shut at around 2pm and reopen at 5pm or 6pm. The Chinese are accustomed to eating much earlier than Westerners, lunching at around midday and having dinner about 6pm.

How Much?

Despite the rich aromas around town, you won't pay through the nose for it all – eating in Beijing can be inexpensive. But if you insist on lavish dining in style you will not be disappointed.

Eating in Beijing is generally inexpensive; listed below are restaurants catering to all budgets. At cheap eateries, meals (for one) will cost less than Y30 to Y40, mid-range dining options will cost between Y40 to Y100 and top-end choices more than Y100.

Credit cards are accepted at most mid-range hotel restaurants and the most expensive eateries, but not at inexpensive or budget eateries, so make sure you take enough cash.

Be warned that some (but by no means all) restaurants in tourist areas still fob off foreigners with an English menu (*yīngwén càipǔ*) with prices in excess of the Chinese menu. Unfortunately, deciphering the Chinese menu (*zhōngwén càipǔ*) will require either assistance or Chinese reading skills. Be also prepared for lamentable English language skills, even in expensive restaurants. Furthermore, waiting staff at elegant restaurants can occasionally be annoyingly snobbish.

You don't have to travel very far to find recommended restaurants in Beijing. Most can be found within the Second Ring Rd and reaching even the most far-flung does not involve a major expedition. The main restaurant neighbourhoods are Dongcheng, Chongwen and South Chaoyang, and Chaoyang, where you can find a wide choice of dining establishments.

Self-Catering

Eating outside of restaurants in Beijing is not as easy as you may be accustomed to, but there are numerous supermarkets and cafés in town.

Supermarkets are plentiful. In the basement of the Henderson Center opposite the Beijing International Hotel is the well-stocked **Yansha Supermarket** (Map pp239–41; ⏰ 10am-8pm) and there is a further 24-hour **Yansha convenience store** by the Henderson Center's south entrance (facing Beijing Train Station). There's a basement branch of **Park N Shop** (Map pp234–5; 18 Chaoyangmenwai Dajie) at Full Link Plaza, and a well-stocked supermarket in the basement of **Scitech Plaza**, a department store on the southern side of Jianguomenwai Dajie where you can find an extensive range of coffee. Just north of the Great Wall Sheraton is the enormous Lufthansa Center, home to Lufthansa Center Youyi Shopping City (p148), a multi-storey shopping mall. The **Yansha Supermarket** is in the basement, chock-a-block with imported goods. Other useful Chinese supermarkets include a branch of **Jingkelong** (Map pp234–5) in Sanlitun and the 24-hour **Super 24** (Map pp234–5) on Sanlitun Lu. Most visitors will find what they need at such supermarkets, but delis (see below) stock wider selections of foreign cheeses, cured meats and wines. Note that some supermarkets annoyingly insist you hand in your other shopping bags before you browse or purchase goods.

Despite being an acquired taste for the Chinese palate, coffee has become a cherished commodity in Beijing's flourishing café culture. Cafés such as Starbucks can be useful for perusing up-to-date international magazines and newspapers that are otherwise difficult to come by in Beijing. Other chains, however, can charge over the odds for coffee while providing a limp array of reading matter, such as *Beijing Weekend*. If you are spending Y25 on a coffee, expect to be able to flick through copies of *Time*, the *Economist* or the *International Herald Tribune*.

Many restaurants can also deliver food, so phone ahead to check. Alternatively, try Beijing Goodies (☎ 6416 7676/7070; www.beijinggoodies.com; ⏰ 11am-11pm), who deliver from over 35 Beijing restaurants.

CRC SUPERMARKET
Map pp239–41   *Supermarket*
Huárùn Liánsuǒ Cháoshì
China World Shopping Mall, Jianguomenwai Dajie;
⏰ 9.30am-9.30pm; subway Guomao

Apart from this handy branch (adjacent to which is a vintner with a fine selection of wines), CRC has several well-stocked branches around town. CRC can also be found in the **Kerry Mall** (Map pp234–5; Shop B25, Basement, 1 Guanghua Lu; ⏰ 8.30am-10.30pm; subway Chaoyangmen), **Oriental Plaza** (Map pp239–41; shop BB10a, Basement, 1 Dongchang'an Jie; ⏰ 8.30am-10.30pm; subway Wangfujing) and **Huanan Building** (Map pp236–8; 2nd fl, 176 Xidan Beidajie; ⏰ 8.30am-10.30pm; subway Xidan).

CARREFOUR
                                     Supermarket
Jiālèfú
☎ 8460 1030; 6b Beisanhuan Donglu; ⏰ 8am-9.30pm

The French hypermarket chain has gone down a storm in Beijing and is packed to the gills with eager consumers. Carrefour (five Beijing branches to date with annual revenue of US$1.6 billion) stocks virtually everything you may need, takes credit cards, provides ATMs and has a home delivery service. There are branches in the following districts: **Xuanwu** (☎ 8636 2155; 11 Malian Dao; ⏰ 8am-9.30pm); **Fengtai** (☎ 6760 9911; 15 No2 district Fangchengyuan Fangzhuang; ⏰ 8am-9.30pm), **Haidian** (☎ 8836 2729; 54a Zhongguancun Nandajie; ⏰ 8am-9.30pm) and **Zhongguancun**.

APRIL GOURMET Map pp234–5   *Deli*
Lüyèzi Shípǐndiàn
☎ 8460 1030; Sanlitun Beixiaojie; ⏰ 8am-9pm; subway Dongzhimen, then bus 416

April Gourmet is a small deli-style provisions store in the Sanlitun embassy district. The nourishing selection runs to cheese, fresh bread, butter, wine, sauces, Western soups, coffee, milk, meats and frozen food (fish fingers!). The wine selection is good and there's a fattening selection of cheeses (Roquefort, Chaumes, mozzarella, Gouda, Emmental, Brie, Pecorino Romano etc). Another **branch** (Sanlitun Lu; subway Dongsishitiao, then bus 701) is conveniently located opposite the entrance to Sanlitun Dongsi Jie.

JENNY LOU'S Map pp234–5   *Deli*
☎ 6501 6249; 1 Nongzhanguan Nanlu, west gate of Chaoyang Park; ⏰ 8.30am-8pm; subway Dawanglu, then bus 31

This welcoming deli-style chain has several branches around town. Stocking wine, bread, cheese, canned goods and other imported foodstuffs, the chain also offers free delivery within 2km. A further branch can be found on **Sanlitun Beixiaojie**, near April Gourmet (above).

KEMPINSKI DELI Map pp234–5 *Deli*

☎ 6465 3388, ext 5741; Kempinski Hotel, Lufthansa Center, 50 Liangmaqiao Lu; ⏱ 7am-10pm; subway Dongsishitiao, then bus 701

Just off the shuddering Third Ring Rd, the deli in the Kempinski Hotel (p159) is well liked for its desserts, breads and cakes (discounted after 8pm). Tables are available for patrons to park themselves for coffee and a chat in a smart environment.

PATISSERIE Map pp239–41 *Chocolatier*
Sùyuán

☎ 8518 1234, ext 6362; Grand Hyatt Beijing, 1 Dongchang'an Jie; subway Wangfujing

This small outlet is a fine choice if you have to get your hands on quality chocolate – either as a present or to satisfy an admittedly costly (if you shop here) craving.

SCHLOTZSKY'S DELI Map pp239–41 *Deli*
Sìlèsìjì

☎ 6505 0806; 2nd fl, Tower Two, China World Trade Center; ⏱ 8am-9pm Mon-Thur & 11am-8pm Fri-Sun; subway Guomao

This deli offers a great range of its own breads, huge sandwiches on freshly baked sourdough, rye or wheat bread, as well as a range of pizzas. There's another branch in the **Oriental Plaza** (Map pp239–41; ☎ 8518 6810; 1st fl, Oriental Plaza, 1 Dongchang'an Jie; ⏱ 9.30am-9.30pm; subway Wangfujing).

CHONGWEN & SOUTH CHAOYANG

Busy with shoppers and tourists alike, these districts are packed with dining options and have places to suit all budgets. You can dine in style at any of the top-end hotels that gather along Chang'an Jie or delve into the areas around the embassy district of Jianguomen for reliably good food. Some of Beijing's most well known Peking duck restaurants can be found around the bustling Qianmen district and some excellent restaurants are located in the catchment area of the Forbidden City and Wangfujing Dajie.

Eating – Chongwen & South Chaoyang

BE THERE OR BE SQUARE

Map pp239–41 *Cantonese*
Bú Jiàn Bú Sàn

☎ 8518 6518; shop BB71 Oriental Plaza, 1 Dongchang'an Jie; meals Y40; ⏱ 24 hr; subway Wangfujing

This funky chain is a slick yet affordable pit stop for Cantonese favourites including *cha siu* (barbecue pork slices), *siu ngap* (duck), *cha siu bao* (sweet pork-filled buns), *chun kuen* (spring rolls) and noodles. You can also hunt down Western dishes on the menu but they are more so-so. Dishes arrive promptly on the gimmicky tables, and there's a busy efficiency about the staff and the way young professional diners hoover up the chow. Look out for other braches, including the **Henderson Center** (Map pp239–41; Level 2, 18 Jianguomennei Dajie; ☎ 6518 6515; ⏱ 24 hr; subway Jianguomen) and in the **Landmark Tower** (Map pp234–5; 1st fl, 8 Dongsanhuan Beilu; ☎ 6590 6999; ⏱ 6.30am-11pm).

BIANYIFANG Map pp239–41 *Peking Duck*

☎ 6712 0505; 2a Chongwenmenwai Dajie; economy/standard half duck Y44/69; ⏱ 11am-11pm; subway Chongwenmen

Dating back to the reign of the Qing emperor Xianfeng, Bianyifang offers mid-range comfort reminiscent of a faded Chinese three-star hotel with sparse decoration. Roasted in the *menlu* style, the cheaper half ducks cost Y44 to Y69 (plus Y2 for pancakes, scallions and sauce), while ducks prepared in the more expensive Huaxiangsu style are Y84 (half) or Y168 (whole). Ducks find their way into numerous other preparations, including boiled duck blood in hot soup (Y22) and duck hearts in chilli (Y28). A bottle of *Maotai* will set you back Y430, but if you simply require the effect of the alcohol, why not settle for the rougher, locally distilled Erguotou (Y12). Otherwise, jasmine tea will cost you Y10. Be warned that waiting staff will steer you towards the special (read: pricier) duck, so be vigilant.

BLEU MARINE Map pp239–41 *French*
Lán Mǎlì

☎ 6500 6704; 5 Guanghua Xili; mains Y85; ⏱ 11.30am-11.30pm; subway Yonganli

Well-located, civilised and attractively decorated (if you can ignore the traffic outside), this French restaurant manages to put together a new menu daily. Satisfactory dishes include the rich and wholesome onion soup and the veal stew with mushrooms, served on a huge platter. There is an OK wine list too.

DANIELI'S Map pp239–41 *Italian*

☎ 6460 6688, ext 2440/2441; 2nd fl, St Regis, 21 Jianguomenwai Dajie; mains Y100+; ⏱ 11.30am-2pm & 6-10pm

Ensconced in the St Regis, this gorgeous and classy restaurant is Beijing's finest Italian dining choice (the rest of the competition is rather hit and miss), boasting a generous menu and wine list. Glide up the sumptuous marble staircase, past the crackled glass doors to a splendid alcove interior and sit down to a meal served upon marvellously decorated plates.

FENGZEYUAN Map pp239–41 *Shandong*

☎ 6318 6688, ext 125; 83 Zhushikou Xidajie; meals Y60; subway Qianmen

This Beijing institution attracts crowds of locals who toast each other with rounds of snake wine and devour Fengzeyuan's Shāndōng (*lǔcài*) specialities, such as sea cucumber with scallion or sautéed fish slices.

GONGDELIN VEGETARIAN RESTAURANT

Map pp239–41 *Chinese Vegetarian*
Gōngdélín Sùcàiguǎn

☎ 6511 2542; 158 Qianmen Nandajie; meals Y25-40; ⏱ 10.30am-8.30pm; subway Qianmen

One of Beijing's best bloodless dining experiences; restore your karma with dishes of mock meat that taste better than the real thing. A poet has been to work on the menu ('the fire is singeing the snow-capped mountains') even though service is pedestrian and the décor

strictly no-frills. The food is not to be missed and being a card-holding carnivore is simply no excuse.

HENRY J BEAN'S Map pp239–41 *American*
Hēnglì Jiǔba

☎ 6505 2266, ext 6569; shop L129 West Wing, China World Trade Center, 1 Jianguomenwai Dajie; meals Y80; ⏱ 11.30am-11pm; subway Guomao

This may not be your first port of call in Beijing, but Henry J Bean's' baked French onion soup (Y35) is well worth it and the burgers (Y60) are first rate (succulent and cooked as you want it). The fisherman's burger (Y55) is ample and tasty and there's a range of pizzas. The cocktails are a tad pricey, but you can order beer by the pint and there's live music nightly after 9pm.

LIQUN ROAST DUCK RESTAURANT

Map pp239–41 *Peking Duck*
Lìqún Kǎoyādiàn

☎ 6702 5681; 11 Beixiangfeng Hutong; roast duck Y68; ⏱ 10am-10pm; subway Qianmen

Buried away in a maze of *hútong* in east Qianmen is this tiny eatery. It's well known and very busy – chefs scamper about as waiters scurry by with sacks of garlic and crates of Erguotou; no medals for service. Troll past the flaming ovens (fruit tree wood is exclusively used, piled up outside) to reach your table, which may be next to a frame of ducks hanging from hooks. Waiting staff insist you phone first to reserve a table; otherwise turn up off-peak (eg 2.30pm) when most punters have moved on. You will

---

Story of the Duck

Without argument, most people would agree that Peking (or Beijing) duck is the capital's most famous dish. Once imperial cuisine, now the legendary duck dish is served at restaurants around the world.

The culinary history of Peking duck goes as far back as the Yuan dynasty, where it was listed in royal cookbooks as an imperial food. The Qing poet Yuan Mei once wrote in a cookbook, 'roast duck is prepared by revolving a young duckling on a spit in an oven. The chief inspector Fang's family excel in preparing this dish'. When the Qing dynasty fell in 1911, former palace chefs set up restaurants around Beijing and brought the dish to the public.

To prepare the duck, chefs go through a lengthy process. First the ducks are inflated by blowing air between the skin and body. The skin is then pricked and boiling water poured all over the duck. Sometimes the skin is rubbed with malt sugar to give it an amber colour and then is hung up to air dry before being roasted in the oven. When roasted, the flesh becomes crispy on the outside and juicy on the inside. The bird is meticulously cut into 120 slices and served with fermented bean paste, light pancakes, sliced cucumbers and green onions.

Two of the most famous restaurants in Beijing that serve Peking duck are the **Quanjude Restaurant** (p120), which first opened in 1864. Its current location is at Hepingmen. Ducks here are roasted with fruit tree wood, giving the dish a special fragrance.

Another famous restaurant is **Bianyifang Roast Duck Restaurant** (p115), founded in 1855. Instead of fruit tree wood, the ducks here are cooked in an oven with straw as fuel. Prior to being put in the oven the duck is filled with soup.

have to wait about an hour for your duck. The duck is scrummy and there are other dishes on the menu.

MAKYE AME Map pp239–41 *Tibetan*
Mǎjí Āmǐ

☎ 6506 9616; 2nd fl, A11 Xiushui Nanjie; dishes from Y20; ⊙ 11.30am-2am; subway Jianguomen or Yonganli
Tucked behind the Friendship Store, this is one of Beijing's few Tibetan restaurants. There's a comfy upstairs room with atmosphere, an excellent menu and a generous crop of Tibetan ornaments. Go all out for the lamb ribs (Y40), boiled yak with chilli (Y40), *champa* (roasted barley meal) and yoghurt, butter tea and cooling salads (from Y20).

QIANMEN QUANJUDE ROAST DUCK
RESTAURANT Map pp239–41 *Peking Duck*
Qiánmén Quànjùdé Kǎoyādiàn

☎ 6511 2418; 32 Qianmen Dajie; half duck Y58, scallions, sauce Y2; ⊙ 11am-1.30pm & 4.30-8.30pm; subway Qianmen
As fundamental to a Beijing trip as a visit to the Great Wall, the sampling of Peking duck is an absolute must – to miss out you'd have to be completely quackers. Despite the restaurant's name and pedigree (dating back to 1864), service at this branch is pretty lousy (staff sling you sachets of sauce like dealing cards); it's geared mainly to the tourist hordes (with marketing devices and duck props) and it needs to get its act together. Enter to photos of George Bush poking a duck with his finger and Fidel Castro sizing up an imaginary duck with his hands (perhaps they were dining here at the same time), plus other luminaries doing something or other at Quanjude. There is another branch nearby (☎ 6301 8833; 14 Qianmen Xidajie) and a superior branch just off Wangfujing Dajie (p120). There is an English menu and you can get your duck to go at the booth outside (vacuum packed duck Y68; vacuum packed pancakes Y5; vacuum packed duck sausage Y9.80).

TAJ PAVILION Map pp239–41 *Indian*
Tàijí Lóu Yìndù Cāntīng

☎ 6505 5866; 1st fl, West Wing, China World Trade Center; meals from Y100; ⊙ 10.30am-2.30pm & 6-10.30pm; subway Guomao
This relaxing and popular restaurant – voted as the 2003 Best Restaurant in Beijing by expat rag *City Weekend* – has a well-deserved reputation among Beijing expats. There's mild-mannered

service and some mild and not so-mild curries from the land of mouth-burning cuisine. For creamy textures and subtle flavourings try the *palak panir* (Y50), a creamy spinach dish with cottage cheese, or to have smoke jetting from your ears, sample the chicken vindaloo (Y80). There's also a branch in **Chaoyang** (Map pp228–9; ☎ 6436 7678; 3rd fl, Holiday Inn Lido; Jiangtai Lu).

TIANDI YIJIA Map pp239–41 *Chinese Mixed*
Tiāndì Yījiā

☎ 8511 5556; 140 Nanchizi Dajie; meals Y300 ⊙ 11am-2pm & 2-10pm; subway Tiananmen Dong
Doing business from a restored building alongside Changpu River Park (p65), this civilised and refined traditional Chinese courtyard-style restaurant is decked out with traditional furniture, water features and side rooms for snug hotpot dinners come winter. Further rooms upstairs include a banquet room and a balcony overlooking the Imperial Archives (p64). The expensive dishes – from Beijing, Shāndōng, Zhèjiāng and beyond – include shark's fin and abalone. Cantonese dim sum (11am-2pm & 5-9.30pm) is also served. The elegantly presented menus (manufactured from traditional Chinese paper; English version available) may be delivered to your table by snobbish waiting staff – a fly in the ointment. MasterCard, Visa and American Express are all accepted.

TONY ROMA'S Map pp239–41 *American*
Duōlì Luómǎ

☎ 8518 6432; A305 Oriental Plaza, 1 Dongchang'an Jie; meals Y100; ⊙ noon-8.30pm; subway Wangfujing
Not just 'Famous for ribs', Tony Roma's also grills up chicken, shrimp and burgers at this slick outlet. Take all your relatives along to tuck into the family feast platter (Y280), park the kids with the crayons and colouring mats and tune into the funky tableside TV sets.

XIAO WANG'S HOME RESTAURANT
Map pp239–41 *Beijing/Chinese*
Xiǎowáng Fǔ

☎ 6594 3602/6591 3255; 2 Guanghua Dongli; meals Y70; ⊙ 11am-2pm & 5-11pm; subway Guomao or Yonganli
Treat yourself to home style Beijing cuisine from this excellent, bustling restaurant and go for one of Xiao Wang's specials. The deep-fried spareribs with pepper salt (*piāoxiāng páigǔ*; Y38) are simply delectable. Xiao Wang's fried

hot and spicy Xīnjiāng-style chicken wings (zīran jīchì; Y35) are deservedly famous, as is the crispy and lean Peking duck (Y88 per duck, Y5 for sauce, scallions and pancakes). Also try the deep-fried crispy bean curd with mild chilli sauce (Y18) or the barbecue mutton slices with coriander (zīran yángròu; Y28). Xiao Wang – the cordial entrepreneurial owner – has devised a formula that goes down well with both expats and local Chinese. A more sedate, branch can be found in Sanlitun (p123), but the branch that existed on Jianguomenwai Dajie was mercilessly flattened by property developers.

CHEAP EATS

DUYICHU

Map pp239–41 *Chinese Buns*
Dùyīchù Fànzhuāng
☎ 6702 1555; 36 Qianmen Dajie; dishes Y15; subway Qianmen

On the corner of Dashalan Xijie, Duyichu has served delicious steamed *bāozi* for over a century. This is a great place to come to snack on dumplings and buns (veggie options available).

FOOD COURT

Map pp239–41 *Chinese Mixed*
basement, Oriental Plaza, 1 Dongchang'an Jie; dishes from Y10; subway Wangfujing

This hygienic fast food emporium puts yummy Cantonese, Yúnnán, Sìchuān, teppanyaki, clay pot, Korean and porridge (zhōu) outlets all under one roof. Look out for outlets like Hokkien Delights, Lanzhou Noodles, Hotplate Specials, Indian Roti Prata, Shànghǎi and Chinese Dumplings – the latter puts together some great dumplings (jiǎozi; pork, lamb and other fillings) and buns (bāozi). Sichuan Delights serves up a fine chilli-oil red dàndanmiàn (Sìchuān noodles in peppery sauce; Y9). The layout is both intelligent and spacious, and the food generous and good value – you can eat very well for around Y20. Don't pay in cash for your dish – buy a card (Y5 deposit; cards come in denominations of Y30, 50, 100, 200, 500 and 1000 units) at the kiosk at the entrance. Credits are deducted with each dish ordered so you can pick and mix your plates from different outlets (check the expiry date of your card). Don't get timid at the sight of half of Beijing eating here, it's very easy to order. Food is either cooked in front of you canteen-style or arrayed uncooked on plates – it's simply a case of pointing at what you want.

NIUGE JIAOZI

Map pp239–41 *Chinese Dumplings*
Niúgē Jiǎozi
☎ 6525 7472; Nanheyan Dajie; meals Y15; subway Tiananmen Dong

East of the Forbidden City, this pocket-sized and homely restaurant dishes up dozens of varieties of Chinese dumplings (jiǎozi). All the jiǎozi are listed on red plaques on the four walls but there's no English menu. Here's a sample of what you can order: lamb (yángròu; Y5 per liǎng), pork (zhūròu; Y3 per liǎng), beef (niúròu; Y4 per liǎng), donkey (lǘròu; Y8 per liǎng) and mushroom and cabbage (xiāngsū báicài; Y4); but there are many other fillings, from pork and aubergine, to chicken and garlic, celery and chicken and shrimp. There are only around 10 tables draped in simple, embroidered tablecloths, busied over by the restaurant's unfussy and polite owners. The restaurant is opposite the building with the sign on the roof saying 'Hualong St'.

PIZZA FACTORY

Map pp239–41 *Pizza*
☎ 6518 6840; Shop L-1008 Henderson Center, 18 Jianguomennei Dajie; ☽ 10am-10pm; subway Dongdan or Jianguomen

This handy outlet just north of Beijing Train Station (the outlet is on the west side of the Henderson Center, on Beijingzhan Jie), serves sandwiches (Y18-23) and a range of mini to large pizzas (Y23-95), including a vegetarian option, and has a salad bar (Y24).

WANGFUJING SNACK STREET

Map pp239–41 *Chinese Mixed*
west off Wangfujing Dajie; kebabs from Y3, dishes from Y5; ☽ 11am-8pm; subway Wangfujing

Fronted by an ornate archway, this quadrant has bright and cheery restaurants and stalls overhung with colourful banners and bursting with character and flavour. This is a good place to pick up Xīnjiāng or Muslim Uyghur cuisine such as lamb kebabs and flat bread. Also on offer are other dishes from all over China, including málà tàng, zhájiàngmiàn (noodles in fried bean sauce) and noodles in peppery sauce. Also being scoffed by the bowl here are Lánzhōu lāmiàn (Lanzhou noodles), Shāndōng jiānbing (Shandong pancake), Yúnnán guòqiáo mǐxiàn (Yúnnán across-the-bridge noodles) and oodles of Sìchuān food. At most outlets you have to sit outside elbow to elbow with other diners.

DONGCHENG

This historic part of Beijing is ideal for atmospheric and traditional dining options. Snackers can pick up tasty bite-sized morsels at the **Donghuamen Night Market** (p121) or at hole-in-the-wall outlets scattered through the local *hútong*. On the west side of Qianhai Lake is a strip called **Lotus Lane** (Map pp232–3; Tianhe Fang), a trendy batch of recently opened cafés, restaurants and crafts shops. All have views over the lake and sit alongside a newly paved walkway and boardwalk. Many of the bars and cafés in the Houhai and Qianhai Lake area also serve food.

BAGUO BUYI Map pp232–3   *Sichuan*
☎ 6400 8888; 89-3 Dianmen Dongdajie;
dishes from Y8; subway Andingmen or Gulou

This celebrated and award-winning Chengdu restaurant chain delivers fine Sichuan dishes from a marvellous Chinese inn-style setting with balconies, a central stairway and dolled up waiting staff. Enter through huge red doors to a traditional-style building just off Dianmen Dongdajie. There's music, occasional operatic events and a range of very good value dishes for Y8, including *Chóngqìng làzi jī* (Chongqing hot pepper chicken) and *xiānjiāo yúpiàn* (chilli fish slices). The food is first rate and the ambience bursts with both character and theatre. There's a branch in **Xicheng** (☎ 6615 2230; 68 Xizhimen Nanxiaojie).

COURTYARD Map pp232–3   *Fusion*
Sìhé
☎ 6526 8882; 95 Donghuamen Dajie; meals from Y50;
subway Tiananmen Dong

The Courtyard enjoys a peerless location overlooking the Forbidden City. You may have to forage to find the entrance (up the steps curtained by fronds of bamboo), but once inside you will be guided to a table and through a fine menu. The minimalist **art gallery** (☎ 6526 8883) in the basement provides cerebral nutrition and the cigar divan upstairs the perfect conclusion to a meal, but it's the view and the menu that hog the limelight. Among dishes on the menu are New Zealand mussel soup (Y65), steamed Shandong sea bass (Y165), roast half chicken with green olive salsa, chick pea *frites* and sweet Thai soy (Y165) and grilled US Kobe beef (Y245). Sunday lunch is an affordable option at Y150 per person for an aperitif, appetizer, main course, dessert and tea or coffee.

FANGSHAN RESTAURANT
Map pp232–3   *Imperial Chinese*
Fángshàn Fànzhuāng
☎ 6401 1889; Jade Islet, Beihai Park; set menus
Y100-500; ⏱ 11am-1.30pm & 5-7.30pm

Beijing's most elaborate imperial cuisine is served up in this restaurant in a pavilion overlooking the lake in Beihai Park (enter through either the west or south gate). All dishes are elaborately prepared, and range from delicately filled pastries to sea cucumber with deer tendon, peppery inkfish-egg soup and camel paw with scallion (no, it's not a real camel paw). The Y500 menu will get you rare delicacies such as bird's nest soup, abalone and turtle meat. Reservations are a must. Another less expensive **branch** (Map pp239–41; ☎ 6523 3555; 12 Dongzongbu Hutong) can be found to the east of Chaoyangmen Nanxiaojie.

GOUBULI
Map pp232–3   *Chinese Buns*
Gǒubùlǐ
12 Dayuanfu Hutong; set meals Y10; ⏱ 11am-8pm;
subway Wangfujing

The renowned Tiānjīn *bāozi* (filled buns) outlet has set up several branches in Beijing. This branch just south of the Beijing Department Store serves up fine meat-filled buns (Y10 for nine pork or mushroom and vegetable *bāozi*). The restaurant sign is only in Chinese; as you head down Dayuanfu Hutong west of Wangfujing Dajie, look out for the bright yellow sign on the left. There is another branch in **Shuaifuyuan Hutong** (Map pp239–41; ☎ 6525 7314) east of Wangfujing Dajie, and a huge branch in **Dashilar** (☎ 6315 2389; 31 Dazhalan Jie).

GREEN TIANSHI VEGETARIAN
RESTAURANT   *Chinese Vegetarian*
Lǜsè Tiānshí Sùcàiguǎn
☎ 6524 2349/2476; 57 Dengshikou Dajie;
meals from Y50; ⏱ 10.30am-9pm

Mount the stairway past the shop on the 1st floor to the 2nd floor restaurant and one of Beijing's longest serving vegetarian dining experiences. Green Tianshi cooks up simulated meat dishes entirely fashioned from vegetables and presented in a relaxed and attractive environment. There is no alcohol served on the premises; a handy picture menu helps steer you to the right dish.

Eating – Dongcheng

HUANG TING Map pp232–3 *Chinese*

☎ 8516 2888, ext 6707; Peninsula Palace, 8 Jinyu Hutong; meals Y150; 🕐 11.30am-2.30pm & 6-10pm; subway Dongdan

Faux Old Peking is taken to an extreme in the courtyard setting of Huang Ting. Enter though a *sìhéyuàn* (courtyard house) entrance with carved lintels and a wooden portal to an interior fashioned from grey bricks with stone lions, water features, bird cages, stone floor flagging, decorated lanterns and Ming and Qing dynasty-style mahogany and sandalwood furniture – it's like a Fifth Generation film set. Despite its artificiality and location (in the bowels of a five star hotel), the setting is impressive, caressed by the sounds of *zhēng*, *pípa* and other traditional Chinese instruments. With so many of Beijing's *hútong* falling to the sledgehammers of property developers, diners can toast their demise from the comfort of this simulacrum. Even the loos have their own wooden door and brass courtyard-style handles. Despite the Beijing setting there are also Cantonese dishes (including dim sum). Dishes include whole Peking duck (Y220), roast suckling pig (Y100), braised spareribs in tangy brown sauce (Y70) and braised 'Beijing style' meatball with cabbage (Y40).

KAOROUJI Map pp232–3 *Chinese Muslim*

☎ 6404 2554; 14 Qianhai Dongyuan; meals Y55; 🕐 11am-10pm; subway Gulou

Near Silver Ingot Bridge (Yíndìng Qiáo) close to the Drum Tower (p76) is this old Beijing stand-by that has been firing its ovens since Qing times. If joining our Lakeside Walk (p106) or Beijing Bike Ride (p107) you will pass nearby, so you can stock up on calories with the flavoursome coriander-laced roast mutton (Y45), barbecue lamb (Y38) along with hot and sour soup (Y18), sesame buns (*gōngbào jīdīng*; Y14) and roast duck (Y48). Although the décor won't have you jumping for joy, the lakeside positioning is a plus.

KOSMO Map pp232–3 *Café*

☎ 6611 0214; 5 Tianhe Fang (Lotus Lane), Qianhai Xiyan; coffee Y10; subway Gulou

This trendy and relaxing café serves up ultra-health conscious organic herbal teas, fruit juices and a range of coffees (organic as well) from its two-storey glass fronted premises overlooking Qianhai Lake. You can also purchase a variety of organically grown coffee from around the world, including Peruvian *Montealto* and Colombian *Supremo Condor*

de la Sierra. Daily brew (Y10) and walnut cake slice (Y10).

LIUJIA GUO Map pp232–3 *Hunan*

☎ 6524 1487; 19 Nanheyan Dajie; meals Y80; subway Tiananmen Dong

Eye-poppingly hot Húnán (*Xiāngcài*) cuisine is a cauldron of flaming flavour, marked by a rampant use of chilli and other spices. Liujia Guo, however, goes easy on the seasoning, serving up medium-hot dishes that won't have you gagging. The grilled beef (Y28) is sizzlingly excellent and the 'Mao family fashion braised pork' (Y28) is fantastic – rich chunks of fatty pork steeped in a strong sauce. There are also a few vegetarian dishes such as mock mutton (Y20) and 'peasant family fashion eggplants' (Y16). Service is good and the restaurant is finely positioned east of the Forbidden City. There's no English sign; look for the one-storey building capped in traditional green tiles and hung with red lanterns on the west side of Nanheyan Dajie.

PURPLE VINE TEAHOUSE

Map pp232–3 *Chinese Teahouse*

Zǐténglú Cháyúguǎn

☎ 6606 6614; 2 Nanchang Jie; tea from Y40; subway Dongsishitiao or Dongzhimen

Experience a traditional tea ceremony at the Purple Vine Teahouse, where you'll be greeted with the gentle sounds of *gǔzhēng* music and the smell of incense. Traditional Chinese furniture and century-old Shanxi wooden screens decorate this tiny oasis just outside the west gate of the Forbidden City. Choose from the menu of jasmine, black, green or oolong teas; a pot ranges in price from Y40 up to Y250 for oolong. There's another branch in **Sanlitun** (Map pp234–5). The teahouse accepts all major credit cards.

QUANJUDE ROAST DUCK RESTAURANT Map pp232–3 *Peking Duck*

Quànjùdé Kǎoyādiàn

☎ 6525 3310; 9 Shuaifuyuan Hutong; standard/special duck Y108/168; 🕐 11am-1.30pm & 4.30-8.30pm; subway Wangfujing

This huge and well-presented restaurant is less famous than its Qianmen sibling (p117), but more convenient if you're shopping along Wangfujing Dajie and less touristy. Examine the English menu under the light of the glittering chandeliers and go for a half duck (Y54, minus pancakes, scallions and sauce) or a range of other duck dishes including ducks' webbed feet with mustard sauce (Y32), salted duck liver (Y24) or deep fried duck heart (Y80). There's also seafood and a variety of vegetable dishes.

RED CAPITAL CLUB Map pp232–3 *Beijing*
Xīnhóngzī Jùlèbù

☎ 6402 7150 day, 8401 8886 night & weekends; 66 Dongsi Jiu Tiao; dishes from Y60; subway Dongsishitiao, then bus 113

Hidden away down a quiet *hútong* is this meticulously restored Qing-styled courtyard house, offset by props from a 1950s Politburo meeting room and cuisine from Zhōngnánhǎi (p90). It's pricey, leans heavily on the nostalgia pedal and the prolix menu requires dedication and patience (every dish has an accompanying myth), but the food hits the mark. Look for the big red doors with no sign. Reservations required. The restaurant is next door to the Red Capital Residence (p158).

SICHUAN RESTAURANT
Map pp232–3 *Sichuan*

☎ 6513 7591/7593; 37a Dong'anmen Dajie; meals Y50; subway Wangfujing

This spacious restaurant decorated with traditional Chinese eaves is rather worn in its old age and the manager's office is still forlornly hung with a portrait of Mao, but the dishes are well worth your time and portions are generous. Try the filling crispy tinfoil-wrapped mutton (*zhǐbāo yángròu;* Y22), while the deep fried eggplant with garlic and chilli sauce (*yúxiāng qiézi;* Y26) is tender and swimming in a sea of hot red chilli oil. The menu extends to shark's fin and abalone, and other seafood such as the hot, sweet and spicy crab (*xiānglà xiè;* Y58). You can sweat over a *yuānyang huǒguō* (literally Mandarin duck hotpot) – the celebrated Sichuan hotpot that is divided into hot (*là*) and not-hot (*búlà*) sections. Note the countertop array of home fermented wines infused with various flora and fauna (for around Y20 a shot). The restaurant takes Visa.

TIANWAITIAN ROAST DUCK RESTAURANT Map pp232–3 *Peking Duck*
110 Dianmenwai Dajie; meals Y50; ⏰ 10am-10pm; subway Gulou

This reliable chain of Peking duck specialists is dotted around town. The chefs do a fine job on the tasty duck morsels, served alongside a thick wad of pancakes. Order beer by the pint; the *méicài kòuròu* is a delicious dish of melt-in-the-mouth strips of fatty pork atop a small mound of cabbage.

YUELU SHANWU Map pp232–3 *Hunan*
☎ 6617 2696; 10-11 Tianhe Fang (Lotus Lane); subway Gulou

With a marvellous view over the lake of Qianhai, this pretty, neat and civilised Hunan restaurant and bar – the name means 'House at the foot of the mountain' – serves a range of hot and mild dishes from the province renowned for its searing flavours. There's an English menu but credit cards are not accepted.

CHEAP EATS
DONGHUAMEN NIGHT MARKET
Map pp232–3 *Snacks*
Dōnghuāmén Yèshì

Dong'anmen Dajie; ⏰ 3-10pm, closed Chinese New Year; subway Wangfujing

A sight in itself, the bustling night market near Wangfujing Dajie is a veritable food zoo: lamb kebabs, beef and chicken skewers, corn on the cob, smelly *dòufu*, cicadas, grasshoppers, kidneys, quail's eggs, squid, fruit, porridge, fried pancakes, strawberry kebabs, bananas, Inner Mongolian cheese, stuffed aubergines, chicken hearts, pitta bread stuffed with meat, shrimps and that's just the start. Expect to pay around Y5 for a lamb kebab, far more than you would pay for the same snack from a *hútong* vendor.

Donghuamen Night Market (above)

CHAOYANG

While restaurants can be found throughout the district, the dining action focuses on the Sanlitun bar and embassy area and the district around the Workers' Stadium. If you are on the hunt for non-Chinese dishes, this is a good place to start, and there's a lively entertainment and bar culture to help round off a meal.

BEIJING DADONG ROAST DUCK
RESTAURANT Map pp234–5   *Peking Duck*
Běijīng Dàdǒng Kǎoyā Diàn
☎ 6582 2892/4003; 3 Tuanjiehu Beikou; duck Y98;
⏰ 11am-9.30pm; subway Dongsishitiao

A long-term favourite of the Peking duck scene, this restaurant has a tempting variety of fowl. The hallmark bird is a crispy, lean duck without the usual high fat content (trimmed down from 42.38% to 15.22% for its 'superneat' roast duck, the brochure says), plus plum (or garlic) sauce, scallions and pancakes. Also carved up is the skin of the duck with sugar, an old imperial predilection. Fork out an extra Y20 and get the duck of your choice. The menu also dishes up some fine local non-duck dishes.

BERENA'S BISTRO Map pp234–5   *Sichuan*
Bóruìnà Jiǔjiā
☎ 6592 2628; 6 Gongrentiyuchang Donglu; meals Y50; ⏰ 11.30am-11.30pm; subway Dongsishitiao

This tastefully laid out restaurant (despite the Chen Yifei fakes on the wall) delivers some yummy Chinese food. The slant is towards Sichuan dishes with the *suānlà tāng* (hot and sour soup; Y25) thick, plentiful and heavily laced with chilli – easily enough for two. The *làzi jīdīng* (chicken in spicy sauce; Y25) is excellent and the *hēijiāo niúliǔ* (sizzling beef platter with black pepper) a feast. The bar in the entrance – decked out in football memorabilia – says it all: Berena's is expat-oriented, but it's very popular and has been going for yonks. Go under the Beckham Real Madrid shirt to get to the restaurant.

DOWNTOWN CAFÉ Map pp234–5   *Western*
☎ 6415 2100; 26 Sanlitun Lu; meals Y70;
⏰ 10am-3pm; subway Dongsishitiao

This popular Western café seems to hog the lion's share of hungry expats on Sanlitun Lu. The menu delivers dependable European dishes from salads, pasta, pizza and sandwiches or burgers. Try the crispy Croque Monsieur (Y35), a tuna sandwich (Y40) or sample the large range of vegetarian dishes, including vegetarian lasagne (Y40). There's a friendly and relaxed atmosphere, and it's ideal for long lunches and watching the CD/DVD hawkers and masseurs trolling by on Sanlitun Lu outside.

FLO Map pp234–5   *French*
☎ 6595 5139; 2nd fl, Rainbow Plaza, 16 Dongsanhuan Beilu; mains Y100+; ⏰ 11am-2.30pm & 5.30-10pm; subway Dongsishitiao

Over the years Flo has maintained a reputation as a reliable French restaurant with a decent menu. Try the onion soup (Y48), the smoked Norwegian salmon with poached egg (Y78) or the roasted lamb fillet (Y108).

FOUR SEASONS RESTAURANT
Map pp234–5   *Cantonese/Sichuan*
Měiwèi Sìjì Cāntīng
☎ 6508 5823; east gate of the Workers Stadium, Gongrentiyuchang Donglu; meals Y50;
subway Dongsishitiao

This is a clean, efficient and stylish restaurant with a large and tempting range of Cantonese seafood, Sichuan and hotpot dishes. It's newly opened so there's a fresh and un-jaded feel to the place, reflected in the efficient staff. Try the fizzing and spitting *niúròu tiěbǎn* (sizzling beef platter; Y28), the *chuānlà hǎixiān bāo*, a spicy seafood hotpot (Y48) or the more standard but stomach-filling *yúxiāng qiézi bāo*, a scorching clay pot of tender aubergines laced with garlic and pork mince (Y22). There is also a range of vegetable dishes. At the time of writing there was no English menu but one is in the pipeline.

FRANK'S PLACE Map pp234–5   *American*
☎ 6507 2617; Gongrentiyuchang Donglu;
dishes from Y30; ⏰ 11am-midnight;
subway Dongsishitiao

It may be simple and getting a bit hoary in its old age (it opened in 1989), but American-style Frank's is an old original and the menu a trusted favourite of regulars who seem to have nowhere else to go. The burgers (Y40) really do the job (Y5 extra for bacon, cheese and other toppings), as do the jumbo-sized hot dogs (Y30). Otherwise there is the chicken and chips (Y55) or steak. Service is more personal and the atmosphere more congenial than at the Hard Rock Café. The Cuban cigars at the bar go down a treat and the huge screen for live football matches is not unpopular with the wall of punters at the bar.

LAO HANZI Map pp234–5 *Chinese Hakka*

☎ 6415 3376; Sanlitun Beijie; meals Y40; ☼ 11am-2.30pm & 5-10pm; subway Dongsishitiao or Dongzhimen

Kejia (Hakka) cuisine may not be one of China's main cooking styles (the Hakka live principally in Fujian and Guangdong), but the dishes at the Lao Hanzi (Old Character) are deservedly popular; the place is frequently packed and the ambience is superb.

LOUISIANA Map pp234–5 *American*
Lùyìsiānnà

☎ 6466 2288, ext 7420; 2nd fl, Hilton Hotel, 1 Dongfang Lu; meals Y200; ☼ 11.30am-2pm & 6-10pm

Not to be outshone by what is a very famous wine list, the kitchen crew work hard to dish up excellent Cajun and Creole cuisine in a top of the range setting. Main attractions on the menu are the steaks and seafood. It's not cheap, but it's a class act.

OUTBACK STEAKHOUSE
Map pp234–5 *Australian*
Àobàikè

☎ 6506 5166; north entrance of Workers' Stadium; meals Y120; ☼ 5-10.30pm Mon-Fri & 11am-10.30pm Sat & Sun; subway Dongsishitiao

The Australian-themed Outback is one of Beijing's most popular destinations for grilled slabs of meat and massive, stomach-stretching portions. Another branch can be found at the foot of **Wangfujing Dajie** (Map pp239–41; ☎ 6528 2858; ☼ 11am-11pm), adjacent to the Beijing Hotel.

RED BASIL Map pp234–5 *Thai*

☎ 6460 2339; Sanyuan Dongqiao; ☼ 11.30am-2pm & 5.30-10pm

This long-running Thai restaurant may be expensive, but the elegant décor creates a fine ambience and the menu is first rate. Reservations are recommended.

SORABOL Map pp234–5 *Korean*

☎ 6465 3388, ext 5720; basement, Lufthansa Center, 50 Liangmaqiao Lu; meals Y150; ☼ 10am-10pm

This dependably good Korean chain restaurant is the place to come for barbecue and *banfan* (rice, egg, meat, vegetables and hot pepper sauce), as well as *paigu* (roast spareribs). Other branches can be found at **Landmark Towers** (Map pp234–5; ☎ 6590 6688, ext 5119; 2nd fl, 8 Dongsanhuan Beilu) in Chaoyang and the **Novotel Peace Hotel** (☎ 6512 8833, ext 6605; 1st fl, 3 Jinyu Hutong).

SERVE THE PEOPLE Map pp234–5 *Thai*
Wèi Rénmín Fùwù

☎ 8454 4580; 1 Sanlitun Xiwujie; meals Y50; ☼ 11am-11pm; subway Dongzhimen

Serve the People is widely acknowledged as Beijing's trendiest Thai restaurant. Its warm décor, *tom yam* (spicy, lemongrass flavoured soup) and other dishes are deservedly popular.

1001 NIGHTS Map pp234–5 *Middle Eastern*
Yìqiānlíngyī Yè

☎ 6532 4050; opposite the Zhaolong Hotel, Gongtrentiyuchang Beilu; meals Y100; ☼ 11am-2am; subway Dongsishitiao

Widely acknowledged as the best Middle Eastern food in Beijing, 1001 Nights (not far east of the Sanlitun bar district) throws together an excellent concoction of kebabs, falafel, hummus, pitta bread and belly dancing shows in the evening. No credit cards.

XIAO WANG'S HOME RESTAURANT
Map pp234–5 *Beijing/Chinese*
Xiǎowáng Fǔ

☎ 6594 3602/6591 3255; 4 Gonrentiyuchang Beilu; meals Y70; ☼ 11am-2pm & 5-11pm

This branch of Xiao Wang's has a classier and quieter ambience than the Guanghua Dongli branch (p117) cavernous interior and train carriage/office-style seating (the no-smoking section is housed in an old train carriage). There's polite service and it's deservedly popular. The food is again excellent, with the same menu; the sizzling beef slices with pepper and onion in black bean sauce (Y38) is a scorching and peppery delight. There's a take out menu, so you can order over the phone (☎ 6591 3255, 800 810 8988) and eat your deep fried chicken breast with chilli, egg fried rice or stir fried kale from the comfort of your hotel bed (if you want). Tucked away, the restaurant is up the steps inside the Success Club, opposite the Sanlitun Yashou Clothing Market (p148).

XINJIANG RED ROSE RESTAURANT
Map pp234–5 *Xinjiang*

☎ 6415 5741; Xingfuycun Qixiang; opposite Workers Stadium north gate; meals Y40; ☼ 1pm-midnight; subway Dongsishitiao

The south entrance to the Xinjiang Red Rose on Gongrentiyuchang Beilu leads to a small and unassuming restaurant with good value and tasty dishes from Xīnjiāng province. It's just a front, however, for the maelstrom of tabletop dancing, live Uyghur music and belly dancers in the building behind. Meander through the restaurant or use the entrance off Xingfucun Qixiang to get to the action, which kicks off every night at 7.30pm. You can pass on the whole roast lamb (Y800) unless you're a crowd, but the roast leg of lamb (Y30 per *jin*) is filling and chunky lamb kebabs (Y3 each) good value.

FENGTAI & XUANWU

JI GU GE TEAHOUSE

Map pp236–8   *Chinese Teahouse*
Jígǔgé Cháyuán
☎ 6301 7849; 2nd fl, 132-136 Liulichang Dongjie; tea from Y20; ☻ 9am-11pm; subway Hepingmen
In Liulichang, the Ji Gu Ge infuses its teas with mineral water. Head upstairs through an art gallery to the teahouse, where you can nose around and take in the atmosphere. Otherwise, a cup of tea will cost you around Y20. The teahouse also sells a range of specially wrapped gift teas for souvenir hunters and gift givers. It also sells loose tea – but prices are high, like everything else here, so you are better off buying it from Ten Fu's Tea (p146) or even the Friendship Store (p144).

HAIDIAN & XICHENG

NENGRENJU Map pp230–1   *Hotpot*
☎ 6601 2560; 5 Taipingqiao; meals Y80;
☻ 10.30am-2am; subway Fuchengmen
This is one of Beijing's most renowned hotpot restaurants. The lamb slices are scrumptious and the sesame sauce rich, but in winter it's wall to wall so be sure to come early or make a reservation.

BEIJING

LONG HWA TREE ORGANIC VEGETARIAN RESTAURANT

Map pp228–9   *Vegetarian*
3 Mai Mai Jie; meals Y30
Run by the Fan family, this place is filled with a unique peacefulness. The menu changes daily, with tasty dishes such as spicy Indian curry, delicious Taiwanese rice noodles and thick vegetable sandwiches. Food is laid out buffet-style – create your own portions and then pay 'according to your own good heart and mind'. Drop your money into the large ceramic jar in the corner.

Entertainment

Entertainment

Deng Xiaoping's maxim, 'When you open the window for fresh air, expect some flies to blow in', gauged the tolerable risks of China's open-door policy. Just 20 years ago, strait-laced Beijing might have flinched at the notion of having a good time. Today's Beijing has seen a revolution in leisure, and the entertainment industry is in full throttle. It might not be Swinging Shanghai or Highballing Hong Kong, but Beijing is a city whose denizens work and play hard.

Some pastimes, such as Beijing opera (*jingjù*) or acrobatics, are fixtures on the tourist circuit and draw regular crowds. Others are more contemporary events: art exhibitions, concerts and modern theatre are receiving an enthusiastic welcome. On the live music front, the city snaps its fingers to a motley medley of beats, so there should be something up your street most nights of the week, whether jazz, classical, blues, soul, R&B, rock, independent or whatever.

If you want to sway to the latest sounds, a host of clubs can put a beer in your hand and a dance floor under your feet. Or if you'd rather have your beer sitting down, parts of Beijing are a virtual checkerboard of bars, some of which take their profession seriously enough to line up a wide range of foreign brews.

Thanks to the regularly updated expat magazines (p204) circulating in town, events listings can easily be found.

Preparing for a Beijing Opera performance (p25)

PUBS & BARS

Necessity being the mother of invention in Beijing, as everywhere else, first came beer (circa 1903), which gradually dislodged *báijiǔ* (the strong stuff) as the nation's favourite tipple. Later came the bars (circa late 1980s). It wasn't until somewhere in the mid-1990s, however, that the gift-wrapping truly came off Beijing's tavern scene.

Seemingly shrugging off threats by the authorities to sweep away the whole shebang, Sanlitun in the Chaoyang district forms the hub of expat drinking life in town. This is where about 75% of expat bar-cafés are amassed. Drawn moth-like by the lights, droves of drinkers populate the two main bar streets in Sanlitun: the main one that runs between Gongrentiyuchang Beilu and Dongzhimenwai (Sanlitun Lu), and a smaller alleyway that runs south from Gongrentiyuchang Beilu (Sanlitun Nanlu). The bars here are going strong, but rumours of major redevelopment darken the horizon, and a relocation of bartenders and punters could take place if these pubs disappear. Remember, this is China; *change* and *flux* are buzzwords. Taking a leaf from Sanlitun's page, other parts of town are trying to recreate the whole bar experience. After a few bars around the lakes of Qianhai and Houhai (north of Beihai Park) struck gold a few years back, a swarm of prospectors has followed suit. The lakeside street running south of Houhai (Houhai Nanyan) is now a long strip of bars, and Yandai Xijie – a small street just east of Silver Ingot Bridge – has recruited a new population of cafés, bars and souvenir shops, many of which are particularly samey.

With Beijing bars, don't judge a book by its cover. There's been a rush to open bars in recent years; some look slick and smart on the exterior, but once you get past the wrapping, you discover it's all a bit drab and lacklustre. Conversely, some outsides might not warrant a second glance, but the bar turns out to be a gem.

CHONGWEN & SOUTH CHAOYANG

CHARLIE'S BAR Map pp239–41
☎ 6500 2233; Jianguo Hotel, 5 Jianguomenwai Dajie; beer Y25; ⊙ 11.30am-2am; subway Yonganli

An old-timer in the august Jianguo Hotel, Charlie's enjoys fond patronage from embassy staff and a regular complement of long-term expats. Enjoying the yesteryear feel, middle-aged drinkers sit down for nights of spirits, beers (Qingdao Y25) and evening singers.

JOHN BULL PUB Map pp234–5
Zūnbó Yīngshì Jiǔbā
☎ 6532 5905; 44 Guanghua Lu; beer Y25; ⊙ 9am-midnight; subway Jianguomen

Servicing legions of Brit expats in the embassy district, this English-style pub has particularly tasty steak-and-kidney pie and other pub grub, plus a snug weeknight atmosphere (often as quiet as a library), comfy furniture, Foster's Lager (Y25), pool, sports TV, English breakfasts and pleasant staff who speak good English.

PALACE VIEW Map pp239–41
☎ 6515 7788; 10th fl, Grand Hotel Beijing, 35 Dongchang'an Jie; subway Tiananmen Dong or Wangfujing

For liquid refreshment with a top-notch panorama, the Palace View is in a league of its own. Bar winter, outdoor tables graced by a string of palm trees make this a wonderful place to escape the city and size up the view overlooking Dongchang'an Jie, the Forbidden City and Tiananmen Square.

PJ O'REILLY'S Map pp239–41
Àiěrlán
☎ 6559 4218; Henderson Center, 18 Jianguomennei Dajie; subway Jianguomen or Dongdan

Far from the madding crowd, Irish pub PJ O'Reilly's is a quiet and neglected tavern on the corner of the Henderson Center, north of Beijing Train Station. It's nothing special and the Guinness (Y45) might rapidly empty your

wallet, but punters can peruse up-to-date in-house copies of USA Today.

PRESS CLUB Map pp239–41
☎ 6460 6688; St Regis, 21 Jianguomenwai Dajie; beer Y35; ⊙ 4.30pm-1am; subway Jianguomen

If Sanlitun is just too sordid, seek out the dignified repose of the wood-panelled Press Club in the top-drawer St Regis off Ritan Lu. Its five-star bar has five-star prices, a large-screen sports TV and a lounge with library-like ambience.

RED MOON BAR Map pp239–41
Dōngfāng Liàng
☎ 8518 1234, ext 6366; Grand Hyatt Beijing, 1 Dongchang'an Jie; beer Y40, cocktails from Y45; ⊙ 11.30am-2.30pm & 5pm-1am; subway Wangfujing

Arriving at the Red Moon, customers are met by a svelte female attendant and ushered through a looking-glass door to a gorgeous lounge bar blessed with a huge selection of wines. The lighting is subdued, soporific jazz wafts over a very chilled-out clientele, and the evening's live music goes down well with those who are not in a rush to go anywhere else. The overall effect is particularly seductive and the perfect antidote to some of Beijing's rawer bar spots. Japanese snacks are nearby, and a private function room at the rear is available for more intimate gatherings. There's also a cigar bar.

SPORTS CITY CAFÉ Map pp239–41
Yùndòngchéng
☎ 6515 8855, ext 3349; 3rd Fl, Gloria Plaza Hotel, 2 Jianguomenwai Dajie; ⊙ 11am-2am; subway Jianguomen

This is a sprawling American sports bar, just off Jianguomen Nandajie, which airs live matches on a vast TV screen amid a constellation of smaller sets. A live band cranks out cover hits every night except Mondays. Perhaps not a choice setting, but it's a harmless kind of place and there's essential sports coverage on ESPN for football fans.

DONGCHENG

Bars and cafés have overrun the area around the Shichahai lakes in recent years, especially along Houhai Nanyan, running south of Houhai Lake. Yandai Xijie (Chinese Pipe Cross St) has also been ambushed by a mob of recently opened bars, cafés, arts and crafts shops, and purveyors of trinkets. Both the economics and character of the lane have been redefined. There's little to differentiate the competition, and the **Paradise Bar** (Mèngyún Tái; Map pp232–3 ☎ 6402 7825; 16 Yandai Xijie; Qingdao Y25, cocktails Y30) at the eastern end of Yandai Xijie is perhaps typical. It has a comfy, albeit minute, bar with a miniature garret space up a very steep flight of steps. On the same street, the **Guangfuguan Greenhouse** (below) is unique in its exclusive address within a former Taoist temple.

BUDDHA BAR Map pp232–3
Búdà Jiǔba
☎ 6617 9488; 2 Yinding Qiao; beer Y15;
🕑 1pm-1am; subway Gulou, then bus 60
Its name in Chinese is a clever play on the word 'not big' or 'small'. This tiny and reclusive bar is excellent for those on the run from Beijing's noisy, sprawling and brash taverns.

GUANGFUGUAN GREENHOUSE
Map pp232–3
Guǎngfúguàn de Wēnshì
☎ 6400 3234; 36 Yandai Xijie; 🕑 2pm-2am;
subway Gulou, then bus 60
This laid-back place (the manager was wandering about brushing his teeth when I last popped in) on the bar-cluttered Yandai Xijie gets full marks for novelty. Formerly the Guanfu Taoist Temple (according to the characters carved on the lintel above the arched doorway), the shrine has been requisitioned for the city's exploding bar scene and simply decked out with art posters, including one of Allen Ginsberg. The temple's roof guardians are still intact, and the presence of religious statuary reminds visitors that they drink on sacred turf.

HOUHAI CAFÉ & BAR Map pp232–3
☎ 6613 6209; 20 Houhai Nanyan; 🕑 noon-late;
subway Gulou, then bus 60
This low-key, beautifully decorated café and bar has large rattan chairs from which you can enjoy a vista of cyclists, vendors, and sightseers and locals ambling alongside Houhai Lake. It serves teas, coffees (Y25), beers (Qingdao Y12) and liqueurs, and is one of the best in a long strip of bars and cafés.

LEFT BANK Map pp232–3
Zuǒàn
11 Qianhai Beiyan; beer Y15; 🕑 3.30pm-2am;
subway Gulou, then bus 60
Situated west of Qianhai Lake, the analogy with the Parisian Rive Gauche might be far-fetched,

but an unruffled, lazy equilibrium hangs over the place. Bring along a good book and join guests lounging in wicker furniture and comfy couches (although young night owls might seek wilder pastures).

NO NAME BAR Map pp232–3
Bái Fēng
☎ 6401 8541; 3 Qianhai Dongyan; beer Y15;
🕑 12pm-2am; subway Gulou, then bus 60
Perched beside Qianhai Lake in one of Beijing's more historic and pleasant reaches, this rather cliquey bar (its name in Chinese means 'White Maple') sees a lot of customers. The weekend sees the bar's small array of seats under a dislodgeable contingent of bums. This was one of the very first bars to open up lakeside – but now the area is jam-packed with look-alike operations. There's no sign, so search out the bar with the green shutters to the south of the restaurant **Kaorouji** (p120), east of Yinding Bridge.

PASSBY BAR Map pp232–3
Guòkè
☎ 8403 8004; www.gk01.com; 108 Nanluogu Xiang;
beer Y18, meals from Y40; 🕑 7pm-2am;
subway Andingmen or Gulou
A necessary alternative to Sanlitun's more formulaic bar scene, Passby Bar caters to tumbleweed travellers barrelling in for a fine concoction of beer, travel tales and tongue wagging. The bar operates from a courtyard house, which has polished beams, low-ceiling, a mezzanine floor (up the ladder) and a useful and growing library of books with book exchange. It's not cheap but is well worth investigating: the travel-oriented staff in this historic *hútong* (alleyway) haunt is always keen to help, and the ambience is peerless. There is also a menu with Italian, Chinese and Western food, so you can settle down to a Beijing Hutong pizza (Y40), a US Angus sirloin steak (Y108), or even (believe it or not) a Gongbao Jiding pizza (Y40). There's also a large selection of wines (Y150-Y688).

CHAOYANG

Beijingers refer to Sanlitun Lu as Jiǔbā Jiē (Bar St). Many bars leave the impression of living on borrowed time, and the old-timers have a pedigree of not much beyond five years. Local Chinese drinkers tend to stick to this main reach, which is patrolled by CD/DVD hawkers and employees of nearby massage parlours. Prices for a bottle of Tsingtao hover at around Y15; a draught Beijing or Yangjing beer should set you back Y15 to Y25, but cheapskate dives with a cheaper tariff constantly crop up. Besides beer, you can fork out plenty for coffee and Western food. In summer, outdoor tables are set up on the sidewalk (although authorities periodically ban them).

The narrow lane tucked away southwest of Sanlitun Lu is known as Sanlitun Nanlu (although its official name is Dongdaqiao Xijie). It's cosier and has more character than its sibling, and it's possibly the most popular nightlife area for Beijing expats. Some bars here do not open until after 7pm, but they stay open until dawn. Enter the alley from the northern end and walk south.

CENTRO Map pp234–5
Xuànkù
☎ 6561 8833, ext 6388; Kerry Center Hotel, 1 Guanghua Lu; beer Y40; ☽ 24hr; subway Guomao

Swish and stylish, Centro is a highly seductive and impressive lounge bar with low mood lighting, illuminated table tops, a black glossy bar (with a range of cigars) and discreet, quiet corners caressed by relaxing chill-out tunes and ambient sounds. It's an excellent place to seek refuge and a Qingdao (Y40) at the conclusion of a hectic day, and it offers respite from the frantic clutter of contemporary Beijing. There's live music (including jazz) at night, and a DJ spins sounds at weekends (10pm–midnight Fri–Sun). Chinese music gets airplay on Sunday evenings (5pm–9pm).

CLUB FOOTBALL CENTER Map pp234–5
☎ 6417 0497; www.wanguoqunxing.com; Red House Hotel, 10b Chunxiu Jie; beer Y10; ☽ 11am-2am; subway Dongsishitiao, then bus 701

With its wall-to-wall football trophies, scarves, Liverpool FC memorabilia, live English premiership action, big screen and yelping punters at the bar, this is probably the most genuine British pub in town. A must for anyone obsessed with the beautiful game and/or beer (Beijing Y10) and/or pool and/or rugby (not necessarily in that order). Become a member and get on their email list for forthcoming matches. It's in the Red House Hotel, up the stairs on the left, and past the sign that says 'The Angler's Arms'.

DURTY NELLIE'S Map pp234–5
Dūbǎilín Jiǔbā
☎ 6502 2808; www.durtynellies.com.cn; 11a Dongdaqiao Xijie, Sanlitun Nanlu; ☽ 5.30pm-1.30am; subway Dongsishitiao, then bus 701

This cavernous Irish pub serves Guinness (Y50 per pint), unless the Eire shipment is stranded somewhere, as well as Kilkenny's (Y50). The tavern seems to go on forever once you get past the main bar, and there's pool, table football, darts and acres of stone-flagged space behind. Adding to the atmosphere are wobbly tables straight from Dublin, snugs and regular bands cranking out ballads and covers from the Emerald Isle. There's another branch with more of the same at 1/B Liangmaqiao Flower Market (Map pp234-5; ☎ 6593 5050), also in Chaoyang. The bar takes Visa and Mastercard.

GOOSE & DUCK PUB Map pp234–5
Éhéyā
☎ 6538 1691; 1 Bihuju Nanlu; beer Y15; ☽ 24hr; subway Dawanglu, then bus 31

This is a sprawling Brit bar that comforts expats pining for Blighty with bangers and mash, table football, darts, sports TV and pool. It has live music and a basement, and is opposite the west gate of Chaoyang Park. The Goose & Duck offers two drinks for the price of one between 4pm and 8pm.

HALF & HALF Map pp234–5
Haitōng
☎ 6416 6919; Yaxiu Donglu; beer Y20; ☽ to 2am; subway Dongsishitiao

Perhaps Beijing's most famous and long-standing gay and lesbian bar, Half & Half lies in an alley east of the Sanlitun Yashou Clothing Market (p148). This bar, with a dark and low-key interior, is secretively tucked away, without any attempt to project itself, on the right-hand side of the road as you head north. Look for the sign saying 'Half' on the road outside.

HART SALON Map pp234–5
Hātè Yìshù Shālóng
☎ 6504 6010; 17 Dongdaqiao Xijie, Sanlitun Nanlu; ☽ 3pm-1am; subway Dongsishitiao, then bus 701

This appealing bar on Sanlitun Nanlu appears small and uneventful downstairs, but things get better on the 2nd floor. Beijing's creative intelligentsia descends on the bar for discussions and forums on film, dance, literature, drama and art. Movies are also screened, and it's a good place to hang out and penetrate the city's cultural underground.

HIDDEN TREE Map pp234–5
Yinbì de Shù

☎ 6509 3642; 12 Dongdaqiao Xijie, Sanlitun Nanlu; beer Y15; ☽ 10am-4am; subway Dongsishitiao, then bus 701
Looking for a Belgian Leffe, Duvel or Trappist monastery-brewed Chimay, to flush away that sour flavour of the local beer? Look no further; the deep-rooted (it's been in business for years) Hidden Tree has a cellar of Belgian brews. There's a beer garden that opens from late spring, the interior is cosy (with the namesake tree growing in the bar), and there's a Mediterranean menu (pizzas around Y70), soft candlelight in the evening and occasional live music of the Filipino band variety (after 10pm Tue, Thur & Sun).

JAZZ-YA Map pp234–5
Juéshì

☎ 6415 1227; 18 Sanlitun Beijie; beer Y15; ☽ 10.30am-2am; subway Dongsishitiao, then bus 701
This veteran (established circa 1995) bar is in many an expat's address book. It's a nifty Japanese-style bar and restaurant hidden down a small alley across the way from the China Industrial and Commercial Bank. It gets busy only after 8pm.

NEO LOUNGE Map pp234–5
99 Jiǔláng

☎ 6416 1077; 99 Xingfu Yicun Zhonglu; ☽ 6pm-2am; subway Dongsishitiao, then bus 701
This swish and stylish bar, not too far east of the On/Off Bar and hidden behind smoked windows, is one of town's more sophisticated options for those trying to score image points. Irregular live jazz, in-house DJs and occasional live acts create a cultivated mood designed for the young and neat professional set.

ON/OFF BAR Map pp234–5
Shàngxiàxiàn

☎ 6415 8083; Lianbao Apartments, Xingfu Yicun Zhonglu; beer Y15; ☽ 10am-2am; subway Dongsishitiao, then bus 701
A quiet and seductive outfit well managed by a squad of helpful staff, On/Off caters to both gay and straight clientele.

POACHERS INN Map pp234–5
☎ 6417 2632, ext 8506; 43 Beisanlitun Lu; subway Dongsishitiao, then bus 701
Cavernous Poachers literally heaves with exuberant throngs and a thumping, hammering bass at the weekend when it's party central and the volume reaches pathological levels. If you want a conversation, take turns with a loudhailer and if you want a beer, grease yourself down to get to the besieged bar. The floor a writhing knot of liúxuéshēng (foreign students) and partygoers, this is probably the most popular bar in Beijing, with prices to match and occasional live acts. Follow the crowds/ruckus to the entrance next door to the (surely soundproofed?) You Yi Youth Hostel (p160).

FENGTAI & XUANWU

WORLD FOR TWO CAFÉ Map pp236–8
Liǎngrén Shìjiè

☎ 6607 9184/6617 4200; 81 Xuanwumen Xidajie; beer Y15; subway Changchunjie or Xuanwumen
Tucked away just west of the entrance to main office of Xinhua (Beijing's official news agency), this very small bar and restaurant (meals Y30) is quietly cultured and off the beaten track. It's snug with an understated jazzy mood, a small lounge at the back and a simple menu. Managing to create some style from a ramshackle and unlikely location, it's easy to miss – the sign outside says 'café' – and there's a little patio outside with tables.

On/Off Bar (left)

CLUBBING

Beijing's discos might not be cutting edge, but they pack in loyal, sweaty patrons and should wow Westerners who thought the city was still stuck on the hard shoulder. Most budgets meet their match, from student dives to sharper Sanlitun venues and top-end clubs. Most outfits idle along in low gear early in the week before the high-octane Friday and Saturday rush and dance floor pile-up.

CLUB BANANA Map pp239–41
Bānànà

☎ 6526 3939; SciTech Hotel, 22 Jianguomenwai Dajie; Y20-50; ⏰ 8.30pm-4am Sun-Thu, 8.30pm-5pm Fri & Sat; subway Jianguomen or Yonganli

Mainstay of Beijing club land, Banana is loud and to the point. Select from the techno, acid jazz and chill-out sections according to your energy levels as the night progresses.

CLUB NIGHTMAN Map pp234–5
Láitèmàn

☎ 6466 2562; 2 Xibahe Nanli; ⏰ 8.30pm-2am; subway Dongzhimen

Old-timer Nightman has undergone recent renovation and is still packing in the crowds on its multilevel dance floors with regular appearances by international DJs.

LOFT Map pp234–5
Cángkù Jiŭbā

☎ 6501 7501; 4 Gongrentiyuchang Beilu; ⏰ 11am-2am; subway Dongsishitiao, then bus 701

The Loft delivers a fresh world of live jazz, techno and house music, funky TV screens and art space. There is a European fusion menu as well as regular DJs and live music. It's tucked away behind the huge Pacific Century Place office and apartment complex.

VICS Map pp234–5
Wēikèsī

☎ 6593 6215; Workers' Stadium north gate; Fri Y35, Sat Y50; ⏰ 7pm-late; subway Dongsishitiao

South of the Outback Steakhouse, Vics is decked out with couches, a pool table and a sweaty dance floor. Perhaps Beijing's most popular club, this place offers a selection of hip-hop, R&B, pop and soul that attracts solid crowds. Wednesday is ladies night, and Friday and Saturday nights see things thumping and jumping until 7am.

WORLD OF SUZIE WONG Map pp234–5
Sūxī Huáng

☎ 6593 7889; 1a Nongzhanguan Lu, Chaoyang Amusement Park west gate; ⏰ 7pm-3.30am; subway Dawanglu, then bus 3

This elegant lounge bar attracts glamorous types who recline on traditional wooden beds piled with silk cushions, sipping daiquiris. There's attentive service, fine cocktails and beer (Y15+), and the music is varied, from house, through chill-out, to techno, pop and rock. Enter through the Q Bar entrance.

BEIJING OPERA & TRADITIONAL CHINESE MUSIC

For details of this remarkable operatic style see the Beijing Opera boxed text (p25).

CHANG'AN GRAND THEATRE
Map pp239–41
Chángān Dàjùchăng

☎ 6510 1309; Chang'an Building, 7 Jianguomennei Dajie; Y40-150; ⏰ performances 7.15pm; subway Jianguomen

This theatre offers a genuine experience, and the erudite audience chatters knowledgably among themselves during weekend matinee classics and evening performances.

HUGUANG GUILD HALL Map pp236–8
Húguăng Huìguăn

☎ 6351 8284; 3 Hufangqiao Lu; tickets Y100-380; ⏰ performances 7.15pm ; subway Hepingmen, then bus 25

Similarly decorated to the Zhengyici Theatre (p132), with balconies surrounding the canopied stage, this theatre dates back to 1807. It is the site where the Kuomintang, led by Dr Sun Yat-sen, was established in 1912. The interior is magnificent, coloured in red, green and gold, and decked out with tables and a stone floor. There's also a very small opera museum (Y10) opposite the theatre displaying operatic scores, old catalogues and other paraphernalia. There are also colour illustrations of the *liănpŭ* (types of Beijing opera facial makeup) – examples include the *hóu liănpŭ* (monkey face) and the *chŏujué liănpŭ* (clown face). Sadly, there are few English captions.

LAO SHE TEAHOUSE

Map pp239–41
Lăo Shě Cháguăn
☎ 6303 6830, 6304 6334; www.laosheteahouse.com; 3rd fl, 3 Qianmen Xidajie; evening tickets Y60-130; ☾ 7.30pm; subway Hepingmen or Qianmen

Lao She Teahouse (west of the large KFC on Qianmen Xidajie) has nightly shows, mostly in Chinese. The performances here are a combination of Beijing opera, cross-talk and acrobatics. Prices depend on the type of show and where you sit. Enter the teahouse past statues of Weituo, Sakyamuni and Guanyin on your left and an effigy of President Bush on your right. There are several halls; in the small hall there is folk music (2.30-5pm Mon-Fri), and in the large hall there are folk music and tea ceremony performances (3-4.30pm Fri), theatrical performances (2-4.30pm Wed & Fri), and matinee Beijing opera performances (3pm-4.30pm Sun). Evening performances of Beijing opera, folk art and music, acrobatics and magic (7.50-9.20pm) are the most popular. Phone ahead or check online for the schedule. The teahouse is named after the celebrated Beijing writer Lao She, who has a museum dedicated to him (p80). Major credit cards accepted.

LIYUAN THEATRE

Map pp236–8
Líyuán Jùchăng
☎ 8315 7297; Qianmen Jianguo Hotel, 175 Yongan Lu; tickets Y30-200; ☾ martial arts 12.30pm, opera 7.30pm; subway Hepingmen, then bus 25

This touristy theatre, across the lobby of the Qianmen Jianguo Hotel (p161) and past the mannequins outside, has regular performances for Beijing opera greenhorns, performed over servings of Peking duck and other local delicacies. The setting isn't traditional and it resembles a cinema auditorium (the stage façade is the only authentic touch), but there are also matinee shows of *gōngfu* (kungfu) performed by Shaolin monks (p136).

OLD STATION THEATER

Map pp239–41
Lăo Chēzhàn Jùshè
☎ 8284 3316; 3rd Fl, Qianmen Old Railway Station building, Qianmen; Y30-180, students & senior discounts; ☾ performances 7.15pm Sat, 2pm Sun; subway Qianmen

On the top floor of the historic Old Qianmen Railway Station to the east of the Qianmen Arrow Tower and southeast of Zhengyang-men is this new theatre offering weekend performances of Beijing opera. The railway building dates from 1901, was China's first railway and was officially called the Zhifeng Railway Zhengyangmen Station. The theatre is located on the same floor as the **Qian Yi Internet Café** (p201).

PRINCE GONG'S RESIDENCE

Map pp230–1
☎ 6618 6628; 14 Liuyin Jie; Y80-120; ☾ performances 7.30pm Mar-Oct; subway Gulou, then bus 60

A good place to enjoy Beijing opera is within the Qing dynasty Grand Opera House in one of Beijing's landmark historic courtyards (p94). Phone ahead to check on performance times; note that performances are held only in summer.

SANWEI BOOKSTORE

Map pp236–8
☎ 6601 3204; 60 Fuxingmennei Dajie; cover charge Y30; ☾ performances 8pm; subway Xidan

Opposite the Minzu Hotel (p161), this place has a small bookshop on the ground floor and a teahouse on the second. It features music with traditional Chinese instruments on Saturday night.

ZHENGYICI THEATRE

Map pp236–8
Zhèngyīcí Jùchăng
☎ 6303 3104; 220 Xiheyan Dajie; Y50+; ☾ performances 7.30pm; subway Hepingmen

Originally an ancient temple, this ornately decorated building is the oldest wooden theatre in the country and the best place in the city to experience Beijing opera and other operatic disciplines like Kunqu. The theatre was restored by a private businessman with an interest in reviving the dying art, and it was reopened in 1995 after a long period of disrepair. Opera can be appreciated over a dinner of Peking duck.

LIVE MUSIC
ROCK, POP, JAZZ, BLUES & COUNTRY

There might be an instinctive Chinese fondness for the syrupy musical genre of Canto pop, but some of Beijing's residents have grittier tastes that have needed something with more bite and imagination. Nodding its head to a growing medley of sounds, China's increasingly brazen capital (see p23) has found an exciting language with which to articulate the new *Zeitgeist*. On the downside, international pop and rock acts of any worth rarely make it to Beijing, but there are several places around town where you can take in Beijing's home-grown music scene. Taking up the rear are the usual Filipino cover bands performing at American-style burger bars.

You can find musical events of varying quality lifting Beijing's roofs every night of the week, and there should be something up your street, whether it be jazz, rock, classical, indie, blues, R&B, soul, funk or punk. Check the listings in the expat mags (p204) for full listings of what's playing.

BIG EASY Map pp234–5
☎ 6508 6776; south gate of Chaoyang Park;
☽ live music 7pm-2am; subway Dawanglu, then bus 31
Big Easy delivers Cajun dishes accompanied by live jazz, blues, African music and reggae seven days a week – phone for details.

CD CAFÉ Map pp234–5
Sēndì
☎ 6586 5532; C16 Dongsanhuan Beilu;
☽ 8pm-2.30am; subway Dongsishitiao, then bus 416
Tilted heavily towards jazz, but rock, blues and techno (every Fri and Sat) also get airplay at this popular two-floor outfit. The CD Café also hosts an international jazz festival every November. You can find it hidden away south of the Agricultural Exhibition Centre, a ramshackle place tucked away behind an overhead walk-way vaulting over Dongsanhuan Beilu.

CD JAZZ CAFÉ Map pp234–5
Sēndì Juéshì Jùlèbù
☎ 6506 8288; main gate of the Agricultural Exhibition Centre, Dongsanhuan Beilu; ☽ 2.30pm-2.30am Wed-Sun; subway Dongzhimen
Cui Jian's saxophonist owns this small but popular club, where jazz aficionados arrive from Wednesday to Sunday for live jazz performances. Dance events are also held, including swing lessons.

JAM HOUSE Map pp234–5
Jièmofáng
☎ 6506 3845; Dongdaqiao Xijie, Sanlitun Nanlu;
☽ 7.30pm-2.30am; subway Dongsishitiao, then bus 701
One of the oldest places on Sanlitun Nanlu, this old-timer has live music (rock and flamenco) and free-for-all jam sessions. If you need a musical interlude, head up to the rooftop terrace.

NASHVILLE Map pp234–5
Xiāngyáo Jiǔbā
☎ 6502 4201; www.nashville.com.cn; Dongdaqiao Xijie, Sanlitun Nanlu; ☽ 6pm-2am; subway Dongsishitiao, then bus 701
In the bar heartland of Sanlitun Nanlu, Nashville is a long-running country pub (all wood rusticity, stone floor etc). Every evening there's country, folk, blues and rock on stage and Boddingtons at the bar. Visa card is accepted.

RED BAR Map pp234–5
Zhǔchàng
Dongdaqiao Xijie, Sanlitun Nanlu; ☽ 6.30pm-2am
On the west side of Sanlitun Nanlu, this bar (formerly the River bar) has regular rock and folk music on its small stage.

SWEETNESS Map pp234–5
☎ 8456 4868/2899; 19 Liangmaqiao Lu;
subway Dongsishitiao, then bus 701
Rough and ready and flung out in the northeast of town, Sweetness stages rock and indie music acts sandwiched between more standard live fare. Head along Liangmaqiao Lu from the Kempinski Hotel for around 1km, then turn north onto a street containing other music bars (including B-52) and Sweetness is further up on the left – just follow the noise.

TWO POINTS ONE LINE Map pp234–5
Liǎngdiǎn Yìxiàn
☎ 6506 3965; north of Pengli Apartment Block, Dongsanhuan Beilu; Y30; subway Guomao, then bus 703
No points for style, but this no-frills venue is a focal point for Beijing's rock musicians and the place to come for a sample of the local sound. It's located west of Tuanjiehu Park.

CLASSICAL MUSIC

As China's capital and the nation's cultural centre, Beijing has several venues around town where the city's increasingly cosmopolitan residents can satisfy their highbrow needs. The annual 30-day Beijing Music Festival takes place between October and November, and is an excellent time to catch international and homegrown classical music. By the time you read this the Beijing Opera House to the west of Tiananmen Square should be completed. Again, refer to the listings in *That's Beijing* and other events magazines (p204) for details of current musical events.

BEIJING CONCERT HALL

Map pp236–8
Beijing Yīnyuè Tīng
☎ 6605 5812; 1 Beixinhua Jie; Y50-500;
⏲ performances 7.30pm; subway Tiananmen Xi or Xidan

The 2000-seat Beijing Concert Hall showcases performances of classical Chinese music as well as international repertoires of Western classical music. The building was undergoing renovation at the time of writing.

CENTURY THEATRE

Map pp234–5
☎ 6466 4805; 40 Liangmaqiao Lu; Y100-500;
⏲ 7.30pm; subway Dongsishitiao, then bus 701

Musical presentations here are perhaps smaller in scale than those at other venues, featuring smaller orchestras and solo performances where the violin, cello and flute get centre stage. Ballet performances are also presented.

FORBIDDEN CITY CONCERT HALL

Map pp239–41
Zhōngshān Gōngyuán Yīnyuè Táng
☎ 6559 8285; Zhongshan Park; Y50-500;
⏲ performances 7.30pm; subway Tiananmen Xi

Located on the eastern side of Zhongshan Park, this is the most central venue for performances of classical and traditional Chinese music. Tickets can be purchased at the concert hall box office inside the **Friendship Store** (p144).

POLY PLAZA INTERNATIONAL THEATRE Map pp234–5

Bǎolì Dàshà Guójì Jùyuàn
☎ 6500 1188, ext 5682; 14 Dongzhimen Nandajie; Y100-680; ⏲ performances 7.30pm; subway Dongsishitiao

Located in the Poly Plaza right by Dongsishitiao subway station, this venue hosts a wide range of performances including classical music, ballet and traditional Chinese folk music. Operatic works from the good old bad old days, such as *Red Detachment of Women*, have made a reappearance here in recent years.

THEATRE

Gong Li and Zhang Ziyi, big names of the big screen, might have learned their art at the **Central Academy of Drama** (Zhōngyāng Xìjù Xuéyuàn), but theatre (*huàjù*) never commanded much of a following in China. Spoken drama appeared in China only in the 20th century, but never won the hearts of the masses. The great 20th-century playwright Cao Yu penned tragic family tableaux, such as the stifling *Thunderstorm* and *Daybreak*. Lao She is also famed for his ironic social commentary and observations of Beijing life, with *Teahouse* being his most famous play.

Much of the last century saw drama stubbing its toe on unexpected political corners, such as the Cultural Revolution. As a literary art, creative drama is still unable to express itself fully and remains sadly gagged and sidelined. Plays do, however, make it to the stage, so if you want to know what's walking the floorboards in Beijing, try some of the venues below.

BEIJING NORTH THEATRE

Map pp232–3
Běi Bīngmǎsī Jùchǎng
☎ 6404 8021, 6406 0175; Beibing Masi Hutong, 67 Jiaodaokou Nandajie; Y100-360; ⏲ performances 7.30pm

This theatre can be found in Beibing Masi Hutong, a *hútong* famous for its theatrical associations southeast of the Drum Tower. Staged here are modern and folk Chinese dramas, work from experimental theatre companies, comedies and international touring productions.

Capital Theatre (below)

CAPITAL THEATRE Map pp232–3
Shǒudū Jùyuàn

☎ 6524 9847/6512; 22 Wangfujing Dajie;

⊙ performances 7pm Tue-Sun; subway Wangfujing

Located in the heart of the city on Wangfujing Dajie, this central theatre has regular performances of contemporary Chinese productions from several theatre companies. Classic plays in the Chinese language often feature, and there's a bookstore within the theatre.

CENTRAL ACADEMY OF DRAMA THEATRE Map pp232–3
Zhōngyāng Xìjù Xuéyuàn Jùchǎng ☎ 6401 3958/3959; 39 Dongmianhua Hutong; subway Andingmen

Situated in the *hútong* district southeast of the Drum Tower, this reputed academy stages regular performances of Chinese language plays.

CENTRAL EXPERIMENTAL DRAMA THEATRE Map pp232–3
Zhōngyāng Shíyàn Huàjùyuàn

☎ 6403 1099; 45 Mao'er Hutong; subway Gulou

Located in a district famous for its thespian associations, this theatre has regular performances of experimental and avant-garde Chinese-language productions.

CHINA PUPPET THEATRE
Map pp228–9
Zhōngguó Mùǒu Jùyuàn

☎ 6422 9487; 1a Anhua Xili, Beisanhuan Zhonglu; subway Andingmen or Gulou

This popular theatre has regular events, including shadow play, puppetry, music and dance.

CINEMAS

Cinemas (*diànyǐngyuàn*) in Beijing are on a slide, propelled downwards by expensive tickets, an annual limit on the number of imported foreign films and a public turning to the latest movies on pirate DVDs. With police turning a blind eye to the deluge of pirated DVDs, cinemas are fighting a desperate battle to woo customers.

There are about 50 cinemas in Beijing with most showing Chinese films that are seldom subtitled. Owing to the limit on the number of foreign films screened, the turnover rate of English language movies is painfully slow, and you will have to wait ages for the next batch to arrive. When you find a Western film, don't forget to check whether it is screened with subtitles (*zìmù*) or dubbed (*pèiyin*) into Chinese. Listings magazines such as *That's Beijing* (p204) advertise film schedules. There is a growing number of cinema cafés in town screening art house movies and classic cinema; check the cinema listings in the expat rags for the latest developments. Apart from futile prayers for a good movie on CCTV, you could tune into your hotel HBO, Cinemax or Star Movies film channel or visit some of the following cinemas. Cinema tickets cost in the region of Y40 to Y120, with cheaper tickets for morning sessions. Note that some bars such as **Hart Salon** (p129) periodically stage cinematic events, so it is worth phoning ahead to find out what's on.

B2M Map pp232–3

☎ 6426 1091; Dongheyan Xiaoqu, Dongcheng;
🕙 5pm until late

This small and simple place has regular screenings of Chinese movies and classic Western cinema from the black and white movie age to the present day. Phone for the latest films. B2M is around 150m to the west of Ditan Park's south gate, along the river (Hucheng He).

CHERRY LANE THEATRE

Map pp234–5

☎ 6430 1398; www.cherrylanemovies.com.cn; Experience Peking Opera Photo Studio, Kent Center, 29 Liangmaqiao Lu; Y50; subway Dongsishitiao, then bus 701

This theatre has Chinese films – often screenings of art films or underground Chinese flicks – with English subtitles. The place is popular, but there is only one screening every two weeks (always on a Friday night). Screenings by Cherry Lane Theatre also take place at the **Hilton Hotel** (Map pp234–5; ☎ 6466 2288, ext 7370; 1 Dongfang Lu, Chaoyang).

STAR CINEMA CITY Map pp239–41

☎ 8518 5399; www.xfilmcity.com; shop BB65, basement, Oriental Plaza, 1 Dongchang'an Jie; Wed-Mon Y50, Tue Y35; subway Wangfujing

This six-screen cinema might have a central location and plush leather reclining sofa chairs, but you pay a hefty prices for the location and luxury.

SUNDONGAN CINEMA CITY

Map pp232–3

☎ 6528 1988; 5th fl, Sundongan Plaza, Wangfujing Dajie; Y40

Don't expect a huge selection, but this is one of Beijing's most conveniently located cinemas, and there's usually a Hollywood feature plus other English-language movies among the Hong Kong dross. Morning screenings are cheaper. Next door to the cinema is a Segaworld entertainment centre.

Other cinemas around town worth trying your luck at include the **Capital Cinema** (Shǒudū Diànyǐngyuàn; Map pp236–8; ☎ 6605 5510; 46 Xichang'an Jie, Xidan); **Dahua Cinema** (Dàhuá Diànyǐngyuàn; Map pp232–3; ☎ 6527 4420; 82 Dongdan Beidajie, Dongcheng); **UME International Cineplex** (☎ 6255 5566; 44 Kexueyuan Nanlu, Haidian) and **Victory Theatre** (Shènglì Diànyǐngyuàn; Map pp230–1; ☎ 6617 5091; 55 Xixi Beidajie). At the time of writing, a **Movie City** was due to open in the popular Henderson Center on Jianguomennei Dajie.

ACROBATICS & MARTIAL ARTS

Two thousand years old, Chinese acrobatics is one of the best deals in town. Most of today's acrobatic repertoire originates from the works of Zhang Heng (AD 25–120), who is credited with creating acts including balancing on a high pole, jumping through hoops, swallowing knives and spitting fire. Wuqiao County in Héběi province is said to be the original bastion of Chinese acrobatics. As well as the following listings, acrobatic performances are also held at the **Dongyue Temple** (p86).

The monks of Shaolin from Songshan in Hénán province have gained an international reputation for their legendary fighting skills honed from a recipe of physical deprivation, spiritual illumination, patience and ironclad willpower. They can be seen in action at the **Liyuan Theatre** (p132).

CHAOYANG THEATRE

Map pp234–5

Cháoyáng Jùchǎng

☎ 6507 2421; 36 Dongsanhuan Beilu; Y80;
🕙 performances 7.30pm; subway Chaoyangmen

Probably the most accessible place for foreign visitors and often bookable through your hotel, this theatre is the venue for visiting acrobatic troupes filling the stage with plate-spinning and hoop-jumping.

UNIVERSAL THEATRE (HEAVEN AND EARTH THEATRE)

Map pp234–5

Tiāndì Jùchǎng

☎ 6416 0757, 6416 9893; 10 Dongzhimen Nandajie; Y60-200; 🕙 performances 7.15pm; subway Dongsishitiao or Dongzhimen

Around 100m north of Poly Plaza, young performers from the China Acrobatic Circus and the China National Acrobatic Troupe perform their mind-bending, joint-popping contortions. This is a favourite with tour groups, so book ahead. Tickets are pricier the further from the stage you sit. You can also visit the circus school to see the performers training (☎ 6502 3984). Find the awful white tower that looks like it should be in an airport – that's where you buy your tickets (credit cards are not accepted).

WAN SHENG THEATRE Map pp239–41
Wànshèng Jùchǎng
☎ 6303 7449; Tianqiao; Y100-150; ☻ performances 7.15pm; subway Qianmen, then bus 819
West of the Temple of Heaven Park, the Wan Sheng Theatre offers one of Beijing's best acrobatic displays performed by the Beijing Acrobatics Troupe. The entrance is down the eastern side of the building.

SPORTS, HEALTH & FITNESS

It's worth getting in touch with your embassy's cultural section, which should have useful information about teams, sports clubs, health centres and other health and fitness-related questions you might have.

WATCHING SPORT

The main venue for national and international athletic championships is the Workers Stadium (Gōngrén Tǐyùguǎn; Map pp234-5) in the Sanlitun area. Athletics events are also held at the Asian Games Village, just within the Fourth Ring Rd in the north of town. As the 2008 Olympics approaches and with China's successful medal haul at the 2004 Athens Olympics, expect increasing emphasis to be put on athletics.

The Chinese are avid football (zúqiú) fans, but they almost universally lament the poor performance of the national team (who nonetheless managed to get to the World Cup in 2002, hosted in Japan and South Korea). Despite being slightly outclassed by the Japanese football team, the

Playing football, Beijing (p138)

Chinese team (guójiaduì) is technically proficient. Several Chinese players have gained experience abroad, including a number with English Premiership teams including Li Tie, Sun Jihai and Fan Zhiyi. In 2004, Manchester United signed Dong Fangzhuo. Foreign football players are also heading for China; even former English football hero Paul Gascoigne played for a period in Chinese 3rd division Tianshui in Gansu province. China's most famous football teams are from Dalian (Shide) and Shanghai (Shenhua), but you can catch the Beijing Team (Guoan), which plays at the Workers Stadium on Sundays.

Basketball is also big news in China, and there is a professional basketball league. Players have been recruited by teams in the USA, including Yao Ming, who (at the time of writing) plays in the NBA. Basketball games are held at the Workers Stadium.

HEALTH & FITNESS
Ballet

The **Western Ballet School** (Map pp234-5; ☎ 6507 1426; 1st fl, Kempinski Hotel, 50 Liangmaqiao Lu) in Chaoyang is a popular ballet school offering courses for both children and beginners.

Fencing

Swashbucklers can find a place in Beijing to practise their epee, sabre and foil strokes. The **Fenxing Fencing Club** (☎ 6492 9041; Olympic Sports Center, Yayuncun, Chaoyang) provides equipment and tuition at a range of levels. Classes are held seven days a week from 10am.

Fitness Clubs

EVOLUTION FITNESS CENTRE

Map pp239–41

☎ 6567 0266; Jianguomenwai Dajie & Dongsanhuan Zhonglu; Y100 per day

Exercise on your own or join a class for aerobics, *tàijíquán* (also known as *taichi*), hip-hop dancing, kick boxing, Latin dancing, yoga or aquaerobics. Personal training programs, fitness consultation and sports therapy are also available, and there's a 25m, five-lane pool.

Football

Several expat five-a-side and 11-a-side teams play in Beijing, including the International Friendship Football Club (iffc@public .east.net.cn), which takes players at all levels and ages, and the Inter United Football Club (interunitedsc@hotmail.com). If you are interested in joining a team or watching a team play, get in touch with the Club Football Center (p129), where you can meet like-minded folk over a pint of beer who should be able to steer you in the right direction.

It is also possible to catch international league games from Europe on CCTV5 and BTV on your hotel TV. Alternatively, try Beijing sports bars like the Club Football Center (p129), Sports City Café (p127) or Frank's Place (p122) for live matches on ESPN or Star Sports. Phone ahead to find out what's on.

Golf

The sport of golf (*gāoěrfúqiú*) enjoys high prestige in China, although Beijing's winters are frost-bitingly cold. If you want to get into the swing of things in warmer seasons, there are a few places you can check out. Frank's Place (p122) is the meeting place for Beijing Golfers Club (golf@franksbar.com), an association of expatriate golfers who meet regularly for golf-related outings and events.

BEIJING GOLF CLUB

Běijīng Gāoěrfúqiú Jùlèbù

☎ 8947 0248; Shunyi; green fees Y1000 Mon-Fri, Y1400 Sat & Sun ◷ 7.30am-dusk

The Beijing Golf Club's 36-hole golf course is northeast of town on the eastern bank of Chaobai River (Chaobai He).

BEIJING INTERNATIONAL GOLF CLUB

Map pp228–9

Běijīng Guójì Gāoěrfúqiú Jùlèbù ☎ 6076 2288; Changping; green fees weekdays Y550, weekends & public holidays Y1270; ◷ 7am-7pm

Considered the best in Beijing, this 18-hole course is 35km north of town, close to the Ming Tombs (p171) and north of Shisanling Reservoir. Hitting that little ball around is not cheap, but the course is in top condition and the scenery is spectacular. You can rent a set of golf clubs and shoes for an additional fee.

Hiking & Biking

Several groups in Beijing organise hiking and biking expeditions to villages and temples outside town. Needless to say, this can be an excellent way for visitors to get out and see the more difficult to reach and remote sights. Beijing Hikers (☎ 139 1002 5516; www.bjhikers.com) organises regular hikes (Y100 per person) and is open to everyone, including children. Mountain Bikers of Beijing (themob@404.com.au) coordinate one-day weekend mountain bike rides at locations outside town (Y70).

Ice Skating

Beijing's winter chill clamps the city's lakes in sheets of ice – but the usual warnings apply about safety and ice thickness for those who want to skate (*liū bīng*). Popular outdoor venues include the lake in Beihai Park, Kunming Lake at the Summer Palace and the Shichahai lakes southwest of the Drum Tower. Skating on the moat around the Forbidden City is not allowed.

LE COOL ICE RINK Map pp239–41

☎ 6505 5776; basement 2, China World Shopping Mall, 1 Jianguomenwai Dajie; per 90 min Y30-50; ◷ 10am-10pm; subway Guomao

This is probably the best and most accessible indoor ice rink in town. It's easy to reach, surrounded by the shops of the China World Trade Center and perfect for the kids. It costs Y30-50 per 90 minutes (charges vary depending on time of day you skate); skate hire is extra.

XIDAN RINK Map pp236–8

☎ 6606 3283; Basement 3, Culture Center, 180 Xidan Beidajie, Xicheng; ◷ 9am-10pm; subway Xidan

Depending on when you go, prices here are Y25-35 per 90 minutes, and skate hire is extra.

Martial Arts

Beijing is an excellent place to stretch a leg. Legions of elderly folk start the day with a bout of *tàijíquán*, and you'll probably get used to seeing octogenarians doing the splits without a wince. Certainly, if you have any interest in China's martial arts heritage, you won't want to miss out on this opportunity to learn from the experts.

Most of you will probably settle for a dose of *taijiquan* and some *qigong* (exercise that channels *qi* or energy) to limber up, learn some breathing techniques and get the blood circulating. More adventurous visitors can dig a bit deeper into China's exciting fighting arts; you never know what you'll unearth.

Visiting Beijing's parks early in the morning and approaching practitioners is possible, if you speak Chinese. You might encounter that grand master of Eight Trigram Palm *(Bāguàzhǎng)* willing to instruct you in some deadly device. Or you might catch an early morning glimpse of a White Eyebrow Boxing *(Báiméiquán)* expert going through clandestine moves. Unfortunately it's easy to get out of one's depth. Chinese martial arts can be bewilderingly enigmatic and some are deeply esoteric; on top of which you might find yourself learning tae kwon do (a Korean martial art), kickboxing or some jazzy health system. Another problem is that many teachers insist that students show patience and loyalty by waiting for an eternity before tuition commences. Also, you will probably encounter communication problems if you don't speak Chinese.

Martial arts lessons in English are held at the **Beijing Language and Culture Institute** (Map pp228-9; ☎ 6232 7531; 15 Xueyuan Lu, Haidian), **FESCO** (p197) and **Evolution Fitness Centre** (p138). Otherwise, check the classified pages of the expat mags (p204), as English-speaking *gongfu* teachers occasionally advertise here. Be aware that some martial artists exploit the gullible, and a great number of teachers are decidedly substandard. Try to get a personal recommendation from other enthusiasts if possible.

Massage

Walking around Beijing's vast distances can put serious stresses on both ligaments and musculature. Thankfully, there are several places in town where you can have your feet and body massaged and reinvigorated. **Beijing Tai Pan Foot Massage** (Map pp239-41; ☎ 6512 0868; 6th fl, Gangmei Dasha, Xiagongfu Jie) is centrally located off Wangfujing Dajie (behind the Beijing Hotel) and can do wonders for body and sole.

Running

Beijing's toxic atmosphere might deter you from sampling extra lungfuls of air, but some groups organise runs in, around and outside town. **Hash House Harriers** (hhhbj@public3.bta .net.cn) – the eccentric expat organisation ('drinkers with a running problem') that originated with the British in Malaysia – has sporadic trips beyond Beijing and are worth contacting for their weekend runs, followed by meals and beer (Y50).

Skiing

Several ski resorts within reach of Beijing lure skiers during the winter months.

BEIJING SNOW WORLD SKI PARK
☎ 8976 1886; Xiaogongmen, Shisanling, Changping

Not far from the Ming Tombs close to town, this resort features lodging, equipment hire and two modest ski runs. Take bus No 345 from Deshengmen; get off at Zhengfa Daxue and change to minibus No 3 to the ski park.

JUNDUSHAN SKI RESORT
☎ 8464 1845, 8462 5486; Cuizhencun 588 Zhenshuncun, Changping; entrance Y20

Just 34km from Beijing, Jundushan advertises that skiing can help people 'relieve psychic tension and return themselves to nature for intimacy with God'. Skiing charges vary according to the day of the week and how long you want to ski (1 hr Mon-Fri Y60, Sat-Sun Y80; 2 hrs Mon-Fri Y100, Sat-Sun Y140; whole day Mon-Fri Y220, Sat-Sun Y340). The resort also offers discounts for regular users and has a team of 'more than 30 professional skimeisters'. The resort provides ski clothing (Y30), sledge hire (Y20), lessons (in Chinese only), a cable car (one way/return Y15/20) and accommodation in wooden villas.

NANSHAN SKI VILLAGE
☎ 6445 0990/91/92; www.nanshanski.com

This resort in Miyun county has beginner and intermediate trails, 90 minutes from Beijing. Packages are available (including transport, meals, equipment and use of slopes), otherwise it's Y20 to enter the resort and Y220 per day Mon-Fri and Y340 Sat-Sun. The resort also has villas and cabins, restaurants, a car park and equipment hire.

SAIBEI SKI RESORT
Beijing ☎ 6711 2847 **or Hebei** ☎ 0313 477 2012/ 2053; sales@saibeiski.com

Located 270km north of Beijing in Hebei province, this resort operates from December to March, and boasts a number of slopes of varying difficulty. Equipment, clothing and snowmobiles are available, but getting here is quite an excursion. Take a train from Beijing south train station to Zhangjiakou and then catch a local bus or taxi; or take a bus from Xizhimen long-distance bus station. The Saibei Ski Resort also runs its own bus to the resort.

Snooker, Billiards & Pool
Snooker and pool are both very popular with the Chinese. Pool is available in several bars around town including the **Club Football Center** (p129), the **John Bull Pub** (p127) and **Durty Nellie's** (p129). For snooker and billiards, you can try the **Xuanlong Pool Hall** (☎ 8425 5566; 179 Hepingli Xijie, Chaoyang; per hr Y28; ☻24hr) or the **Baizhifang Amusement Club** (☎ 6351 4490; 13 Baizhifang Beili, Xuanwu; per hr Y25; ☻ 10am-2am).

Squash
Several five-star hotels hire out squash courts. You could try the **Pulse Club** (Map pp234-5; ☎ 6465 3388, ext 5722; Kempinski Hotel, Lufthansa Center, 50 Liangmaqiao Lu; non-members Y85 per hr), the **Health Club & Spa** (Map pp239-41; ☎ 6460 6688; St Regis, 21 Jianguomenwai Dajie; Y160 per 45 minutes) or the **Kerry Centre Hotel** (p159).

Swimming
You can find pools at some four-star and all five-star hotels, but although access is free for guests, as a non-guest you will have to pay a fee (typically around Y50). Outside hotels, the pool at the **Dongdan Sports Center** (Map pp239-41; ☎ 6523 1241; 2a Dahua Lu,

Dongcheng; Y30; ☻noon-10pm Mon, 10am-10pm Tue-Fri, 9am-10pm Sat & Sun) is popular. You can also try the **Ditan Swimming Pool** (Map pp232-3; ☎ 6426 4483; 18 Anwai Hepingli Zhongjie, Chaoyang; Y20; ☻ 9am-3pm Mon-Fri, noon-9.30pm Sat & Sun).

Tennis
Tennis *(wǎng qiú)* is a popular sport in Beijing that draws enthusiastic crowds, so phone well in advance to make reservations. Many top-end hotels have tennis courts, which can be used for free by guests and by non-guests for a fee. You can try the **Kerry Centre Hotel** (p159). Alternatively, try the **Beijing Gymnasium** (Map pp239-41; ☎ 6711 2266, 2 Tiyuguan Lu; per hr Y150; ☻ 8am-10pm), east of the Temple of Heaven Park or the **Chaoyang Tennis Club** (☎ 6501 0959/0953; 1a Nongzhanguan Nanlu; nonmembers per hr Y200; ☻ 8am-12pm) by the south gate of Chaoyang Park. The **International Tennis Center** (Map pp239-41; ☎ 6711 3872, 50 Tiantan Lu; per hr Y300, Y100 for members; ☻ 10am-10pm) has indoor and outdoor courts and is southeast of the Temple of Heaven Park. The **Beijing International Club** (Map pp239-41; ☎ 6532 2046/2188, ext 3015; 21 Jianguomenwai Dajie; per hr Y120, per hr Y200 after 5pm & weekends; ☻ 8am-9pm) has indoor courts and is south of the St Regis hotel.

Yoga
Older Chinese might choose the more homegrown methods of *qigong* and *tàijíquán* over the imported variant of yoga, but the disciplines have much in common. Both focus on the circulation of energy, called *qì* by the Chinese and *prana* by Indians. **Yoga Yard** (Map pp232-3; ☎ 5102 6108; www.yogayard.com; 108, Bldg 4, Yonghe Jiayuan), just north of the Lama Temple, charges Y80/300/700 for one/four/ten classes and also offers an unlimited monthly pass for Y600. An introduction to yoga course costs Y350, and the class has regular schedules. Drop in on classes and ask about discounts. Class instruction is largely in English.

Shopping

Shopping

Although not exactly a dictum of the late Mao Zedong, 'shop till you drop' has become a mantra of the Communist Party's popular reform drive. Historically China has stressed self-sufficiency and, with domestic demand a major linchpin of economic growth, it's China's magic formula when exports are hit. When the Chinese population of 1.3 billion goes shopping, it shops big time. Beijing is no exception.

Beijing has a diverse range of shopping haunts, from vast malls and department stores to roadside markets, street-side vendors and itinerant hawkers, all of them feeding China's consumer revolution. Travellers won't want to get weighed down with heavy and useless junk, but Beijing is a good place for sought-after curios and souvenirs. It's worth spending a bit of time getting to know where the markets are and trawling through them with a careful eye and the bargaining gloves off.

There are several notable Chinese shopping districts offering abundant goods and reasonable prices, including Wangfujing Dajie, Dongdan Beidajie, Xidan Beidajie, Qianmen (including Dashilar) and Xidan Beidajie. More luxurious shopping areas can be found around the embassy areas of Jianguomenwai and Sanlitun; also check out five-star hotel shopping malls. Shopping at open air markets is an experience not to be missed. Beijing's most popular markets are the Xiushui Silk Market (p146), Panjiayuan (p145) and Hongqiao Market (p144). There are also specialised shopping districts such as Liulichang.

Those on the hunt for silks, jade, Mao memorabilia, pearls, chops (carved name seals), brushes, inks, scrolls, handicrafts, clothing and antiques won't leave Beijing empty-handed. Small or light items to buy are silk scarves, embroidered purses, paper cuttings, wooden and bronze Buddhas, paper lanterns and kites.

You'll also be tripping over fakes by the bundle-load. The latest DVDs and music CDs come smoking off the pirate's press seven days a week, to be hawked from roadsides across the city. Pirate DVDs retail for around Y10, but can be of very bad quality and occasionally the film on the disc is not what you thought you were buying. Top brand names – including Dunhill, Burberry and North Face – are faked wholesale, so if you want the real thing, check the quality of the product carefully. For pharmacies, see p205.

Top Five Shopping Haunts

- **Wangfujing Dajie** (right) Beijing's foremost shopping drag can be found in the Dongcheng area.
- **Liulichang** (p149) Curios and souvenirs amid flavours of old Beijing in Xuanwu district.
- **Dashilar** (right) Bustling street of historic Qing dynasty shops not far from Tiananmen Square.
- **Xiushui Silk Market** (p146) A deluge of pirated labels and low-cost knock-offs.
- **Panjiayuan** (p145) Antiques and collectibles in a market atmosphere; only at weekends.

Clothing Sizes

Measurements approximate only, try before you buy

Women's Clothing

Aus/UK	8	10	12	14	16	18
Europe	36	38	40	42	44	46
Japan	5	7	9	11	13	15
USA	6	8	10	12	14	16

Women's Shoes

Aus/USA	5	6	7	8	9	10
Europe	35	36	37	38	39	40
France only	35	36	38	39	40	42
Japan	22	23	24	25	26	27
UK	3½	4½	5½	6½	7½	8½

Men's Clothing

Aus	92	96	100	104	108	112
Europe	46	48	50	52	54	56
Japan	S		M	M		L
UK/USA	35	36	37	38	39	40

Men's Shirts (Collar Sizes)

Aus/Japan	38	39	40	41	42	43
Europe	38	39	40	41	42	43
UK/USA	15	15½	16	16½	17	17½

Men's Shoes

Aus/UK	7	8	9	10	11	12
Europe	41	42	43	44½	46	47
Japan	26	27	27½	28	29	30
USA	7½	8½	9½	10½	11½	12½

Shopping Tips

Most shops in this chapter are open Monday to Saturday from 8.30am to 8pm, and department stores are open seven days a week from around 9am to 9pm. Open-air markets are generally open from dawn to around sunset, but might open later and close earlier. If the opening times of outlets listed below differ from standard opening hours, their opening times are listed below with the individual entry.

Always remember that foreigners are very likely to be quoted an inflated price for goods and services in Beijing. Prices at department stores are generally fixed (although a 10% discount might be possible if you ask), but bargaining is very much standard practice everywhere else and vendors have factored some latitude into their prices. In markets such as the Xiushui Silk Market (p146), haggling is definitely a prerequisite. When haggling keep the proceedings good natured, so that neither of you feel under pressure. Unless you really want the item in question and can't find it anywhere else, simply walking away from the vendor's stall might achieve the price you are after.

Most large department stores take credit cards, but you should always check that your type of card is accepted. Smaller stores might take only Chinese credit cards, so come armed with cash. Many large department stores and hotels also sport ATMs with international access.

It's worth noting that in many shops, you can't just pay for your goods and walk out in one movement. The salesperson will give you a ticket for your goods. You then go to a till, hand over your ticket and pay for your goods; the stamped ticket is then returned to you. You then return to the salesperson who takes the stamped ticket and hands you your purchase. The whole process can take a long time and involve considerable legwork, so be prepared.

Many tourist shops can arrange shipping overseas, but you should go into the details of the costs and charges with the vendor before proceeding.

CHONGWEN & SOUTH CHAOYANG

A prestigious partly pedestrianised shopping street heading north just west of Oriental Plaza, Wangfujing Dajie boasts a solid strip of stores and cafés and is a favourite commercial haunt of locals, out-of-towners and tourists. Also called Gold St (Jin Jie) by Beijing locals, in pre-liberation days Westerners knew it as Morrison St. The present name of Wangfujing Dajie remembers a 15th-century well. East of Wangfujing is Dongdan Beidajie where you can find fashionable clothes, small speciality shops and a number of music shops where you can pick up cheap CDs.

If Wangfujing Dajie is too organised for you, the place to go and rub shoulders with the proletariat is Dashilar, a *hútong* (alleyway) running west from the top end of Qianmen. Imperial Beijing's shops and theatres were not permitted near the city centre, and the Qianmen-Dashilar District was outside the gates. Many of the city's oldest shops can be found along or near this crowded *hutong*. It's a heady jumble of silk shops, tea shops, department stores, theatres, herbal medicine stores, food and clothing specialists and some unusual architecture. If you take the Beijing bike ride (p107), it finishes near the entrance to Dashilar.

A medieval flavour hangs over Dashilar, a hangover from the days when bustling markets plying specialised products thronged each *hutong*: lace in one *hutong*, lanterns in the other, jade in the next. Dashilar was Silk St, but its official name referred to a wicket gate that was closed at night to keep prowlers out. Many of Beijing's oldest shops can be found here, including Ruifuxiang (p146), Tongrentang (p146) and the Zhang Yiyuan Teastore.

Top Five Clothing

- **Sanlitun Yashou Clothing Market** (p148)
  Beijing's best multi-floor clothing emporium
- **China World Shopping Mall** (p144) Top names and top prices
- **Oriental Plaza** (p145) Swish and splendid
- **Xiushui Silk Market** (p146) Haggle, haggle, haggle
- **Beijing Silk Store** (p144) Well-priced silk material

BEIJING ARTS & CRAFTS CENTRAL
STORE Map pp239–41   *Arts & Crafts/Jade*
Gōngyè Dàshà
☎ 6523 8747; 200 Wangfujing Dajie; subway Wangfujing
This centrally located store (with a sign outside saying Artistic Mansion) is well known for its good selection of jade (with certificates of authenticity), jadeite, *cloisonné* vases, carpets and other Chinese arts and crafts. Jewellery (gold, silver, jade and pearl) is on the ground floor, with glass, paintings, calligraphy and fans on the 2nd floor. You can find woodcarvings, *cloisonné*, lacquer ware and silks on the 3rd floor and jade carvings on the 4th floor.

BEIJING CURIO CITY
Map pp239–41   *Arts & Crafts/Antiques*
Běijīng Gǔwán Chéng
☎ 6774 7711; 21 Dongsanhuan Nanlu;
⊙ 9.30am-6.30pm; subway Guomao, then bus 28
South of **Panjiayuan** (right), Curio City is four floors of gifts, scrolls, ceramics, carpets, duty-free shopping and furniture. This is an excellent place to find knick-knacks and souvenirs, especially on Sundays.

BEIJING SILK STORE Map pp239–41 *Silk*
Běijīng Sīchóu Shāngdiàn
☎ 6301 6658; 5 Zhubaoshi; subway Qianmen
This store near **Ruifuxiang** (p146) and off Qianmen Dajie is an excellent place to pick up quality silk fabric and ready-made clothes at low prices.

CHINA WORLD SHOPPING MALL
Map pp239–41   *Shopping Mall*
☎ 6505 2288; 1 Jianguomenwai Dajie; subway Guomao
Adjacent to the first-rate China World Hotel (p154), this is where Beijing's well-heeled come to be seen shopping. It's a lavish and potently snobbish display – the shops are usually devoid of customers, as many are alienated by its exclusivity and stratospheric prices. It must be seen, however, and kiddies will love **Le Cool Ice Rink** (p138)! If you are hunting for jewellery, **Cartier** (☎ 6505 6660; shop L104) might have what you are after. Other names here include Prada, Louis Vuitton and Moschino.

FLOWER AND BIRD MARKET
Map pp239–41   *Flowers/Birds*
Yùtíng Huāniǎo Shìchǎng
Yuting Shimin Cultural Sq; subway Chongwenmen, then bus 39
Alive with a cornucopia of fauna and flora, this market seethes with pigeons, parrots, turtles, rabbits and all sorts of other birds, beasts and knick-knacks. You can find it off the southeast corner of the Temple of Heaven Park (p68), just south of the canal and north of the railway line.

FRIENDSHIP STORE
Map pp239–41   *Department Store*
Yǒuyì Shāngdiàn
☎ 6500 3311; 17 Jianguomenwai Dajie; subway Jianguomen or Yonganli
The Friendship Store could be worth a perusal for its upstairs touristy junk and its ground floor books and magazine hide-out (excellent for coffee table titles and travel books on China), supermarket and deli.

HAOYUAN MARKET
Map pp239–41   *Souvenirs*
Háoyuán Shìchǎng
west off Wangfujing Dajie; subway Wangfujing
Branching off from **Wangfujing Snack Street** (p118) is this small and bustling souvenir market, full of knick-knacks, curios and whatnots. Swords, calligraphy, toys, handicrafts, masks, kites and all sorts of other goodies make up the picture. It's a good place to pick up a last-minute souvenir or present; haggling is imperative.

HENDERSON CENTER
Map pp239–41   *Shopping Mall*
Jianguomennei Dajie; subway Dongdan or Jianguomen
The high post-modern tower of this centrally located multi-level shopping mall boasts numerous shops and several decent restaurants, including **Be There or Be Square** (p115) and the Irish pub **PJ O'Reilly's** (p127), as well as some useful **supermarkets** (p114).

HONGQIAO MARKET
(PEARL MARKET) Map pp239–41   *Market*
Hóngqiáo Shìchǎng
☎ 6711 7429; 16 Hongqiao Lu; ⊙ 8.30am-7pm; subway Chongwenmen, then bus 610
Besides a cosmos of clutter (shoes, clothing, electronics and much more), you'll also find Chinese arts and crafts and antiques, flanking the vendors who sell pearls. A huge range of pearls is available – freshwater and seawater, white pearls and black pearls – and prices vary incredibly with quality. Pop down to the basement for a selection of scorpions, snake meat, snails and more. Hongqiao Market is across from east gate of the Temple of Heaven Park.

JINGDEZHEN CERAMIC CITY

Map pp239–41 _Ceramics_

☎ 6512 4925/4867; www.jdtcc.com.cn;
277 Wangfujing Dajie; subway Wangfujing

Just off Wangfujing Dajie, this huge emporium is spread over several floors with displays of well-lit ceramics from the Jingdezhen kilns. Pieces are modern, but many works on view employ traditional decorative styles and glazes, such as _doucai_, _fencai_ (famille rose) and _qinghua_ (blue and white).

LIUBIJU Map pp239–41 _Sauces_

Liùbijū Jiàngyuán

3 Liangshidian Jie; subway Qianmen

This 400-year-old pickle-and-sauce emporium patronised by discriminating shoppers is just off the beginning of Dashilar. Nearby is the Zhimielou Restaurant, which serves imperial snacks. On your right as you go down Dashilar across the way is a green concave archway with columns at No 5; this is the entrance to the century-old **Ruifuxiang** (p146), one of the better-known material and silk stores.

LIULIGONGFANG

Map pp239–41 _Glassware_

☎ 8518 6855; www.liuli.com; 1st fl, Oriental Plaza,
1 Dongchang'an Jie; subway Wangfujing

This superbly laid-out shop displays spectacular coloured glass jewellery and ornaments with designs that incorporate traditional Chinese and Western motifs. Even if you don't buy anything, it's worth coming here to examine the delicious items on view, all of which are designed by the famous Taiwanese actress Yang Huishan. Further branches can be found in the **Lufthansa Center Youyi Shopping City** (☎ 6465 1188, ext 109; p148), the **China World Shopping Mall** (☎ 6505 4597; p144), **SciTech Plaza** (☎ 6515 8045) and **Pacific Century Place** (☎ 6539 3888, ext 1123).

NEILIANSHENG SHOE SHOP

Map pp239–41 _Shoes_

Nèiliánshēng Xiédiàn

☎ 6301 4863; 34 Dazhalan Jie; subway Qianmen

They say this is the oldest existing cloth shoe shop in China (it opened in 1853), and it has a factory that still employs more than 100 workers. Mao Zedong and other luminaries had their footgear made here, and you too can pick up ornately embroidered shoes or simply styled cloth slippers from this historic Beijing shop.

ORIENTAL PLAZA

Map pp239–41 _Shopping Mall_

1 Dongchang'an Jie; subway Wangfujing

You could spend a day in this staggeringly large shopping mega-complex at the foot of Wangfujing Dajie. Prices might not be cheap, but window shoppers will be overjoyed. There's a great range of shops and restaurants and the **Food Court** (p118) in the basement is a popular and eclectic Asian eatery. Many top names are here, including Rolls Royce, Swarovski, Valentino and others. It's kid friendly, with nappy-changing rooms and a playroom downstairs.

PANJIAYUAN MARKET

Map pp239–41 _Antiques/Crafts/Collectibles_

off Dongsanhuan Nanlu (Third Ring Rd); ⏺ dawn-around 3pm Sat & Sun; subway Guomao, then bus 28

Hands down the best place to shop for arts (_yìshù_), crafts (_gōngyì_) and antiques (_gǔwán_) in Beijing is Panjiayuan (aka the Dirt or Sunday Market). The market takes place only at weekends and has everything from calligraphy, Cultural Revolution memorabilia and cigarette ad posters to Buddha heads, ceramics and Tibetan carpets.

The market hosts up to 50,000 visitors a day scoping for treasures. Serious collectors are the early birds, swooping here at dawn to snare that precious relic someone will unwittingly let go for Y10. If you want to join them, early Sunday morning is the best time. You might not find that rare Qianlong doucai stem cup or late Yuan dynasty qinghua vase that will ease you into early retirement, but what's on view is no less than a compendium of Chinese curios and an A-Z of Middle Kingdom knick-knacks. Bear in mind that this market is chaos – especially if you find crowds or hard bargaining intimidating. Also, ignore the 'don't pay more than half' rule here – some vendors might start at 10 times the real price. Make a few rounds to compare prices and weigh it all up before forking out for anything.

QIANMEN CARPET COMPANY

Map pp239–41 _Carpets_

Qiánmén Dìtǎnchǎng

☎ 6715 1687; 59 Xingfu Dajie; ⏺ 9.30am-5.30pm;
subway Chongwenmen

This store, just north of the Tiantan Hotel, stocks a good selection of handmade carpets and prayer rugs with natural dyes from Tibet, Xīnjiāng and Mongolia. Prices start at around Y2000.

RUIFUXIANG Map pp239–41 *Silk*
Ruìfúxiáng Sīchóudiàn

☎ 6303 2808; 5 Dazhalan Jie; subway Qianmen

Housed in a historic building on Dashilar, this is one of the best places in town to browse for silk. There's an incredible selection of Shāndōng silk, brocade and satin-silk. Ruifuxiang also has an outlet in the **Sanlitun Yashou Clothing Market** (p148) and at **190 Wangfujing Dajie**.

TEN FU'S TEA Map pp232–3 *Tea*
Tiānfú Míngchá

☎ 6527 4613; www.tenfu.com; 88 Wangfujing Dajie; subway Wangfujing

This excellent shop has top-quality loose tea (prices start at Y10 for a bag) from all over China. Staff can line you up with a free tea tasting, and there are free tea ceremony demonstrations upstairs at the **Dashilar branch**. Why not try the flowery aroma of jasmine tea or some black-tea candy for a caffeine buzz? There is another branch at **65 Liulichang Dongjie** (Map pp236-8; ☎ 6304 8671).

TONGRENTANG
Map pp239–41 *Chinese Medicine*
24 Dazhalan Jie; subway Qianmen

This famous, now international, herbal medicine shop has been peddling pills and potions since 1669. It was a royal dispensary in the Qing dynasty, and its medicines are based on secret prescriptions used by royalty. Its colourful ingredients will cure you of anything from fright to encephalitis, or so they claim. Traditional doctors are available on the spot for consultations. You can find the three-storey shop just west of the Zhang Yiyuan Teastore, with a pair of *qilin* standing outside.

XIUSHUI SILK MARKET
Map pp239–41 *Silk/Clothing*
Xiùshuǐ Shìchǎng
off Jianguomenwai Dajie; subway Yonganli

This market on the northern side of Jianguomenwai, between the Friendship Store and the Jianguo Hotel, is awash with the silkworm's finest. You can also find top brand and designer labels such as Gucci, Burberry and North Face (much of it fake) here. Bargaining is imperative, although it's often a struggle with so many foreign tourists handing over thick wads of cash. Rumours abound of the market being shut down and moved indoors, but at the time of writing it was still thriving. Be extra

vigilant against pickpockets in the crowded quadrants; your wallet could well be taking a walk as you haggle.

YUANLONG SILK CORPORATION
Map pp239–41 *Silk*
Yuánlóng Gùxiù Chóuduàn Shāngháng

☎ 6702 4059; 15 Yongdingmen Dongjie; subway Qianmen, then bus 803

This well-known outlet has a large selection of silk fabric and ready-made clothes at reasonable prices.

ZHAOJIA CHAOWAI MARKET
Map pp239–41 *Furniture*
Zhàojiā Cháowài Shìchǎng

☎ 6770 6402; 43 Huawei Beili; subway Guomao, then bus 28

This huge four-storey warehouse is packed to the gills with traditional Chinese furniture – from opium beds to barrel stools to ornately carved side tables and carpets. Prices are reasonable, but remember to factor in shipping costs (which vendors can arrange). Many stallholders say their wares are genuine Ming or Qing items, but take it all with a pinch of *yán* (salt). The stalls get fancier the higher the floor, and prices rise accordingly. The 4th floor contains ceramics and other antiques. The market is located on the southern part of Dongsanhuan Nanlu at Panjiaqiao, a short distance south of **Beijing Curio City** (p144).

DONGCHENG
FOREIGN LANGUAGES BOOKSTORE
Map pp232–3 *Books*
Wàiwén Shūdiàn

☎ 6512 6911; 235 Wangfujing Dajie; subway Wangfujing

This bookshop has a reasonable selection of English-language novels, as well as a plentiful children's section. There's a good range of travel books, including Lonely Planet titles, on the third floor.

NEW CHINA CHILDREN'S TOY WORLD
Map pp232–3 *Toys*
Zhōngguó Értóng Yòngpin Shāngdiàn
Wangfujing Dajie; subway Wangfujing

If you need to find somewhere to occupy kids, bring them to this maze of toys, model cars and trains, gadgets, puzzles, flashing lights and electronic noises, overseen by helpful staff.

Making a Name for Yourself

The traditional Chinese name chop or seal has been used for thousands of years. It's likely that people began using name chops because Chinese characters are so complex, and few people in ancient times were able to read and write.

A chop served both as a unique personal statement and as a valid signature. All official documents in China needed a chop to be valid. Naturally, this made a chop quite valuable, for with another person's chop it was possible to sign contracts and other legal documents in their name.

Today most Chinese are literate but the tradition lives on. In fact, without a chop it is difficult or impossible to enter into a legally binding contract in China. A chop is used for bank accounts, entrance to safe-deposit boxes and land sales. Only red ink is used for a name chop.

If you live in China for work or study, you will almost certainly need to have a chop made. On the other hand, if you're staying a short time a chop makes a great souvenir. A chop can be made quickly, but first you will need to have your name translated into Chinese characters.

There are many different sizes and styles of chops. Inexpensive small chops can be carved from wood or plastic, while expensive ones can be carved from ivory, jade, marble or steel. Most Chinese people have many chops to confuse a possible thief, although they run the risk of confusing themselves as well. One chop might be used for their bank account, another for contracts and another for a safe-deposit box. Obviously, a chop is important, and losing one can be a big hassle.

Since the people who carve chops don't check your ID, it might occur to you that obtaining a fake or forged chop would be very easy. Indeed, it is. It's also a very serious crime in China.

SHOPPING ARCADE, PENINSULA PALACE HOTEL

Map pp232–3 *Shopping Mall*
8 Jinyu Hutong; subway Wangfujing or Dongdan
There's a host of top names at this exclusive and very hushed basement-level shopping haunt beneath the Peninsula Palace hotel (p158), including **Chanel** (☎ 6512 8899, ext 3590) and **Tiffany & Co** (☎ 6512 9048). There's also a very useful ATM with international access and fine dining at **Huang Ting** (p120).

ZEN CAT GALLERY *Art*

☎ 6651 5392; 14 Houhai Nanyan;
🕙 9am-10am & noon-1pm
Dong Zi is a growing sensation on the Beijing art scene, and her creations, which fill this small room, will show you why. This unique gallery, on the banks of Houhai Lake, contains some very imaginative work at reasonable prices.

ZHAOYUANGE

Map pp232–3 *Kites*
☎ 6512 1937; 41 Nanheyan Dajie;
subway Tiananmen Dong
If you love Chinese kites, you will love this minute shop on the west side of Nanheyan Dajie, south of the **Liujia Guo restaurant** (p120). There's a range of traditional Chinese paper kites here, starting at around Y10 for a simple kite, up to around Y300 for a dragon. You can

also pick up Beijing opera masks. The owner does not speak much English, but you can browse and make a selection.

CHAOYANG

The vast Chaoyang district, home to the Sanlitun Embassy area with its numerous bars and restaurants and the cluster of top-end hotels around the Lufthansa Center, is also one of Beijing's foremost shopping areas.

BLACK ANT BAR

Map pp234–5 *Hiking*
Hēiyǐ Ba
☎ 6506 7202/7196; 3 Baijiazhuang Lu;
subway Chaoyangmen or Dongsishitiao
The Black Ant Bar is indeed a bar, but it doubles as a mountaineering gear shop during daylight hours, when you can pick up hiking kit. The bar-cum-shop also runs hiking and climbing trips outside town.

CASA BELLA Map pp234–5 *Ceramics*

Tongli Studio Lifestyle & Arts, Sanlitun;
subway Dongsishitiao, then bus 701
This marvellous porcelain emporium at the funky Tongli displays a splendid range of reproduction ceramics, many of which are flawless replicas of exquisite pieces that have passed through auction houses. It's worth

coming here just to wander round the well-illuminated pieces on display. The celadon, *fencai* (famille rose), *doucai*, *qinghua* (blue and white) and monochromes here are far superior to the usual junk.

EXTREME BEYOND

Map pp234–5 *Hiking*
☎ 6505 5121, 6506 5121; 6 Gongrentiyuchang Donglu; subway Dongsishitiao

This small shop has a good selection of real brand-name hiking boots, waterproof jackets, backpacks and sleeping bags. Prices here are not cheap (eg Y650 for hiking boots), but you can bargain. The store takes JCB cards.

GANGCHEN CARPETS

Map pp234–5 *Carpets*
☎ 6465 3388; Kempinski Hotel, Lufthansa Center, 50 Liangmaqiao Lu; subway Dongsishitiao, then bus 701

You might pay more for your carpets here (ranging from Y2000 to Y16,000), but you can be assured that what you are buying are genuine, handmade carpets from Tibet. All carpets are made from Changphel sheep wool (characterised by its durable fibres) and decorated with traditional Tibetan motifs.

GEGE QIPAO Map pp234–5 *Clothing*
☎ 6747 1917/2811; Tongli Studio Lifestyle & Arts, Sanlitun; subway Dongsishitiao, then bus 701

This retail outlet upstairs at the Tongli in Sanlitun has a splendid range of silk *qipao* (*cheongsam*) in various designs and colours, some embroidered and others hand-painted. Prices range from Y700 to Y1800. The name of the outlet is a form of address for Manchurian princesses.

KERRY MALL Map pp234–5 *Shopping Mall*
Kerry Center Hotel, 1 Guanghua Lu; subway Chaoyangmen

In a similar league to the China World Shopping Mall, the Kerry Mall has an exclusive range of boutiques. Here you can get your hair styled, relax with some aromatherapy, sample fine wines, send postcards, develop your photos and wander through this smart enclave.

LUFTHANSA CENTER YOUYI SHOPPING CITY

Map pp234–5 *Shopping Mall*
Yànshā Yǒuyì Shāngchǎng

50 Liangmaqiao Lu; subway Dongsishitiao, then bus 701
The gigantic Lufthansa Center is a smart, well-stocked and long-established multi-level

shopping mall. You can find most of what you need here, including several restaurants (Korean, German and Italian), and there are international access ATMs on the ground floor.

PACIFIC CENTURY PLACE

Map pp234–5 *Department Store*
2 Gongrentiyuchang Beilu; subway Dongsishitiao, then bus 701

This upmarket store has clothing for all, as well as electronics and cosmetics, a pharmacy, laundry and a supermarket.

QUINTERO Map pp234–5 *Cigars*
☎ 8529 9496; shop 121, 1st fl, Kerry Mall, 1 Guanghua Lu; ⏳ 11am-2am; subway Chaoyangmen
Come to this exclusive cigar lounge and bar where you can sample a 1989 Chateau Lafite Rothchild (Y5800), Montecristo No. 1 (Y243) or Romeo y Juleta Mille Fleurs (Y108).

SANLITUN YASHOU CLOTHING MARKET Map pp234–5 *Clothing*

Sānlǐtún Yǎxiù Fúzhuāng Shìchǎng
58 Gongrentiyuchang Beilu; subway Dongsishitiao, then bus 701

Five floors of all virtually anything you might need. Basement: shoes, handbags and suitcases. First floor: jackets. Second floor: hiking gear, suits and ladies wear. Third floor: silk, silk and more silk: clothes, cloth, a branch of **Ruifuxiang** (p146) and carpets. Fourth floor: jade, pearls, souvenirs, ethnic jewellery and toys. Fifth floor: sustenance to keep you going.

TONGLI STUDIO LIFESTYLE & ARTS

Map pp234–5 *Arts & Crafts*
⏳ 11am-9pm; subway Dongsishitiao, then bus 701
This impressive lifestyle and arts market in Sanlitun has four floors of excellent outlets selling ceramics, clothing, jewellery and jade, and arts and crafts. You can find **Casa Bella** (p147), **Gege Qipao** (left) and **Things of the Jing** (silver accessories) here among loads of other outlets. **Bar Blue** on the 3rd floor is a smooth and stylish tavern where you can recuperate after shopping.

YANSHA BOOKSTORE Map pp234–5 *Books*
Túshū Tiāndì
☎ 6465 1188; 4th fl, Lufthansa Center Youyi Shopping City , 50 Liangmaqiao Lu; subway Dongsishitiao, then bus 701

The titles here are largely Chinese, but there's also a selection of English-language travel guides, novels and coffee table books on China.

FENGTAI & XUANWU

LIULICHANG

Not far west of Dashilar is Liulichang, Beijing's premier antique street. Worth delving into for its quaint, albeit dressed-up, age-old village atmosphere, the shops on Liulichang (meaning glazed tile factory) trade in (largely fake) antiques. Alongside ersatz Qing monochrome bowls and Cultural Revolution kitsch, you can also rummage through old Chinese books, paintings, brushes, ink and paper. Prepare yourself for pushy sales staff and stratospheric prices – wander round and compare price tags. If you want a chop made, you can do it here.

At the western end of Liulichang Xijie, a collection of ramshackle stalls flog bric-a-brac, Buddhist statuary, Cultural Revolution pamphlets and posters, fake Tang dynasty three-colour porcelain (*sāncǎi*), shoes for bound feet, silks, handicrafts, Chinese kites, swords, walking sticks, door knockers and so on. Moving east along Liulichang Xijie, the **China Cultural Heritage Bookstore** (below) has a fascinating collection of literature and old maps. Across the way from **Rongbaozhai** (p150) is **Parson's** (☎ 6302 0585; 36 Liulichang Xijie), with its collection of musical instruments. Also on Liulichang are several branches of **Cathay Bookshop** (below). And when you're all shopped out, you can put your feet up at the **Ji Gu Ge Teahouse** (p124).

CATHAY BOOKSHOP Map pp236–8   *Books*
Zhōngguó Shūdiàn
☎ 6303 2104; 34 Liulichang Xijie; subway Hepingmen
There are several branches of the Cathay Bookshop on Liulichang. This branch (Gǔjí Shūdiàn), on the south side of Liulichang Xijie opposite Rongbaozhai, is worth checking out for its wide variety of colour art books on Chinese painting, ceramics and furniture, most of which are in Chinese. There is also an extensive range of books on religion (also in Chinese). Upstairs has more art books, stone rubbings and antiquarian books (in what is called the Gǔjí Shūdiàn). The store takes Mastercard and Visa. There's another branch just further along at **18 Liulichang Xijie** that has a paper cuts exhibition on the 2nd floor. It also sells an interesting set of bookmarks (Y10) of photographs of the old Qing Imperial household, including snapshots of Reginald Johnson (Last Emperor Henry Puyi's English tutor), Puyi practising shadow boxing, eunuchs and Cixi dressed as Avalokiteshvara (Guanyin). Another branch of Cathay Bookshop can be found at **106 Liulichang Dongjie** (Map pp236-8).

CHINA CULTURAL HERITAGE BOOKSHOP (CATHAY BOOKSHOP)
Map pp236–8   *Books/Museum Pieces*
Wénhuà Yíchǎn Shūdiàn
☎ 6303 1602; 57 Liulichang Xijie; subway Hepingmen
This branch of the Cathay Bookshop on the north side of the road has a marvellous museum on the ground floor containing a fascinating collection of literature and maps relating

Traditional masks for sale on Liulichang (above)

Best Buys in Beijing

Arts and crafts and antiques are all tempting buys in Beijing, but it takes an expert eye to sort the wheat from the chaff, and even connoisseurs end up getting fleeced. Don't forget it's not just DVDs that are pirated; ceramics, oils and carvings regularly get the facsimile treatment. Those after real treasures will be looking for special certificates to take genuine antiques out of China (see Customs p197) and checking for the red wax seal that allows the owner to export it. Technically, items dating from before 1795 cannot be exported from China, but it is unlikely you will find anything genuinely that old. If buying a convincing reproduction or fake, ask the vendor to provide paperwork proving it does not infringe export regulations. Don't expect to unearth anything of real value; China has largely been sieved of nuggets.

Silk (*sīchóu*) is an important commodity in Beijing, and excellent prices for both silk fabrics and clothing can be found. The top places for silk in Beijing include the **Xiushui Silk Market** (p146), **Beijing Silk Store** (p144) and **Ruifuxiang** (p146).

Carpets (*dìtǎn*) can be found at several stores, and Beijing is an excellent place to shop for rugs, both antique and new, from all over China – from Xīnjiāng and Níngxià to Gānsù and Tibet. Antique carpets are often preferred for their richness in colour, attained through the use of natural dyes, and because they are handmade. As well as specialist stores, carpet vendors can be found at **Panjiayuan Market** (p145), **Beijing Curio City** (p144), **Zhaojia Chaowai Market** (p146) and some five-star hotels, including the **Kempinski Hotel** (p159). It pays to know that some rugs advertised as Tibetan are actually made in factories in mainland China, so try to visit a reputable dealer rather than hunting out the cheapest item. Other carpets are woven from imported Australian wool, the fibres of which are not particularly suitable for rugs. A carpet should be woven from a durable rather than a soft wool. The quality of the dye is something else to ask about.

Tailor-made clothes can be an excellent idea if you have the time, and made-to-measure clothing, including traditional Chinese gowns (*qípáo*, or *cheongsam* in Cantonese) and Mao suits, can be a bargain in Beijing. Most tailors supply material, or you can bring your own.

Cashmere (*yángróngshān*) from Inner Mongolia is another good buy in Beijing. The Silk Market is a good place to hunt for cashmere bargains; however, as with other things here, eye it up carefully as synthetics sometimes pose as the real thing.

When looking for bookstores, don't expect to find a wide range of decent literature. The selection in town remains sporadic, limited and very expensive. Our advice is to bring your own reading material. Bookshop buyers don't know what to order: you'll find wildly improbable titles and plenty of omissions. However, if what you are after are coffee table books on China in English, you'll be in seventh heaven.

to Beijing, some accompanied by English captions. Among the antique cartography is a map published by the *Peiping Chronicle* called 'A bird's eye view of Beiping and Environs'. Also on view is a colour map of Beijing from the early days of the Republic and photos of old Peking, including the old city wall gates, some of which are for sale. There is also an extensive collection of calligraphy at the rear and displays of antiquarian books.

RONGBAOZHAI

Map pp236–8   *Chinese Artwork*

☎ 6303 6090; 19 Liulichang Xijie; subway Hepingmen

Spread over two floors and sprawling down quite a length of the road, this store has a selection of scroll paintings, woodblock prints, paper, ink and brushes. As it's state-run, the effect is rather uninspiring and the collection

somewhat flat. Prices are generally fixed, although you can usually get 10% off. The shop accepts JCB credit cards.

XIDAN BOOKSHOP Map pp236–8   *Books*
Xīdān Túshū Dàshà

☎ 6607 8477; 17 Xichang'an Jie; subway Xidan

The titles at this absolutely vast bookshop (Beijing's largest) are largely Chinese, but there is a good range of English language titles in the basement. The gang of writers – Heroditus, Homer, Clausewitz, Machiavelli, Maupassant, Victor Hugo et al. – are hardly cutting edge, but there's a smattering of modern pulp fiction. You can also find works with titles like *Theory of Marx and Engels* and *History and Construction of the Communist Party*. Maps of Beijing are handily located on the 6th floor.

Sleeping

Sleeping

As with the rest of China (bar Hong Kong, Macau and Shànghǎi), Beijing's hotels do not make for an inspiring selection, and few establishments have real character or distinction. That said, hotels come in all shapes and sizes to meet most wallet widths. This chapter will guide you through all options, however large or small your budget.

Beijing's mid-range (three- to four-star) hotels offer a uniform product largely indistinguishable from each other in their blandness and ordinariness. Many hotels in this price range have little if any history and therefore hardly any character or appeal, although service standards are acceptable. An exception are the old, historic courtyard hotels (sihéyuàn bīnguǎn) buried away down Beijing's hútong (alleyways). Staying at courtyard hotels allows guests to reside in the old part of town rather than being encapsulated in a fabricated, modern shell in an overdeveloped district.

Top Five Places to Stay

- **St Regis** (p155) First-rate, top-notch elegance complemented by professionalism and a superb location.
- **Grand Hyatt Beijing** (p154) Gorgeous hotel at the foot of Wangfujing Dajie and in the heart of Beijing.
- **Lusongyuan Hotel** (p159) The courtyard ambience and historic hútong locale make this a charming base for exploring the old city.
- **Hao Yuan Guesthouse** (p157) Delightful and quiet Qing courtyard hotel with pleasant staff and a modest handful of tastefully finished rooms.
- **Far East International Youth Hostel** (p161) Loads of character, good-value rooms and the thumbs up from enthusiastic travellers.

Unlike hotels in Hong Kong, Macau or Shanghai, Beijing's top-end accommodation options (four- to five-star hotels) are similarly practically devoid of history or real class, although the best offer a standard equal to five-star international hotels abroad.

Be warned that China's hotels regularly award themselves five and four stars, when they are patently a star lower in ranking. This might not be immediately obvious to guests approaching the reception desk, so take time to wander round and make a quick inspection of the overall quality. This is particularly important when travelling to destinations outside Beijing.

Beijing used to present dire options for the economy traveller, but the battle for budget rooms is in full swing. Beijing's successful 2008 Olympic bid has further turned the screw, and a growing variety of youth hostels and budget accommodation is becoming available.

Until 2003, the Public Security Bureau (PSB; Gōngānjú) operated a policy of barring foreigners from the cheapest guesthouses (called zhāodàisuǒ, lǚdiàn or lǚguǎn), ostensibly for security reasons. In 2003 it was announced that foreigners would be able to stay anywhere, even at the lowest of the low. At the time of research, this message had yet to filter down to the reception desks of most budget Chinese guesthouses, and they were still turning foreigners away. If you are looking for very cheap accommodation, however, enquire at zhāodàisuǒ (招待所), as they are required to take foreigners; don't expect anyone to speak English, and do expect grubby rooms. Cheap hotels are also known as lǚdiàn (旅店) or lǚguǎn (旅馆).

A far superior option in the budget category are youth hostels that offer central, affordable accommodation and are staffed by English speakers. All of the Hostelling International (HI) hostels open in Beijing at the time of writing have been reviewed.

English-language skills can be minimal even in five-star hotels. Three-star hotels that mainly deal with Chinese and overseas Chinese guests might have no English-speaking staff, while HI hostels often have someone who can speak decent English at reception, as they are used to dealing with Westerners.

Hotels tend to fill quickly (especially cheaper, smaller options) during the peak summer season, and you might have to scramble to find something affordable.

When you check into a hotel, you will have to complete a registration form, a copy of which will be sent to the local PSB office.

Price Ranges & Reservations

It often pays to reserve a hotel room through the hotel's website, where discounts are regularly offered. Also visit travel agencies and websites that can get you discounts at top-end hotels. Such sites as www.asia-hotels.com and www.redflag.info offer discounted advance booking.

If you are arriving in Beijing without a reservation and are planning to stay in mid-range or top-end accommodation, stop by one of the airport hotel reservations counters, which could secure you a discount of up to 50% off the rack rates. Counters are located just outside the arrivals area, after you pass through customs.

Bargaining for a room at hotels is often possible; just ask whether a 'discount' (*dǎzhé*) is in effect. Outside peak times (during the Chinese New Year, May to September and the first week of October), you can often get a discount of 30% to 40%. But make sure you check whether the discounted price includes the service charge, as this will eat up 10% to 15% of your discount. Also ask about special promotional packages at top-end hotels, especially newly opened ventures. If staying long-term, you should be able to get good deals, especially at top-end hotels.

Top-end hotels usually list their room rates in US dollars, but you will have to pay in local currency. Practically all hotels will change money for guests, and most mid-range and top-end hotels accept credit cards. All hotel rooms are subject to a 10% or 15% service charge, but many cheaper hotels don't bother to charge it.

Longer-Term Rentals

Accommodation options for those planning to live, work or study in Beijing have grown now that the restrictions on where foreigners can live have been lifted.

New housing laws stipulate that foreigners can live in Chinese housing as long as the owners of the apartment register the foreign resident with the local PSB. Failure to do so could well incur foreigners a fine of around Y3000 (per person).

The advantage of living in Chinese housing, rather than in housing designed for expat residents, is that the rent is far more attractive. Expat housing developments are generally first-rate, with expensive management fees, 24-hour security, guards, sports facilities, swimming pools and kindergartens. Rates for such properties are stratospheric, with rents reaching as high as US$9500 per month for a four-bedroom flat in Beijing. Modern Chinese housing (eg, apartment blocks), however, offers substantially lower rents, and although standards are lower than typical foreign housing, they're much higher than average Chinese housing (there will be tiles on the floor, decent plumbing etc).

If you're coming to study, your school will probably have a dormitory. It's possible to move in with a Chinese family and simply pay rent, but make sure you are officially registered. Families typically charge Y1000 per month for a room. If you teach or work for the government, your housing will likely be provided free or at the Chinese price (next to nothing).

Some long-term residents prefer to live in a courtyard house, as they have more personality and charm than sterile modern high-rises and expat housing developments. What you gain in history and character, however, you might sacrifice in amenities: there is usually nowhere to park the car, the toilet might be outside, heating might be wanting and the chances are there won't be any satellite TV. But many courtyard homes on the rental market now have air-con, shower rooms, lavatories and fully equipped kitchens, and have been recently redecorated. Check the expat magazines, where you will find monthly rents in the region of US$1000 to US$10,000. Such places, however, might deal specifically with expats and will be far more expensive; if you manage to find a courtyard residence through a Chinese estate agent, it could be much, much cheaper. If you are interested, look around and compare prices.

If you live in a hotel, you should be able to negotiate a discount for a long-term stay. Some cheaper hotels, such as the **Red House Hotel** (p160), have facilities for long-staying residents.

Foreigners expecting to make Beijing their permanent home can buy property (at a price), and by doing so also gain a residence permit. In most cases, buying actually means leasing the property for 75 years, after which it reverts to state ownership.

Besides word of mouth, the best way to find housing in Beijing is through a real estate agent or by checking housing ads in the expat mags. *That's Beijing* (www.thatsmagazines.com) is a useful source of rental information and advertisements.

CHONGWEN & SOUTH CHAOYANG

This area is probably Beijing's most popular hotel district, at least for mid-range and top-end accommodation. Local hotels all offer either proximity or simple transport access to Tiananmen Square, the Temple of Heaven Park, Wangfujing Dajie and Beijing's commercial and business district in the east. Some of Beijing's best top-notch and mid-range hotels are found here, as well as a handful of decent budget alternatives.

ASCOTT Map pp239–41

☎ 6567 8100; www.the-ascott.com; 108b Jianguo Lu; 1/2/3 bedroom Y1300/1900/2400; subway Guomao

Located opposite the China World Trade Center in Beijing's business district, the Ascott offers a range of stylish and fully equipped serviced apartments for rent on a daily or monthly basis. Of undeniable appeal to those doing long-term business in Beijing, Ascott's residents benefit from 24-hour security and a full range of amenities, including a children's playground and babysitting service, an indoor swimming pool, a mini supermarket and fine dining options. Also available are 12 penthouses with long views over town.

BEIJING HOTEL Map pp239–41

Běijīng Fàndiàn

☎ 6513 7766; www.chinabeijinghotel.com.cn; 33 Dongchang'an Jie; tw US$180–290, ste US$320–590; subway Wangfujing

This is Beijing's oldest hotel, dating from Boxer Rebellion days, when the nearby Foreign Legation Quarter was a mass of smoking ruins. The hotel was neglected for years, but a refit several years ago re-launched the 900-room Beijing Hotel as a contender in a highly competitive market, despite persistent murmurs of casual service. The hotel is finely perched on Wangfujing Dajie's southern extremity a hop away from Wangfujing subway stop.

CHINA WORLD HOTEL Map pp239–41

Zhōngguó Dàfàndiàn

☎ 6505 2266; www.shangri-la.com; 1 Jianguomenwai Dajie; d/ste US$300–500, ste US$410–3500; subway Guomao

This excellent five-star hotel has all the hallmarks of the Shangri-La chain (reliability and style), and all your shopping and dining needs can be met at the China World Trade Center. Well suited to the executive traveller, the hotel has a sumptuous foyer with pronounced Chinese motifs, along with glittering chandeliers, robust columns and smooth acres of marble.

As with all Shangri-La hotels, an extra degree of luxury awaits on Horizon Club floors. Full tariff rate includes free airport transfer, laundry, dry cleaning, breakfast and local phone calls.

GRAND HOTEL BEIJING Map pp239–41

Guìbīnlóu Fàndiàn

☎ 6513 7788; www.grandhotelbeijing.com.cn; 35 Dongchang'an Jie; standard tw/ste US$275/330; subway Tiananmen Dong or Wangfujing

This 10-storey hotel has unparalleled views over its imperial neighbour, the Forbidden City, which might be the reason to come here (expect to pay more for palace views). The location is splendid, but the effect is spoiled by a wanting and unimpressive interior; compared to the spotless five-star competition, this place is in need of a refit. The tariff is not very competitive, so try for discounts or stay somewhere else. The hotel is adjacent to the Beijing Hotel; the Palace View bar (p127) on the 10th floor has an excellent view.

GRAND HYATT BEIJING Map pp239–41

Běijīng Dōngfāng Jūnyuè Dàjiǔdiàn

☎ 8518 1234; www.hyatt.com; 1 Dongchang'an Jie; d US$320; subway Wangfujing

This stunning hotel has an exclusive address right on the shopping strip of Wangfujing Dajie, with all you could need at the attached Oriental Plaza (p145). Blessed with top-notch design, a splendid interior, exemplary service and undeniable opulence, the Grand Hyatt is only 10 minutes walk from the Forbidden City and Tiananmen Square. The hotel features an indoor swimming pool and four restaurants – including smart Cantonese at Noble Court and northern cuisine at Made in China – as well as several bars, including the Red Moon (p127).

HADEMEN HOTEL Map pp239–41

Hādémén Fàndiàn

☎ 6711 2244; hademen@ public.gb.com.cn; 2a Chongwenmenwai Dajie; s Y420, d Y480–580; subway Qianmen or Chongwenmen

The three-star Hademen Hotel might be unexceptional, but it benefits from a decent location near the Beijing Train Station and the restored Ming City Wall Ruins Park (p66). Rooms are good value (ask for a discount). The hotel is just south of Chongwenmen Dajie, known as Hademen Dajie during foreign Legation days, which was the site of the murder of the German minister, Baron von Ketteler, by the Boxers. Hademan's standard doubles are reasonably decorated and comfy, with small shower rooms. Bike rental is available (Y50 per day, Y200 deposit). You can satisfy your roast duck cravings at the Bianyifang Roast Duck restaurant (p115) adjacent to the hotel.

HUAFENG HOTEL Map pp239–41
Huáfēng Bīnguǎn
☎ 6524 7311; fax 6524 7495; 5 Qianmen Dongdajie; d/ste Y420/780; subway Chongwenmen or Qianmen

Situated on the former site of the more illustrious Grand Hotel des Wagon-Lits (Liùguó Fándiàn) but now rather a more dismal Chinese-style outfit, the three-star Huafeng is nevertheless well located in the former Foreign Legation Quarter (p63). Tiananmen Square and Wangfujing Dajie are within walking distance. There's a Chinese restaurant and a billiard room.

JIANGUO HOTEL Map pp239–41
Jiànguó Fàndiàn
☎ 6500 2233; sales@ hoteljianguo.com; 5 Jianguomenwai Dajie; d/ste US$220/310; subway Yonganli

This four-star Jianguo Hotel has a very cosy, but slightly yesteryear atmosphere. The recently decorated rooms are stylish, clean and tastefully furnished in dark wood, while the rest of the hotel slowly goes to seed. The hotel is also home to Charlie's Bar (p127) and a host of restaurants, including the excellent French restaurant, Justine's. There is an executive floor at hand for business travellers in need of a bit more. The hotel offers good off-season rates.

ST REGIS Map pp239–41
Běijīng Guójì Jùlèbù Fàndiàn
☎ 6460 6688; www.stregis.com/beijing; 21 Jianguomenwai Dajie; d/ste US$340/500-5300; subway Jianguomen

With first-rate, top-notch elegance complemented by professionalism and a superb location, the St Regis is a marvellous choice. The splendid foyer and an enticing complement of restaurants compound this hotel's undeniable allure. In the Club Wing you can find a bowling centre, squash courts, cigar and wine lounges and the Astor Grill. Enter off Ritan Lu.

XIAOXIANG HOTEL Map pp239–41
Xiāoxiāng Dàjiǔdiàn
☎ 8316 1188; fax 6303 0690; 42 Beiwei Lu; s/d/ste Y480/580/880

This three-star hotel is getting a bit worn, but the location is close to the west gate of the Temple of Heaven Park (p68) and it's worth fishing for discounts. The hotel restaurant specialises in fiery Hunan cuisine as well as Cantonese dishes.

CHEAP SLEEPS

DONGFUYUAN HOTEL Map pp239–41
Dōngfúyuàn Bīnguǎn
☎ 6528 2019; 277 Wangfujing Dajie; d Y128-258, tr Y158; subway Wangfujing

This two-floor hotel has very simple, grubby rooms and would not normally warrant a mention but for its location just west of Wangfujing Snack Street (p118). The cheaper doubles have no shower, but the more expensive ones come with shower and balcony. There's no English sign, but the hotel is around 100m down along Wangfujing Snack Street on your right. Don't expect much English to be spoken here, but it's worth trying hard to bargain the room price down.

EASTERN MORNING SUN YOUTH HOSTEL
Map pp239–41
Běijīng Dōngfāng Chénguāng Qīngnián Lǚguǎn
☎ 6528 4347; www.easytour.com.cn in Chinese; fl B4, Oriental Plaza, 8-16 Dongdansantiao; s/d/tr Y80/120/180; subway Wangfujing

Despite the sign outside, this is not a bona fide Hostelling International hostel, but the location is peerless. Single rooms are simple and small with tiled floors; the better doubles have TV (no phone). Showers and phones are all communal. There is a tourist information office, Internet (Y10 per hour), ticketing office, lockers and IP cards on sale. If staying, memorise where the fire escape is as the hostel is a subterranean four floors below ground level.

DONGCHENG

As this ancient district of Beijing is riddled with *hútong* and history, you'll find the best courtyard hotels here, as well as some historic guesthouses. High-calibre top-end hotels tend to cluster close to the shopping street of Wangfujing Dajie, and a few decent budget options can also be found.

BAMBOO GARDEN HOTEL Map pp232–3
Zhúyuán Bīnguǎn
☎ 6403 2229; www.bbgh.com.cn; 24 Xiaoshiqiao Hutong; s/d/ste Y380/530/680; subway Gulou

This cosy, intimate and tranquil courtyard hotel is pleasantly located in a *hútong* not far from the Drum and Bell Towers. The buildings date back to the late Qing dynasty, and the gardens belonged to a eunuch from Empress Cixi's entourage. The hotel gets good reviews, despite occasionally unhelpful staff. The atmosphere can seem contrived, but rooms are tastefully decorated with reproduction Ming furniture and the abundant foliage pleasant. Reception is through the gates on your left.

CROWNE PLAZA HOTEL
Map pp232–3
Guójì Yìyuàn Huángguān Jiàrì Fàndiàn)
☎ 6513 3388; www.crowneplaza.com;
48 Wangfujing Dajie; s US$200-260, d US$220-280;
subway Wangfujing

The Crowne Plaza enjoys an excellent central location on Wangfujing Dajie. Entered via a vast atrium, this is a slightly faded (scuffed brass and marble work) five-star hotel of the early 1990s ilk, but the staff is pleasant and service is good. There's a quiet bar on the 2nd floor (with CNN) and a collection of art galleries on the ground floor.

Hútong Life

A few years ago, my wife, my baby son and I hit upon a small, tidy two-bedroom maisonette in a Qing dynasty *sìhéyuàn* (courtyard house) just off Chaoyangmen Nanxiaojie to rent at Y2500 per month. A white plaque outside trumpeted it as the former residence of a high-ranking official called Zhu Qiqian. At first glance, the cheap rent didn't bode well for modern amenities. The owner, however, gaily spun open hot water taps, zapped the air-con with a remote and flung open a curtain to reveal a fully equipped shower room. Capping all of this was a finely crafted traditional Qing roof with upturned eaves, along which slunk a lethargic cat. We were right in the heart of Beijing, but all we could hear was a dry rustling of leaves in the wind and the click of chess pieces at the gate. Bet your bottom dollar we signed and sealed on the spot.

Our neighbour Mr Ma, a cheerful *yùchú* (imperial chef), gave us a warm welcome that quickly developed into a feast attended by many of the courtyard's residents. Our host regaled us with anecdotes about the domicile. Mr Ma insisted the same pair of hands that fashioned the celebrated Long Corridor at the Summer Palace designed the corridor that linked our courtyards (much nodding from the old-timers). Waving a contemptuous hand at the high-rises beyond, Mr Ma pledged that his courtyard house was sturdy enough to ride out an earthquake.

After a few glasses of Erguotou (white spirit), Mr Ma was even hinting at an ancient, carved stone tablet in the *siheyuan*, surely worth a bob or two. He never actually pointed it out; perhaps he thought I would take advantage of a moonless night to crowbar it from the wall and get it under Sotheby's gavel in Hong Kong.

Two huge red doors, each around seven inches thick, fronted the *siheyuan*. There were nine courtyards in all, strung out along a bicycle-lined wooden corridor. At night the men of the courtyard would gather by the ancient drumstones in the doorway, with beer, cigarettes, stories or a chess set. Come 10.30pm, they would slip indoors and the gates would be shut by a family paid around Y150 a month to act as *chuándàshì* (gatekeeper) and lookout. If you wandered out for a beer (Y1.50 per bottle from the local) after 10.30pm, you had to take a key and rummage through a sliding hatch on the door for the huge bolt fastening it from the inside.

All of this made us feel very secure. So secure that we would leave our front door open all day; in London that would have been unforgivable stupidity, but here in Beijing it is the norm. My 18-month-old son could usually be found playing with Mr Ma's young daughter, Xiao Yue ('Little Moon'), or enveloped in a Chinese world at the home of Mr Ma's parents opposite.

Night-time was magical, with the Qing rooftops silhouetted against the evening sky and the courtyard deep in a nocturnal reverie. Most residents would have returned from work, but the corridor would give the occasional squeak as a straggler returning late wheeled their bicycle home. A gorgeous hush would then invariably settle over the courtyard. At moments like this, we were no longer in Beijing but had been transported back to Peking.

Damian Harper

CUI MING ZHUANG HOTEL Map pp232–3
Cuìmíng Zhuāng Bīnguǎn
☎ 6513 6622; www.cuimingzhuanghotel.com.cn;
1 Nanheyan Dajie; d/ste Y600/1200;
subway Tiananmen Dong

Located diagonally across the road from the former site of Dongan Men (p76) and fronted by a reproduction Chinese roof with green tiles, this pleasant and quiet three-star hotel dates from the 1930s. During the 1940s, the building was an office of the Chinese Communist Party, which helped agree to the ceasefire between the Kuomintang and the communists. It largely caters to Chinese guests, but is excellently located for the Forbidden City and Wangfujing Dajie. Facilities include a billiard room, ticketing office, Sunshine Café and shuffleboard.

FRIENDSHIP GUESTHOUSE Map pp232–3
Yóuhǎo Bīnguǎn
☎ 6403 1114; fax 6401 4603; 7 Houyuan Ensi Hutong;
s/d/ste Y296/392/800; subway Andingmen

In a *hútong* just off Jiaodaokou Nandajie, this hotel was built in 1875 and was once the residence of Chiang Kai-shek and the Yugoslav Embassy. Today it survives as a pleasant courtyard-style hotel with a Japanese restaurant, managed by the Chinese People's Association for Friendship with Foreign Countries. The hotel has a socialist-era feel to it, and the rooms are yesteryear in feel, but they have a pleasant outlook over a courtyard. It's about 200m down Houyuan Ensi Hutong on the north side of the road; reception is in the brick building through the gate on your right.

HAO YUAN GUESTHOUSE Map pp232–3
Hǎoyuán Bīnguǎn
☎ 6512 5557; www.haoyuanhotel.com; 53 Shijia
Hutong; d Y468-572; subway Dongdan, then bus 807

This delightful quiet Qing courtyard hotel has pleasant staff and a handful of tastefully finished rooms. Laid out with trees, the courtyard at the rear is gorgeous and boasts the best room, in which the owner used to live. At the time of writing the buildings opposite had been razed, leaving a flattened wasteland waiting for the developers, robbing the *hutong* of some charm. The hotel is about a 10-minute walk from Wangfujing Dajie's main drag. Walk north on Dongdan Beidajie and about 25m before Dengshikou Dajie, you'll see a small alley – Shijia Hutong – off to the right. The hotel is about 200m down the alley on your left with big red gates and guarded by two stone lions. There is a restaurant as well as bike rental; breakfast is included; and Internet access is available (Y10 per hr). Rooms have showers.

NOVOTEL PEACE HOTEL Map pp232–3
Běijīng Nuòfùtè Hépíng Bīnguǎn
☎ 6512 8833; www.novotelpeace.bj.com; 3 Jinyu
Hutong, Wangfujing Dajie; West Wing d US$80-110,
ste US$100-130; subway Wangfujing or Dongdajie

This efficient and inviting refurbished four-star hotel has a fresh and cosmopolitan touch and a fantastic central location. Eschewing the gaudiness of some top-league places, Novotel Peace delivers a straightforward elegance without the ostentatious frills. As a result, it is popular and appealing. There's a useful travel

Hao Yuan Guesthouse (above)

service and bookshop (for newspapers) and the location is excellent, with Wangfujing Dajie just around the corner. The ground-floor Western restaurant is well known for its filling buffets. The cheaper rooms – not huge but perfectly serviceable – are in the older, more scuffed West Wing. Ask for promotional rates.

PENINSULA PALACE Map pp232–3
Wángfǔ Fàndiàn

☎ 8516 2888; www.peninsula.com; 8 Jinyu Hutong; d/ste US$320/360; subway Wangfujing or Dongdan

Owned by the Peninsula Group, the recently renovated Peninsula Palace Hotel is an elegant composition, making for a consummate residence while in the capital. It boasts two excellent restaurants, including the popular Huang Ting (p120), a sparkling multi-tiered, exclusive shopping mall (p147), a fine location off Wangfujing Dajie, a fitness centre and luxurious styling all round. The Club floors offer an executive lounge with complimentary breakfast and evening cocktails. Promotional prices frequently take the sting out of the tariff, so ask. Rolls-Royce and Mercedes-Benz limousines are available for airport transfer, and an ATM can be found in the sub-basement.

PRIME HOTEL Map pp232–3
Huáqiáo Dàshà

☎ 6513 6666; www.primehotel.cn; 2 Wangfujing Dajie; d US$200, ste US$320-1500; subway Wangfujing

With an excellent location at the northern end of Wangfujing Dajie, this hotel (advertised as five-star) also has Beijing's largest standard double rooms at 42 sq metres. The hotel is perhaps a bit gaudy and decoratively gauche (eg the sky and clouds in the atrium, white tiles and upturned eaves outside), but the spacious rooms have broadband Internet access, satellite TV and there's a choice of Western, Chinese and Japanese restaurants. Other facilities include indoor swimming pool, gym and a nightclub. Ask for promotional rates, especially during the off-season.

RED CAPITAL RESIDENCE Map pp232–3
Xīnhóngzī Kèzhàn

☎ 6402 7150; www.redcapitalclub.com.cn; 9 Dongsi Liutiao; r US$148-188; subway Dongsishitiao

Dressed up with Liberation-era artefacts and established in a glorious Qing dynasty courtyard, this unusual guesthouse is heady with the nostalgia of a vanished age. Make your choice from five rooms decked out with stuff that wouldn't look out of place in a museum:

Top Courtyard Hotels

- **Lusongyuan Hotel** (right) Centrally located Qing dynasty courtyard residence originally built by a Mongolian general.
- **Red Capital Residence** (below) Historic courtyard hotel with a mere handful of nostalgically styled rooms.
- **Hao Yuan Guesthouse** (p157) Well-preserved Qing dynasty courtyard once home to Hua Guofeng, Communist Party chairman after Mao Zedong.
- **Bamboo Garden Hotel** (p157) Quiet and spacious courtyard hotel with pleasant grounds in the vicinity of the Drum and Bell Towers.

the Chairman's Residence, the Concubine Suites (each with their own courtyard), or the two author suites named after Edgar Snow and Han Suyin. Also in the spirit of the pastiche is the Bomb Shelter Bar, pampering its guests with wine, cigars and propaganda films from a shelter excavated on the orders of Vice-Chairman Lin Biao. For those who really want to get into the swing, the hotel can also arrange cruises of Beijing's streets in the Red Flag limousine that belonged to Jiang Qing (Mao's doomed wife and Gang of Four member).

WANGFUJING GRAND HOTEL
Map pp232–3
Wángfǔjīng Dàfàndiàn

☎ 6522 1188; www.wangfujinghotel.com; 57 Wangfujing Dajie; d/ste US$180/300; subway Wangfujing

This Chinese-managed 16-storey hotel enjoys a splendid location and offers good service, and considerable latitude is generally given for discounts. However, the hotel has lost some of its freshness. Rooms come with satellite TV and in-house films, executive floors exist for business travellers and the hotel has an indoor swimming pool. Reserve your room on line and secure a standard double for as low as Y580 off-season.

CHEAP SLEEPS
BEIJING SAGA INTERNATIONAL YOUTH HOSTEL Map pp232–3
Shíjiā Guójì Qīngnián Lǚshè

☎ 6527 2773/8607 7516; sagayangguang@yahoo.com; 9 Shijia Hutong; dm/d/tr Y40/Y160/Y180, Y10 extra for non-HI members; subway Beijingzhan

This recently opened youth hostel sits on this famous *hútong* east off Chaoyangmen Nanxiaojie (look for the signpost) and operates over three floors. All of the clean and well-kept rooms above dorm level have TV. Communal phone, laundry service (Y10 per load), bike rental (Y20 per day) and Internet access (Y8 per hour) are available, and there's a small array of essentials at reception (biscuits, washing powder etc). Great Wall trips can be arranged, as well as outings to watch acrobats.

FANGYUAN HOTEL Map pp232–3
Fāngyuán Bīnguǎn
☎ 6525 6331; www.cbw.com/hotel/fangyuan; 36 Dengshikou Xijie; d Y198-280, ste Y422; subway Wangfujing or Tiananmen Dong

This good value two-star hotel – its front door guarded by a pair of stone cats – could do with a refit, but it is handily located just east of Wangfujing Dajie. The cheapest rooms are the downstairs junior rooms (with shower room, and clean and toasty in winter). The suites are also downstairs while the standard doubles upstairs are larger. All rooms come with air-con, TV and phone. A simple breakfast (boiled eggs, rice porridge etc) is included (7.30am–9.30am). The staff is friendly and well used to dealing with Westerners and the place is well run, with a restaurant, ticketing service, bicycle rental and Internet access (Y10 per hour).

LUSONGYUAN HOTEL Map pp232–3
Lǔsōngyuán Bīnguǎn
☎ 6404 0436; 1syhotel@263.net; 22 Banchang Hutong; dm/s/d/ste US$10/35/60/110; bus 104 to Bei Bingma Si stop

North of the Forbidden City, this *hútong* hotel certainly has character. Built by a Mongolian general during the Qing dynasty, its location among Beijing's historic alleys makes this an excellent base for exploring the city, and guests can sit out drinking in the courtyard during spring and summer. There is bike rental at Y30 per day, but Internet access is expensive. For a double bedroom, book ahead as the hotel has only two (the other rooms have two single beds). Pocket-sized singles come with pea-sized baths (albeit quite cute); dorms have three beds (with TV), and there is just one suite. All rooms facing onto the courtyard are slightly more expensive. Check out the fascinating old map of Beijing on the wall to the right of reception. There is a small sign (in English) on Jiaodaokou Nandajie. The hotel is about 50m down the alley. Walk a short distance south then turn right down the first alley.

CHAOYANG

Most top-end options in this district can be found near the Sanlitun Embassy area and the Lufthansa Center. Mid-range options are more limited, but there are some excellent hotels for those on a budget. This might not be the most historic part of town and only a few of Beijing's top sights can be found here, but travellers looking for Beijing's nightlife will love the proximity to the bar streets of Sanlitun.

GREAT WALL SHERATON Map pp234–5
Chángchéng Fàndiàn
☎ 6590 5566; www.sheratonbeijing.com; 10 Dongsanhuan Beilu; d US$260; subway Dongsishitiao, then bus 701

Despite getting long in the tooth, this landmark five-star hotel (one of Beijing's first international quality hotels) on the Third Ring Rd has refurbished many of its rooms (ask for the cheaper promotional room rate). It offers a very comfortable sojourn for visitors to Beijing. The breakfast buffet is recommended, and there's a fine choice of dining options.

KEMPINSKI HOTEL Map pp234–5
Kǎibīnsījī Fàndiàn
☎ 6465 3388; www.kempinski-beijing.com; Lufthansa Center, 50 Liangmaqiao Lu; d US$270; subway Dongsishitiao, then bus 701

The location next to the Lufthansa Center Youyi Shopping City (p148) might be convenient for shopping sprees, but this corner of Beijing has precious little history. If you want gleaming shoes, stop off at the shoe-shine man and his marvellous, glittering brass shoe rest in the lobby (he operates from 7am to 10pm). There's also a large range of shops, including carpet shops and art galleries (with insipid art work). There is also a decent gym and a good deli and bakery.

KERRY CENTER HOTEL Map pp234–5
Jiālì Zhōngxīn Fàndiàn
☎ 6561 8833; www.shangri-la.com; 1 Guanghua Lu; d US$240-320, ste US$360-2000; subway Guomao

Another hotel from the Shangri-La chain, this modern, slick and stylish hotel with trendy decor and smart dining options is aimed at the business traveller market. The spacious rooms are neat, with broadband Internet connection, minibar, shower and bath, iron and ironing board. The foyer is clutter free, spacious and sleek. Chill out at Centro (p129) or head to the adjacent Kerry Mall (p148). Facilities include indoor swimming pool, children's playground, and tennis and squash courts.

ORIENTAL GARDEN HOTEL Map pp234–5
Dōngfāng Huāyuán Fàndiàn

☎ 6416 8866; fax 6415 0638; 6 Dongzhimen Nandajie; s/d/ste US$80/120/160; subway Dongsishitiao or Dongzhimen

This four-star Chinese-run business hotel has comfortable and attractive guest rooms, Cantonese and Shanghai restaurants and a coffee shop. A short walk north of Dongsishitiao subway station and the Poly Plaza International Theatre (p134), the hotel is near the Sanlitun nightlife. Facilities include an indoor swimming pool and health club. A superior standard of service can be found on executive floors.

SWISSÔTEL Map pp234–5
Ruìshì Jiǔdiàn

☎ 6553 2288; www.swissotel-beijing.com; 2 Chaoyangmen Beidajie; d/ste US$230/320; subway Dongsishitiao

Located just outside the Dongsishitiao subway station, this hotel (managed by Raffles International) has decent-sized rooms (ask for discounts) and an excellent gym and swimming pool. But despite its five-star billing, it is past its prime. There is also a post office, an ATM on the ground floor in the shopping mall, a branch of Panda Tours, and Chinese, Japanese and Western restaurants.

CHEAP SLEEPS

BEIJING GONGTI INTERNATIONAL YOUTH HOSTEL Map pp234–5
Běijīng Gōngtǐ Qīngnián Lǚshè

☎ 6552 4800; bih-yh@sohu.com, gongti@hotmail .com; east gate, Workers' Stadium; 2-/4-bed dm Y70/50, s Y100; subway Dongsishitiao

This clean and appealing hostel offers both excellent value and excellent positioning for the Sanlitun district nightlife and restaurants around the Workers' Stadium. The dorm rooms (Y10 extra for non-HI members) are bright, clean and spacious, and are equipped with phone, TV (incoming only) and radiator. Communal showers are clean, and a self-service washing machine is provided. Internet access costs Y10

per hour. Non-HI members pay an extra Y20 for single rooms. A camping area is planned outside for the summer months, so enquire at reception. The hostel also has a bar and Chinese restaurant, lockers, a book exchange (although at time of writing it was devoid of books) and a useful notice board used by travellers. The absence of a lift is, however, frustrating. If you want more luxurious accommodation, check into the smarter Gongti Hotel next door.

RED HOUSE HOTEL Map pp234–5
Ruìxiù Bīnguǎn

☎ 6416 7500; www.redhouse.com.cn; 10 Chunxiu Lu; dm Y70, ste solo/shared Y400/200; subway Dongzhimen

Dorm bed rooms come with attached shower room. All recently refurbished suites come with living room, cable TV, shower rooms and kitchen, while the shared suites have two separate bedrooms. There's Internet access (Y10 per hour), lockers and laundry facilities, and breakfast is included. It has a great location near Beijing's expat area (Sanlitun), and the hotel is also home to the Club Football Center (p129). The hotel takes all major credit cards (except Visa).

YOU YI YOUTH HOSTEL Map pp234–5
Yǒuyì Qīngnián Jiǔdiàn

☎ 6417 2632; fax 6415 6866; 43 Beisanlitunnan; dm/tw Y70/180; subway Dongsishitiao or Dongzhimen

This hostel has a peerless location in Sanlitun bar ghetto district, next door to the thunderously loud Poacher's Inn (p130). Note, however, that the hostel is not a Hostelling International member. Twins (with phone, TV, air-con and radiator) are bright and spacious with large beds, but doors only have one lock, so if you have valuables, plonk them in a hotel locker. Rooms are comfortable enough, and there's the free laundry service – dump your dirty rags in the cart for washing and drying – which is a hospitable gesture (although the facility can be erratic). There is Internet access (Y10 per hour), and room rates include breakfast (7.30am–9am; toast, coffee, eggs and sausage). Signs say: 'Gambling, prostitution and drunkenness are strictly forbidden.'

ZHAOLONG INTERNATIONAL YOUTH HOSTEL Map pp234–5
Zhàolóng Qīngnián Lǚshè

☎ 6597 2299; outdoor@etang.com; 2 Gongrentiyuchang Beilu; 2-/4-/6-bed dm Y70/60/50; subway Dongsishitiao

A six-floor block tucked away off Dongsanhuan Beilu behind the Zhaolong Hotel, this is a first-rate place with clean rooms, laundry (Y10 to Y20), Internet (Y10 per hour), shop (selling IP and IC cards), kitchen, reading room, air-con, safe, bike rental (Y20 per day) and 24-hour hot water (there are communal showers). Non-HI members pay an extra Y10 for all room types. There's also a recreation room with table football and a coffee machine. The hostel is well positioned for the nearby bars at Sanlitun, but the door shuts at 1am.

FENGTAI & XUANWU

BEIJING NINGBO HOTEL Map pp236–8
Běijīng Níngbō Bīnguǎn
☎ 6605 2226; fax 6607 7320; 25 Xizhong Hutong; s/d/ste Y280/360/720; subway Hepingmen

This very clean, small and central two-star modern hotel is set in a historic *hútòng* district west of Tiananmen Square. The singles and doubles are clean, and rates include breakfast. The hotel has a restaurant.

MARCO POLO BEIJING Map pp236–8
Běijīng Mǎgē Bóluó Jiǔdiàn
☎ 6603 6688; www.marcopolohotels.com; 6 Xuanwumennei Dajie; d/ste US$170/280; subway Xidan or Xuanwumen

Rising up south of Xidan just north of the South Cathedral (p89), this new four-star hotel is the best in this part of town. Shopping is easy at the nearby Capital Times Square shopping complex. The hotel has a fine indoor swimming pool, a fitness centre and a decent selection of bars and restaurants, including Cantonese cuisine at Heichinrou. The old Qing dynasty map of Beijing on the stairs to the right of the foyer is well worth perusing.

MINZU HOTEL Map pp236–8
Mínzú Fàndiàn
☎ 6601 4466; fax 6601 4849; 51 Fuxingmennei Dajie; tw/ste US$120/205

The huge Chinese-run four-star Minzu has a yesteryear feel, and is located near the huge and distinctive Nationalities Cultural Palace, west of Xidan. The hotel's restaurants specialities include hotpot and Chaozhou and Turkish cuisine.

QIANMEN JIANGUO HOTEL Map pp236–8
Qiánmén Jiànguó Fàndiàn
☎ 6301 6688; fax 6301 3883; 175 Yong'an Lu; s/d/tr/ ste Y620/760/910/1100; subway Hepingmen

Well situated to visit Tiananmen Square (p70), Temple of Heaven Park (p68) and Liulichang

(p149), this hotel has a very attractive interior (marbled lobby with a glistening chandelier) and sees a lot of tour groups. You can find the Liyuan Theatre (p132) to the right of the domed atrium at the rear of the hotel. Rooms are spacious, clean and attractively carpeted, and have broadband Internet access as standard. Housed in a red brick and white shell, the hotel has gift shops and numerous restaurants serving roast duck, Chaozhou cuisine and Western food.

CHEAP SLEEPS

BEIJING FEIYING INTERNATIONAL YOUTH HOSTEL
Map pp236–8
Fēiyíng Qīngnián Lǚshè
☎ 6315 1165; iyhfy@yahoo.com.cn; no 10 Bldg; Changchun Jie Hou Jie, Xuanwumen Xidajie; 10-/5-bed dm Y30/50, d Y160; subway Changchunjie

All rooms have shower rooms and air-con at this newly opened youth hostel. Non-HI members will pay Y10 extra for five-bed dorms and Y20 for double rooms. At hand are bicycle hire, Internet access (Y10 per hour), washing machine, kitchen and tourist info. The hostel does not have a lift. To reach the hostel, take the subway to Changchun Jie, exit the station (exit C) and head east pass the McDonald's, walking for around 150m.

FAR EAST INTERNATIONAL YOUTH HOSTEL Map pp236–8
Yuǎndōng Guójì Qīngnián Lǚshè
☎ 6301 8811, ext 3118; courtyard@elong.com; 113 Tieshuxie Jie, Qianmen Wai; Youth Hostel dm high/low season Y60/45; subway Hepingmen

This hostel is in a pretty old courtyard opposite the hotel of the same name. It is an extremely pleasant and clean place with loads of character, Internet (Y10 per hour), bike rental (Y20 per day, Y200 deposit), kitchen, washing facilities and a fine bar–café. There is also a table tennis room, a shop (selling IP cards), a tourist office (7.30am–11.30pm), pricey VDC rental (Y2 to Y5) and guests can lounge around in the courtyard when the weather's warm. Rooms come without TV, phone or shower. The **Far East Hotel** (s/d/tr Y238/398/378, q Y75 per bed) opposite is an unremarkable two-star hotel, but the quads downstairs are clean with wood flooring strips and well-kept bunk beds. The hotel has a decent café–bar with sports TV downstairs (noon-midnight), plus a kitchen with two washing machines and a fridge. To get here head south on Nanxinhua Jie. About 200m after you pass Liulichang you'll see a sign (in English) on the right-hand side of the street saying 'Far East Hotel'. Follow the *hútong* for about 50m.

QIAOYUAN HOTEL

Map pp236–8

Qiáoyuán Fàndiàn

☎ 6301 2244; fax 6303 0119; 135 You'anmen Dong-binhe Lu; dm Y31, d Y132-192; subway Beijing South Train Station

This place has a large range of cheap rooms, bike rental (Y5), laundry service, Internet access and a useful backpacker info office (☎ 8315 1553). But it is hampered by a non-central location to the northwest of Beijing South Train Station.

HAIDIAN & XICHENG

BEIJING MARRIOTT WEST

Map pp230–1

Běijīng Jīnyù Wànháo Jiǔdiàn

☎ 6872 6699; www.marriotthotels.com; 98 Xisanhuan Beilu; d US$260

The Marriott is a fine hotel with vast, fully equipped and very comfortable rooms, but the location, near the intersection of Fucheng Lu and the Third Ring Rd, is a big drawback. Amenities include an indoor pool, tennis courts, bowling centre and health club.

SHANGRI-LA HOTEL Map pp230–1

Xiānggé Lǐlā Fàndiàn

☎ 6841 2211; www.shangri-la.com; 29 Zizhuyuan Lu; d US$130

Located in West Beijing and well positioned for trips to the Summer Palace, the Shangri-La has a top-notch selection of restaurants, bars and shops, as well as a fine spread of rooms.

STATE GUEST HOTEL Map pp230–1

Guóbīn Jiǔdiàn

☎ 6800 5588; www.stateguesthotel.com; 9 Fucheng-menwai Dajie; d US$175; subway Fuchengmen

This five-star hotel has a choice range of serv-ices and facilities, including three restaurants, an indoor pool and gym. Rooms are well geared to the business traveller and discounts can bring prices down, but the hotel is located in an uninteresting part of town and the gaudy foyer suggests a lack of taste.

FURTHER AFIELD

HOLIDAY INN LIDO Map pp228–9

Lìdū Jiàrì Fàndiàn

☎ 6437 6688; www.beijing-lido.holiday-inn.com; cnr Jichang Lu & Jiangtai Lu; d US$76

This hotel might be on the road out to the airport and a bit stranded for other parts of town, but it's a highly popular and first-rate establishment, with excellent amenities and a resourceful shopping mall.

Excursions

0 — 40 km
0 — 20 miles

To Chengde

To Shanhaiguan (150km)

Yuqiao Reservoir

To Chengde (50km)

Mt Wuling (2116m)

Eastern Qing Tombs

Haizi Reservoir

Simatai Great Wall

HEBEI

Jinshanling Great Wall

Gubeikou

Bailong Pool

Hudongshui

Jingdudyu Falls & Heilong Pool

Miyun Reservoir

Tianxian Falls

Miyun

Beijing Golf Club

Beijing Rural Golf Club

Shunyi

Huairou

Capital Airport

Tongxian

Mutianyu Great Wall

Hongluo Temple

Huairou Reservoir

Mutianyu

Bat River

Beijing International Golf Course

See Beijing Map pp228-9

BEIJING

Daxing

Huanghua Great Wall

Duijiu Valley

Changping

Yongding Ri

Marco Polo Bridge

Fahai Temple

Hetai Temple

Badachu

Fangshan

HEBEI

Longqing Gorge

Ming Tombs

Tomb of Seventh Prince

Mt Haituo (2241m)

Kangxi Grasslands

Juyong Pass

Tanzhe Temple

Stone Flower Cave

Peking Man Site

Songshan Nature Reserve

Badaling Great Wall

Fang Mountains Yunshui Caves

Yunju Temple

HEBEI

Guanting Reservoir

Zhaitang

Chuandixia

To Western

Mt Ling (2303m)

Shidu

To Zhangjiakou (50km); Saibei Ski Resort

Excursions

For those with a wandering instinct and some time up their sleeves, there are fantastic attractions and destinations surrounding Beijing that add an extra dimension to a visit. They can provide an excellent reason to escape town and offer a glimpse of more rugged and exciting terrain. And having made it to China and travelled this far already, it's worth dipping a little deeper into the China experience, so why not venture a bit further afield?

Perhaps more importantly, some of China's most famous monuments lie within Beijing Municipality, outside the city proper. The **Great Wall** is a mandatory fixture for any traveller to Beijing and several restored stretches can be visited on day trips beyond Beijing. Trips to the Great Wall are often combined with visits to the **Ming Tombs**, the stately burial place of 13 of the Ming emperors. For those who are interested in the remains of dynastic China or who appreciate the unique formula of Chinese tomb architecture, the tombs of many of the Qing emperors can also be explored at the Eastern and Western **Qing Tombs**.

If the city's temple culture has whetted your appetite, several other temples worth exploring lie within reach of town, including **Tanzhe Temple, Jietai Temple, Fahai Temple** and **Yunju Temple**. Also within Beijing Municipality are some less well-known sights that are worth a diversion. The remoteness of the ancient hillside village of **Chuandixia** has protected its charming streets and buildings from modernisation and provides a fascinating snapshot of disappearing China.

More distant from Beijing, the Ming dynasty garrison town of **Shānhǎiguān** gives travellers the chance of combining a trip to the edge of China's mighty northeast (formerly known in the West as Manchuria) with visits to a section of the Great Wall north of town. Shanhaiguan may be poor, bedraggled and its tourist economy suffering from under-investment, but the town is an appealing place that is commensurate with real China.

A one- or two-day trip to the imperial retreat of **Chéngdé**, 255km northeast of Beijing, should be a high priority for travellers to Beijing. Not only is the scenery magnificent, but also beyond the grounds of the imperial estate is a scattering of notable and important temple architecture.

THE GREAT WALL

Also known to the Chinese as the '10,000 Li Wall', the Great Wall (Chángchéng) stretches from its scattered remains in Liáoníng province to Jiāyùguān in the Gobi Desert.

Standard histories emphasise the unity of the Wall. The 'original' Wall was begun over 2000 years ago during the Qin dynasty (221–207 BC), when China was unified under Emperor Qin Shihuang. Separate walls, constructed by independent kingdoms to keep out marauding nomads, were linked together. The effort required hundreds of thousands of workers, many of them political prisoners, and 10 years of hard labour under General Meng Tian. An estimated 180 million cubic metres of rammed earth were used to form the core of the original Wall, and legend has it that one of the building materials used were the bones of deceased workers.

The Wall never really did perform its function as an impenetrable line of defence. As Genghis Khan supposedly said, 'The strength of a wall depends on the courage of those who defend it'. Sentries could be bribed. However, it did work very well as a kind of elevated highway, transporting people and equipment across mountainous terrain. Its beacon tower system, using smoke signals generated by burning wolves' dung, transmitted news of enemy movements quickly back to the capital. To the west was Jiayuguan, an important link on the Silk Road, where there was a customs post of sorts and where unwanted Chinese were ejected through the gates to face the terrifying wild west.

During the Ming dynasty a determined effort was made to rehash the bastion, this time facing it with bricks and stone slabs – some 60 million cubic metres of these. This project took over 100 years, and the costs in human effort and resources were phenomenal.

The Great Wall was largely forgotten after that. Lengthy sections of it have returned to dust and the Wall might have disappeared totally had it not been rescued by the tourist industry. Several important sections have been rebuilt, kitted out with souvenir shops, restaurants and amusement-park rides, and formally opened to the public. Not impressed with the tourist-oriented sections, explorative travellers

Injuries on the Great Wall

Never in his most disturbing dreams could the Great Wall's first architect Emperor Qin Shihuang imagine barbarians wobbling around his masterpiece in 'I climbed the Great Wall' T-shirts. His edifice occasionally retaliates, however, against ill-prepared or over-adventurous tourists.

Despite being a generally hazard-free outing for most day-trippers, more elderly or unfit travellers can drag a twisted ankle or even a broken leg back with them through customs. Certain parts of the rampart, especially the steeper reaches, can exhaust the unfit and the steps are often uneven. Remember to take bottled water and shoes with a good grip.

Simatai can be precarious and Huanghua, with its wilder sections, can be quite treacherous; a few years ago, a traveller fell off a section of this wall, ending up with severe injuries. Fortunately, he was part of a group; if he had been alone he might not have been found.

have sought out unrestored sections of the Wall for their more genuine appeal. The Chinese government has, however, begun periodically slapping fines on visitors to such sections. The authorities argue that they are seeking to prevent damage to the unrestored Wall by traipsing visitors, but they are also very keen to keep the tourist revenue flowing to restored parts of the Wall. Furthermore, the Wall has suffered far more from farmers pillaging its earthen core for use on the fields. The Wall also provided a useful and free supply of stone, stripped from the rampart for use on road and building construction.

The myth that the Great Wall is visible with the naked eye from the moon was finally laid to rest in 2003, when China's first astronaut Yang Liwei failed to see the barrier from space. The Great Wall is certainly not visible from the moon, where even individual continents are barely perceptible. The myth is to be edited from Chinese textbooks, where it has cast its spell over generations of Chinese.

The most touristed area of the Wall is Bādálǐng. Also renovated but less touristed are Sīmǎtái and Jīnshānlǐng. The Jiǎo Shān section at Shanhaiguan is also worth seeing. Other travellers swear by seeing the Wall *au naturel*, such as at the Yellow Flower Fortress (Huánghuā Chángchéng).

When choosing a tour, it is essential to check that it visits the places you want to see. Tours to the Great Wall are often combined with trips to the Ming Tombs, so ask beforehand and if you don't want to visit the Ming Tombs, choose another tour. Far more worryingly, less reputable tours make painful and expensive diversions to gem exhibition halls and Chinese medicine centres. At the latter, tourists are herded off the bus and analysed by white-coated doctors, who diagnose ailments that can only be cured with high-priced Chinese remedies (supplied there and then). The tour organisers receive a commission from the gem showroom/medicine centre for every person they manage to funnel through, so you are simply lining other people's pockets. When booking a tour, it is essential to check that such scams and unnecessary diversions are not on the itinerary; more reliable operators include **Dragon Bus** (☎ 6515 8565) and **Panda Tours** (☎ 6525 8372; www.pandatourchina.com), outfits that have desks in several top-end hotels (including Swissôtel, p160). They may still make scheduled stops at jade factories en route to the Great Wall – so ask beforehand what is on the itinerary and compare. As with most popular destinations in China, try to avoid visiting the Great Wall at weekends.

BADALING

Most visitors see the Great Wall's most artificial incarnation at Bādálǐng at an elevation of 1000m. The section of masonry at Badaling was first built during the Ming dynasty (1368–1644), and was heavily restored in the 1950s and 1980s. Punctuated with watch-towers (*dílóu*), the 6m wide wall is clad in brick, typical of the stonework employed by the Ming when they restored and expanded the fortification. Prior to the Ming era, the Wall was largely constructed of tamped earth, without an outer brick cladding.

The surrounding scenery is raw and impressive and this is the place to see the Wall snaking off into the distance over the undulating hills. Also come here for guardrails, souvenir stalls, a fairground feel and the companionship of squads of tourists surging over the ramparts. If you time your visit to coincide with a summer weekend, you won't be able to move against the wall of humanity on the battlements. Come during the week instead and, if possible, during the colder months:

THE GREAT WALL AND THE FORBIDDEN CITY, IN MY OPINION, ARE MOST BEAUTIFUL IN THE WINTER AS THEY ARE COVERED IN SNOW AND NOT JAM-PACKED WITH TOURISTS.

Adam Dunnett

Cable cars exist for the weary (Y50 round trip), but don't take the 'slide' (*huádào*; Y30) as it's a colossal waste of money (unless you like getting winched along in a slow moving plastic vehicle).

There are two sections of wall, trailing off to the left and right of the main entrance. The restored sections crawl for a distance before nobly disintegrating into ruins; unfortunately you cannot realistically explore these more authentic fragments.

Apart from the pristine battlements, you can be conveyed back into history via 15-minute films about the Great Wall at the **Great Wall Circle Vision Theatre**, a 360-degree amphitheatre. The admission fee also gets you into the **China Great Wall Museum**.

Transport

Distance from Beijing 70km

Direction Northwest

Tours China International Travel Service (CITS; ☎ 6515 8566), China Travel Service (CTS), the Beijing Tourist Information Centre, Panda Tours (see above), Dragon Bus (see above), big hotels and everyone else in the tourist business does a tour to Badaling. Some hotels charge astronomical prices for tours to the Great Wall (up to Y300 per person), but they can be convenient to arrange and you can depart from your hotel. Hotel tours should not include the infuriating side trips to jewellery exhibitions and Chinese medicine centres listed previously – but check.

Local Bus The cheapest and easiest way to get to Badaling is to take bus 919 from Deshengmen, about 500m east of the Jishuitan subway stop. Buses leave regularly from 5.30am from just north of the old gate of Deshengmen. Ordinary buses take two hours and cost Y5, while the faster, nonstop luxury air-con buses take one hour and cost Y12. The last bus leaves Badaling for Beijing at 6.30pm.

Tour Bus Several tour buses run to Badaling, taking around 90 minutes to two hours. Many of these visit the Ming Tombs on the way back. Tour bus 1 (☎ 6303 5066) runs to Badaling and leaves from a departure point east of Zhengyang Men (Front Gate) at Qianmen, across the street from the southeastern corner of Tiananmen Square, between 6.30am and 11.30am (Y50). Tour bus 2 (☎ 6764 3687) runs to Badaling and leaves from the same location as tour bus 1 (standard bus Y45; luxury bus Y50). Tour bus 2 also departs from the South Cathedral at Xuanwumen (☎ 6601 8285) between 6.30am and 8.30am (Y50). Tour bus 5 also departs in the morning from the western side of Qianmen for both Badaling and the Ming Tombs (Y50). Tour bus 4 will get you to Badaling from the Zhanlanguan Lu tour-bus station, near the zoo. Plan about nine hours for the whole trip. Touts for inexpensive Chinese tour buses patrol the Beijing Train Station forecourt, but they could well detour to the scam destinations mentioned earlier and are best avoided.

Taxi A taxi to the Wall and back will cost a minimum of Y400 for an eight-hour hire with a maximum of four passengers.

MUTIANYU

The 2250m-long granite section of wall at Mùtiányù, in Huáiróu County, dates from Ming dynasty remains built upon an earlier Northern Qi-dynasty conception. It was developed as a decoy alternative to Badaling and is, on the whole, a less commercial experience. Despite some motivated hawking and tourist clutter, the stretch of Wall is notable for its numerous Ming dynasty guard towers and stirring views. The Wall is also equipped with a **cable car** (Y50 round trip; ☼ 8.30am to 4.30pm). October is the best month to visit, for the autumn colours of the trees that envelop the surrounding countryside.

Transport

Distance from Beijing 90km

Direction Northeast

Local Bus From Dongzhimen long-distance bus station (☎ 6467 4995) take either bus 916 (Y8; one hour) or 936 (Y5) to Huairou then change for a minibus to Mutianyu (Y25). Alternatively, the less frequent 916 branch line (*zhīxiàn*) goes all the way from Dongzhimen to Mutianyu (Y15).

Tour Bus Bus 6 (☎ 6601 8285) from outside the South Cathedral at Xuanwumen runs to Mùtiányù for Y50 between 6.30am and 8.30am Saturday, Sunday and public holidays from April to October. The bus also visits the Hongluo Temple (Hóngluó Sì).

Climbing the Great Wall at Badaling (p167)

JUYONGGUAN

Originally constructed in the 5th century and rebuilt by the Ming, Jūyōngguān (Juyong Pass) was considered one of the most strategically important because of its position as a link to Beijing. However, this section in Changping County has been thoroughly renovated to the point where you don't feel as if you're walking on a part of history. Still, if you're in a hurry, it's the closest section of the Wall to Beijing and is usually quiet. You can do the steep and somewhat strenuous circuit in under two hours.

Transport

Distance from Beijing 50km

Direction Northwest

Local Bus Juyongguan is on the road to Badaling. Any of the buses for Badaling listed earlier can get you here – but tell the bus driver you want to be dropped off at Juyongguan Changcheng.

SIMATAI

In Mìyún County near the town of Gǔbĕikŏu, the stirring remains at Sīmǎtái make for a more exhilarating Great Wall experience. Built during the reign of Ming dynasty emperor Hongwu, the 19km stretch is marked by watchtowers, steep plunges and scrambling ascents.

It's not for the faint-hearted: This rough section of the Wall is very steep. The eastern section of wall at Simatai sports 16 watchtowers and from around the 12th watchtower, the climb gets precarious. A few slopes have a 70-degree incline and you need both hands free, so bring a day-pack to hold your camera and other essentials. One narrow section of footpath has a 500m drop, so it's no place for acrophobics. The cable car (Y50 round trip) could be an alternative to a sprained ankle. Take strong shoes with a good grip.

Simatai has some unusual features, like 'obstacle-walls' – walls-within-walls used for defending against enemies who'd already scaled the Great Wall. Small cannon have been discovered in this area, as well as evidence of rocket-type weapons, such as flying knives and flying swords. Another peculiar feature of Simatai is the toboggan ride (Y30) and, unfazed by the dizzying terrain, hawkers make an unavoidable appearance:

I WOULD LIKE TO STATE HERE AND NOW THAT THEY ARE THE MOST RELENTLESS AND IRRITATING THING I HAVE EVER ENCOUNTERED ON A TRIP. THE OLD LADY WHO CLAMBERED UP THE GREAT WALL'S PRECIPICE AFTER US FOR TWO HOURS SHOUTING ABOUT HER POSTCARDS TAKES THE CROWN FOR QUEEN OF ANNOYANCE.

Ross van Horn

But you won't be short-changed by what are some exhilarating views.

Transport

Distance from Beijing 110km

Direction Northeast

Local Bus Early morning direct minibuses leave from Dongzhimen long-distance bus station (☎ 6467 4995) for Y20, from 6am. Otherwise take a minibus to Miyun from Dongzhimen (Y8; 1¼ hours) and change to a minibus to Simatai or a taxi (round trip Y120).

Tour Bus Weekend tour-bus 12 (☎ 6601 8285) from outside the South Cathedral at Xuanwumen leaves for Simatai for Y50 between 6.30am and 8.30am on Saturday, Sunday and public holidays. The bus also stops at Bailong Tan.

Hotel Tours Backpacker hotels often run morning trips by minibus (Y60, not including ticket). Also ask at your hotel to see if tours are offered.

Taxi Hiring a taxi from Beijing for the day costs about Y400.

Excursions – The Great Wall

JINSHANLING

Though not as steep (and therefore not as impressive) as Simatai, the Great Wall at Jīnshānlǐng (Jīnshānlíng Chángchéng; admission Y40) has 24 watchtowers and is considerably less developed than any of the sites previously mentioned, despite undergoing some restoration work.

Perhaps the most interesting thing about Jinshanling is that it's the starting point for a hike to Simatai. The distance between Jinshanling and Simatai is only about 10km, but it takes nearly four hours because the trail is steep and stony. Parts of the Wall

Transport

Distance from Beijing 110km

Direction Northeast

Local Bus From Dongzhimen long-distance bus station (☎ 6467 4995) take a minibus to Miyun (Y8; 1¼ hours), change to a minibus to Gubeikou and get off at Bakèshíyíng (Y7). If you are heading to Chengde (see p181) you will pass Jinshanling en route.

Train Take a train to Jinshanling, followed by a local minibus to Jinshanling.

between Jinshanling and Simatai have collapsed and much is in a state of ruin, but it can be traversed without too much difficulty. Arriving at Simatai, however, you may have to buy another ticket.

You can do the walk in the opposite direction, but getting a ride back to Beijing from Simatai is easier than from Jinshanling. Of course, getting a ride should be no problem if you've made arrangements with your driver to pick you up (and didn't pay him in advance).

HUANGHUA

For a genuine Wall experience close to Beijing, the Yellow Flower Fortress (Huánghuā Chángchéng) section is ideal. The Great Wall at Huánghuā lies in two sections, clinging to hillsides adjacent to a reservoir. Huanghua is a classic and well-preserved example of Ming defence with high and wide ramparts, intact parapets and sturdy beacon towers. The Wall here has not benefited from restoration, which makes the experience that much more genuine. Anxious to preserve the Wall, the authorities are, however, considering putting Huanghua off limits to hikers, so it would be a good idea to check with your hotel before you set out.

It is said that Lord Cai masterminded this section, employing meticulous quality control. Each *cùn* (inch) of the masonry represented one labourer's whole day's work. When the Ministry of War got wind of the extravagance, Cai was beheaded for

Transport

Distance from Beijing 60km
Direction North

Local Bus Take bus 961 (Y8; two hours; two morning and afternoon departures) to Huanghua from the Dongzhimen long-distance bus station (☎ 6467 4995). The last bus back to Beijing is at 2.30pm. Ask for Huánghuāchéng and don't get off at the smaller Huánghuāzhèn by mistake. Also from Dongzhimen long-distance bus station, bus 916 (Y8; air-con) and 936 (Y6) to Huairou leave frequently from 5.30am to 6.30pm and take just over an hour to get to Huairou. Same number minibuses run the same route a little quicker for Y5. From Huairou you can take a minibus directly to Huánghuā Chángchéng (Y4; 40 minutes) or hire a minicab from Huairou to Huánghuā Chángchéng (Y60 round trip).

his efforts. In spite of the trauma, his decapitated body stood erect for three days before toppling. Years later a general judged Lord Cai's Wall to be exemplary and he was posthumously rehabilitated.

The section to the east, accessed across the dam and via a ticket collector (Y1) rises abruptly from a solitary watchtower. Be warned that it's both steep and crumbling – there are no guardrails here and the Wall has not been restored. There may be further tickets ahead, depending on how far you venture. It's possible to make it all the way to the Mutianyu section of the Wall, but it'll take you a few days and some hard clambering (pack a sleeping bag). Local hawkers have got wind of foreigners in the vicinity, but they won't follow you up the Wall.

The section of Wall immediately to the west is in bad shape, so you'll have to clamber up the hillside from the south. Alternatively (and for ticket-free access and a great walk), walk south and take the first turning (about 500m down) on the right, walk through the village, keep going until the river bends to the right and take the right fork following the river. Keep bearing right all the way (you'll pass fading Cultural Revolution characters on a corner that proclaim 'Long Live Chairman Mao' and just around the corner 'The Red Heart Faces the Communist Party' – if you can read Chinese). Soon, you'll see a watchtower ahead – the path leads up to it. The whole jaunt should take 45 minutes and you can continue along the Wall. Be warned that the Wall here can be quite narrow and perilous, so don't carry on unless you feel confident (see p166).

Several places have sprung up offering beds. The shack at the entrance to the eastern section of the Wall, **Xiaohong's Shop** (☎ 6165 1393/2350; damatthewall@hotmail.com) can get you a simple bed for Y50 or less and you can get something to eat here as well. **Jìntáng Shānzhuāng** (☎ 6499 4812/4813) has doubles for Y258 and triples for Y288. This is a more upmarket, resort-style establishment overlooking the reservoir, north of Xiaohong's Shop. It's fine if you like the white-tile effect and security guards.

MING TOMBS

Shísān Líng

The Ming Tombs are the final resting-place of 13 of the 16 Ming emperors. The Confucian layout and design may intoxicate erudite visitors, but some find the necropolis lifeless and ho-hum. Confucian shrines lack the vibrancy and colour of Buddhist or Daoist temples, and their motifs can be bewilderingly inscrutable.

The first Ming emperor, Hongwu, is buried not here but in Nánjīng, the first capital of the Ming dynasty. Three tombs have been opened up to the public – Cháng Líng, Dìng Líng and Zhāo Líng.

The Ming Tombs follow a standard layout for imperial tomb design. The plan typically consists of a main gate (Líng Mén), leading to the first of a series of courtyards and the main hall, the Hall of Eminent Favours (Língēn Diàn). Beyond lie further gates or archways, leading to the Soul Tower (Míng Lóu), behind which rises the burial mound (tumulus).

Cháng Líng, burial place of the emperor Yongle, is the most impressive, with its series of magnificent halls lying beyond its yellow-tiled gate. Seated upon a three-tiered marble terrace, the most notable structure is the Hall of Eminent Favours, containing a recent statue of Yongle and a breathtaking interior with vast *nanmu* (cedar wood) columns. The pine-covered burial mound at the rear of the complex is yet to be excavated and is not open to the public.

Dìng Líng is the burial place of the emperor Wanli, and contains a series of subterranean interlocking vaults and the remains of the various gates and halls of the complex. Excavated in the late 1950s, some visitors find this tomb of more interest, as you are allowed to descend into the underground vault. Accessing the vault down the steps, visitors are confronted by the simply vast marble self-locking doors that sealed the chamber after it was vacated. Note the depression in the floor where the stone prop clicked into place once the door was finally closed.

Zhāo Líng, the resting-place of the 13th Ming emperor Longqing, follows an orthodox layout and is a tranquil alternative if you find the other tombs too busy. The rest of the tombs are in various stages of dilapidation and are sealed off by locked gates.

The road leading up to the tombs is a 7km stretch called the **Spirit Way** (shéndào). Commencing with a triumphal arch, the path enters the Great Palace Gate, where officials once had to dismount, and passes a giant *bìxì* (a mythical tortoise-dragon like animal), which bears the largest stele in China. A guard of 12 sets of stone animals

Excursions – Ming Tombs

MING TOMBS

| 0 | 2 km |
| 0 | 1 mile |

To Duijiu Valley (5km)
Tianshou Mountains
To Huairou
To Tongliao
International Friendship Forest 国际友谊林
North New Village
Seven Arch Bridge 七孔桥
Beijing International Golf Club 北京国际高尔夫球俱乐部
Lingxing Gate 棂星门
Shisanling Reservoir
Small Palace Gate 小宫门
Dragon Hill
Fairy Cave 仙人洞
Changping North Train Station 昌平北火车站
To Beijing (45km)
Changping Village

171

Transport

Distance from Beijing 50km

Direction Northwest

Local Bus Take bus 345 (branch line, *zhīxiàn*) from Deshengmen (500m east of Jishuitan subway station) to Chāngpíng (Y6; one hour). Take the bus to the Changping Dongguan stop and change to bus 314 for the tombs. Alternatively, take the standard bus 345 to Changping and then take a taxi to the tombs (Y20). You can also reach the Changping Dongguan stop on bus 845 (Y10) from Xizhimen long-distance bus station, just outside the Xizhimen subway stop. It's about a 10-minute ride from Changping to the entrance to the tombs.

Tour Bus Most tour buses usually combine a visit to the Ming Tombs with a visit to the Great Wall at Badaling. Tour bus 1 (☎ 6303 5066) runs to Badaling and leaves from a departure point east of Zhengyang Men (Front Gate) at Qianmen, across the street from the southeastern corner of Tiananmen Square between 6.30am and 11.30am (Y50). Tour bus 2 (☎ 6764 3687) runs to Badaling and the Ming Tombs and leaves from the same location as Tour Bus 1 (standard bus Y45; luxury bus Y50). Tour bus 2 also departs from the South Cathedral at Xuanwumen (☎ 6601 8285) between 6.30am and 8.30am (Y50). Tour bus 5 also departs in the morning from the western side of Qianmen for both Badaling and the Ming Tombs (Y50).

and officials follows this. Your tour-bus driver may well speed past them (preferring to spend half an hour at the routine Shisanling Reservoir instead), so insist if you want to see them.

Other interesting features are the loos at the Ming Tombs. The toilets at Cháng Líng must be the best in China outside of a five-star hotel. The English notice advising visitors to behave at Cháng Líng is also peerless. It reads: 'No fight and scrap. No rabble, no feudal fetish and sexy service. After close, don't stay or sleep in the open'.

WESTERN QING TOMBS

Qing Xī Líng

The Western Qing Tombs are set in fabulous surroundings in Yixian County. The vast tomb area houses the mausoleums of emperors Yongzheng, Jiaqing, Daoguang and Guangxu, along with the tombs of empresses, princes, concubines and royal retainers, comprising over 70 tombs in all. The tomb of Emperor Guangxu (r 1875–1908), called **Chóng Líng**, was the last of the grand imperial tombs and was constructed between 1905 and 1915. There are also **Chāng Líng** (tomb of 5th Qing emperor Jiaqing), **Mù Líng** (tomb of 6th Qing emperor Daoguang) and **Tài Líng** (tomb of 3rd Qing emperor Yongzheng), the latter being both the earliest and the most imposing.

Unlike the Ming Tombs, two Qing Tomb sites exist for the bodies of the Qing emperors, the result of Yongzheng's guilty conscience, or more likely fear of being buried

Transport

Distance from Beijing 110km

Direction Southwest

Tours Few tours reach these tombs, so your best bet may be to share a chartered taxi (three hours from Beijing) or hiring a car (p192), but ask at your hotel for suggestions as they may be able to arrange something.

Train You can take a train part of the way to the tombs. From Beijing West Station take a train to Gaobeidian, then change to a bus to the tombs from the long-distance bus station (unfortunately, not many Beijing-bound trains stop at Gaobeidian, so returning can be problematic).

next to his father, Emperor Kangxi. When Yongzheng's father appointed a younger son to ascend the throne, Yongzheng took matters into his own hands – killing his brothers and his father's ministers so that he could take his father's seat at the head of the empire. If you poke around at the tombs, you can also find a **simple tomb** where the ashes of the Last Emperor (Henry Puyi) lie.

EASTERN QING TOMBS

Qīng Dōng Líng

The area of the Eastern Qing Tombs could be called Death Valley, housing as it does five emperors, 14 empresses and 136 imperial consorts. In the mountains ringing the valley are buried princes, dukes, imperial nurses and others.

A spirit way is a principal feature here, as at the Ming Tombs. Five emperors are buried here: Qianlong (Yù Líng), Kangxi (Jǐng Líng), Shunzhi (Xiào Líng), Xianfeng (Dìng Líng) and Tongzhi (Huì Líng). Emperor Qianlong (1711–99) started preparations when he was 30 and by the time he was 88 he had used up 90 tonnes of his silver. His resting place covers half a square kilometre. Some of the beamless stone chambers are decorated with Tibetan and Sanskrit sutras, and the doors bear bas-relief Bodhisattvas. Apart from Hui Ling, all of the tombs listed above are open to visitors.

Empress Dowager Cixi also got a head

Transport

Distance from Beijing 125km

Direction East

Tour Bus A special tour bus line departs when full for the Eastern Qing Tombs on Saturday and Sunday from South Cathedral (☎ 6601 8285; by Xuanwumen subway station) at Xuanwumen between 6.30am and 8.30am (Y60; air-con Y80). Pedicabs can convey you around the tombs upon arrival (Y15).

Local Bus Take a morning bus from the Majuan bus station in Beijing to Zunhua (Y20; four hours; first bus 7am), followed by a minibus to the tombs.

Taxi A taxi from Beijing should cost around Y350 for the day trip to the tombs.

start. Her tomb, **Dìng Dōng Líng**, was completed some three decades before her death and also underwent considerable restoration before she was finally laid to rest. Her tomb lies alongside the tomb of Empress Cian. The phoenix (symbol of the empress) appears above that of the dragon (the emperor's symbol) in the artwork at the front of the tomb – not side by side as on other tombs. Both tombs were plundered in the 1920s.

Located in Zūnhuà County, Héběi province, the Eastern Qing Tombs are blessed with a more dramatic setting than the Ming Tombs, although getting there is an expedition and getting around is difficult without a vehicle.

TANZHE TEMPLE

Tánzhè Sì

Tanzhe Temple is the largest of all the Beijing temples. The Buddhist complex has a very long history dating as far back as the 3rd century and structural modifications date from the Tang, Liao, Ming and Qing dynasties.

The temple is attractively set amid trees in the mountains, but most of the statuary is, sadly, very new. The ascending temple grounds are covered with towering cypress and pine trees, many so old that their gangly limbs have to be supported by metal props. The highlight of a trip to the temple is the small **Talin Temple** (Tǎlín Sì), by the forecourt where you disembark the bus, with its collection of stupas reminiscent of the Shaolin Temple. You can tour them while waiting for the return bus. An excellent time to visit Tanzhe Temple is around mid-April, when the magnolias are in bloom.

JIETAI TEMPLE

Jiètái Sì

About 10km southeast of Tanzhe Temple is this smaller but more engaging temple. Jietai (Ordination Terrace) Temple was built around AD 622 during the Tang dynasty, with major improvements made during the Ming dynasty. The main complex is dotted with ancient pine trees, all of which have been given quaint names. One of these, **Nine Dragon Pine**, is claimed to be over 1300 years old, while the **Embracing Pagoda Pine** does just what it says.

EIGHT GREAT SITES

Bādàchù

Bādàchù is named after the eight monasteries, nunneries and temples scattered through its attractive wooded valleys. The second site contains the Buddha's Tooth Relic Pagoda, built to house the sacred tooth accidentally discovered when the allied army demolished the place in 1900. Relics of Buddha (Sanskrit name *sarira*) are scattered throughout China (eg at Famen Temple outside Xī'ān) and are often associated with the Indian monarch Ashoka, who distributed them throughout the Buddhist world. There's a cable car for trips to the top of the hill (Y20).

The mountain has numerous apricot trees, which makes for some cheerful and sweet-smelling scenery around April when the trees bloom briefly. As with other sights, it is inadvisable to visit at the weekend, which is particularly busy.

FAHAI TEMPLE

Fǎhǎi Sì

The peaceful Fahai (Sea of the Law) Temple on the western edge of Beijing is unremarkable apart from the Ming-dynasty murals on the walls of the **Mahavira Hall** (*Dàxióng Bǎodiàn*). Sadly, the frescoes suffer from such bad lighting you can't make much out from the fading photon-challenged pigment (flickering strip lighting and glass screens don't help). One option is to stand in the dark and wait for your pupils to sufficiently dilate, or take a torch (flashlight).

YUNJU TEMPLE

Yúnjū Sì

Just south of the Fáng Shān mountains there are limestone hills riddled with small cave temples, some of which date as far back as the Sui dynasty (AD 581–618). The best-known cave temple in the area is Yúnjù Temple. China's state-controlled Buddhist Association declared in 1987 that a box found in the temple contained two bone fragments that belonged to none other than Siddhartha Gautama (563–483 BC) himself, the Buddha.

In 1990 a new structure was built to house more than 77,000 engraved wooden blocks containing the Chinese Tripitaka (Buddhist scriptures). This Tripitaka did not originate in Yunju Temple, but has been shipped in from other collections throughout China, such as the one at Beijing University. Only eight such sets of Tripitaka are known to exist in China.

Transport

Tanzhe Temple 45km west of Beijing. Take the subway to the Pingguoyuan stop and then take bus 931 to the temple (Y3), which is at the namesake final stop (don't take the bus 931 branch line, *zhīxiàn*, however). This bus will also stop near Jietai Temple (see entry following). Alternatively, take tour bus 7 (☎ 6779 7546; Y40) from the tour-bus station east of Zhengyang Men (Front Gate), which runs on Saturday and Sunday between mid-April and mid-October (☉ 7am to 8.30am) and also stops at Jietai Temple.

Jietai Temple You can visit the temple on the 931 bus on the way back from, or en route to, Tanzhe Temple. It's a 10-minute walk uphill from the bus stop. Alternatively, take tour bus 7 (see above), which visits both Tanzhe Temple and Jietai Temple.

Badachu The easiest way to reach Badachu is by taking the East–West subway line to the Pingguoyuan stop and then catching a taxi (Y10). You can also take bus 347, which runs from Badachu to Beijing Zoo.

Fahai Temple Take the East–West subway line to the Pingguoyuan station and then take bus 311 from Pingguoyuan and get off at the Moshikou stop, which is not far from the temple. Alternatively, take a taxi van (Y10) from the Pingguoyuan stop.

Yunju Temple Take bus 917 from Tianqiao bus station (western side of Temple of Heaven Park) in Beijing to Fang Shan and then a minibus to the temple. Alternatively, take tour bus 10 (☎ 6779 7546; Y43) from the tour bus station east of Zhengyang Men (Front Gate), which departs when full between 7am and 8.30am on Saturday, Sunday and public holidays between mid-April and mid-October. The bus stops at Shidu and Yunju Temple.

Marco Polo Bridge Take bus 6 from the north gate of Temple of Heaven Park to the last stop at Liuli Bridge (Liúlí Qiáo), and then either bus 339 or 309 to Lúgōu Xīnqiáo; the bridge is just ahead.

Tomb of the Seventh Prince Take bus 346 from the Summer Palace to the Caochang stop (Y2) and then take a minibus heading west for 1km or walk.

Excursions – Eight Great Sites

MARCO POLO BRIDGE

Lúgōu Qiáo

Described by the great traveller himself, the 266m-long grey marble bridge is host to 485 carved stone lions. Each animal is different, with the smallest only a few centimetres high, and legend maintains that they move around during the night.

Dating from 1189 the stone bridge is Beijing's oldest, but is a composite of different eras (it was widened in 1969) and spans the river Yŏngdìng Hé near the little walled town of Wǎnpíng.

Long before the China International Travel Service, Emperor Qianlong did his bit to promote the bridge, composing calligraphy now engraved into stone tablets on the site.

Despite the praises of Marco Polo and Emperor Qianlong, the bridge wouldn't have rated more than a footnote in Chinese history were it not for the famed Marco Polo Bridge Incident, which ignited a full-scale war with Japan. On 7 July 1937 Japanese troops illegally occupied a railway junction outside Wanping. Japanese and Chinese soldiers started shooting, and that gave Japan enough of an excuse to attack and occupy Beijing.

The **Memorial Hall of the War of Resistance Against Japan** is a gory look back at Japan's occupation of China, but the there are no captions in English. Also on the site are the Wanping Castle, Daiwang Temple and a hotel.

TOMB OF THE SEVENTH PRINCE

Qīwáng Fén

The land around Beijing is scattered with ancient graves and mounds, some of which are decidedly heavy going, while others are not. This well-preserved tomb (near Beixan He in Haidian district) is a splendid spot, with no ticket collectors and blessed by gorgeous countryside. It's not that easy to get to, but worth the effort for its dignified and quiet repose. The tomb, housing the remains of a Qing-dynasty prince and constructed in 1874, is made up of a series of small halls rising steeply uphill, encompassed with trees. An ornate marble bridge survives and there are very few visitors, making it an ideal getaway for a picnic and some solitude.

Cycling over Marco Polo Bridge (above)

CHUANDIXIA VILLAGE

Nestled in a valley and overlooked by towering peaks is the land that time forgot – Chuāndǐxià Village, a gorgeous cluster of historic courtyard homes and old-world charm. The bucolic backdrop is divine: terraced orchards and fields, with ancient houses and alleyways rising up the hillside, all the while swept by winds funnelling through the valley.

Apart from the rural beauty of the village, Chuandixia is also a museum of **Maoist graffiti and slogans**, especially up the incline among the better-preserved houses. Some choice poetry daubing the walls includes 'Proletariats of the world unite!', 'Long live Mao Zedong', 'Courageously advance holding high the mighty red flag of Mao Zedong Thought' and 'Arm our minds with Mao Zedong Thought'.

Despite their impressive revolutionary credentials, Chuandixia's residents have sensed the unmistakable whiff of the tourist dollar on the north-China breeze, and have flung open the doors to their antique homesteads. The village is a hamlet of rustic simplicity – despite obvious restoration work and the occasional naff intrusion of pine.

Two hours is more than enough to wander around the village as it's not big, although it's possible to ascend the path through the terraces above the village. Some homesteads are derelict and a few walls look dangerous and in a state of collapse, so be careful when wandering about.

Entrance to the village is Y20, for which you can patrol these ancient abodes at your leisure. If you want to stay the night, residents will find you a bed for a further Y15 or so and cook you food – many of the courtyard houses offer food and lodging. A number of houses also sell local produce, including honey (fēngmì) and walnuts (hétao).

Transport

Distance from Beijing 90km

Direction West

Local Bus Take bus 929 (make sure it's the branch line, or *zhīxiàn*, not the regular bus) from the bus stop to the right of Pingguoyuan subway station to Zhaitang (Y7; two hours), then hire a taxi van (Y10). If going off season, arrange with the taxi van to return to pick you up. The last bus returns from Zhaitang to Pingguoyuan at 4.20pm. If you miss the last bus, a *xiali* taxi will cost around Y80 to Pingguoyuan, but look out for stray minibuses piling travellers in for around Y30. It's not easy to get to Chuandixia and if taking public transport bank on taking well over three hours from central Beijing.

SHIDU

Shídù is Beijing's answer to Guìlín. Its pinnacle-shaped rock formations, pleasant rivers and general beauty make it a favourite with expats. Shidu means '10 ferries' or '10 crossings': before the new road and bridges were built, visitors had to cross the Juma River 10 times while travelling along the gorge from Zhangfang and Shidu village.

Transport

Distance from Beijing 110km

Direction Southwest

Train There are trains (Y15; two hours) departing from Beijing South Train Station (Yǒngdìngmén) for Shidu at 6.36am, 7.30am and 5.40pm. Trains leave Shidu for Beijing at 9.36am, 3.50pm and 7.40pm. If you take the morning train the trip can be completed in one day.

Tour Bus Weekend tour bus 10 (☎ 6779 7546) heads to Shidu (Y43) from the tour bus station east of Zhengyang Men (Front Gate), departing when full between 7am and 8.30am on Saturday, Sunday and public holidays between mid-April and mid-October. The bus also stops at the Yunju Temple (p174).

Sights & Information

Badaling Great Wall (☎ 6912 1338/1423/1520; admission Y45; ☺ summer 6am-10pm, winter 7am-6pm)

China Great Wall Museum (☺ 9am-4pm)

Chuandixia (admission Y20)

Eastern Qing Tombs (admission Y55; ☺ 8am-5pm)

Eight Great Sites (☎ 6887 5211; admission Y5)

Fahai Temple (☎ 6880 3976; admission Y20; ☺ 9am-5pm)

Great Wall Circle Vision Theatre (admission Y25; ☺ 9am-9.45pm)

Jietai Temple (admission Y20; ☺ 8am-6pm)

Jinshanling Great Wall (admission Y40)

Juyongguan Great Wall (☎ 6977 1665; admission Y40; ☺ 6am-4pm)

Marco Polo Bridge (☎ 8389 3919; 88 Lugouqiaochengnei Xijie; admission Y15; ☺ 8am-5pm)

Ming Tombs (☎ 6076 1156/1334/1435; admission for each tomb Y20; ☺ 8am-5.30pm)

Mutianyu Great Wall (☎ 6162 6873/6022; admission Y35; ☺ 6.30am-5.30pm)

Simatai Great Wall (☎ 6903 5025/5030; admission Y30; ☺ 8am-5pm)

Tanzhe Temple (admission Y30; ☺ 8.30am-6pm)

Yunju Temple (☎ 6138 1612; admission Y30; ☺ 7am-5.30pm)

Western Qing Tombs (admission Y50; ☺ 8am-5pm)

SHANHAIGUAN

The Great Wall meets the sea at Shanhaiguanin in Héběi province (a mere whisker away from Liaoning province and what was called Manchuria). The area was originally part of the state of Guzhu during the Shang and Zhou dynasties but came into its own in 1381, when it was developed under General Xuda. He converted it into a garrison town with a square fortress, four gates at the compass points and two major avenues running between the gates. Shanhaiguan sits on a strategic pass that leads to northeast China. Considerable charm remains within the remains of the old walled enclosure, despite its dilapidation. Part of Shanhaiguan's appeal lies in its manageable size, its grid-like streets and tenacious sense of history. The Wall here has been extensively rebuilt and is now a major tourist drawcard, so it's best to sample it early in the morning when the crowds are thinner.

Its proximity to the beach resort of Běidàihé guarantees Shanhaiguan a summer tourist bonanza, but winter is a much mellower and more frigid experience. The town is a poor and ragged reminder that the benefits of economic reform remain unevenly spread. Facilities for Western visitors are, as a result, basic at best, but this allows you to see China's rawer reaches.

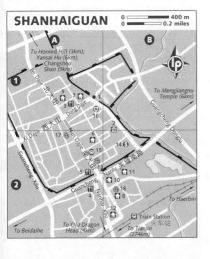

The **First Pass Under Heaven** (Tiānxià Dìyī Guān) is also known as East Gate (Dōng Mén). Shredded by the wind, tattered flags flap along a restored section of Wall, itself studded with watchtowers, dummy soldiers and tourist paraphernalia. Long views of factories stretch off to the east as decayed sections of battlements trail off into the Jiaoshan and Yanshan hills. The Wall here is 12m high and the principal watchtower – a two-storey structure with double eaves and 68 arrow slit windows – is a towering 13.7m high. Several other watchtowers (named Linlulou and Muyinglou) can also be seen and there's a *wengcheng* (enceinte) extending out east from the Wall. Along the western edge of the Wall south of the entrance is a pleasant grassy park where you can stretch your legs.

The calligraphy at the top (attributed to the scholar Xiao Xian) reads 'First Pass Under Heaven'. The words reflect the Chinese custom of dividing the world into civilised China and the 'barbarians'. The

Transport

Distance from Beijing 300km

Direction East

Train Shanhaiguan is accessible by train from Beijing. Trains are frequent, but don't always arrive at convenient hours. The fastest trains take around three hours from Beijing (Y70). Slower trains go via Tiānjīn and take around five hours. Alternatively, take the night sleeper from Beijing (Y70; seven hours). Tiānjīn is three to four hours away (Y41).

Long-Distance Bus There are departures for Beijing from Qínhuángdao (Y80; three hours), a city sandwiched between the beach resort town of Beidaihe and Shanhaiguan. You can also take direct buses from Qínhuángdao to Chengde (Y70; seven hours), departing at 6am, 7am and 8am.

Air There's a small airport between Shanhaiguan and Qinhuangdao, with flights to several cities.

barbarians (Manchus) got the upper hand when they stormed this gate in 1644 and enslaved China for 250 years (see p46).

Down the street the **Great Wall Museum** (Chángchéng Bówùguǎn) is housed in a pleasant, one-storey traditional Chinese building with upturned eaves. This is perhaps overall a more interesting way to explore the history of the Wall through its collection of photographs and memorabilia. Sadly, there is a lack of captions in English.

Old Dragon Head (Lǎolóngtóu) was the serpentine conclusion of the Great Wall as it made a grand finale at the sea's edge. The name derives from the legendary carved dragon head that once faced the waves. This is traditionally considered to be the Wall's easternmost extent, but other fragments of the Wall extend east into Liaoning province.

There are beaches on either side of the Wall; avoid buying the extortionate ticket and take the left-hand road to the sea where you can walk along the beach or ride a horse (Y2) to Old Dragon Head (but don't get caught by the tide). The views are spectacular and you can join the winkle-pickers and cockle-hunters on the rocks. Minibuses speed to Old Dragon Head from Shanhaiguan's South Gate, as do bus 13 and 23.

A half-hour walk (taxi Y10; motor tricycle Y5) beyond the North Gate brings you to a steep section of rebuilt masonry, where the Great Wall mounts its first high peak, called **Horned Hill**. It's a trying 20-minute clamber from the base, but a cable car can yank you up for Y20 (return trip). The views are ace on a clear day. The path behind the hills to the **Qixian Monastery** (Qixián Sì) is thorny and it's easy to lose the trail, which peters out, but the tranquillity is peerless.

Mengjiangnu Temple (Mèngjiāngnǚ Miào) is a Sung-Ming reconstruction 6km east of Shanhaiguan. It has coloured sculptures of Lady Meng and her maids, and calligraphy on Looking for Husband Rock. The story is famous in China:

Meng's husband, Wan, was press-ganged into wall building because his views conflicted with those of Emperor Qin Shihuang. When winter came Meng Jiang set off to take her husband warm clothing, only to discover that he had died from the backbreaking labour. Meng tearfully wandered the Great Wall, thinking only of finding Wan's bones to give him a decent burial. The Wall, a sensitive soul, was so upset that it collapsed, revealing the skeleton entombed within. Overcome with grief, Meng hurled herself into the sea from a boulder.

The temple itself is washed out and a little tacky. Take bus 23 from Guancheng Nanlu; a taxi should cost around Y12.

Sights & Information

21st Century Internet Café (21st Shìjì Wǎngbā; 24 Nan Dajie; per hr Y2) This place is in between Wutiao and Liutiao Hutong; there's no English sign but look for the large white placard.

Bank of China (Diyiguan Lu; ☯ 8.30am-noon & 1.30-5.30pm) Housed in a building with a splendid roof south of the Great Wall Museum, no international ATM.

First Pass Under Heaven (cnr Dong Dajie & Diyiguan Lu; admission Y40; ☯ 7.30am-5.30pm) Open longer hours in summer.

Great Wall Museum (Diyiguan Lu; admission incl in First Pass Under Heaven ticket Y5; ☯ 8am-6pm)

Horned Hill (Jiaoshān; 3km north of Shanhaiguan; admission Y15; ☯ 5am-sunset)

Mengjiangnü Temple (6km east of town; admission Y40; ☯ 7am-5.30pm)

Old Dragon Head (4km south of Shanhaiguan; admission Y40; ☯ 8am-5.30pm)

Post Office (eastern side of Nan Dajie; ☯ 8am-5.30pm)

PSB (☎ 0335 505 1163) Opposite entrance to First Pass Under Heaven on corner of small alleyway slightly to the south.

Qixian Monastery (Qixián Sì; admission Y5)

Shiji Internet Café (Shìjì Wǎngbā; 85 Nan Dajie; per hr Y2) There's no English sign, look for the big red sign that says 'Shiji Wangba' in pinyin. It's across the way from the People's Hospital.

Yimei Internet Café (Yìmèi Wǎngbā; Xinglong Jie; per hr Y2; ☯ 24hr)

Eating

Small restaurants and food vendors congregate along Nan Dajie, Shanhaiguan's main north–south thoroughfare, and several streets running east–west of it. Come sundown, gregarious kebab sellers set up barbecue ovens outside many of the shops along Nan Dajie, where you can feast on lamb kebabs (*yángròu chuàn*) and pick up cheap beers (Y2) – the kebabs are very good value at around Y1 for five *chuàn*. Larger restaurants can be found along the road south of the city wall heading towards the train station.

Lida Restaurant (Lìdá Hǎixiān Jiǔlóu; ☎ 0335 505 1476; Dong Dajie; meals Y35) A cheerful, colourful eatery serving local, northern and northeastern fare, plus some Sìchuān dishes. Try *huíguōròu* (a dish of oily pork strips with vegetables; Y25), pick up a bowl of steaming *jiǎozi*

(dumplings; Y5) or the *gānzhá hǎixiā* (dry fried shrimps; Y18).

Mike Hamn Fast Food (Màikè Hànmǔ; Guancheng Nanlu) If you want the Hebei fast-food experience (chicken meals, chips, piped muzak) come here. The food is actually not bad, but you'll have to wait while they fry it all up for you.

Shanghai Mianbao (Shanghai Bread; 123 Nan Dajie) In between Batiao and Jiutiao Hutong. Worth trying for tasty cakes, bread, buns, pastries or sandwiches

Sleeping

Jiguan Guesthouse (Jīguǎn Zhāodàisuǒ; ☎ 0335 505 1938; 17 Dongsitiao; d Y100-180, ste Y320) This pleasant hotel has rooms off two courtyards. The simple doubles come without bathrooms, but have clean, tiled floors and TVs. The Y180 doubles have showers.

Jingshan Hotel (Jīngshān Bīnguǎn; ☎ 0335 505 1130; Dong Dajie; tw Y140-300) Large and charmless hotel, built in imitation traditional Chinese style and the top tourist option. Among check-in papers is a voucher for a free breakfast at the hotel's restaurant.

Lida Restaurant (Lìdá Hǎixiān Jiǔlóu; ☎ 0335 505 1476; Dong Dajie; d/q Y30/Y40) Very simple lodgings at the rear of the Lida Restaurant (see above). The rooms are behind an attractive little courtyard, but are small and frugal. No air-con (but there's heating and TV), no shower, public loo.

Longhua Hotel (Lónghuá Dàjiǔdiàn; ☎ 0335 507 7698; 1 Nanhai Dajie; s/d/large d/tr Y168/188/288/368) This hotel has spacious, so-so rooms with reproduction traditional furniture in the block at the rear, and the smaller doubles in the main building at the front.

North Street Hotel (Běijiē Zhāodàisuǒ; ☎ 0335 505 1680; 2 Mujia Hutong; 6-bed dm/d Y30/100+) Attractive courtyard hotel in need of renovation. Doubles have no phones, huge Victorian baths with mismatched plugs, leaking taps, collapsing curtain rails, antique radiators, flickering TVs, scalding hot water etc.

Shangye Hotel (Shāngyè Bīnguǎn; ☎ 0335 505 1684; 91 Guancheng Nanlu; q/d/superior d Y80/120/228) This two-star hotel near the South Gate is good value, with decent doubles.

Shanhaiguan Grand Hotel (Shānhǎiguān Dàjiǔdiàn; ☎ 0335 506 4488; 107 Guancheng Nanlu; d/ste Y288/580) This mid-range glass and white tile hotel just outside the city walls offers reasonable rooms and rates.

Yihe Hotel (Yìhé Jiǔdiàn; ☎ 0335 505 1033; 4 Nanhai Xilu; d/tr Y288/388) This large hotel has large, clean double rooms, with water coolers, TVs, phones and bathrooms. Staff are pleasant and there's a restaurant next door.

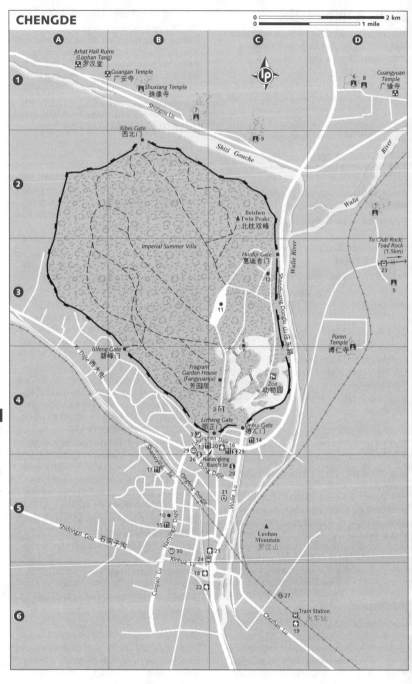

CHENGDE

0 _____ 2 km
0 _____ 1 mile

A   **B**   **C**   **D**

Arhat Hall Ruins
(Luohan Tang)
罗汉堂

Guangan Temple
广安寺

Shuxiang Temple
殊像寺

Shizigou Lu

6
8
Guangyuan
Temple
广缘寺

7

9

Xibei Gate
西北门

Shizi Gouche

Wulie

River

Beizhen
Twin Peaks
北枕双峰

Wulie River

Imperial Summer Villa

Huidiji Gate
惠迪吉门

1

To Club Rock;
Toad Rock
(1.5km)

12

23

5

11

Bifeng Gate
碧峰门

Xi Dajie 西大街

4

Puren
Temple
溥仁寺

Fragrant
Garden House
(Fangyuanju)
芳园居

Zoo
动物园

2

Lizheng Gate
丽正门

Dehui Gate
得汇门

3

Lizhengmen Dajie

13   20   16

29   25

26

28

17

Shanxijie lie

Nanxinglong
Xiaochi lie

Qingong Donglie

Nanyingzi Dajie

Wulie Lu

31

Shidongzi Gou 石洞子沟

10

15

Luohan
Mountain
罗汉山

30

21

Xinhua Lu

24

Cangao Lu

18

22

27

Chezhan Lu

Train Station
火车站

19

CHENGDE

Once known as Jehol, Chéngdé is an 18th-century imperial resort area boasting the remnants of the largest regal gardens in China.

Chengde was an obscure town until 1703 when Emperor Kangxi began building a summer palace with all the court trappings, including a throne room. More than a home away from home, Chengde became a seat of government, since wherever the emperor went his seat went too. Kangxi called his summer creation the **Imperial Summer Villa** or **Fleeing-the-Heat Mountain Villa** (Bìshǔ Shānzhuāng).

By 1790, during the reign of Kangxi's grandson Qianlong, it had grown to the size of Beijing's Summer Palace and the Forbidden City combined. Qianlong extended an idea started by Kangxi, to build replicas of minority architecture in order to make envoys feel comfortable. In particular he was keen on promoting Tibetan and Mongolian Lamaism. This explains the Tibetan and Mongolian features of the monasteries north of the Imperial Summer Villa, one of them a replica of the Potala Palace in Lhasa. Emperor Xianfeng died in Chengde in 1861, an event that initiated the gradual demise of the imperial retreat: it was never used again by the emperors, who associated it with misfortune.

Today Chengde has slipped back into being the provincial town it once was, its grandeur long decayed and its emperors long gone. Chengde is on Unesco's World Heritage list, but sadly this does not guarantee a programme of full restoration and some features are gone for good. Nonetheless, recent restoration work has tidied the place up and restored an element of grandeur.

The town of Chengde is drab and unexciting, but the park and temples are fine. Grab a bike, pedal through some enchanting countryside and make sure you take in the jaw-dropping statue of Guanyin at **Pǔníng Temple** – one of Buddhist China's most incredible monuments.

Visiting Chengde in autumn is an option as tourists choke the place in summer. Autumn adds its own rich colours to the landscape and sees far less visitors in town, while remaining warm enough to be comfortable. The train from Beijing to Chengde passes level fields, dark mountains, factories, terraced slopes, occasional pagoda-capped hills and crumbling lengths of the Great Wall. The dryness of the land and the terrace-striated slopes of distant hills exemplify China's agricultural problems, with all vestiges of usable terrain scooped from hillsides.

IMPERIAL SUMMER VILLA
Bìshǔ Shānzhuāng

This fanciful park covers a huge 590 hectares and is bounded by a splendid 10km wall. Emperor Kangxi decreed that there would be 36 'beauty spots' in Jehol; Qianlong delineated 36 more. A combination of rampaging warlords and Japanese invaders added their own brand of devastation to the park, and even the forests have suffered cutbacks. Even so, the park is a great place to stroll in the shade of the trees and slowly take in the scale of the place.

Passing through the **Main Gate** (Lìzhèng Mén) you reach the **Front Palace** (Zhèng Gōng), containing the main throne hall. The refreshingly cool **Hall of Simplicity and Sincerity** is built of an aromatic hardwood called *nánmù;* on display is a carved throne. There are also the emperor's fully-furnished bedrooms, as well as displays of ceramics, drum stones and calligraphy.

The double storey **Misty Rain Tower** (Yǔ Lóu), on the northern side of the main lake, was an imperial study. While here, you can also take boats out for trips around the lake (Y10 per hour). Further north is the **Wenjin Chamber** (Wénjīn Gé) built in 1773 to house a copy of the *Sikuquanshu*, a major anthology of classics, history, philosophy and literature commissioned by Qianlong.

In the east, the tall green and yellow **Yongyousi Pagoda** (Yǒngyòusì Tǎ) soars above the fragments of its vanished temple and dominates the area. Wander in here and inspect the layout of this temple, which was levelled by the Japanese. You see where the temple halls formerly stood from the forlorn terraces and pillar stumps.

About 90% of the Imperial Summer Villa is composed of lakes, hills, mini-forests and plains (where visitors now play football). At the northern end of the park the emperors reviewed displays of archery, equestrian skills and fireworks. Horses were also chosen and tested here before hunting sorties.

Just beyond the Front Palace is a ticket office (☎ 0314 203 7720) for tourist buggies that whiz around the grounds (Y40).

GUANDI TEMPLE

Guāndì Miào

Requisitioned years ago by the local government to house generations of Chengde residents, the restored Guāndì Temple (west of the main gate of the Imperial Summer Villa) is a welcome addition to Chengde's temple population. Also called the **Wumiao**, the Guandi Temple is a Daoist temple first built during the reign of Yongzheng, in 1732. Enter the temple with the Green Dragon (or Blue Dragon) on your right and the White Tiger (or White Lion) on your left (both are protective guardians) in the **Shanmen Hall** (Shānmén Diàn). The **Chongwen Hall** on the right contains modern frescoes of Confucius while in the **Shengmu Hall** on the left is a statue of the **Princess of Azure Clouds**, the patron deity of Tài Shān, holding a baby. The hall ahead contains a statue of Guandi himself, the Daoist God of War and patron guardian of business. In the courtyard at the rear are two steles, supported on the backs of a pair of disintegrating *bìxì* (mythical tortoise-dragon like creatures). The right-hand hall here is dedicated to the God of Wealth (Caishen) and the left-hand hall to the God of Medicine and his co-practitioners. The **Hall of the Three Clear Ones** stands at the rear to the left. The central hall at the rear contains a further statue of Guandi. The former inhabitants of the temple grounds (the citizens of Chengde) have been moved on and the temple is now home to a band of Daoist monks, garbed in distinctive jackets and trousers, their long hair twisted into topknots.

EIGHT OUTER TEMPLES
Wàibā Miào

Some fine examples of religious architecture can be found in the foothills outside the northern and northeastern walls of the Imperial Summer Villa. The number of temples is down on its original complement and some remain closed, but there are enough to keep you busy. The surviving temples and monasteries were all built between 1750 and 1780 and are 3km to 5km from the garden's front gate; bus 6 taken to the northeastern corner will drop you in the vicinity – going by bike is an excellent idea.

Puning Temple
Pǔníng Sì

Puning Temple (Temple of Universal Tranquillity) is a Chinese-style *(hànshì)* temple. You'll find chubby Milefo (see p90) welcoming visitors and more Tibetan-style *(zàngshì)* features at the rear.

Enter the temple grounds to a stele pavilion with inscriptions by the Qianlong emperor in Chinese, Manchu, Mongol and Tibetan. Behind are halls arranged in a typical Buddhist temple layout, featuring the **Hall of Heavenly Kings** and the **Mahavira Hall** (Dàxióngbǎo Diàn) beyond. The Chinese name of the hall is typical of the name of the main hall of most Buddhist temples (Dàxióng means Mahavira and is a respectful form of address for Buddha by his disciples and followers). The hall contains three images of the Buddhas of the three generations; the central image is Sakyamuni, flanked by the past and future Buddha. Behind lie some very steep steps (the temple is arranged on a mountainside) leading to a gate tower, which you can also climb.

On the terrace at the top of the steps is the huge **Mahayana Hall**. To the right and left are stupas and square, block-like, Tibetan-style buildings, decorated with beautiful water spouts. Some of the buildings on the terrace have been converted to shops, while others appear to be solid, serving a purely decorative purpose.

The absolute highlight of any trip to Puning Temple is the heart-arresting golden statue of the Buddhist **Goddess of Mercy** (Guanyin) in the Mahayana Hall. The effigy is astounding: it's over 22m high (the highest of its kind in the world) and radiates a powerful sense of divinity. Mesmerising in its scale, the labour of love for those who fashioned her is hewn from five different kinds of wood (pine, cypress, fir, elm and linden). Guanyin has 42 arms, with each palm bearing an eye, and each hand holds instruments, skulls, lotuses and other Buddhist devices. Tibetan features include the pair of hands in front of the goddess, below the two clasped in prayer; the right one holds a sceptre-like *dorje* (*vajra* in Sanskrit), a masculine symbol, and the left a *dril

Traditional Manchurian costume on display in Chengde (p181)

bu (bell), a female symbol. On Guanyin's head sits the **Teacher Longevity Buddha** (Shizunwuliang-shoufo). To her right stands a male guardian and disciple called **Shancai**, opposite his female equivalent, **Longnü** (Dragon Girl). Unlike Guanyin, they are both painted, although their paintwork is in poor condition. On the walls are hundreds of small effigies of Buddha.

You can clamber up to the first gallery (Y10) for a closer inspection of Guanyin; torches (flashlights) are provided to cut through the gloom so you can pick out the uneven stairs (take care). When last visited the galleries were inaccessible, but a notice indicated that further effigies could be seen upstairs, including the Buddhas of the three generations and eight Buddhist pagodas. Sadly, the higher galleries are often out of bounds, so an eye-to-eye with the goddess may be impossible. Guanyin's golden sheen is dulled by a copious sprinkling of dust. If you want to climb the gallery, try and come in the morning, as it is often impossible to get a ticket in the afternoon (especially outside of summer).

Puning Temple has a number of friendly lamas who manage their domain, so be quiet and respectful at all times. You can catch bus 6 from in front of the Mountain Villa Hotel to Puning Temple.

Putuozongcheng Temple

The largest of the Chengde temples, Putuozongcheng Temple (Pǔtuózōngchéng Zhī Miào) is a minifacsimile of Lhasa's Potala Palace and houses the nebulous presence of Avalok-iteshvara (Guanyin), who manifests herself in earthly form in the Dalai Lama. The temple is a marvellous sight on a clear day, its vast red walls standing out against its mountain backdrop. Enter to a huge stele pavilion, followed by a huge triple archway topped with five small stupas in red, green, yellow, white and black. Note the two large stone elephants, between the two gates, whose knees bend impossibly. The scale of the place comes into relief when you get up to the White Palace and look up – it's an astonishing sight, especially when framed against the blue sky. Note that most of the windows are fake and painted in.

Fronted by a collection of **prayer wheels** and flags, the **Red Palace** (also called the Great Red Terrace) contains most of the main shrines and halls. Continue up and past an exhibition of *Tanka* in a restored courtyard and look out for the marvellous sandalwood pagodas further up. Both are 19m tall and contain 2160 effigies of the Amitabha Buddha. Among the many exhibits on view are displays of Tibetan Buddhist objects and instruments, including a *kapala* bowl, made from the skull of a young girl (all captions are in Chinese). The main hall is housed at the very top, surrounded by several small pavilions (most of which now house souvenir stalls); the climb to the top is worth it for the views. In the uppermost hexagonal pavilion in the northwestern part of the roof is a small statue of Guanyin. The temple's sacred aura is sadly ruined by graffiti, but you can buy a bust of Chairman Mao from the Buddhist Statue Shop.

Other Temples & Sights

The **Temple of Sumeru, Happiness and Longevity** (Xūmífúshòu Zhī Miào) is a further huge temple, around 1km to the east of the Putuozongcheng Temple. It was built in honour of the sixth Panchen Lama, who stayed here in 1781; and being an imitation of a temple in Shigatse, Tibet, it incorporates elements of Tibetan and Han architecture. Note the eight, huge, glinting dragons (each said to weigh over 1000kg) that adorn the roof of the main hall.

Pule Temple (Pǔlè Sì) was built in 1776 for the visits of minority envoys (Kazakhs among them). At the rear of the temple is the unusual Round Pavilion, reminiscent of the H). It's a 30-minute hike to **Club Rock** (Bàngchuí Fēng) from the Temple of Universal Happiness – the rock is said to resemble a club used for beating laundry dry. Nearby is **Toad Rock** (Hámá Shí). There is pleasant hiking, good scenery and commanding views of the area. You can save yourself a steep climb to the base of Club Rock (Y20) and Toad Rock by taking the chairlift (Y40 return), but it's more fun to walk if you're reasonably fit. Bus 10 will take you to Pule Temple. East of Puning Temple is **Puyou Temple** (Pǔyòu Sì). While it is in a somewhat sad state, there is a plentiful contingent of merry gilded *luohan* (see p90) in the side wings.

Anyuan Temple (Ānyuǎn Miào) is a copy of the Gurza Temple in Xīnjiāng. Only the main hall remains and it contains deteriorating Buddhist frescoes. **Puren Temple** (Pǔrén Sì) is not open to the public. Surrounded by a low red wall, **Shuxiang Temple** (Shūxiàng Sì) also appears to be

Guanyin

The boundlessly compassionate countenance of Guanyin, the Buddhist Goddess of Mercy, can be encountered in temples all over China. The goddess (more strictly a Bodhisattva or a Buddha-to-be) goes under a variety of aliases: Guanshiyin, literally meaning 'Observing the Cries of the World', is her formal name, but she is also called Guanzizai, Guanyin Dashi and Guanyin Pusa or, in Sanskrit, Avalokiteshvara. In Japan she is known as Kannon and in Cantonese as Guanyam. Guanyin shoulders the grief of the world and dispenses mercy and compassion. Christians will note a resemblance to the Virgin Mary in the aura surrounding the goddess.

In Tibetan Buddhism her earthly presence manifests itself in the Dalai Lama and her home is the Potala Palace in Lhasa. In China her abode is the island mount of Pǔtuóshān in Zhèjiāng province, whose first two syllables derive from the name of her palace in Lhasa.

In temples throughout China Guanyin is often found at the very rear of the main hall, facing north (most of the other divinities, apart from Weituo, face south). She typically has her own little shrine and stands on the head of a big fish, holding a lotus in her hand. On other occasions she has her own hall, which is generally towards the rear of the temple.

The goddess (who in earlier dynasties appears to be male rather than female) is often surrounded by little effigies of the *luohan* (*arhat*, those freed from the cycle of rebirth), who scamper about (the Guanyin Temple in Dàlǐ is a good example of this). Guanyin also appears in a variety of forms, often with just two arms, but sometimes also in a multi-armed form (a statue of the goddess in Xīyuán Sì in Sūzhōu bristles with arms). The 11-faced Guanyin, the horse head Guanyin, the Songzi Guanyin (literally 'Offering Son Guanyin') and the Dripping Water Guanyin are all manifestations, and there are many more. She was also a favourite subject for white *dehua* porcelain figures, which are typically very elegant.

---

closed, although it may open in the summer months (unless it is being restored). You can try your luck, or at least look at the pair of huge stone lions sitting outside. Just to the west of Shuxiang Temple is a sensitive military zone where foreigners are not allowed access, so don't go wandering around.

Sights & Information

Anyuan Temple (admission Y10; ☉ 8am-5.30pm)

Bank of China (3 Dong Dajie & east of the Mountain Villa Hotel)

Bank of China ATM (Nanyingzi Dajie) Outside the Wankelong Supermarket just south of the Chengde Theatre (Chéngdé Jùchǎng), takes MasterCard and Visa.

Chaosu Internet Café (High Speed Internet Café; Chezhan Lu; per hr Y2; ☉ 24hr) North of the train station.

CITS (☎ 0314 202 6418; 11 Zhonghua Lu, Wulie Lu, 1st fl) It's the building on your right in a dishevelled courtyard on the western side of Wulie Lu, a dreadful looking place but someone should be able to speak English.

CTS (☎ 0314 203 5322/202 1621; Block 2, Shiwei Zonghelou, Wulie Lu)

Guandi Temple (Lizhengmen Dajie; admission Y20; ☉ 8am-5pm),

Imperial Summer Villa (☎ 0314 216 3761/202 5918; admission Y60; tour guides summer/winter Y90/60; ☉ 5.30am- 6.30pm)

Luggage Storage Long-distance bus station ticket hall and train station ticket hall

Post Office (Nanyingzi Dajie; ☎ 8am-6pm) The main post office is on Nanyingzi Dajie and there's a smaller branch on Lizhengmen Dajie just east of the Main Gate (Lizheng Men) of the Imperial Summer Villa.

PSB (☎ 0314 223 091; Wulie Lu)

Pule Temple (admission Y20; ☉ 8am-6pm)

Puning Temple (Puningsi Lu; admission Y40; ☉ summer 8am-5.30pm, winter 8.30am-4pm)

Putuozongcheng Temple (Shizigou Lu; admission Y30; ☉ 8am-6pm)

Puyou Temple (admission Y10; ☉ 8am-6pm)

Supermarket (Wankelong Supermarket; Nanyingzi Dajie) South of Chengde Theatre (Chéngdé Jùchǎng).

Temple of Sumeru, Happiness and Longevity (Shizigou Lu; admission Y20; ☉ 8am-5.30pm)

Tourist Appeal (☎ 0314 202 4548; ☉ 8.30am-5pm) May be able to help if you have a tourism-related problem.

Xiandai Internet Café (Chezhan Lu; per hr Y2; ☉ 24hr) North of train station.

Eating

For street food, try the restaurants along **Shaanxiying Jie** (at the northern end of Nanyingzi Lu), with its plentiful barbecue (*shāokǎo*) restaurants (and dog meat outlets). **Qingfeng Dongjie** just north of the railway line and south of Dong Dajie has a brightly lit and colourful spread of restaurants – you can't miss the lights at night. Also try **Nanxinglong**

Xiaochi Jie (across from the Lizhèng Mén, the main gate of the Imperial Summer Villa), where you can get all kinds of local dishes, including pheasant and dog meat, as well as many of China's staple dishes. Opposite the Mountain Villa Hotel is a string of smart restaurants housed in dolled up, reproduction, traditional style Chinese buildings, hung with lights at night and aimed at tour groups. Chengde's local speciality is wild game – deer (lùròu) and pheasant (shānjī), which you can find all over town.

Beijing Roast Duck Restaurant (Běijīng Kǎoyādiàn; ☎ 0314 202 2979; 22 Wumiao Lu; duck Y50) Central restaurant with tasty duck roasted over fruit tree wood. It's opposite Guandi Temple.

Dongpo Restaurant (Dōngpō Fànzhuāng; ☎ 0314 210 6315; Shanzhuang Donglu; meals Y30+) With red lanterns outside, steaming shāguō (clay pot) at the door and a large aquarium, this lively and popular restaurant has no English menu but a large choice of Sichuān dishes.

Henghexiang Roast Duck Restaurant (Hénghéxiáng Kǎoyādiàn; ☎ 0314 207 5568; 2 Wenjiagou; roast duck Y60; deer Y30) A small, clean and well-decorated restaurant (no English sign) offering slightly spicy deer fried in a crisp coating of batter (gānpēng lùròu) and deep-fried pheasant (qīngzhá shānjī), among others.

Maihamu Fast Food (Màihāmǔ Kuàicān; Lizhengmen Dajie; meals Y15) Hamburgers, chicken burgers, chips. It's east of Mountain Villa Hotel.

Saiwai Roast Duck Restaurant (Sàiwài Kǎoyādiàn; ☎ 0314 213 9791; Shaanxiying Jie; meals Y30-40) Corner restaurant with check tablecloths, cheap duck (Y25) and a range of traditional dishes including clay pot, doufu and spareribs.

Sleeping

For such an important tourist destination, Chengde has a particularly unremarkable range of hotels. As with other parts of China, hoteliers can be seriously lazy and incompetent (perhaps even more so here than elsewhere).

Dianli Hotel (Diànlì Bīnguǎn; ☎ 0314 217 3735; Daqiaotou; d/q/tr/ste Y120/150/280/260) This large, blue glass and white tile block hotel offers clean, simple and functional tile-floor rooms, all with air-con. The cheapest doubles have no showers, there are grim carpets up the stairs and a large restaurant.

Jingcheng Hotel (Jīngchéng Fàndiàn; ☎ 0314 208 2027; next to train station; q per bed Y30, d Y200) This is a so-so place that greets you at the station. The quad rooms have a shared bathroom, but be warned there are no smoke alarms.

Mountain Villa Hotel (Shanzhuang Resort Hotel; Shānzhuāng Bīnguǎn; ☎ 0314 202 3501; fax 202 2457; 127 Xiaonanmen Lu; d Y140, tw Y240-480) This hotel has clean, cheap rooms and offers pole positioning for a trip inside the Imperial Summer Villa. Take bus 7 from the train station and from there it's a short walk.

Shenghua Hotel (Shènghuá Dàjiǔdiàn; ☎ 0314 227 1000; s/d/ste Y600/680/1200) This glossy, three-star hotel has a modern exterior of glass and steel and a voluminous marble foyer, and is well located for the long-distance bus station and the train station.

Yunshan Hotel (Yúnshān Dàjiǔdiàn; ☎ 0314 205 5888; 6 Nanyuan Donglu; d/ste Y680/1600) Despite the ghastly exterior (white tiles, office block style), the rooms (minibar on request video CD movies, Internet access, bathroom) at this four-star hotel are clean, elegant and spacious.

Directory

Directory

TRANSPORT

As it's the nation's capital, getting to Beijing is straightforward. Rail and air connections link the capital to virtually every point in China, and fleets of buses head to abundant destinations from Beijing. Using Beijing as a starting point to explore the rest of the land makes perfect sense.

Central Beijing might be of orderly design, but getting around much of the city can be gruelling as the huge distances and overburdened transport options make navigation exhausting. The city is undergoing rapid development to haul its transport infrastructure into the modern age and to prepare it for the growing number of visitors as the 2008 Olympics approaches. Road widening, extending the subway system, laying a light rail link and providing new buses all aim to ease the flow of traffic, but Beijing's roads remain congested and its infrastructure overstretched. China's unprecedented growth has meant that Beijing's road expansion schemes have failed to keep pace with the increasing volume of vehicular traffic, leaving many of Beijing's roads regularly congested. There are now more than two million cars on the roads of Beijing, and the number is growing. It is attempting to move in the right direction with 15 express roads planned to link the outer ring roads with the city centre by 2006 and US$4 billion earmarked for traffic improvements during 2003–04. The roads remain heavily burdened with traffic, however, which makes travelling on buses an exercise in patience. Taking taxis is far preferable, if you have to take to the road at all. They are cheap and efficient, as long as you avoid the rush hour. Apart from jumping on a bicycle, the best way to get about, however, is to use the subway. It might be limited in scope (it is being expanded), but it can get you close to where you want to head. Then you can take a taxi, walk or take a bus to your final destination.

AIR

You can purchase tickets for Chinese carriers flying from Beijing at the Aviation Building (Map pp236-8; Mínháng Yíngyè Dàshà; ☎ domestic 6601 3336; ☎ international 6601 6667; 15 Xichang'an Jie). The same tickets can be bought from numerous other ticket outlets and service counters around Beijing, and through most midrange and top-end hotels. Chinese speakers can call the ticket reservation hotline on ☎ 962581.

You can make inquiries for all airlines at Beijing's Capital Airport (☎ 962580 from Beijing only). Call ☎ 6459 9567 for information on international arrivals and departures and ☎ 1689 6969 for information on domestic flights.

Airlines

Chinese carriers in Beijing include:

China Northwest Airlines (Map pp236-8; ☎ 6601 7755, ext 2141; www.cnwa.com in Chinese; Aviation Building, 15 Xichang'an Jie)

China Southern Airlines (☎ 6567 2203; 2 Dongsanhuan Nanlu)

Shanghai Airlines (☎ 6456 9019; www.shanghai-air.com in Chinese; Bldg 3, Capital Airport)

International airlines in Beijing include:

Air Canada (Map pp234-5; ☎ 6468 2001; www.aircanada.ca; room C201, Lufthansa Center, 50 Liangmaqiao Lu)

Air France (Map pp234-5; ☎ 6588 1388; www.airfrance.com.cn; room 512, 5th fl, Full Link Plaza, 18 Chaoyangmenwai Dajie)

British Airways (Map pp239-41; ☎ 6512 4070; room 210, 2nd fl, SciTech Tower, 22 Jianguomenwai Dajie)

Dragon Air (Map pp239-41; ☎ 6518 2533; www.dragonair.com; room 1710, Office Tower 1, Henderson Center, 18 Jianguomennei Dajie)

Japan Airlines (Map pp239-41; ☎ 6513 0888; www.jal.com; 1st fl, Changfugong Office Bldg, Hotel New Otani, 26a Jianguomenwai Dajie)

KLM (Map pp239-41; ☎ 6505 3505; www.klm.com; W501, West Wing, China World Trade Center, 1 Jianguomenwai Dajie)

Lufthansa Airlines (Map pp234-5; ☎ 6465 4488; www.lufthansa.com; room 101, Lufthansa Center, 50 Liangmaqiao Lu)

Qantas Airways (Map pp234-5; ☎ 6467 4794/3337; www.qantas.com.au; room 120, Lufthansa Center, 50 Liangmaqiao Lu)

Singapore Airlines (Map pp239-41; ☎ 6505 2233; www.singaporeair.com; room L109, China World Trade Center, 1 Jianguomenwai Dajie)

Thai Airways International (Map pp234-5; ☎ 6460 8899; www.thaiairways.com; room S102B, Lufthansa Center, 50 Liangmaqiao Lu)

United Airlines (Map pp239-41; ☎ 6463 1111; www.united.com; Lufthansa Center, 50 Liangmaqiao Lu)

Airports

Beijing's Capital Airport is 27km northeast of the city centre. The arrivals hall is located on the first floor, and the departure hall is on the second floor. For currency exchange, you can find several banks (the Agricultural Bank of China and the Industrial and Commercial Bank of China) in the arrivals hall. They are open 24 hours and offer a similar exchange rate to banks in the city and probably a better rate than your hotel. Here you can also find several ATMs (Bank of China, China Construction Bank and the Industrial and Commercial Bank of China) with international access, such as Maestro, Plus and Cirrus (and take Visa and MasterCard), where you can draw local currency. There's a small post office in the departure hall as you enter the airport; you can buy IC and IP phonecards and maps of Beijing here. Phones can be found at each end of the arrivals hall; you must buy a phonecard (available in denominations of Y50 and Y100) or have some small change ready. Left-luggage facilities (from Y5) are on the first floor, where luggage can be stored for a maximum of seven days. Trolleys are available for free. A small Airport Clinic can be found on the first floor.

There is a branch of the **Beijing Tourist Information Center** (see p208) in the arrivals hall, but it's not of much use and is more a hotel booking service, but you might be able to score a map. Other desks in the arrivals hall also provide hotel bookings, and you can often obtain substantial discounts on accommodation.

The airport restaurants are unimaginative and overpriced; you will pay upwards of Y50, or around ten times the price in town, for a bowl of noodles. The absence of competition from fixed-price fast-food chains means that the outfits here can charge whatever they like. If you're doing last-minute souvenir shopping, you'll find prices are astronomical at the airport trinket stores.

International/domestic departure tax is Y90/50. The tax is not included in the price of your ticket and is paid before check in. It is only payable in Renminbi, so ensure that you have enough local currency when you depart.

To/From Capital Airport

Beijing's **Capital Airport** is 27km from the centre of town or about 20 minutes by car.

Several bus companies run services to and from the airport. Inside the airport terminal there's a service desk where tickets are sold, and a further desk can be found outside, alongside a bus timetable. All buses into town cost Y16, so just pay for your ticket and tell them where you want to go. Almost any bus that gets you into town will probably do; then you can hop in a taxi and drive to a hotel.

Several express bus routes (☎ 6459 4375/ 4376) run regularly to Beijing every 15 minutes between 5.30am and 7pm daily. Some lines also operate outside these hours during peak time. Route A runs 24 hours, with less frequent services after 10pm, and it's probably the most popular with travellers. From the airport it goes to Sanyuanqiao, passes the Kunlun Hotel, Dongzhimen and Dongsishitiao, and terminates at the Beijing International Hotel (Guójì Fàndiàn), north of Beijing Train Station. Route B goes to Jinganzhuang, Xibahe, Hepingjie, Anzhenqiao, Beitaipingzhuang, the Friendship Hotel, Zizhuqiao, Huayuanqiao, Hangtianqiao and Gongzhufen. Both of these buses can drop you at a subway station. Route C goes to Xinyuanli, Gongti, Dongdaqiao and the China Art Gallery (Zhōngguó Měishù Guǎn) north of Wangfujing Dajie. Other buses follow the same route as Route A, but terminate at the CAAC office west of the Forbidden City in Xīdān; another follows Route B, but terminates at Beijing West Train Station (Běijīng Xī Zhàn).

Going from the city to the airport, the most useful place to catch the bus is at the west door of the Beijing International Hotel (Map pp239-41), where buses leave every half hour between 6.30am and 7.30pm (Y16). You can also pick up the bus that leaves every 30 minutes from the east end of the Aviation Building (Map pp236-8) on Xichang'an Jie, Xidan District (the CAAC ticket office; ☎ 6601 7755) between 6am and 7.30pm (Y16). Buy your tickets from the office in the corner of the building.

Many top-end hotels runs shuttle buses from the airport to their hotels. Check at the hotel desks at the airport upon arrival or check with the hotel beforehand. You do not necessarily have to be a guest of the hotel to use these, but you do have to pay for the service. The price for the minibuses is higher than that for the regular airport buses.

A light rail link from Capital Airport to Beijing is under construction, but is not due for completion until 2007.

A taxi (using its meter) should cost about Y85 from the airport to the centre, including the Y15 airport expressway toll. A well-established illegal taxi operation at the airport attempts to lure weary travellers into a Y300-plus ride to the city. One man acts as a taxi pimp for a squad of drivers – he will usually solicit you while you're still inside the airport terminal building.

To the Rest of China

Daily flights connect Beijing to every major city in China. There might not be daily flights to smaller cities throughout China, but there should be at least one flight a week. Tickets can be purchased at the Aviation Building (see p188) or one of the numerous airline offices in Beijing or through your hotel. Discounts are generally available, so it is important to ask. The domestic airfares listed here are approximate only and represent the non-discounted air fare from Beijing.

Destination	One-way fare
Chéngdū	Y1300
Dàlián	Y640
Guǎngzhōu	Y1510
Guìlín	Y1580
Hángzhōu	Y1050
Hong Kong	Y2800
Kūnmíng	Y1600
Lhasa	Y2040
Nánjīng	Y930
Qīngdǎo	Y660
Shànghǎi	Y1040
Ürümqi	Y2080
Wǔhàn	Y990
Xī'ān	Y970

BICYCLE

Getting around Beijing by bike is an excellent idea. The city is flat as a chessboard, and there are ample bicycle lanes. The increase in traffic in recent years has made biking along major thoroughfares more dangerous and nerve-racking, however. Cycling through Beijing's *hútòng* is far safer and an experience not to be missed (see p107).

Parking your bike in one of the more secure pavement bike parking lots found all over town is around Y0.20. Very cheap roadside repairs can be found down Beijing's numerous alleyways.

If you have the option of buying your own bike, good-quality bikes can be bought at the **Qianmen Bicycle Shop** (Map pp239-41; Qianmen Zixingche Shangdian; 97 Qianmen Dajie), opposite the post office, or you can try the **bike shop** next to the Beijing Gongti International Youth Hostel (Map pp234-5).

Despite the convenience of cycling, take care when you're on your bike. Watch out for ice in winter; the fierce sand storms during springtime present another challenge. Riding at night can also be hazardous, mainly because few Chinese bikes are equipped with lights. But your greatest concern will probably be Beijing's pernicious traffic conditions and bad drivers.

Hire

Budget hotels are good places to rent bicycles, which cost around Y10 per day (plus a deposit); rental at upmarket hotels is far more expensive. A few tourist-oriented rental outfits have been established, including **Universal Bicycle Rental Outlet** (Map pp232-3; ☎ 1330 1195288), which has two outlets in the vicinity of Qianhai Lake. The clearly signposted outlets are convenient, but expensive. Tandems (*shuǎngrén zixíngchē*) are Y20 per hour, single bikes Y10 per hour (Y500 deposit). You might find the location of the outlets convenient but at this price, it might make more sense to buy your own bike. When renting a bike it's safest to use your own lock(s) in order to prevent bicycle theft, a common problem in Beijing.

BUS

Relying on buses (*gōnggòng qìchē*) to get swiftly from A to B can be frustrating unless it's a short hop. Getting a seat can also be impossible. Fares are typically Y1 or under depending on distance, although plusher, air-conditioned buses are more expensive. You generally pay the conductor, rather than the driver, once aboard the bus. Beijing's fleet of aged cream-coloured, dented leviathans is being gradually replaced with modern low-pollution green buses.

Buses run 5am to 11pm daily or thereabouts, and stops are few and far between. It's important to work out how many stops you need to go before boarding. If you can read Chinese, a useful publication is available (Y5) from kiosks listing all the Beijing bus lines; alternatively, tourist maps of Beijing illustrate some of the bus routes.

One- and two-digit bus numbers are city-core; 100-series buses are trolleys; 200-series are night buses (*yèbān gōnggòng qìchē*) and 300-series are suburban lines. Minibuses (*xiǎobā*) follow many of the main bus routes and are slightly more expensive, costing from around Y2. Some of the buses are air-conditioned, and an increasing number run on natural gas. If you work out how to combine bus and subway connections the subway will speed up much of the trip.

Special double-decker buses run in a circle around the city centre and are slightly more expensive but spare you the traumas of normal public buses and you should be able to get a seat.

The following double-decker routes are useful:

No 1 Beijing West Train Station, heading east on Fuxingmen Dajie, Xichang'an Jie, Dongchang'an Jie, Jianguomennei Dajie, Jianguomenwai Dajie, Jianguo Lu, Bawang fen (intersection of Jianguo Lu and Xidawang Lu)

No 2 shangxing Qianmen, north on Dongdan Beidajie, Dongsi Nandajie, Dongsi Beidajie, Lama Temple, Zhonghua Minzu Yuan (Ethnic Minorities Park), Asian Games Village

No 3 Jijia Miao (the southwest extremity of the Third Ring Rd), Grand View Garden, Leyou Hotel, Jingguang New World Hotel, Tuanjiehu Park, Agricultural Exhibition Center, Lufthansa Center

No 4 Beijing Zoo, Exhibition Center, Second Ring Rd, Holiday Inn Downtown, Yuetan Park, Fuxingmen Dajie flyover, Qianmen Xidajie, Qianmen

Useful standard bus routes include:

No 1 Runs along Chang'an Jie, Jianguomenwai Dajie and Jianguomennei Dajie: Sihuizhan, Bawangfen, Yonganli, Dongdan, Xidan, Muxidi, Junshi Bowuguan, Gongzhufen, Maguanying

No 4 Runs along Chang'an Jie, Jianguomenwai Dajie and Jianguomennei Dajie: Gongzhufen, Junshi Bowuguan, Muxidi, Xidan, Tiananmen, Dongdan, Yonganli, Bawangfen, Sihuizhan

No 5 Deshengmen, Dianmen, Beihai Park, Xihuamen, Zhongshan Park, Qianmen

No 15 Beijing Zoo, Fuxingmen, Xidan, Hepingmen, Liulichang, Tianqiao

No 20 Beijing South Train Station, Tianqiao, Qianmen, Wangfujing, Dongdan, Beijing Train Station

No 44 outer ring Xinjiekou, Xizhimen Train Station, Fuchengmen, Fuxingmen, Changchunjie, Xuanwumen, Qianmen, Taijichang, Chongwenmen, Dongbianmen, Chaoyangmen, Dongzhimen, Andingmen, Deshengmen, Xinjiekou

No 54 Beijing Train Station, Dongbianmen, Chongwenmen, Zhengyi Lu, Qianmen, Dazhalan (Dashilar), Temple of Heaven Park, Yongdingmen, Haihutun

No 103 Beijing Train Station, Dengshikou, China Art Gallery, Forbidden City (north entrance), Beihai Park, Fuchengmen, Beijing Zoo

No 332 Beijing Zoo, Weigongcun, Renmin Daxue, Zhongguancun, Haidian, Beijing University, Summer Palace

To the Rest of China

No international buses serve Beijing, but there are plenty of long-distance domestic routes. Although most domestic travel is by train, roads are improving, buses are cheaper and it's easier to book a seat. Sleeper buses are widely available and recommended for overnight journeys. Twelve national highways radiate from Beijing to major cities nationwide, including Shěnyáng, Tiānjīn, Harbin, Guǎngzhōu, Nánjīng, Fúzhōu and Kūnmíng.

Beijing has a total of 12 long-distance bus stations (*chángtú qìchēzhàn*), so figuring out which bus station to depart from is confusing. The rule of thumb is that long-distance bus stations are on the perimeter of the city in the direction you want to go. The major stations are at **Xizhimen** (☎ 6218 3454/6217 6767) in the west and **Dongzhimen** (☎ 6467 1346) in the northeast. Other important stations are at **Zhaogongkou** bus station (☎ 6722 9491/6723 7328) in the south (useful for buses to Tianjin), **Deshengmen** and **Beijing South Train Station** (☎ 6303 4307).

Buses range in both type and quality, from simple minibuses (*xiǎobā*) to air-conditioned Volvo (*wòěrwò*) buses, equipped with TV sets, reclining seats and hostesses. On long journeys, it is advisable to spend a bit more so that you can travel in comfort.

There are a few small bus stations where tour buses and minibuses gather (usually just in the morning) looking for passengers heading for the Great Wall and other sites in the outlying areas. The most important of these is east of Zhengyang Men (Front Gate) in Qianmen, in the vicinity of Tiananmen Square. Also useful is the **Zhanlanguan Lu tour bus station**, which is just to the south of Beijing Zoo, and the **tour bus station** at Xuanwumen in front of the South Cathedral.

CAR

If you are willing to endure the appalling driving conditions of Beijing's roads, you can hire a car. You will need an International Driving Licence or a Chinese driving licence and will be limited to driving within Beijing proper (you will not be allowed to drift off to, say, Shanghai). The current absence of car hire outlets at Beijing's Capital Airport signals a reluctant industry. **Hertz** used to have an office opposite the arrivals hall, but when last inspected, the sign remained even though the staff had long moved out. They have another branch (Map pp239-41; ☎ 800-810 8833 countrywide; 5 Jianguomenwai Dajie; ☽ 9am-5pm) outside the Jianguo Hotel (p155).

It must be emphasised that the Chinese drive dangerously and give very little consideration to other drivers. The law of the road is one of carelessness, and it is a far better and safer idea not to get involved at all (unless you are staying in Beijing long term and have no option). Taxis are cheap, and even hiring a driver is a better proposition; it can be arranged at major hotels, CITS or other travel agencies. Depending on the type of vehicle, a chauffeur-driven car could cost you as much as Y1000 per day. It's cheaper to hire a *xiali* taxi by the day for about Y350 (see below).

TAXI

Taxis are everywhere, and finding one is only a problem during rush hour and (infrequent) rainstorms.

Beijing taxis come in different classes. All taxis sport a red sticker on the side rear window declaring the rate per kilometre. Red *xiali* taxis are the most economical (Y10 for the first 4km; Y1.20 per kilometre thereafter). Next are the larger Y1.60 taxis (Y10 for the first 3km; Y1.60 per kilometre thereafter), many of these are red Citroens; it pays to take them if you are going a long distance as there's more leg room and they're cleaner. Volkswagen Santana 2000

taxis cost Y12 for the first 4km and Y2 for each kilometre thereafter. Taxis are required to switch on the meter for all journeys. Between 11pm and 6am daily there is a 20% surcharge added to the flag fall metered fare. Always insist that the meter is used, unless taking a long trip out of town.

Beijing taxi drivers speak little if any English. If you don't speak Chinese, bring a map or have your destination written down in characters. It helps if you know the way to your destination; sit in the front with a map.

Cabs can be hired for distance, by the hour or by the day (a minimum of Y350 for the day). Taxis can be hailed in the street or summoned by phone, or you could wait at one of the designated taxi stopping zones. Call ☎ 6835 1150 to register a complaint. Remember to collect a receipt (ask the driver to *fāpiào*) – if you accidentally leave anything in the taxi, the driver's number appears on the receipt so he or she can be located.

Don't expect rear seatbelts in any but the best cabs, and be prepared to find the front seat belt possibly locked solid or filthy through neglect. The taxi driver might try to dissuade you from wearing a seatbelt – don't listen to him/her. You won't find child seats. Be prepared for bad driving, and try to position yourself so that you don't lose an eye on one of the sharp corners and edges of the security cage the driver inhabits if he or she suddenly halts (or crashes). Watch out for tired drivers – they work long and punishing shifts.

If you're staying for a long time and you meet a taxi driver you like or trust, ask for a name card. Most drivers have home phones or mobile phones and can be hired for the day.

SUBWAY & LIGHT RAILWAY

The subway (*dìtiě*) is probably the best way to travel around. The Underground Dragon can move at up to 70km per hour – a jaguar compared with the lumbering buses. The system is modest and trains are showing their age, but five new subway lines are being constructed to take the strain off the roads before the 2008 Olympics. Three lines exist: the Circle Line (*Huánxiàn*), the East-West Line (*Yīxiàn*) and Line 13 (*shísān hào xiàn*), the last being a light rail link. The fare is a flat Y3 on all lines, regardless of distance. Only a few platforms have seats, but none have toilets. Trains run at a frequency of one every few minutes during peak times. They can get very crowded, but the carriages have seats for 60 and standing room for 200. The subway runs from 5am to 11pm daily; platform signs are in Chinese characters and pinyin. You'll find a detailed subway map of Beijing in the colour map section at the back of this book.

To recognise a subway station (dì tiě zhàn), look for the subway symbol, which is a blue English capital 'D' with a circle around it. Another way of recognising a subway station is to look for an enormous cluster of bicycles.

In addition to the lines described here, Line 5 is under construction and is due for completion in 2007. When it opens, it will run north–south, intersecting the Circle Line at Yonghegong and Chongwenmen and intersecting the East–West Line at Dongdan. Extending into the eastern suburbs from the East-West Line from Sihuixi to Tuqiao (13 stations in all) is the Batong Line, which opened in late 2003. Fares on the Batong Line are Y2.

Circle Line

This 16km line presently has 18 stations: Beijing Zhan (Beijing Train Station), Jianguomen, Chaoyangmen, Dongsishitiao, Dongzhimen, Yonghegong, Andingmen, Gulou, Jishuitan, Xizhimen (the north train station and zoo), Chegongzhuang, Fuchengmen, Fuxingmen, Changchunjie, Xuanwumen, Hepingmen, Qianmen and Chongwenmen. The Circle Line intersects with the East–West Line at Fuxingmen and Jianguomen.

East–West Line

This line has 23 stations and runs from Sihuidong to Pingguoyuan, a western suburb of Beijing. The stops are Sihuidong, Sihuixi, Dawanglu, Guomao, Yonganli, Jianguomen, Dongdan, Wangfujing, Tiananmen Dong, Tiananmen Xi, Xidan, Fuxingmen, Nanilishilu, Muxidi, Junshibowuguan, Gongzhufen, Wanshoulu, Wukesong, Yuquanlu, Babaoshan, Bajiaocun, Guchenglu and Pingguoyuan.

Line 13

Classified as part of the subway system but actually a light rail link, Line 13 runs in a northern loop from Xizhimen to Dongzhimen in the north of Beijing, stopping at 14 stations (approximately three minutes per station) in between (first/last train 6am/9pm). As with the subway, tickets are Y3, but Y5 gets you a ticket to any station on the other lines of the underground system. It's not of great use for tourist sights, apart from the Dazhongsi stop (for the Great Bell Temple) and the Wudaokou stop, for the Old Summer Palace and Summer Palace. An extension to the line that will link Dongzhimen to Beijing's Capital Airport is being built (due for completion in 2007).

The stations on Line 13 (heading west to east) are Xizhimen, Dazhongsi, Zhichunlu, Wudaokou, Shangdi, Xierqi, Longze, Huilongguan, Huoying, Lishuiqiao, Beiyuan, Wangjingxi, Shaoyaoju, Guangximen, Liufang and Dongzhimen.

TRAIN

China's extensive rail network covers every province except Tibet (rail link under construction). Travelling China by train is an excellent way to voyage, especially by hard sleeper, as it offers an entertaining ride and brings you together with Chinese travelling the land. Intercity trains are largely air-conditioned, fast and comfortable, and varying classes of travel are often available.

Buying Tickets

Tickets can be bought up to only four days in advance, which includes the day you buy the ticket and the day you depart; so you don't turn up at the station a week before you want to travel.

It's cheapest if you buy tickets at the train station, but for a small surcharge you can get them at most hotel counters and ticket counters around the city or through travel agents. Avoid buying from the touts who gather outside the train station, unless you are desperate for a ticket. If you do buy from a tout, examine the ticket carefully to check the date of travel and destination, before handing over your money.

You might want to avoid buying tickets in the main ticket hall at the station, as the crowds there can be overwhelming. A **ticketing office for foreigners** exists at **Beijing Train Station** in the northwest corner of the first floor (5.30am-7.30am, 8am-6.30pm, 7pm-11pm), accessed through the soft-seat waiting room (guìbīn hǒ'chēshì). This is an excellent place to sit down and take a breather in the comfy armchairs provided. You can also book return tickets here and tickets for trains departing from other cities, eg from Nánjīng to Shanghai, as long as there are seats available.

There is also a foreigners ticketing office on the second floor of **Beijing West Train Station** (24hr). Your chances of getting a sleeper (hard or soft) are good if you book ahead. Never just turn up and expect to be able to buy a ticket to a distant destination for same-day travel. Train tickets to and from Beijing can be booked solid for almost a week around National Day (1 October); the rail network is also totally congested during Chinese New Year. Chinese speakers can call ☎ 962586 to book tickets in advance.

Classes

Trains on longer routes are divided into classes. Hard-seat (yìng zuò) is actually generally padded, but the hard-seat section can be hard on your sanity (it can be very dirty, noisy and smoky, and painful on the long haul) but the tourist, express trains or newer trains are more pleasant, less crowded and air-conditioned.

Since hard-seat is the only thing most locals can afford, it's packed to the gills. You should get a ticket with an assigned seat number, but if seats have sold out, ask for a standing ticket (wúzuò), which at least gets you on the train, where you might find a seat or you could upgrade (see below). Because hard-seat tickets are relatively easy to obtain, you might have to travel hard-seat even if you're willing to pay for a higher class.

On short express journeys (such as Beijing to Tianjin) some trains have soft-seat (ruǎn zuò) carriages. The seats are two abreast and comfortable, and overcrowding is not permitted. Soft-seats cost about the same as hard-sleeper, and carriages are often double-decker.

Hard-sleeper (yìng wò) carriages are made up of doorless compartments with half a dozen bunks in three tiers, and sheets, pillows and blankets are provided. It does very nicely as an overnight hotel. There is a small price difference between berths, with the lowest bunk (xiàpù) the most expensive and the top bunk (shàngpù) the cheapest. You might wish to take the middle bunk (zhōngpù) as all and sundry invade the lower berth and use it as a seat during the day, whereas the top one has little headroom and puts you near the speakers. Tall passengers might prefer the top bunk, however, as the beds are short, and passengers in the aisle will bash into your overhanging feet. As with all other classes, smoking is prohibited in hard-sleeper. Lights and speakers go out at around 10pm. Each compartment is equipped with its own hot water flask (rèshuǐpíng), which is filled by an attendant. Hard-sleeper tickets are the most difficult of all to buy; you almost always need to buy these far in advance.

Soft sleeper (ruǎn wò) is luxurious travel, with four comfortable bunks in a closed compartment, wood panelling, potted plants, lace curtains, teacups, clean washrooms, carpets and air-con. Soft sleeper costs twice as much as hard sleeper (the upper berth is slightly cheaper than the lower berth), so it is usually easier to purchase soft rather than hard sleeper; however, more and more Chinese are travelling this way.

If you get on the train with an unreserved seating ticket, you can find the conductor and upgrade (bupiào) yourself to a hard-sleeper, soft-seat or soft-sleeper if there are any available.

Services

Travellers arrive and depart by train at **Beijing Train Station** (Běijīng Huǒchē Zhàn; ☎ 6563 3262/3242), southeast of the Forbidden City, or **Beijing West Train Station** (Běijīng Xī Zhàn; ☎ 6321 6253), near Lianhuachi Park. Beijing Train Station is served by its own underground station, making access simple. International trains to Moscow, Pyongyang and Ulaan Baatar arrive at and leave from Beijing Train Station; trains for Hong Kong and Vietnam leave from Beijing West Train Station.

There are also two other stations of significance in the city: **Beijing South Train Station** (Yǒngdìngmén Huǒchē Zhàn; ☎ 6563 5222) and **Beijing North Train Station** (Běijīng Běizhàn; ☎ 6563 6122/6223) on the Second Ring Rd.

You can find left luggage counters (jìcúnchù) at most train stations. Useful lockers exist just to the right as you enter the soft-seat waiting room (see Tickets above) of Beijing Train Station. They are automatic and have English instructions, and you receive a printed ticket (12 hours Y25).

Directory – Transport

Paperback train timetables for the entire country are published every April and October, but they are available in Chinese only (Y8). Thinner versions listing the major trains from Beijing can be bought at train stations for about Y2 – again in Chinese only. An English translation of the timetable is provided by Duncan Peattie, listing the most important routes. Contact chinatt@eudoramail.com for details on how to get hold of a copy.

Typical train fares and approximate travel times for hard-sleeper tickets to destinations from Beijing include: Chéngdū (Y418; 26 hours), Dàlián (Y257; 12 hours), Guangzhou (Y458; 22 hours), Hángzhōu (Y363; 15 hours), Jǐ'nán (Y137; 4½ hours), Kūnmíng (Y578; 40 hours), Nánjīng (Y274; 11 hours), Nánníng (Y499; 28 hours), Shànghai (Y327; 13½ hours), Tiānjīn (Y30 hard seat; 80 minutes) and Xī'ān (Y274; 12 hours).

PRACTICALITIES

ACCOMMODATION

The hotels, hostels and guesthouses in the Sleeping chapter are listed alphabetically within each neighbourhood. Mid-range and top-end hotels are first, followed by budget options.

Hotel rooms are generally easy to find, although it can be harder during the peak tourist season from June to September. Finding a hotel room during the 1 May and 1 October holiday periods can be taxing, so book ahead if visiting during these times.

For information on rates and discounts, reservations and other aspects of accommodation in Beijing, consult the Sleeping chapter (p151).

Accommodation websites that could be useful for travellers booking accommodation include www.redflag.info and www.asia-hotels.com. Before booking compare online rates with those offered by the hotel itself, as rates might be similar.

BUSINESS

Doing business in China has long been fraught for Westerners since Lord Macartney's turkey of a mission to Chengde in 1793 to develop trade relations.

Things are easing up rapidly, but even simple things can still be difficult. Renting properties, getting licences, hiring employees, having a telephone installed and paying taxes can generate mind-boggling quantities of red tape. Many foreign businesspeople who have worked in China say that success is usually the result of dogged persistence and finding cooperative officials.

Countless Western businesses have been beached by the lure of the Chinese market, and only a few have made money, although that could be changing. Anyone planning on doing business in China is advised to read *The China Dream: The Elusive Quest for the Greatest Untapped Market on Earth* by Joe Studwell (Profile Books Ltd, 2002). It's not all doom and gloom, but the book affords a sober and balanced perspective on the Chinese economy and how it all fits together.

If yours is a high-tech company, you can go into certain economic zones and register as a wholly foreign-owned enterprise. In that case you can hire people without going through the government, enjoy a three-year tax holiday, obtain long-term income tax advantages and import duty-free personal items for corporate and expat use (including a car!). The alternative is listing your company as a representative office, which doesn't allow you to sign any contracts in China – these must be signed by the parent company.

It's easier to register as a representative office. First find out where you want to set up (the city or a special economic zone), then go through local authorities (there are no national authorities for this). Go to the local Commerce Office, Economic Ministry, Foreign Ministry, or any ministry that deals with foreign economic trade promotion. Contact your embassy and national trade organisation first – they can advise you.

Taxation rates vary from zone to zone, authority to authority. They seem to be negotiable, but 15% is fairly standard in economic zones. Every economic zone has a reasonably comprehensive investment guide, which is available in English and Chinese – ask at the economic or trade section of your embassy, which might have copies of them.

Anyone thinking of doing serious business in China is advised to do a lot of preliminary research. In particular, talk to other foreigners who are already doing business in China. Alternatively, approach a firm of business consultants for advice or approach the business associations listed below.

Business Associations

The following organisations can be found in Beijing:

American Chamber of Commerce (☎ 8519 1920; www
.amcham-china.org.cn; room 1903, 8 Jianguomen Beidajie,
China Resources Bldg, Dongcheng)

British Chamber of Commerce (☎ 6593 2153; info@
britaininchina.com; 31 Technical Club, 2nd fl, 15 Guang-
huali, Jianguomenwai Dajie, Chaoyang)

Canada-China Business Council (☎ 6512 6120; www
.ccbc.com; suite 18-2, 18th fl, CITIC Bldg, 19 Jianguomenwai Dajie, Chaoyang)

China-Australia Chamber of Commerce (☎ 6595 9252;
admin@austcham.org; room 314, Great Wall Sheraton
Hotel, 8 Dongsanhuan Beilu, Chaoyang)

European Union Chamber of Commerce in China
(☎ 6462 2065; www.euccc.com.cn)

French Chamber of Commerce & Industry (☎ 8451 2071;
S123, Office Bldg, Lufthansa Center, 50 Liangmaqiao Lu)

US-China Business Council (☎ 8526 3920; www
.uschina.org)

Business Cards

The Chinese hand business cards around in place of handshakes, and if you don't have one, it can be embarrassing. They are essential items, even if you don't do business. If you can get your name translated into Chinese and have it printed on the reverse, all the better. In Beijing small copy shops can usually print name cards; you can also try **Empire Printing** (Map pp239-41; ☎ 6595 9013; empire@public.bta.net.cn; 5 Jianguomenwai Dajie), near the Jianguo Hotel.

BUSINESS HOURS

China officially has a five-day working week. Banks, offices and government departments are normally open Monday to Friday, open roughly from 9am (some closing for two hours in the middle of the day) until 5pm or 6pm. Saturday and Sunday are both public holidays, but most Beijing museums stay open on weekends and make up for this by closing for one day (usually Monday). Museums tend to stop selling tickets half an hour before they close. Bank of China branches are generally open weekdays from 9.30am to 11.30am and 1.30pm to 4.30pm, and most now have 24-hour ATMs (see ATMs, p203). Travel

agencies, the Friendship Store, foreign-exchange counters in the tourist hotels and some of the local branches of the Bank of China have similar opening hours, but are generally open on weekends as well, at least in the morning. Note that businesses in Beijing close for three week-long holidays (p201).

Many parks, zoos and monuments have similar opening hours; they're also open at weekends and often at night.

Long-distance bus stations and train stations open their ticket offices around 5am, before the first trains and buses pull out. Apart from a one- or two-hour break for lunch, they often stay open until midnight.

Beijing's entertainment sector is working increasingly long hours, and it's possible to find something to eat and somewhere to drink at any hour of the day.

CHILDREN

The treatment you'll receive if you're travelling with a young child or baby can often make life a lot easier in Beijing (especially if they have blond hair).

Don't be surprised if a complete stranger picks up your child or tries to take them from your arms: Chinese people openly display their affection for children.

Baby food and milk powder is widely available in supermarkets, as are basics like nappies, baby wipes, bottles, creams, medicine, clothing, dummies (pacifiers) and other paraphernalia. Virtually no cheap restaurants, however, have baby chairs, and finding baby-changing rooms is next to impossible. Check the health section for information on recommended vaccinations (p199).

Numerous international schools where children are educated in the English language, serve the city. One example is the International Academy of Beijing (☎ 6430 1600; www.iabchina.net; Lido Office Tower 3, Lido Place, Jichang Lu, Chaoyang).

CLIMATE

Autumn is the optimal season to visit Beijing as the weather is gorgeous and fewer tourists are in town. Local Beijingers describe this short season as '*tiāngāo qìshuǎng*', literally 'the sky is high and the air is fresh' – with clear skies and breezy days. Arid spring is OK, apart from the (worsening) sand clouds (see p15) that sweep in from Inner

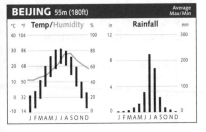

| BEIJING 55m (180ft) | | | Average Max/Min |

Temp/Humidity °C °F % in Rainfall mm

Mongolia and the ubiquitous static electricity that discharges everywhere. Spring also sees the snow-like *liǔxù* (willow catkins) wafting through the air like snow and collecting in drifts. From May onwards the mercury can surge well over 30°C. Beijing simmers under a scorching sun in summer (reaching more than 40°C), which also sees heavy rainstorms late in the season. Surprisingly, this is also considered the peak season, when hotels typically raise their rates and the Great Wall nearly collapses under the weight of marching tourists. In winter there are few tourists in town and many hotels offer substantial discounts – but it's glacial outside (dipping as low as -20°C) and the northern winds cut like a knife through bean curd. Note that air pollution can be very harsh in summer and winter (although Beijing is obliged to clean up its act for the 2008 Olympics).

COURSES

When walking down Wangfujing Dajie, men will be press-ganged into English lessons by persistent female students, who then try to haul them off to art studios to purchase overpriced art works. If what you are after, however, is a language exchange partner, consult the classified pages of English magazines such as *That's Beijing* (www.thatsmagazines.com). The following language schools are reputable and offer tuition in the Chinese language:

Australia-China Cultural Interchange Foundation (☎ 6213 2128; www.accif.org; room 12A06, Qingyun Modern Plaza, Western Road 43, Bei Sanhuan Lu)

FESCO (Map pp234-5; ☎ 8561 6180; www.fesco-training .com.cn; 1st fl, FESCO Bldg, 14 Chaoyangmen Nandajie) This long-established institution has courses in Chinese language, Chinese painting, calligraphy, seal cutting, music, dance, martial arts, acupuncture, moxibustion and other traditional crafts and skills. FESCO also holds regular seminars on subjects relating to Chinese history and culture.

CUSTOMS

Chinese customs generally pay tourists little attention. There are clearly marked 'green channels' and 'red channels'. Duty-free, you're allowed to import 400 cigarettes or the equivalent in tobacco products, 2L of alcohol, 50g of gold or silver and 72 rolls of still film. Importation of fresh fruit and cold cuts is prohibited. You can legally bring in or take out only Y6000 in Chinese currency. There are no restrictions on foreign currency; however, you should declare any cash that exceeds US$5000 (or its equivalent in another currency).

Objects considered as antiques require a certificate and red seal to clear customs. To get the proper certificate and red seal your antiques must be inspected by the **Relics Bureau** (Wénwù Jiàndìng; ☎ 6401 4608), where no English is spoken. Anything made before 1949 is considered an antique and needs a certificate, and if it was made before 1795 it cannot legally be taken out of the country.

DISABLED TRAVELLERS

If you are wheelchair-bound or you have a walking disability, Beijing will be a major obstacle course. Pavements are often crowded, in an appalling and dangerous condition, and high curbs prevent wheelchair access. Many streets can be crossed only via an underground or overhead walkway with many steps. You will also have to stick to the main roads, as cars and bicycles often occupy the pavements of smaller alleys and lanes, forcing pavement users on to the road. Those with sight, hearing or walking disabilities must be extremely cautious of the traffic, which almost never yields to pedestrians. Most, but not all, hotels have lifts, and several top-end hotels have rooms for those with disabilities, but there are no lifts in the subway where escalators usually only go up.

DISCOUNT CARDS

An ISIC card is becoming increasingly useful in China, and it carries fringe insurance benefits (see above). It won't work everywhere in Beijing, but you could get half-price entry to some sights. Chinese signs at many sights clearly indicate that students pay half price – so push the point. It's worth trying to get air ticket discounts using your

Directory – Practicalities

ISIC card; some travellers report success. If you are studying in China, your school will issue you with a student card, which is more useful for discounts on admission charges.

Tickets must be purchased for virtually every sight in Beijing and beyond, and there is little that one can do for free (see p66). Furthermore, ticket prices for many temples and historical monuments are increasing ahead of inflation, raising concerns about regulation. Thankfully, Christian churches in Beijing can still be visited for free (as long as they are open), but that does not apply to the rest of the country (St Michael's in Qīngdǎo has begun to levy entrance fees, depriving many Western worshippers of free access to their shrine). Hopefully, the example will not be followed in Beijing.

ELECTRICITY

Electricity is 220 volts, 50 cycles AC. Most plugs take four designs – three-pronged angled pins (as in Australia), three-pronged round pins (as in Hong Kong), two flat pins (US style but without the ground wire) or two narrow round pins (European style). Conversion plugs are easily purchased in Beijing.

EMBASSIES & CONSULATES
Chinese Embassies & Consulates

For a full list of diplomatic representation abroad go to the Ministry of Foreign affairs website at www.fmprc.gov.cn/eng/.

Australia (☎ 02-6273 4780, 6273 4781; www.china embassy.org.au; 15 Coronation Drive, Yarralumla, ACT 2600); consulate in Sydney (☎ 02-9699 2216); consulate in Melbourne (☎ 03-9822 0604); consulate in Perth (☎ 08-9321 8193)

Canada (☎ 613-789 3509; www.chinaembassycanada .org; 515 St Patrick St, Ottawa, Ontario K1N 5H3); consulate in Toronto (☎ 416-964 7260); consulate in Vancouver (☎ 604-736 3910); consulate in Calgary (☎ 403-264 3322).

Denmark (☎ 039-625 806; Oregards Alle 25, 2900 Hellerup, Copenhagen)

France (☎ 01 47 36 02 58; www.amb-chine.fr; 9 Avenue V Cresson, 92130 Issy les Moulineaux, Paris)

Japan (☎ 03-3403 3389, 3403 3065; 3-4-33 Moto-Azabu, Minato-ku, Tokyo 106)

Malaysia (☎ 03-242 8495; 229 Jalan Ampang, Kuala Lumpur)

Netherlands (☎ 070-355 1515; Adriaan Goekooplaan 7, 2517 JX, The Hague)

New Zealand (☎ 04-587 0407; 104A Korokoro Rd, Petone, Wellington)

Singapore (☎ 65-734 3361; 70 Dalvey Rd)

Thailand (☎ 02-245 7032/49; 57 Th Ratchadaphisek, Bangkok)

UK (☎ 020 7636 8845, 24-hr premium-rate visa information 0891 880 808; www.chinese-embassy.org.uk; 31 Portland Place, London, W1N 5AG; consulate in Manchester (☎ 0161-224 7480); consulate in Edinburgh (☎ 0131-316 4789)

USA (☎ 202-338 6688; www.china-embassy.org; room 110, 2201 Wisconsin Ave NW, Washington DC, 20007; consulate in Chicago (☎ 312-803 0098); consulate in Houston (☎ 713-524 4311); consulate in Los Angeles (☎ 213-380 2508); consulate in New York (☎ 212-330 7410); consulate in San Francisco (☎ 415-563 9232)

Embassies in Beijing

Embassies in Beijing are open 9am to 12pm and 1.30pm to 4pm Monday to Friday, but visa departments are often open only in the morning. There are two main embassy compounds: Jianguomenwai and Sanlitun.

The following embassies are in the Jianguomenwai area:

India (Map pp234-5; ☎ 6532 1908; fax 6532 4684; 1 Ritan Donglu)

Ireland (Map pp239-41; ☎ 6532 2691; fax 6532 2168; 3 Ritan Donglu)

Japan (Map pp234-5; ☎ 6532 2361; fax 6532 4625; 7 Ritan Lu)

Mongolia (Map pp239-41; ☎ 6532 1203; fax 6532 5045; 2 Xiushui Beijie)

New Zealand (Map pp234-5; ☎ 6532 2731; fax 6532 4317; 1 Ritan Dong Erjie)

North Korea (Map pp234-5; ☎ 6532 1186; fax 6532 6056; Ritan Beilu)

Philippines (☎ 6532 1872; fax 6532 3761; 23 Xiushui Beijie)

Singapore (☎ 6532 3926; fax 6532 2215; 1 Xiushui Beijie)

Thailand (Map pp234-5; ☎ 6532 1903; fax 6532 1748; 40 Guanghua Lu)

UK (Map pp234-5; ☎ 6532 1961; fax 6532 1937; 11 Guanghua Lu)

USA (Map pp234-5; ☎ 6532 3831; fax 6532 6057; 3 Xiushui Beijie)

Vietnam (Map pp234-5; ☎ 6532 1155; fax 6532 5720; 32 Guanghua Lu)

The Sanlitun compound is home to the following embassies:

Australia (Map pp234-5; ☎ 6532 2331; fax 6532 6957; 21 Dongzhimenwai Dajie)

Cambodia (Map pp234-5; ☎ 6532 2790; fax 6532 3507; 9 Dongzhimenwai Dajie)

Canada (Map pp234-5; ☎ 6532 3536; fax 6532 4072; 19 Dongzhimenwai Dajie)

France (Map pp234-5; ☎ 6532 1331; fax 6532 4841; 3 Dongsan Jie)

Germany (Map pp234-5; ☎ 6532 2161; fax 6532 5336; 17 Dongzhimenwai Dajie)

Italy (Map pp234-5; ☎ 6532 2131; fax 6532 4676; 2 Sanlitun Dong Erjie)

Kazakhstan (Map pp234-5; ☎ 6532 6182; fax 6532 6183; 9 Sanlitun Dong Liujie)

Laos (Map pp234-5; ☎ 6532 1224; 11 Dongsi Jie)

Malaysia (Map pp234-5; ☎ 6532 2531; fax 6532 5032; 13 Dongzhimenwai Dajie)

Myanmar (Map pp234-5; ☎ 6532 1584; fax 6532 1344; 6 Dongzhimenwai Dajie)

Nepal (Map pp234-5; ☎ 6532 1795; fax 6532 3251; 1 Sanlitun Xi Liujie)

Netherlands (Map pp234-5; ☎ 6532 1131; fax 6532 4689; 4 Liangmahe Nanlu)

Pakistan (Map pp234-5; ☎ 6532 2504/2558; 1 Dongzhimenwai Dajie)

Russia (Map pp232-3; ☎ 6532 1381; fax 6532 4853; 4 Dongzhimen Beizhongjie) West of the Sanlitun Compound in a separate compound.

South Korea (Map pp239-41; ☎ 6505 2608; fax 6505 3067; 3rd & 4th fl, China World Trade Center, 1 Jianguomenwai Dajie)

Sweden (Map pp234-5; ☎ 6532 3331; fax 6532 2909; 3 Dongzhimenwai Dajie)

EMERGENCY

Important telephone numbers include:

Ambulance	☎ 120
Directory enquiries	☎ 114
Fire	☎ 119
International assistance	☎ 115
Police	☎ 110
Weather (English and Chinese)	☎ 121

GAY & LESBIAN TRAVELLERS

Generally, the Chinese authorities take a dim view of homosexuality. Certainly a gay and lesbian scene exists in Beijing (and regular haunts are plentiful), but few people dare say so too loudly. For excellent and up-to-date information on the latest gay and lesbian hot spots in Beijing and the rest of China, have a look at the Utopia website www.utopia-asia.com/tipschin.htm. See also such bars as **Half & Half** (p129), which cater to gays and lesbians, in the Entertainment chapter.

HEALTH

Except for the thick layer of air pollution that sometimes blankets the city, Beijing is a reasonably healthy city and you needn't fear tropical bugs like malaria. When weighing up health risks, always bear in mind other, more immediate dangers – the greatest danger you will probably face is crossing the road.

It's a good idea to consult your government's travel health website before departure, if one is available.

Australia (www.dfat.gov.au/travel)

Canada (www.hc-sc.gc.ca/pphb-dgspsp/tmp-pmv/pub_e.htmi)

New Zealand (www.mfat.govt.nz/travel)

United Kingdom (www.doh.gov.uk/traveladvice)

United States (www.cdc.gov/travel)

It's worth taking your own medicine kit so that you have remedies at hand. Antibiotics *(kàngjūnsù)*, sleeping pills *(ānmiányào)*, anti-depressants and other medications can be picked up prescription-free from many chemists in Beijing; but if you require a more specific type of drug, make sure you take an adequate supply. When looking for medications in Beijing, make sure you take along its brand and the generic name so that pharmacy staff can locate it for you.

Required Vaccinations

Yellow Fever Proof of vaccination is required if entering China within six days of visiting an infected country. If you are travelling to China from Africa or South America, check with a travel medicine clinic whether you need the vaccine.

Recommended Vaccinations

Adult diphtheria/tetanus (ADT) A booster is recommended if it is more than 10 years since your last shot. Side effects include a sore arm and fever.

Hepatitis A One shot provides almost 100% protection for up to a year; a booster after 12 months provides another 20 years protection. Mild side effects include a sore arm, fever and headaches.

Hepatitis B Now considered a routine vaccination for most travellers. Given as three shots over six months, this vaccine can be combined with Hepatitis A (Twinrix). In most people the course gives lifetime protection. Mild side effects include a sore arm and headaches.

Measles/Mumps/Rubella (MMR) Two lifetime doses of MMR are recommended unless you have had the diseases. Many adults under the age of 35 require a booster. Occasionally a rash and flu-like illness occur about a week after vaccination.

Typhoid Needed if spending more than two weeks in China. A single injection provides around 70% protection for two to three years.

Varicella (chickenpox) If you haven't had chickenpox discuss this vaccine with your doctor. Chickenpox can be a serious disease in adults and has such complications as pneumonia and encephalitis.

Under certain circumstances or for those at special risk the following vaccinations are recommended. These should be discussed with a doctor who specialises in travel medicine.

Influenza If you are over 50 years of age or have a chronic medical condition such as diabetes, lung disease or heart disease, you should have an influenza shot annually.

Japanese encephalitis There is risk only in rural areas of China. Recommended if travelling to rural areas for more than a month during summer.

Pneumonia (Pneumococcal) This vaccine is recommended for travellers over 65 years of age or with chronic lung or heart disease. A single shot is given, with a booster in five years.

Rabies Recommended if spending more than three months in China. Requires three injections given over a one-month period.

If you are pregnant or breast feeding consult a doctor who specialises in travel medicine before having any vaccines.

Diseases
AIDS & SEXUALLY TRANSMITTED DISEASES
The Chinese government is starting to take AIDS seriously as the country is said to be on the brink of a major epidemic. Although most cases so far have occurred in intravenous drug users or from contaminated blood products, the virus is increasingly being spread via heterosexual sex.

Always use condoms if you have sex with a new partner, and never share needles. If you have had unsafe sex while travelling, get a checkup and immediately seek medical advice if you develop pain, a rash or a discharge.

HEPATITIS A
This virus is transmitted through contaminated food and water, and infects the liver, causing jaundice (yellow skin and eyes), nausea and extreme tiredness. There is no specific treatment available; you just need to allow time for the liver to heal, which might take many weeks.

HEPATITIS B
This disease is common in China and is transmitted via infected body fluids, including through sexual contact. The long-term consequences can include liver cancer and cirrhosis.

INFLUENZA
Flu is common in Beijing in the winter months. This virus gives you high fevers, body aches and general symptoms, such as a cough, runny nose and sore throat. Antibiotics won't help unless you develop a complication, such as pneumonia. Anyone travelling in the winter months should think about vaccination, but it is particularly recommended for the elderly or those with underlying medical conditions.

TRAVELLER'S DIARRHOEA
This is the most common problem faced by travellers in Asia. Most traveller's diarrhoea is caused by bacteria and thus responds rapidly to a short course of appropriate antibiotics. How soon you treat your diarrhoea will depend on individual circumstances, but it is a good idea to carry appropriate treatment in your medical kit.

TUBERCULOSIS (TB)
This is a rare disease in travellers and requires prolonged close exposure to a person with active TB infection. Symptoms include a cough, weight loss, night sweats and fevers. Children under the age of five spend-

ing more than six months in China should receive BCG vaccination. Adults are rarely immunised.

TYPHOID

This serious bacterial infection is contracted from contaminated food and water. Symptoms include high fever, headache, a cough and lethargy. The diagnosis is made via blood tests, and treatment is with specific antibiotics.

Environmental Hazards

AIR POLLUTION

Beijing is one of the 10 most polluted cities in the world. Although the government is working to improve the situation before the 2008 Olympics, those with chronic respiratory conditions should ensure they have adequate personal medication with them in case symptoms worsen.

WATER

Don't drink the tap water or eat ice. Bottled water, soft drinks and alcohol are fine.

HOLIDAYS

New Year's Day 1 January

Spring Festival (Chinese New Year) January or February

International Women's Day 8 March

International Labour Day 1 May

Youth Day 4 May

International Children's Day 1 June

Birthday of the Chinese Communist Party 1 July

Anniversary of the founding of the PLA 1 August

National Day 1 October

The 1 May holiday has been drawn out into a week-long holiday, as has National Day on 1 October. The Spring Festival is also a week-long holiday for many. It's not a great idea to arrive in China or go travelling during these holidays as things tend to grind to a halt (although being in Beijing for the Spring Festival allows you to see the city at its liveliest).

INTERNET ACCESS

Chinese might be shaping up to be the world's largest online language by 2007, but in recent years Beijing has taken to shut-ting down scores of Internet cafés (wǎngbā) after a fire in a Beijing Internet café in 2002 killed 25 people.

Internet cafés have to use filters to strain out irregular content. Rates should be around Y2 to Y3 per hour for a standard outlet with no frills, but comfier and smarter options often charge more. You might also have to endure agonisingly slow connections, especially on congested sites such as Hotmail.

Try to memorise the Chinese characters for Internet café (网吧), as outlets might not sport an English sign. A well-positioned, but expensive choice is the **Qian Yi Internet Café** (Map pp239-41; ☎ 6705 1722; www .qianyi-wb.com; per hr Y20; ☯ 9am-midnight) on the third floor of the Old Station Building at Qianmen, southeast of Tiananmen Square. **Moko Coffee Bar** (Map pp232-3; Mòkè Wǎngbā; ☎ 6525 3712, 6559 8464; 57 Dongsi Nandajie, Dongcheng; per hr upstairs/downstairs Y4/12) is centrally located, but head upstairs for cheap surfing, unless you want a coffee thrown in with your pricey downstairs online time. There's no English sign, but it's next to a chemist.

Dayusu Internet Café (Map pp236-8; Dáyusù Wangbā; 2 Hufangqiao, Xuanwu; per hr Y3; ☯ 8am-midnight) has no English sign, but it's located around three shops before the Bank of China heading south down Hufang Lu, north of the turn-off onto Yong'an Lu and not far from the Jianguo Hotel Qianmen. **Yongning Internet Café** (Map pp232-3; Yǒngníng Wǎngbā; 71 Chaoyangmen Nanxiaojie, Dongcheng; per hr Y2) can be found just north of the intersection between Chaoyangmen Nanxiaojie and Lishi Hutong; there's no English sign, but look for the characters for wangbā.

Use mid-range and top-end hotel business centre computers for going online only if you have no choice, as charges are stratospheric. Many cheaper hotels and youth hostels provide Internet access at around Y10 per hour.

To access the Internet using a laptop from your hotel room in Beijing, free dial-up access can be made by hooking up through the phone line and using the local dial-up number (169). In the dial-up connection box enter 169 as your username and password, and in the phone number box again enter 169. Many mid-range and top-end hotels now provide free broadband Internet access, so ask.

The cheapest way to keep in touch while on the road is to sign up for a free email account with Hotmail (www.hotmail.com) or Yahoo (www.yahoo.com) and access your account from an Internet café.

LEGAL MATTERS

Anyone under the age of 18 is considered a minor in China, and the minimum driving age is also 18. The age of consent for marriage is 22 years for men and 20 years for women. There is no minimum age restricting the consumption of cigarettes or alcohol.

China's laws against the use of illegal drugs are harsh, and foreign nationals have been executed for drug offences (trafficking in more than 50g of heroin can result in the death penalty).

The Chinese criminal justice system does not ensure a fair trial, and defendants are not presumed innocent until proven guilty. Note that China conducts more judicial executions than the rest of the world combined. If arrested, most foreign citizens have the right to contact their embassy.

MAPS

Beijing is huge and it's essential to score a map of town. Lonely Planet publishes a colour waterproof Beijing foldout city map, designed for the traveller and complete with Chinese script. English-language maps of Beijing can also be bought at the airport and train station newspaper kiosks, the Friendship Store and the Foreign Languages Bookstore. They can also be picked up for free at most big hotels and branches of the **Beijing Tourist Information Center** (see p208).

Street vendors hawk cheap maps with Chinese characters near subway stations around Tiananmen Square and Wangfujing Dajie – make sure you check they have English labelling before you purchase from pushy vendors. A better alternative is the Beijing Tourist Map (Y8) which is labelled in both English and Chinese. For those who can read Chinese, look out for the handy, highly detailed A-Z of Beijing with grids called *Běijīng Shíyòng Dìtúcè* (Y12), which you can find at the Wangfujing Bookstore (north of Oriental Plaza). In the meantime, it's available only in Chinese, but the bookstore has a large range of alternative maps of the city.

MEDICAL SERVICES

As the national capital, Beijing has some of the best medical facilities and services in China. Ask at your embassy for a list of English-speaking doctors, dentists and hospitals that accept foreigners.

Health facilities and standards of medical treatment have improved considerably over the past 10 years, and a variety of international clinics can be found in Beijing.

A consultation with a doctor in a private clinic will cost between Y200 to Y800, depending on where you go. It will cost Y10 to Y50 in a state hospital.

Beijing International Medical Centre (Map pp234-5; ☎ 6465 1561/2/3; ☎ emergencies 6465 1560; suites 106/107, 1st fl, Beijing Lufthansa Center, 50 Liangmaqiao Lu) Open 24 hours, this clinic has English-speaking staff; pharmacy, dental and counselling services also available. Both Western and traditional Chinese medicine is offered.

Beijing Union Hospital Xéhé Yīyuàn (Map pp232-3; Xéhé Yīyuàn; ☎ 6529 6114; ☎ emergency 6529 5284; 53 Dongdan Beidajie) A first rate hospital set in a wonderful building near Wangfujing. There is a wing reserved for foreigners and high-level cadres in the back building. Open 24 hours with a full range of facilities for inpatient and outpatient care, plus a pharmacy.

Beijing United Family Hospital (Map pp228-9; ☎ 6433 3960; www.beijingunited.com; 2 Jiangtai Lu; ☼ 24 hrs) This hospital has 50 beds and can provide alternative medical treatments along with a comprehensive range of inpatient and outpatient care, as well as a critical care unit. It is near the Holiday Inn Lido.

International SOS (Map pp234-5; ☎ clinic appointments 6462 9112; ☎ dental appointments 6462 0333; ☎ 24-hr alarm centre 6462 9100; www.internationalsos .com, Bldg C, BITIC Ying Yi Bldg, 1 Xingfu Sancun Bei Jie, Chaoyang; ☼ 9am-6pm Mon-Fri) Offering 24-hour emergency medical care, this clinic is located behind the German embassy and has a high-quality clinic with English-speaking staff.

Hong Kong International Medical Clinic (Map pp234-5; ☎ 6501 4260; www.hkclinic.com; 9th fl Office Tower, Hong Kong Macau Center, Swissôtel, 2 Chaoyangmen Beidajie; ☼ 9am-9pm) The clinic has a 24-hour medical and dental clinic, including obstetric/gynaecological services. The clinic has facilities for ultrasonic scanning, and immunisations can also be performed. Prices are more reasonable than at SOS and the International Medical Center.

METRIC SYSTEM

China officially subscribes to the international metric system. However, you're likely to encounter the ancient Chinese weights and measures system, which features the *liǎng* (tael) and the *jīn* (catty). One jin is 0.6kg (1.32 lb). There are 16 liang to the jin, so one liang is 37.5g (1.32oz).

MONEY

For information regarding exchange rates, see the Quick Reference on the inside front cover. The City Life chapter gives you some idea of costs you are likely to incur during your stay in Beijing.

ATMs

Increasing numbers of Beijing's ATMs now accept foreign credit cards and are linked to international bank settlement systems, such as Cirrus and Plus. The back of your ATM card should tell you which systems work with your card. The network is not citywide, however, and you are more likely to find an ATM you can use in and around the main shopping areas (such as Wangfujing Dajie) and international hotels and their associated shopping arcades. Many of the large department stores also have useful ATMs. The majority of ATMs at banks other than the Bank of China and the Industrial and Commercial Bank of China accept only domestic cards. ATM screens that take foreign cards offer the choice of English or Chinese operation.

Useful ATMs can be found in the arrivals hall at **Capital Airport**. ATMs are also plentiful along **Wangfujing Dajie**, including a handy wall-mounted ATM that takes Visa, MasterCard, Plus and Cirrus at the **Bank of China** next to the main entrance to Sundongan Plaza. On the other side of the road you will find an ATM of the **Industrial and Commercial Bank of China** that takes foreign cards. A further ATM can be found at the Bank of China on the corner of Oriental Plaza, on the corner of Wangfujing Dajie and Dongchan'an Jie. Also try the Bank of China on the second basement level of the **Peninsula Palace hotel** (p158), the 2nd floor of the **Swissôtel**, the World Trade Center, on the ground floor of the **Lufthansa Center** (50 Liangmaqiao Lu), in the foyer of the **Novotel Peace Hotel** in Jinyu Hutong and in the **Bank of China** to the west of the Novotel Xinqiao. The **Hong Kong and Shanghai Banking Corporation** (☎ 6526 0668, 800 820 8878; www.hsbc.com.cn in Chinese; ground fl, block A, COFCO Plaza, 8 Jian-guomen Dajie, Dongcheng; also at 1st fl, Lido Shopping Arcade, Lido Place, Jichang Lu, Chaoyang) has a 24-hour ATM where you can draw money from your overseas HSBC account. A **Citibank ATM** can be found at the branch of **Citibank** (Map pp239-41) east of the International Hotel on Jianguomen-nei Dajie. For your nearest ATM, consult www.visa.com/pd/atm or www.mastercard .com/atmlocator/index.jsp; both have comprehensive listings. For those without their own ATM card or credit card, a PIN-activated Visa TravelMoney card (☎ 1-877-394-2247) gives you access to pre-deposited cash through the ATM network.

Changing Money

Foreign currency and travellers cheques can be changed at large branches of the Bank of China, CITIC Industrial Bank, the airport, hotel money-changing counters and at several department stores (including the Friendship Store), as long as you have your passport. Hotels usually give the official rate, but some will add a small commission. Some upmarket hotels will change money only for their own guests. Useful branches of the Bank of China with foreign exchange counters include a branch next to Oriental Plaza on Wangfujing Dajie, in the Lufthansa Center and in the China World Trade Center.

Keep at least a few of your exchange receipts. You could need them if you want to exchange any remaining RMB you have at the end of your trip. Those travelling to Hong Kong can change RMB for Hong Kong dollars there and then into other currencies.

Credit Cards

Most tourist hotels and restaurants and some major department stores accept credit cards. Many travel agencies also now accept credit cards for air tickets (plus a 4% service charge). Check that the Visa or MasterCard sign pasted up is not for cards issued only in China.

It's possible to get a cash advance on credit cards at CITIC Bank, 19 Jianguomenwai Dajie, or the Bank of China (Sundongan Plaza and Sanlitun branches), but there is a steep (4%) commission. You can also cash personal cheques if you have an Amex card at CITIC Industrial Bank (CITIC Bldg, Jianguomenwai Dajie) and large branches of the Bank of China.

Currency

The basic unit of Chinese currency is the *yuán* – designated in this book by a capital 'Y'. In spoken Chinese, the word *kuài* or *kuàiqián* is often substituted for yuán. Ten *jiǎo* – in spoken Chinese, it's pronounced *máo* – make up one yuán. Ten *fēn* make up one jiao, but these days *fēn* are very rare because they're worth next to nothing.

Renminbi (RMB), or 'people's money', is issued by the Bank of China. Paper notes are issued in denominations of one, two, five, 10, 20, 50 and 100 *yuán*; one, two and five *jiao*; and one, two and five *fēn*. Coins are in denominations of one *yuán*; five, two and one *jiao*; and one, two and five *fēn*. New-style bills were introduced in 2000; both old and new bills are legal tender.

Travellers Cheques

Besides security considerations, travellers cheques are useful to carry in China because the exchange rate is actually more favourable than the rate for cash. Cheques from most of the world's leading banks and issuing agencies are acceptable in Beijing – stick with the major players such as Citibank, American Express (Amex) and Visa and you should be OK. Note that although cashing travellers cheques is easy in Beijing, you can't expect to find anywhere to cash your cheques in small towns.

Amex (Map pp239-41; ☎ 6505 2888; room 2101, Tower 1, China World Trade Center, 1 Jianguomenwai Dajie)

Citibank (Map pp239-41; ☎ 6510 2933; fax 6510 2932; 16th fl, Bright Chang'an Bldg, 7 Jianguomennei Dajie)

MOVING TO BEIJING

If you're moving things like furniture or all your household goods, you'll need an international mover or freight forwarder. In Beijing you can try one of the following:

Allied Pickfords (☎ 8561 8759; www.alliedpickfords .com.cn)

Asian Express (☎ 8580 1471/2/3; www.aemovers.com .hk; room 902, Tower 1, Bright China Chang'an Bldg, 7 Jianguomennei Dajie, Dongcheng) Can also arrange pet import and export.

Crown Relocations (☎ 6585 0640; www.crownrelo.com; room 201, West Tower, Golden Bridge Bldg, 1 Jianguomen-wai Dajie, Chaoyang)

Links Relocations (☎ 6581 5900; www.linksasia.com)

Santa Fe (☎ 8451 6666; 2nd fl, block J, East Lake Villas; www.santaferelo.com)

NEWSPAPERS & MAGAZINES

The anaemic *China Daily* (www.chinadaily .com.cn) is the government's favourite English-language mouthpiece and carries headlines such as 'State grid outperforms expectations' and other banalities. Resort to it only if there is no alternative, although its weekend culture section, *Beijing Weekend*, is useful for arts listings, events and trips out of Beijing. Among the countless other Chinese-language newspapers is the state's flagship paper, the *Renmin Ribao* (People's Daily) and papers of more specialist leanings, such as the *Nongmin Ribao* (Farmer's Daily).

It's easy enough to buy copies of popular imported English-language international magazines, such as *Time*, *Newsweek*, *Far Eastern Economic Review* and *The Economist* from the bookshops of four- and five-star hotels. Such hotels also stock European magazines in French or German and foreign newspapers such as *The Times*, the *International Herald Tribune*, the *Asian Wall Street Journal*, the *Financial Times* and the *South China Morning Post*. Such newspapers are expensive, out of date and occasionally trimmed of opinion, so reading online is a far better idea, especially for breaking news.

Beijing has a lively world of English-language rags available free at most five-star hotels and Sanlitun bars and restaurants. The slick and confident *That's Beijing* (www.thats magazines.com) is well designed, well written and the best of the bunch. Others include *Metropolis*, *Beijing Journal*, *Beijing This Month* and *Focuzine*.

The **Beijing National Library** (Map pp230-1; Běijīng Túshūguǎn; ☎ 6841 5566; 39 Baishiqiao Lu; ☻8am-5pm Mon-Fri) holds around four million periodicals and newspapers, more than a third of which are in foreign languages. The library's even larger book collection contains rare imperial works.

Various embassies also have small libraries of newspapers and magazines in English and other languages. The **Cultural and Educational Section of the British Embassy** (Map pp234-5; ☎ 6590 6903; www.britishcouncil.org.cn; 4th fl, British Embassy Annex, Landmark Tower, 8 Dongsanhuan Beilu, Chaoyang) is worth visiting.

PHARMACIES

There are several pharmacies on Wangfujing Dajie that stock both Chinese *(zhōngyào)* and Western medicine *(xīyào)*, where you should be able to find any medicines you might need. Note that you do not necessarily need a prescription for the drug you are seeking in Beijing, so ask at the pharmacy first. In other parts of China, however, you will probably find that you need a prescription issued by a doctor. As with many other large shops in Beijing, once you have chosen your item, you are issued with a receipt which you take to the till counter *(shòuyíntái)* to pay and then return to the counter where you chose your medicine to collect your purchase. Chemists stocking traditional Chinese medicine can be found all over town. The best known is **Tongrentang Yaodian** (☎ 6308 5413; 24 Dazhalan Jie). Branches of **Watson's** (1st fl, Full Link Plaza, 19 Chaoyangmenwai Dajie; CC17, 19, CC21, 23 Oriental Plaza, 1 Dongchan'an Jie) also purvey medicines, but are more geared to selling cosmetics, sunscreens etc.

Beijing Wanweierkang Chemist (Map pp232-3; Běijīng Wànwéiěrkāng Dàyàodiàn; ☎ 6559 5763/6669; 62 Dongdan Beidajie) Another chemist where you can hunt down over-the-counter Zopiclone sleeping pills, Prozac, Flixonase, Propanalol, Amoxcyllin or whatever you are after. It's handily located on the road parallel to and east of Wangfujing Dajie (the name outside the chemist is in Chinese, but it's bright green).

Quanxin Pharmacy (Map pp232-3; Quánxīn Dàyàofáng; ☎ 652 4123; 153 Wangfujing Dajie; ⊙ 8.30am-10pm) Large pharmacy opposite St Joseph's Church.

Wangfujing Medicine Shop (Map pp232-3; Wángfǔjīng Yīyào Shāngdiàn; ☎ 6524 0122; 267 Wangfujing Dajie; ⊙ 8.30am-9pm) Come here for a large range of Western and Chinese drugs.

POST

There are convenient post offices in the CITIC building next to the Friendship Store, in the basement of the China World Trade Center, east of Wangfujing Dajie on Dongdan Ertiao, on the south side of Xichang'an Jie west of the Beijing Concert Hall and just east of the Jianguo Hotel Qianmen, on Yong'an Lu. You can also post letters via your hotel reception desk, which might be the most convenient option, or at green post boxes around town. Large post offices are generally open daily between 8.30am and 6pm. Check the maps at the rear of this book for locations.

Letters and parcels marked 'Poste Restante, Beijing Main Post Office' will arrive at the **International Post Office** (Map pp234-5; Jianguomen Beidajie; ⊙ 8am-7pm Mon-Sat) 200m north of Jianguomen subway station. If collecting an item, take your passport and Y2.5 for the service charge. Overseas parcels are also sent from here. Both outgoing and incoming packages will be opened and inspected here. If sending a parcel, don't seal the package until you've had it inspected.

Letters take around a week to reach most overseas destinations. Airmail letters up to 20g cost Y5.40 to Y6.40 to all countries except Hong Kong, Macau and Taiwan (Y2.50). Domestic letters/postcards cost Y0.80/0.30.

China charges extra for registered mail, but offers cheaper postal rates for printed matter, small packets, parcels, bulk mailings and so on.

Parcels sent to domestic destinations by Express Mail Service (EMS) cost Y15 (up to 200g; Y5 for each additional 200g). International EMS charges vary according to country and sample minimum rates (parcels up to Y500g) include Australia (Y164), UK (Y224) and USA (Y184). The main EMS office can be found at 7 Qianmen Dajie (☎ 6512 9948).

Courier Companies

Several private couriers in Beijing offer international express posting of documents and parcels, and have reliable pick-up service as well as drop-off centres:

DHL (☎ 6466 2211, ☎ 800-810 8000; www.dhl.com; 45 Xinyuan Jie, Chaoyang) Further branches in the Kempinski Hotel, the China World Trade Center and COFCO Plaza.

Federal Express (FedEx; ☎ 6561 2003, ☎ 800-810 2338; Hanwei Bldg, 7 Guanghua Lu, Chaoyang; office in room 107, No 1 Office Bldg, Oriental Plaza)

United Parcel Service (UPS; ☎ 6593 2932; unit A, 2nd fl, Tower B, Beijing Kelun Bldg, 12A Guanghua Lu, Chaoyang)

RADIO

The BBC World Service can be picked up on 17760, 15278, 21660, 12010 and 9740 kHz. Reception can often be poor, however, and Voice of American is often a bit clearer at 17820, 15425, 21840, 15250, 9760, 5880 and

6125 kHz. You can find tuning information for the BBC on the Web at www.bbc.co.uk/worldservice/tuning, for Radio Australia at www.abc.net.au/ra, and for VOA at www.voa.gov.

China Radio International (CRI) is China's overseas radio service, and it broadcasts in about 40 foreign languages, as well as in *pǔtōnghuà* and several local dialects.

SAFETY

Generally speaking, Beijing is very safe compared to other similarly sized cities in the world. Crime against foreigners is seldom heard of, although it is on the rise due to unemployment and the influx of people from rural areas who come to Beijing in search of work.

Pickpocketing is a problem you need to guard against carefully. In back alleys a thief might try to snatch your bag, but far more common is the razoring of bags and pockets in crowded places like buses and train stations. If you want to avoid opening wallets or bags on the bus, keep a few coins or small notes ready in an accessible pocket before launching yourself into the crowd.

Hotels are usually safe places to leave your stuff; each floor has an attendant watching who goes in and out. Dormitories could be a problem: there have been a few reports of thefts by staff, but the culprits are more likely to be other foreigners.

A money belt is the safest way to carry valuables, particularly when travelling on buses and trains.

Be alert at all times when crossing the road in Beijing. Traffic comes from all directions, and driving standards are poor. Safe crossing points are indicated by zebra crossing markings and/or pedestrian lights, but the green 'cross now' light doesn't necessarily mean that traffic won't try to run you down (as one lane of traffic is usually exempt from having to stop).

Carry several forms of ID with you, but spread them over different pockets. An ISIC card, a driver's licence, birth certificate (or something with your photograph on it) are all suitable. You will need your passport to check into Chinese hotels, regardless of budget. It's a good idea to make photocopies of the visa and information page of your passport, in case of loss. This makes the job of replacing your passport much simpler and faster.

TAXES

Four- and five-star hotels add a service charge of 15%, and smarter restaurants levy a service charge of 10%.

TELEPHONE

Both international and domestic calls can be made easily from your hotel room or from public telephones on the street. Local calls from hotel room phones are free, although international phone calls are expensive and it is preferable to buy a phonecard (see Phonecards). Public telephones are plentiful, although finding one that works can be a hassle. If making a domestic phone call, also look out for public phones at newspaper stands (*bàokāntíng*) and hole-in-the-wall shops (*xiǎomàibù*); you make your call and then pay the owner (a local call is typically around four *jiao*). If using a public phone, most take IC cards (see Phonecards).

Domestic long-distance rates in China vary according to distance, but are cheap. Card-less international calls are expensive (Y8.2 per minute or Y2.2 for calls to Hong Kong and Macau), but calls made between midnight and 7am are 40% cheaper than at other times; it's far cheaper to use an IP card (see Phonecards). Domestic and international long-distance phone calls can also be made from main telecommunications offices.

If you are expecting a call to your hotel room, try to advise the caller beforehand of your room number as hotel operators and staff at reception (*zǒngtái*) frequently have trouble with foreign names. Otherwise, inform the receptionist that you are expecting a call, and write down your name and room number.

If dialling locally, omit the area code (*qūhào*) and just dial the local five- or six-digit number.

The country code to use to access China is 86; the code for Hong Kong is 852, and Macau is 853. To call a number in Beijing, dial the international access code (00 in the UK, 011 in the USA), dial the country code (86) and then the area code for Beijing (010), dropping the first zero, and then dial the local number. For telephone calls within the same city, drop the area code. If calling internationally drop the first zero of the area or city code after dialling the international access code and then dial the number you wish to call.

Important city area codes within China include:

Beijing	☎ 010
Chengdu	☎ 028
Guangzhou	☎ 020
Hangzhou	☎ 0571
Harbin	☎ 0451
Ji'nan	☎ 0531
Kunming	☎ 0871
Nanjing	☎ 025
Shanghai	☎ 021
Shijiazhuang	☎ 0311
Tianjin	☎ 022
Xiamen	☎ 0592

Buying mobile phones with pay-as-you-go or monthly payment cards that slot into the phone from China Telecom in Beijing is relatively easy.

Faxes can be sent from hotel business centres (shāngwùbù), but be warned, the charges are high and a service charge is levied. Faxes can also be sent from the post office, where charges are Y2 for a one-page fax, plus the charge of the call.

Pager operators don't speak English. They will ask for the number you are calling, your name, your return number and extension, in that order.

The English-language Beijing *Yellow Pages* is available at most business centres, and you might find it provided in your hotel room; alternatively, you can go online at www.yellowpage.com.cn or pick up your own copy at 65 Jianguomennei Dajie (☎ 6512 0400).

Phonecards

A wide range of local and international phonecards exists in Beijing. IC (Integrated Circuit) cards, available from kiosks, hole-in-the-wall shops, Internet cafés and from any China Telecom office, are prepaid cards that can be used in most public telephones, in telecom offices and in most hotels. IC cards come in denominations of Y20, Y50, Y100 and Y200, and appear in several varieties. Some cards can be used only in Beijing (or locally, depending on where the card is purchased), while other cards can be used in phones throughout China. If you want to call abroad, make sure the IC card can make international calls *(dǎ guójì diànhuà)*, although international calls using IC cards are much more expensive than those made using IP cards (see below). Purchasing the correct card can be confusing, as the instructions for use on the reverse of the card are usually only written in Chinese.

If you wish to make international calls, it is much cheaper to use an IP (Internet Phone) card. International calls on IP cards are Y2.40 per minute to the USA or Canada, Y1.50 per minute to Hong Kong, Macau and Taiwan and Y3.20 to all other countries; domestic long-distance calls are Y0.30 per minute. You dial a local number, then punch in your account number, followed by a PIN and finally the number you wish to call. English-language service is usually available. IP cards come in denominations of Y50, Y100, Y200 and Y500 and substantial discounts are offered, so bargain (you should be able to buy a Y50 card for around Y30). Extra credits are also regularly included on IP cards. IP cards can be found at the same places as IC cards, and you will see placards for vendors of both IC and IP cards all over town.

TELEVISION

It might appear inept and amateurish, but Chinese TV production is made up of safe, judiciously selected material that is given a carefully weighted spin. As with Chinese newspapers, domestic news stories 'bao xi bu bao you' – they 'report the good news and not the bad'. This has long been common practice in communist China, and the tradition continues unabated. The national TV outfit, Chinese Central Television (CCTV), has an English-language channel – CCTV9 – that offers complacent, self-congratulatory and spineless programmes. It is useful for its new bulletins in English, if you can't get hold of anything else, even though the news reporting on China issues is innocuous, whereas reports on events outside China relentlessly portray a world in disarray. Most in-room TVs in hotels have CCTV9 (along with scores of further channels). Most Chinese prefer to watch sitcoms and soaps imported from South Korea or Japan (collectively called rìhánjù, literally 'series from Japan and South

Korea') or films made in Hong Kong and Taiwan (collectively called *gǎngtáipiān*), rather than those produced locally.

CCTV4 also has some English programmes, including English-language news programmes on weekdays at 7pm and 11pm, and at noon on weekends. Sports programmes and live matches can be picked up on CCTV5 (in Chinese) or on BJTV. Your hotel might have ESPN or Star Sports; otherwise you will have to find a bar with sports TV, such as **Frank's Place** (p122) or **Sports City Café** (p127). Relying on CCTV for news is a frustrating experience; unfortunately, access to CNN is far from widespread, outside expat residences and mid-range and top-end hotels.

Long-term residents in Beijing wishing to install satellite TV have two choices: move into a block with pre-existing satellite TV or make an application for the right to have receivers installed at your current address. For a block to be fitted with satellite receivers, 80% of residents should be foreigners and applicants must be resident in the city; installation costs are around Y2000.

TIME

All of China runs on the same time as Beijing, which is set eight hours ahead of GMT/ UTC (there's no daylight saving during summer). When it's noon in Beijing it's 4am in London, 5am in Frankfurt, Paris and Rome, noon in Hong Kong, 2pm in Melbourne, 4pm in Wellington, 8pm in Los Angeles and 11pm in Montreal and New York.

TIPPING

Taking the sting out of being frequently overcharged with foreigners' rates, Beijing is at least one of those wonderful cities where tipping is not the norm, and almost no one asks for a tip. This applies throughout China. Restaurants (mid-range and above) are increasingly closing the gap with a service charge, however; don't indulge them with a tip. Porters at upmarket hotels will, of course, expect a tip.

TOILETS

Travellers on the road relate China toilet tales to each other like soldiers comparing old war wounds. Despite proud claims to have invented the first flushing toilet, China

really does have some wicked loos. The capital has made a start on making the city's toilets less of an assault course of foul smells and primitive appliances, but many are still pungent and sordid. Make a beeline for fast-food outlets, hotels and department stores for cleaner alternatives. The Ming Tombs outside town have some of the best loos in China, but it's a heck of a hike. Toilet paper is rarely provided – always keep a stash with you. In some Beijing hotels, especially old ones, the sewage system can't handle paper. As a general rule, if you see a wastebasket next to the toilet, that's where you should throw the toilet paper; otherwise the loo could choke up and flood.

Rural toilets are ghastly snapshots of a scatological hell – just a hole in the ground or a ditch over which you squat – and many cannot be flushed at all. Hyperventilate before tackling toilets on the older trains, or go in with a strong cigarette (eg Temple of Heaven brand).

Remember:

| men | 男 |
| women | 女 |

TOURIST INFORMATION

The Chinese state never quite got the hang of tourist offices, but a tentative step in the right direction has been made with **Beijing Tourist Information Centers** (*Běijīng Lǚyóu Zīxún Fúwù Zhōngxīn*), a chain of offices with turquoise façades dotted around town. You can grab a free tourist map of Beijing and other material, but the operation is not very competent and English-language skills are limited. Most branches are open 9.30am to 5.30pm. A branch can be found in the arrivals hall at Beijing Capital Airport (☎ 6459 8148; jichang@bjta.gov.cn). Other addresses include:

Chaoyang (Map pp234-5; ☎ 6417 6627, 6417 6656; chaoyang@bjta.gov.cn; 27 Sanlitun Beilu)

Dongcheng (Map pp232-3; ☎ 6512 3043, 6512 2991; dongcheng@bjta.gov.cn; 10 Dengshikou Xijie)

Fengtai (☎ 6332 3983; fengtai@bjta.gov.cn; Zhongyan Hotel lobby, Guangwai Dajie)

Haidian (☎ 8262 2895; haidian@bjta.gov.cn; 40 Zhongguancun Dajie)

Xicheng (Map pp236-8; ☎ 6616 0108, 6612 0110; xicheng@bjta.gov.cn; 1st fl, Keji Guangchang, Xidan Beidajie)

Xuanwu (Map pp236-8; ☎ 6351 0018; xuanwu@bjta .gov.cn; 3 Hufang Lu)

The Chaoyang branch, west of the Sanlitun Yashou Clothing Market, probably deals with more foreign travellers than any other branch, but you might interrupt the employees playing computer games. They have a 'Help Deformity Service'.

Your hotel can offer you advice or connect you with a suitable tour within and around Beijing. Some bars also informally address themselves to the needs of travellers: **Passby Bar** (☎ 6401 9474; pass_by@sina.com; 108 Nanluogu Xiang; ☾ 7pm-2am) has travel-oriented staff who are keen to help, as long as you order a drink or two; see p128.

There is an English-speaking 24-hour Beijing Tourism Hotline (☎ 6513 0828), which can answer questions and hear complaints.

VISAS

A visa is required for the People's Republic of China (PRC), but at the time of writing visas were not required for most Western nationals to visit Hong Kong or Macau.

For most travellers, the type of visa is an L, from the Chinese word for travel (*lǚxíng*). This letter is stamped right on the visa.

Visas are readily available from Chinese embassies and consulates in most Western and many other countries. A standard 30-day, single-entry visa from most Chinese embassies abroad can be issued in three to five working days. Express visas cost twice the usual fee. You normally pay up front for the visa, rather than on collection. You can get an application form in person at the embassy or consulate, or obtain one online from a consular website. A visa mailed to you will take up to three weeks. Rather than going through an embassy or consulate, you can also make arrangements at certain travel agencies. Visa applications require at least one photo.

When asked on the application form, try to list standard tourist destinations such as Beijing and Chéndgé; if you are toying with the idea of going to Tibet or western Xīnjiāng, just leave it off the form as it might raise eyebrows; the list you give is not binding in any way.

A 30-day visa is activated on the date you enter China, and must be used within three months of the date of issue. The 60-day and 90-day visas are activated on the

date they are issued. Although visas valid for more than 30 days were once difficult to obtain anywhere other than in Hong Kong, 90-day visas are now becoming easier to obtain abroad.

Be aware that political events can suddenly make visas more difficult to procure.

When you check into a hotel, there is a question on the registration form asking what type of visa you hold. The letter specifying what type of visa you have is usually stamped on the visa itself. There are seven categories of visas, as follows:

Type	Description	Chinese name
L	Travel	lǚxíng
F	Business or student	fǎngwèn (less than 6 months)
D	Resident	dìngjū
G	Transit	guòjìng
X	Long-term student	liúxué
Z	Working	rènzhí
C	Flight attendant	chéngwù

Getting a Visa in Hong Kong

Hong Kong is a good place to pick up a visa quickly. Almost any travel agent can get you a standard 30-day visa. The cheapest visas are available from the **Visa Office of the People's Republic of China** (☎ 3413 2300, 3413 2424; 7th fl, lower block, China Resources Centre, 26 Harbour Rd, Wan Chai; ☾ 9am-noon & 2-5pm Mon-Fri). Visas processed in one/two/ three days cost HK400/300/150. Double/ multiple valid six months/multiple valid for a year entry visas are HK$220/400/600 (plus HK$150/250 if you require express/ urgent service). You must supply two photos, which can be taken at photo booths in the MTR or at the visa office for HK$35.

Visas can also be arranged by **China Travel Service** (CTS; ☎ 2998 7888; www.chinatravel1 .com). Many Hong Kong travel agencies can also get you 60- and 90-day visas, six-month visas and multiple-entry visas at prices cheaper than CTS. On the Kowloon side, try **Phoenix Services Agency** (☎ 2722 7378; phoenix1@netvigator.com; room A, 7th fl, Milton Mansion, 96 Nathan Rd, Tsim Sha Tsui; ☾ 9am-6pm Mon-Fri & 9am-1pm Sat). On the Hong Kong Island side, try **Concorde Travel** (☎ 2526 3391; info@concorde-travel .com; 1st fl, Galuxe Bldg, 8-10 On Lan St, Central; ☾ 9.30am-5.30pm Mon-Fri, 9am-1pm Sat).

Residence Permit

The 'green card' is a residence permit, issued to English teachers, foreign expats and long-term students who live in China. Green cards are issued for a period of six months to one year and must be renewed annually. Besides needing all the right paperwork, you must also pass a health exam (for which there is a charge). If you lose your card, you'll pay a hefty fee to have it replaced.

Visa Extensions

The Foreign Affairs Branch of the local Public Security Bureau (PSB; Gōngānjú) – the police force – handles visa extensions. In Beijing the main office is at 2 Andingmen Dongdajie (Map pp232-3; Běijīngshì Gōngānjú Chūrùjìng Guǎnlǐchù; ☎ 8402 0101; ☿ 8.30am-4.30pm Mon-Sat). The visa office is on the 2nd floor on the east side of the building – take the escalator up. You can also apply for a residence permit here. Extensions vary in price, depending on your nationality. American travellers pay Y185, Australians pay Y100, Canadians pay Y165 and UK citizens pay Y160; and prices can go up or down. Expect to wait up to five days for your visa extension to be processed. You can obtain passport photographs here (Y30 for five).

First time extensions of 30 days are easy to obtain and are issued on any tourist visa, but further extensions are harder to get and might give you only a further week. Offices of the PSB outside Beijing might be more lenient and more willing to offer further extensions, but don't bank on it.

The penalty for overstaying your visa in China is up to Y500 per day. Some travellers have reported having trouble with officials who read the 'valid until' date on their visa incorrectly. For a one-month tourist (L) visa, the 'valid until' date is the date by which you must enter the country, not the date upon which your visa expires. Your visa expires the number of days for which your visa is valid after the date of entry into China (but note that you must enter China within three months of the date the visa was issued). Sixty- and 90-day visas are activated on the day they are issued.

Visa extensions can also be obtained through private visa services in Beijing. The legality of these services is questionable, and most of them seem to operate through private connections with the PSB. Although some foreigners have used these services without incident, you are taking a risk. Look in the classified section of the expat mags for listings, or try to get a personal recommendation from someone.

WOMEN TRAVELLERS

Women travellers generally feel very safe in Beijing. Chinese men are not macho and respect for women is deeply ingrained in Chinese culture. Nonetheless, carrying a whistle or alarm with you would offer a measure of defence in any unpleasant encounter.

As with anywhere else, you will be taking a risk if you travel alone. A self-defence course can equip you with extra physical skills and boost your confidence before your trip.

If travelling to towns outside Beijing, stick to hotels near the city centre. For further tips, consult www.oculartravel.com, which has a very useful section on women travellers. Other useful websites include www.journeywoman.com and its sister site, www.hermail.net.

WORK

In recent years it has become easier for foreigners to find work in Beijing, although Chinese-language skills will naturally increase your options. The majority of foreign professionals working in Beijing are recruited from overseas; many have spent years employed in the company in their home countries.

Teaching jobs that pay by the hour are usually quite lucrative. If you have recognised ELT qualifications, such as TEFL and/or experience, teaching can be a rewarding and profitable way to earn a living in Beijing. International schools offer salaries in the region of Y6000 to Y10,000 per month to qualified teachers, and accommodation is often provided. Schools regularly advertise in the English culture magazines, such as That's Beijing; you can visit its classified pages online at www.thatsmagazines.com.

There are also opportunities in translation, marketing, editing, the hotel industry, writing, acting, bar work and beyond. Most people find jobs in Beijing through word of mouth, so networking is the key.

Language

Language

It's true – anyone can speak another language. Don't worry if you haven't studied languages before or that you studied a language at school for years and can't remember any of it. It doesn't even matter if you failed English grammar. After all, that's never affected your ability to speak English! And this is the key to picking up a language in another country. You just need to start speaking.

Learn a few key phrases before you go. Write them on pieces of paper and stick them on the fridge, by the bed or even on the computer – anywhere that you'll see them often.

You'll find that the people of Beijing appreciate travellers trying to speak a little Mandarin, no matter how muddled you may think you sound. So don't just stand there, say something! If you want to learn more Mandarin than we've included here, pick up a copy of Lonely Planet's comprehensive but user-friendly *Mandarin Phrasebook*.

PRONUNCIATION
Pinyin

In 1958 the Chinese adopted a system of writing their language using the Roman alphabet, known as *pīnyīn*. Pinyin is often used on shop fronts, street signs and advertising billboards, but very few Chinese are able to read or write it.

A few consonants in Pinyin may cause confusion when compared to their counterparts in English:

c	as the 'ts' in 'bits'
ch	as in 'chop', but with the tongue curled back
q	as the 'ch' in 'cheese'
r	as the 's' in 'pleasure'
sh	as in 'ship', but with the tongue curled back
x	as the 'sh' in 'ship'
z	as the 'dz' sound in 'suds'
zh	as the 'j' in 'judge', but with the tongue curled back

Tones

Chinese is a language with a large number of words with the same pronunciation but a different meaning; what distinguishes them are 'tones' – rises and falls in the pitch of the voice on certain syllables. The word *ma*, for example, has four different meanings depending on tone:

high tone	mā	(mother)
rising tone	má	(hemp, numb)
falling-rising tone	mǎ	(horse)
falling tone	mà	(to scold, to swear)

Mastering tones is tricky for newcomers to Mandarin, but with a little practice it gets a lot easier.

SOCIAL
Meeting People

Hello.
nǐ hǎo 你好
Goodbye.
zàijiàn 再见
Please.
qǐng 请
Thank you.
xièxie 谢谢
Thank you very much.
tài xièxie le 太谢谢了
Yes.
shìde 是的
No. (don't have)
méi yǒu 没有
No. (not so)
búshì 不是
Do you speak English?
nǐ huì shuō yīngyǔ ma? 你会说英语吗?
Do you understand?
dǒng ma? 懂吗?
I understand.
wǒ tīngdedǒng 我听得懂
I don't understand.
wǒ tīngbudǒng 我听不懂

Could you please ...?
nǐ néng bunéng ...? 你能不能 ...?

repeat that		
chóngfù	重复	
speak more slowly		
màn diǎnr shuō	慢点儿说	
write it down		
xiě xiàlái	写下来	

Going Out

What's on ...?		
... yǒu shénme yúlè huódòng?		
... 有什么娱乐活动？		
locally		
běndì	本地	
this weekend		
zhège zhōumò	这个周末	
today		
jīntiān	今天	
tonight		
jīntiān wǎnshang	今天晚上	

Where are the ...?		
... zài nǎr?		
... 在哪儿？		
clubs		
jùlèbù	俱乐部	
gay venues		
tóngxìngliàn chángsuǒ	同性恋场所	
places to eat		
chīfàn de dìfang	吃饭的地方	
pubs		
jiǔbā	酒吧	

Is there a local entertainment guide?
yǒu dāngdì yúlè zhǐnán ma?
有当地娱乐指南吗？

PRACTICAL
Question Words

Who?		
shuí?	谁？	
What?		
shénme?	什么？	
When?		
shénme shíhou?	什么时候？	
Where?		
nǎr?	哪儿？	
How?		
zěnme?	怎么？	

Numbers & Amounts

1	yī/yāo	一/幺
2	èr/liǎng	二/两
3	sān	三
4	sì	四
5	wǔ	五
6	liù	六
7	qī	七
8	bā	八
9	jiǔ	九
10	shí	十
11	shíyī	十一
12	shí'èr	十二
13	shísān	十三
14	shísì	十四
15	shíwǔ	十五
16	shíliù	十六
17	shíqī	十七
18	shíbā	十八
19	shíjiǔ	十九
20	èrshí	二十
21	èrshíyī	二十一
22	èrshíèr	二十二
30	sānshí	三十
31	sānshíyì	三十一
40	sìshí	四十
50	wǔshí	五十
60	liùshí	六十
70	qīshí	七十
80	bāshí	八十
90	jiǔshí	九十
100	yìbǎi	一百
200	liǎngbǎi	两百
1000	yìqiān	一千
2000	liǎngqiān	两千
10,000	yíwàn	一万
20,000	liǎngwàn	两万
100,000	shíwàn	十万
200,000	èrshíwàn	二十万

Days

Monday		
xīngqīyī	星期一	
Tuesday		
xīngqīèr	星期二	
Wednesday		
xīngqīsān	星期三	
Thursday		
xīngqīsì	星期四	
Friday		
xīngqīwǔ	星期五	
Saturday		
xīngqīliù	星期六	
Sunday		
xīngqītiān	星期天	

Banking

I'd like to ...		
wǒ xiǎng ...	我想 ...	
change money		
huàn qián	换钱	

change travellers cheques
huàn lǚxíng zhīpiào 换旅行支票
cash a cheque
zhīpiào 支票

Excuse me, where's the nearest ...?
qǐng wèn, zuìjìnde ... zài nǎr?
请问, 最近的 ... 在哪儿?
  automatic teller machine
  zìdòng guìyuánjī
  自动柜员机
  foreign exchange office
  wàihuì duìhuànchù
  外汇兑换处

Post
Where is the post office?
yóujú zài nǎlǐ?
邮局在哪里?

I'd like to send a ...
wǒ xiǎng jì ...
我想寄 ...
  letter
  xìn 信
  fax
  chuánzhēn 传真
  package
  bāoguǒ 包裹
  postcard
  míngxìnpiàn 明信片

I'd like to buy (a/an) ...
wǒ xiǎng mǎi ...
我想买 ...
  aerogram
  hángkōngyóujiǎn 航空邮简
  envelope
  xìnfēng 信封
  stamps
  yóupiào 邮票

Phone & Mobile Phones
I want to buy a phone card.
wǒ xiǎng mǎi diànhuà kǎ　我想买电话卡

I want to make ...
wǒ xiǎng dǎ ...
我想打 ...
  a call (to ...)
  diànhuà (dào ...)
  打电话 (到 ...)
  a reverse-charge/collect call
  duìfāng fùfèi diànhuà
  对方付费电话

Where can I find a/an ...?
nǎr yǒu ...
哪儿有 ...?
I'd like a/an ...
wǒ xiǎng yào ...
我想要 ...
  adaptor plug
  zhuǎnjiēqì chātóu
  转接器插头
  charger for my phone
  diànhuà chōngdiànqì
  电话充电器
  mobile/cell phone for hire
  zūyòng yídòng diànhuà
  租用移动电话　or
  zūyòng shǒujī
  租用手机
  prepaid mobile/cell phone
  yùfù yídòng diànhuà
  预付移动电话　or
  yùfù shǒujī
  预付手机
  SIM card for your network
  nǐmen wǎngluò de SIM kǎ
  你们网络的SIM卡

Internet
Is there a local Internet café?
běndì yǒu wǎngbā ma?
本地有网吧吗?
Where can I get online?
wǒ zài nǎr kěyǐ shàng wǎng?
我在哪儿可以上网?
Can I check my email account?
wǒ chá yīxià zìjǐ de email hù, hǎo ma?
我查一下自己的email户, 好吗?

computer
diànǎo 电脑
email
diànzǐyóujiàn 电子邮件 (often
  called 'email')
Internet
yīntè wǎng/hùlián wǎng 因特网/互联网
  (formal name)

Transport
What time does ... leave/arrive?
... jǐdiǎn kāi/dào?
... 几点开/到?
  the bus
  qìchē 汽车
  the train
  huǒchē 火车

the plane
fēijī　飞机

the boat
chuán　船

When is the ... bus?
... qìchē jǐdiǎn kāi?
... 汽车几点开?

first
tóubān　头班

next
xià yìbān　下一班

last
mòbān　末班

Is this taxi available?
zhèi chē lā rén ma?
这车拉人吗?

Please use the meter.
dǎ biǎo
打表

How much (is it) to ...?
qù ... dūoshǎo qián?
去 ... 多少钱?

I want to go to ...
wǒ yào qù ...
我要去 ...

this address
zhège dìzhǐ
这个地址

FOOD

breakfast
zǎofàn　早饭

lunch
wǔfàn　午饭

dinner
wǎnfàn　晚饭

snack
xiǎochī　小吃

eat
chī　吃

drink
hē　喝

Can you recommend a ...?
nǐ néng bunéng tuījiàn yíge ...?
你能不能推荐一个 ...?

bar/pub
jiǔbā/jiǔguǎn　酒吧/酒馆

café
kāfēiguǎn　咖啡馆

restaurant
cānguǎn　餐馆

Is service/cover charge included in the bill?
zhàngdān zhōng bāokuò fúwùfèi ma?
帐单中包括服务费吗?

For more detailed information on food and dining out, see the Food & Drink chapter, pp29-42 and the Eating chapter, pp111-124.

EMERGENCIES

It's an emergency!
zhèshì jǐnjí qíngkuàng!
这是紧急情况!

Could you help me please?
nǐ néng bunéng bāng wǒ ge máng?
你能不能帮我个忙?

Call the police/a doctor/an ambulance!
qǐng jiào jǐngchá/yīshēng/jiùhùchē!
请叫警察/医生/救护车!

Where's the police station?
jǐngchájú zài nǎr?
警察局在哪儿?

HEALTH

Excuse me, where's the nearest ...?
qǐng wèn, zuìjìnde ... zài nǎr?
请问, 最近的 ... 在哪儿?

chemist
yàodiàn　药店

chemist (night)
yàodiàn (yèjiān)　药店 (夜间)

dentist
yáyī　牙医

doctor
yīshēng　医生

hospital
yīyuàn　医院

Is there a doctor here who speaks English?
zhèr yǒu huì jiǎng yīngyǔ de dàifu ma?
这儿有会讲英语的大夫吗?

Symptoms

I have (a/an) ...
wǒ ...
我 ...

diarrhoea
lādùzi　拉肚子

fever
fāshāo　发烧

headache
tóuténg　头疼

Glossary

apsaras – Buddhist celestial beings, similar to angels

arhat – Buddhist, especially a monk who has achieved enlightenment and passes to nirvana at death

běi – north. The other points of the compass are *nán* (south), *dōng* (east) and *xī* (west).

bīnguǎn – tourist hotel

bìxì – mythical tortoise-like dragons often depicted in Confucian temples

bìyùn tào – condom

Bodhisattva – one worthy of nirvana but who remains on earth to help others attain enlightenment

bówùguǎn – museum

bǔpiào – upgrade

CAAC – Civil Aviation Administration of China

cāntīng – restaurant

catty – unit of weight, one catty (*jīn*) equals 0.6kg

CCP – Chinese Communist Party, founded in Shànghǎi in 1921

Chángchéng – the Great Wall

cheongsam (Cantonese) – originating in Shànghǎi, a fashionable tight-fitting Chinese dress with a slit up the side

chop – see *name chop*

CITS – China International Travel Service. The organisation deals with China's foreign tourists.

CTS – China Travel Service. CTS was originally set up to handle tourists from Hong Kong, Macau, Taiwan and overseas Chinese.

CYTS – China Youth Travel Service

dǎ zhé – discounting

dàdào – boulevard

dàfàndiàn – large hotel

dàjiē – avenue

dānwèi – work unit, the cornerstone of China's social structure

dàshà – hotel, building

dàxué – university

dìtiě – subway

dìtiě zhàn – subway station

dōng – east. The other points of the compass are *běi* (north), *nán* (south) and *xī* (west).

dòngwùyuán – zoo

fàndiàn – hotel or restaurant

fēng – peak

fēngshuǐ – geomancy, literally 'wind and water', the art of using ancient principles to maximise the flow of *qì*, or vital energy

Fifth Generation – a generation of film directors who trained after the Cultural Revolution and whose political works revolutionised the film industry in the 1980s and '90s

gānxǐ – dry-cleaning

gé – pavilion, temple (Daoist)

gōng – palace

góngfu – kungfu

gōnggòng qìchē – bus

gōngyì – crafts

gōngyuán – park

gùjū – house, home, residence

gǔwán – antiques

hé – river

hú – lake

huàjù – theatre

huàndēngpiān – colour slide film

Huí – ethnic Chinese Muslims

hútòng – a narrow alleyway

jiāng – river

jiǎo – see *máo*

jiàotáng – church

jìcúnchù – left-luggage counters

jiē – street

jié – festival

jīn – see *catty*

jīngjù – Beijing opera

jiǔdiàn – hotel

jū – residence, home

kàngjūnsù – antibiotics

kǎoyādiàn – roast duck restaurant

kuài – colloquial term for the currency, *yuán*

Kuomintang – Chiang Kai-shek's Nationalist Party, the dominant political force after the fall of the Qing dynasty

lama – a Buddhist priest of the Tantric or Lamaist school. It is a title bestowed on monks of particularly high spiritual attainment.

lǎowài – foreigner

lín – forest

líng – tomb

lóu – tower

lù – road

lǚguǎn – cheap hotel

luóhàn – see *arhat*

máo – colloquial term for *jiǎo*, 10 of which equal one *kuài*

mén – gate

miào – temple

mù – tomb

name chop – a carved name seal that acts as a signature

nán – south. The other points of the compass are *běi* (north), *dōng* (east) and *xī* (west).

páilou – decorated archway

pedicab – pedal-powered tricycle with a seat to carry passengers

Pinyin – the official system for transliterating Chinese script into roman characters

PLA – People's Liberation Army

Politburo – the 25-member supreme policy making authority of the CCP

PRC – People's Republic of China

PSB – Public Security Bureau. The arm of the police force set up to deal with foreigners

Pǔtōnghuà – the standard form of the Chinese language used since the beginning of the 20th century and based on the dialect of Běijīng

qì – flow of vital or universal energy

qiáo – bridge

qìgōng – exercise that channels *qì*

qílín – a hybrid animal that only appeared on earth in times of harmony

qīngzhēnsì – mosque

rénmín – people, people's

Renminbi – literally 'people's money', the formal name for the currency of China. Shortened to RMB

ruǎn wò – soft sleeper

ruǎn zuò – soft seat

shān – hill, mountain

shāngdiàn – shop, store

shěng – province, provincial

shì – city

shìchǎng – market

sì – temple, monastery

sīchóu – silk

sìhéyuàn – courtyard house

tǎ – pagoda

tàijíquán – the graceful, flowing exercise that has its roots in China's martial arts. Also known as taichi

tíng – pavilion

tripitaka – Buddhist scriptures

wǎngbā – Internet café

wǔshù – martial arts

xī – west. The other points of the compass are *běi* (north), *nán* (south) and *dōng* (east).

xī yào – Western medicine

xiàn – county

xiàng – statue

xǐyī – laundry

yángróngshān – cashmere

yìng wò – hard sleeper

yìng zuò – hard seat

yuán – the Chinese unit of currency; also referred to as RMB (see also *Renminbi*)

Yuècài – Cantonese

zhāodàisuǒ – basic lodgings, a hotel or guesthouse

zhēng – 13- or 14-stringed harp

zhíwùyuán – botanic gardens

zhōng – middle, centre

zhōng yào – herbal medicine

zǒngtái – hotel reception

Behind the Scenes

THE LONELY PLANET STORY

The story begins with a classic travel adventure: Tony and Maureen Wheeler's 1972 journey across Europe and Asia to Australia. There was no useful information about the overland trail then, so Tony and Maureen published the first Lonely Planet guidebook to meet a growing need.

From a kitchen table, Lonely Planet has grown to become the largest independent travel publisher in the world, with offices in Melbourne (Australia), Oakland (USA), and London (UK).

Today Lonely Planet guidebooks cover the globe. There is an ever-growing list of books and information in a variety of media. Some things haven't changed. The main aim is still to make it possible for adventurous travellers to get out there – to explore and better understand the world. At Lonely Planet we believe travellers can make a positive contribution to the countries they visit – if they respect their host communities and spend their money wisely. Every year 5% of company profit is donated to charities around the world.

THIS BOOK

This 6th edition of *Beijing* was written by Damian Harper. Julie Grundvig contributed to the Arts & Architecture chapter, and she wrote the Food & Drink chapter. Dr Trish Batchelor wrote the Health section, which appears in the Directory chapter. Russ Kerr wrote the boxed text 'Gong, But Not Forgotten'. Damian Harper wrote the 5th edition of *Beijing;* Caroline Liou and Robert Storey wrote the 4th. This guide was commissioned in Lonely Planet's Melbourne office and produced by the following people:

Commissioning Editors Rebecca Chau, Michael Day
Coordinating Editor Carly Hall
Coordinating Cartographer Hunor Csutoros
Coordinating Layout Designer Vicki Beale
Editors David Andrew, Cathryn Gane, Helen Yeates
Cartographer Jacqueline Nguyen
Layout Designers Adam Bextream, David Kemp, Jacqui Saunders
Index Carly Hall
Cover Designers Pepi Bluck, Maria Vallianos
Managing Editor Kerryn Burgess
Managing Cartographer Corinne Waddell
Project Manager Fabrice Rocher
Language Editor Quentin Frayne

Thanks to Michael Day, Megan Fraser, Glenn van der Knijff, Rebecca Lalor

Cover photographs The Great Wall at dusk, Bādálíng, Holzner & Lengnick/Alamy Images (top); young boys receiving martial arts training, Keren Su/Lonely Planet Images (bottom); bicycles, pedestrians and taxis on the streets of Beijing, Phil Weymouth/Lonely Planet Images (back).

Internal photographs by Phil Weymouth/Lonely Planet Images except for the following: p2 (#1), p56 (#1) Graham Tween; p2 (#4) Manfred Gottschalk; p2 (#5) Nicholas Pavloff; p30, p121 Jonathan Smith; p33 Oliver Strewe; p34, p57 (#2) Hilary Smith; p56 (#4), p168, p183 Keren Su; p62, p98 Glenn Beanland; p109 Damien Simonis; p126 Diana Mayfield. All images are the copyright of the photographers unless otherwise indicated. Many of the images in this guide are available for licensing from Lonely Planet Images: www.lonelyplanetimages.com.

ACKNOWLEDGMENTS

Many thanks to the following for the use of their content:

Readers Adam Dunnett and Ross van Horn for their contributions to the Excursions chapter.

THANKS
DAMIAN HARPER

Warm hugs and kisses to both Timothy and Emma and thanks as ever to my patient wife, Dai Min. Dai Lu is owed a special debt of gratitude for being so hospitable and resourceful. All credit to the fine folk of Shānhǎiguān and a respectful prayer to the monks of Puning Temple in Chéngdé. Big thanks to Carly Hall and all the editorial and cartographic staff at LP who have guided this book through to completion.

JULIE GRUNDVIG

Special thanks to Lu Yipeng for all his encouragement and help while on the road. In Beijing, a big thank you to Holly Guo, Ruiqiang Tang, Yajing Sun and O Sheng for helpful tips and advice. Thanks also to the Lonely Planet staff who worked on this book.

OUR READERS

Many thanks to the travellers who used the last edition and wrote to us with helpful hints, useful advice and interesting anecdotes. Your names follow:

Keith Acker, Tanveer Ahmed, Frida Andrae, Edward Archibald, David Atkinson, Jamie Bacher, David Balfour, Jan Bayer, Jonathan & Penelope Bayl, Rachel Beit-Aryeh, Mira Benes, Christopher Berresford, Rodrigo Bibiloni, Laura Blom, Kate Botkin, Carmen Boudreau-Kiviaho, Meretta Boyer, Candice & Nick Kilpatrick Broom, Marcel Brosens, Renate Buergler, Penny Burke, Marin Buyco, Matt Carr, Beatrice Carroli, Magnus Caullvine, Jennifer Chang, Alejandro Chaoul, Ed Chen, Gabriel Chew, Caroline Child, Simon Clark, Dean Clarke, Nienke Coehoorn, Susan Cook, Paul Cragg, Karen Crawford, Lori Dam, Michael Dann, David de Bhal, Chris de Fries, Philip & Kerry Dean, Andrew DeFrancis, Thomas Degnan, Andrea Dekkers,

M Delange-Wang, Feng Ding, Diane Ditcham, W F Doran, Robert Doub, Tony Dragon, Charles Dudley, Robin Dwyer-Hickey, Michael Eiselt, Amy Eisner, Sara Elinson, Jeff David Entner, Michel Faas, Ansgar Felbecker, Madeleine Fournier, Paul Fowler, Laura French, Maggi Fuchs, Thubten Gelek, Boni Suzanne Gelfand, Anne Geursen, Jo Gibson, David Glashan, Yvonne Gluyas, Ran Gluzman, Elizabeth Godfrey, Sam Golledge, Karleen Gribble, Minna Haapanen, Goran Hallne, Amy Hanser, Eyal Harel, Manfred Hartmann, Frances Haung, Lene Havgaard, James Hawkins, Robert & Tura Heckler, Alf Hickey, Valerie Hoeks, Alfonso Arias Hormaechea, David Horn, Richard Hoskin, Mirjam Hospers, Robin Hujie, John Hutton, Henrietta Irving, David Irwin, Martin Isaac, Fred Isler, Andrew Johns, Michelle Josselyn, Annelie Jung, Charlotte Kan, Pim Kemps, Nick Klensch, Marc Knijn, Pete Knust, Benjamin Kong, Agnieszka Kula, Simon Kull, Shiamin Kwa, Darlene Lee, Samuel Lee, Diane Leighton, Karen Leivers, Sharon Lew, Philip Lewis, Mike Lieven, Jo-Ann Lim, Mikael Lindqvist-Ottosson, Caroline Liou, Mikael Lo, Salvatore Loi, Adam Lotery, Ingrid K Lund, Martin Lundgren, Pawel Maczel, Laura Magliano, Antony Makepeace, Phil Manson, Andre Martino, Jay Mattner, Annette Mayerbacher, Piotr Mazurkiewicz, Fri McWilliams, Yves Mestric, Peter Micic, Sabrina Mileto, Allison Miller, Helen Mills, Kjell Mittag, Antonella Montironi, Ratna Nandakumar, Alex Nikolic, Paul North, Rip Noyes, Loutfi Nuaymi, Roderick O'Brien, Jarlath O'Carroll, Kelly O'Hara, Julien Pagliaroli, Tanya, Jason & Snortie Paterson, Ruth Payne, Renate Pelzl, Mark Pepper, Bawanthi Perera, Matt Peterson, Mikko Pettila, Jerry Pi, Pat Piskulich, Bernadette Quin, Kate Radford, Zgraggen Reto, Mark Reuber, Jurrian Reurings, Stephan Rey, Sylvia Rhau, Samia Riaz, Deborah Ann Rice, Viviane Rochon, Robert Rosenberg, Julia Ross, Peter Ross, Gernot Roth, Ravi C Roy, Angry Russell, Davina Russell, Inbal Sansani, Heidrun Schmitz, Ernst Albert Schneider, Birte Schulz, Melissa Schwaderer, Kolya Schweppe, M T Shea, Craig Simons, Barrie Sims, Catherine Sinclair, Cameron Smith, Edward Smith, Jason Smith, Mara Soplantila, Dawn Sorenson, David Speary, Ben Steele, Edwin Steele, Nora Sun, Chris Sutor, Peter Szikinger, Hugh Tansley, Bill Thames, Shanice Thia, Lucy Tickell, Andreas Tindlund, Kathy Tipler, E P Tissing, Nick & Rose Todd Brown, Mitzi Toney, Simon Tries, Annelies Troost, William Tse, Charlotte Turner, Sebastian van Treeck, Francoise Vooren, Patricia Weickhardt, Jesse Weiner, Julie Weiss, Siw Wikstrom, Nicole Wild, John Woo, Jessi Wu, Simon Yu, Shami Zain, Tymoteusz Zera, Maike Ziesemer

Notes

Index

See also separate indexes for Eating (p225), Drinking (p225), Shopping (p225) and Sleeping (p225).

000 map pages
000 photographs

Index

000 map pages
000 photographs